7-24-64

# THE
# THIRD WORLD
# IN SOVIET
# PERSPECTIVE

*Studies by Soviet Writers
on the Developing Areas*

# THE THIRD WORLD IN SOVIET PERSPECTIVE

*Studies by Soviet Writers on the Developing Areas*

———•———

EDITED, WITH AN INTRODUCTION BY

THOMAS PERRY THORNTON

PRINCETON, NEW JERSEY
PRINCETON UNIVERSITY PRESS
1964

To my mother,
*Catherine B. Thornton*
and the memory
of my father
*Captain Thomas A. Thornton*
*(1896-1955)*

# Foreword

THIS volume presents a significant, though necessarily very small, sample of Soviet writings on the problems of the world's less-developed countries. When the Soviet Union began, after the death of Stalin, its large-scale political activities in the underdeveloped world—not just in areas adjoining the Soviet Union and what used to be called the Sino-Soviet bloc, but farther afield in Asia, Africa, and Latin America—it required a commensurate knowledge of political, social, economic, and cultural conditions in this strange and multitudinous world. Of necessity, the requirement included an academic capability. The increasing competence of this capability is reflected in the following essays.

As Dr. Thornton points out in his Preface, these articles are not only of uneven quality, rarely measuring up to standards of Western scholarship, but are also burdened with the usual ideological, indeed doctrinal, precipitates. Nevertheless, there is much to be learned from reading them. We can see how Soviet writers conceptualize the problems facing the underdeveloped countries, and we may assume that these conceptual formulae are, to some extent, significant in shaping Soviet policy. We may also learn something about these countries that our own, much more loosely structured, ideological guides prevent us from observing properly. And, finally, we appreciate that materials of this kind are read by many students and other literates in the underdeveloped countries—whether from Cuba or Chile, Ghana or Algeria—and are likely to affect how these readers perceive and evaluate the problems of their own communities.

It is for these reasons that the Center of International Studies was ready to support the enterprise from which this book materialized under Dr. Thornton's able management. Its reading should afford an interesting intellectual encounter for students as well as specialists.

KLAUS KNORR

*Princeton*
*January 1964*

vii

# Preface

WITHIN the last decade, there has been a remarkable burgeoning of interest in the developing areas of the "third world." Popular and scholarly periodicals print ever-increasing numbers of pieces dealing with Asia, Africa, and Latin America, and awareness is rapidly growing that the United States has an involvement in these areas beyond the sending of an occasional missionary or investment by a few adventurous businessmen. The problems confronting the developing areas are of great intrinsic interest, and the spectacle of dozens of new nations attempting to find economic and political viability inevitably arouses concern and sympathy. Yet, in all honesty, this concern would be undeniably less intense if the developing areas were not felt to be a crucial arena in our world-wide confrontation with the Communist world, especially the USSR. For better or worse, the cold war has acted as the accelerator of our interest, and of that of the Soviet Union as well.

Although even the daily press duly notes Soviet moves in the developing areas, very limited attention has been given at any level to the increasing volume of relevant material by Soviet scholars. Since about 1955, these writers have produced a large number of books on the various countries and areas of the third world; one bimonthly periodical and a popularizing monthly have been devoted exclusively to material on Asia and Africa; and a substantial portion of standard periodicals in the fields of economics, international affairs, and politics has been taken up by studies on the developing areas. Behind this production stands a growing body of increasingly better-qualified specialists, and the resources of three institutes of the Academy of Sciences concerned specifically with Asia, Africa, and Latin America, as well as support from other institutes. Although there are good bibliographic surveys covering the material produced, a few analyses of it by American and other Western scholars, and a modest number of translations into English, the Soviet view of the developing areas is for the most part little known in the West.[a]

a. For some of the more useful commentaries by Western writers, see the bibliographical note at the end of this volume.

## Preface

The obvious questions arise: What is the significance of this material? Does it give definite indications of Soviet policy and intentions, or is it only the unrelated output of independent scholars? How does it compare in quality and influence with the corresponding body of research done in the United States?

First of all, it is at least a truism that there is no independent scholarship in the Soviet Union. The mere fact that the great upsurge of Soviet writing on the developing areas came at a time when Soviet policy began to look to the third world illustrates that such research is responsive to policy, and many specific examples of research following the party line can be adduced. The converse of the question—the extent to which research influences policy—is much more difficult to establish. Since the various institutes of the Academy of Sciences are "policy-oriented" and continue to prosper, it must be assumed that the policy-making leadership finds their output useful. In addition, top Soviet leaders have little experience with the non-European world and must look somewhere for sources of knowledge. The Academy institutes are logical places to find at least some. Finally, the important role that the trappings of scholarly research play in Marxist theory would increase the esteem in which the institutes' output is held. It may safely be said that there is feedback in both directions between policy and research—probably to much the same extent as exists in any state, including our own. In addition, however, since there is no independent scholarly community in the Soviet Union—all of it is employed by the government—the intensity of interaction must be all the greater within the Soviet research-policy community.

The quality of the Soviet output, when judged by American or Western European standards, is weak indeed. Aside from the inhibitions imposed by a closed society, Soviet writers have been hampered by the lack of a scholarly tradition, very limited opportunities for firsthand research, and a shortage of trained personnel. There are certain exceptions to this picture —notably in the fields of linguistics and historical research in the areas of the Orient bordering on Russia—but for the most part the picture is at best spotty. When compared with Soviet

# *Preface*

output of the Stalin period, however, current production shows an immense improvement.[b] Soviet scholars are learning, they are developing a limited independence in their views, and they are making increasingly good use of non-Communist source material and contacts with non-Communists, both in the advanced countries and in the third world.

The reader who is unfamiliar with the Communist approach to scholarship—or the "Communist" style of writing—will find the Soviet articles on the developing areas to be ponderous, rather repetitive, and at times unimaginative. Even the most objective of Soviet writers will—indeed, must—engage in polemics to a degree that would discredit any Western scholar. There is little or no attempt to present a balanced picture, and the rigid Marxist-Leninist framework within which selected facts are presented inevitably breeds a hostile reaction in the Western reader. In short, anybody who is solely interested in expanding his knowledge of the developing areas would be ill-advised to seek enlightenment in Soviet writings.[c] This is not to say that there is no interesting (and frequently significant) material presented by Soviet writers; rather, such material is buried deep and is frequently presented in such a dis-

---

b. The reason for the intellectual poverty of the Stalin period was basically fear of criticism, as was already recognized during Stalin's lifetime. See S. Tolstov, "For Advanced Soviet Oriental Studies," *Literatura i Zhizn'* [Literature and Life], August 11, 1950; translated in CDSP, III, No. 33, 3–4.

c. It would not be feasible to give here even a rudimentary bibliography of the relevant material produced by non-Communist writers. A good starting place for those who wish to familiarize themselves is the bibliography in Max F. Millikan and Donald L. M. Blackmer, *The Emerging Nations: Their Growth and U.S. Policy* (Boston 1961), 161–67. Since the publication of that list, any number of new books have appeared. Among them, the following seem to me to be the most important: Richard Harris, *Independence and After: Revolution in the Underdeveloped Countries* (London 1962); John J. Johnson, ed., *The Role of the Military in the Underdeveloped Countries* (Princeton 1962); John H. Kautsky, *Political Change in Underdeveloped Countries* (New York 1962); Paul E. Sigmund, ed., *The Ideologies of Developing Nations* (New York 1963); and Lawrence W. Martin, ed., *Neutralism and Nonalignment* (New York 1962). For a technically oriented bibliography, see Saul M. Katz and Frank McGowan, *A Selected List of U.S. Readings on Development* (Washington 1964).

xi

# Preface

torted manner that only the reader who has some familiarity with Marxism will be able to evaluate it properly.

There are numerous errors of omission and commission, even in the articles that have been chosen for this book. For the most part these do not arise from incorrect knowledge, but from conscious imposition of the Marxist framework on the material available.[d] Again, this situation has improved radically in the past decade, but probably no article could be found that would be accepted by an objective Western observer as a fair presentation of its topic. As a matter of basic editorial policy, I have refrained from engaging in polemics; similarly, I have not undertaken to correct errors or distortions.[e] My objective is solely to present the views of these Soviet writers for whatever use the reader may wish to make of them. In such a wide-ranging field, I would not presume to have the competence to quarrel with Soviet specialists; furthermore, to take issue with certain points would imply that I subscribe to others. Rather, I hope that making this material available will perhaps stimulate Western area specialists to initiate a dialogue with their Soviet colleagues and recognize that Soviet scholarship—with all of its faults and limitations—is a matter which must be taken into consideration.[f]

The critical eye with which Western scholars regard most of the Soviet output will not necessarily be shared by the emerging elites of the developing areas. The Marxist analytical framework and even the language in which these materials are couched are no less foreign to, say, a young African econo-

d. T. G. Spear has put it aptly: "The Stalinist notices only those facts which fit his thesis. The post-Stalinist makes some attempt to see the facts as they are and then tries to superimpose the Marxist pattern." *Central Asian Review*, v, No. 1 (1956), 66.

e. Specifically, I wish to avoid the aridities associated with the "anti-falsification" school of Soviet literature which undertakes to "expose" Western scholarship. The weakness of such an approach is well shown in such volumes as *Protiv fal'sifikatsii istorii Vostoka* [Against Falsification of the History of the East] (Moscow 1961).

f. It should not be thought that Soviet writers are oblivious to the reactions that their work evokes in the West. They are immensely proud of the recognition they are begining to get and are themselves generally very well informed as to the views of Western writers.

## *Preface*

mist than is the "objective" approach taken by Western writers.[g] Colonialism and its remnants are not matters for objective assessment by the newly independent, and the sense of outrage that is conveyed in Soviet writings is mild compared with the attitude of many Africans and Asians. The intellectual equipment of a leader such as Sékou Touré derives at least as much from Marxism as from the Western social sciences, and many of his actions, statements, and theories must be understood in this manner. Marxist categories of analysis are very real for some of these emerging elites, and only to the extent that we understand the Soviet prototypes can we recognize the similarities and—more important still—the differences which the two approaches manifest.

Beyond this, the Soviet writings on the third world provide valuable insight into the development and current line of Soviet policy. In view of the feedback between research and policy, they are probably our best source for policy analysis, and considerably more reliable than study confined to the overt manifestations of Soviet policy—aid agreements, diplomatic recognition, and the like—which are sometimes only ephemeral. To be sure, no open source will provide us with a key to the innermost workings of Soviet policy, but by comparing Soviet actions with the open literature, and in turn judging these against the reality perceived by Western observers, we do have an opportunity to acquire a reasonably reliable picture of Soviet policies and prospects in the developing areas. The object of this collection of material is to provide some input for this calculation of how the "other side" sees the problem confronting both of the international systems.

It must be emphasized, however, that the Soviet "view" described in the following pages is essentially a construct. In fact, there are discernible elements of a lively debate among Soviet students of the third world. To some extent this is a

g. On the semi-Marxist intellectual framework of African elites, see Thomas Hodgkin, "A Note on the Language of African Nationalism," *St. Antony's Papers*, No. 10 (Carbondale, Ill., 1961), 22–40; also Kenneth Grundy, "Nkrumah's Theory of Underdevelopment: An Analysis of Recurrent Themes," *World Politics*, xv (April 1963), 438–54.

## Preface

generational conflict, with younger writers pressing a more empirical approach. Yet the picture is not quite this simple, for significant matters of substance are at stake as well.[h] Similarly, it would be unfair to assert that all Soviet writers of the Stalin period were blind to what was going on in the real world. Then, too, there were visible divergencies of view—for instance, in the first selection by Potekhin reprinted below. In both cases, however, it would have been too cumbersome to make allowances for all shades of opinion. Instead, the models of the "Stalinist" and "contemporary" viewpoints offered here represent majority positions that appear to be the closest to observable policy.

The choice of material to be included was necessarily arbitrary. First of all, I limited the selections to scholarly, as distinct from popular, materials; most of the material is drawn from *Narody Azii i Afriki* [Peoples of Asia and Africa] and *Mirovaya Ekonomika i Mezhdunarodnyye Otnosheniya* [World Economics and International Relations]. The orientation of all of the material is politico-economic. I have excluded work in the fields of anthropology, literature, art, linguistics, etc., even though it is in these fields that the highest level of Soviet scholarly attainment is frequently manifested. Such works tend to be devoid of political content or completely stereotyped in this respect, and it is only in the political and economic literature that one can find the sort of guidelines which are needed for a consideration of policy.

In addition to these broad criteria, I have chosen material with certain further objectives in mind. First of all, articles have been included which deal with as many of the developing areas as possible. A variety of subject matter is discussed— economics, class relationships, political factors, agrarian reform, etc.—so that the reader can obtain at least some familiarity with Soviet views on these topics. With the exception of Guber's article on Indonesia, I have not included studies de-

h. One aspect of the debate is discussed by Herbert S. Dinnerstein in *Soviet Doctrine on Developing Areas: Some Divergent Views* (Santa Monica, RAND Corporation Memorandum P-2725, 1963). For other elements, see the running discussion among Stepanov, Avakov, Mirskiy, and Kiselev in MEIMO, Nos. 2, 4, and 10 (1963).

voted to individual countries, since within the relatively restricted length of this volume it seemed better to provide more general, theoretically oriented studies. Wherever possible, I have chosen items written by the more prominent Soviet scholars in the field, so that such names as Potekhin, Ul'yanovskiy, or Guber may become more than entries in inscrutable footnotes.

Naturally, the prime consideration has been to present scholarship that is of high quality when measured by Soviet standards—and in several instances even by our own. Among the hundreds of pieces that came under consideration, there were several dozen that met the above criteria. Of these at least ten were excluded only because of space limitations. I would defend my selection merely by saying that it appeared to me to be the most feasible.

Almost all of the material selected has not previously been readily available in English. A number of the pieces were translated by the Joint Publications Research Service of the Department of Commerce and have been available in a few repository libraries. Other pieces have been translated specifically for use in this volume. The translations were made by Mr. David Ashworth, who also checked and reedited the JPRS material, and I have rechecked all of these translations and assume ultimate responsibility for them.

I have conscientiously attempted to avoid coloring the translations to reflect either favorably or adversely upon the originals. My objective has been to reproduce a readable but reasonably exact English version of the Russian original. If I have failed in this in any way, it is through inadvertence rather than design. Similarly, the few cuts which I made in lengthy articles were intended solely to eliminate irrelevant material. There has been no attempt to remove material that would weaken the writer's argumentation. For the most part, I have refrained from abridging or cutting, in order to present as accurate a version as possible. Specifically, I have not removed frequent repetitions or dogmatic sections that may seem superfluous to the reader. These are important expository techniques used by Soviet writers and I have not attempted to prejudge

# Preface

which are important and which are not. In any event, they are
useful in recreating the flavor of the original.

For a variety of reasons, I have included only Soviet materials in this collection. In no small part, this was due to limitations of space and to my inability to cope with some of the
Eastern European languages involved. What materials were
available to me, in translation or in the original, did not show
any significant departure from the general Soviet line and most
were of incredibly poor quality.[i] To have gone into the production of Marxists outside the Bloc would have turned up
some interesting material but would lie beyond the scope of
this undertaking.

A noteworthy exception is the Chinese material, which differs considerably from the Soviet and Eastern European output (except, of course, that of Albania, which may be safely
disregarded). The Chinese are markedly more strident in tone
and much more critical of non-Communist forces in the third
world. In general, the Chinese output does not rise above the
level of invective and has only a rudimentary empirical base.
In fact, it is rather similar to Soviet output of the late 1940's—
which is hardly surprising in view of the similarity of the Chinese line to that of the USSR in the Stalin-Zhdanov years. Although much can be learned about the Sino-Soviet dispute by
comparing the Chinese and Soviet writings on the developing
areas, this would properly be the subject of a different study.[j]

i. On a rather random basis of selection, among Romanian sources
I found Gh. Ioniţa and P. Tanu, "Popoarele Africii împotriva neocolonial-
ismului" [The Peoples of Africa Against Neo-colonialism], *Probleme
Economice*, No. 9 (1961), 84–101, which gives the appearance of a
pastiche of inferior Soviet material with no independent analysis of any
type. L. Medianu, "Probleme ale economiei ţarilor Americii latine" [Eco-
nomic Problems of Latin American Countries], *ibid.*, No. 9 (1962), 99–
113, is little better and manages to avoid citing a single Spanish-language
source. Is it unfair to assume that the writer does not know Spanish?
JPRS occasionally translates Bulgarian, Albanian, and East German
material, but it is not worth citing.

j. Chinese material is frequently printed in the English-language
weekly, *Peking Review*. An important selection of better-quality Chinese
material was translated in JPRS 8532; special attention should be given
to Ya Nan, "Certain Special Characteristics of the Indian Bourgeoisie."
Also interesting is "The Fundamental Path for the Liberation Movement
in the Colonial and Semi-colonial Areas," JPRS 6024.

# Preface

The introduction is intended to provide some background for the reader who approaches this area of study without much prior acquaintance. The bibliographical note at the end of the volume may serve as a guide for further investigation. Each of the articles translated is preceded by a brief editor's note to aid in placing it correctly in the context of Soviet research. I have also found it advisable to footnote terms, concepts, references, etc., used by the Soviet writers that may be obscure to the Western reader. Such footnotes are designated by letters; numbered footnotes are those of the Soviet authors. In the instances where the Russian text has been abridged, I have retained the original numbering of the footnotes; thus, certain numbers mays be "missing" from the excerpts printed. Unless otherwise noted, references to material by Russian writers are to Russian-language editions and Lenin citations are to the fourth Russian edition. A list of the abbreviations used in the references will be found at the end of the volume.

Funds to support this undertaking were generously provided by the Center of International Studies at Princeton University. To the Center and its director, Klaus Knorr, I owe a considerable debt of gratitude not only for financial support but also for the stimulation I received while I was a Visiting Research Associate of the Center in 1961–1962. Jean MacLachlan of the Center has, through her patience and editorial talents, done much to improve the readability of unbelievably recalcitrant material. It is, I hope, obvious that the opinions expressed by the Soviet writers whose work is reproduced here are in no way those of the Center or of the Department of State; similarly, my own opinions and views expressed herein are just that—my own.

It is perhaps rare for an editor to disassociate himself totally from the views of his "contributors," yet obviously I must do so. Nevertheless, they too have in a very real sense made this book possible, not only by the fact of having written the material, but also by implanting scholarship where before only dogmatism and polemic grew. I hope they will agree that I have presented their positions fairly and that by making their work available I have contributed to the development

## Preface

of a scholarly dialogue in which both sides should engage.

David Ashworth has been an excellent translator and I am most grateful to him. Several of the translations were first made by the Joint Publications Research Service, an organization to which any student of Communist affairs is deeply indebted. Finally, my wife, Dr. Karin Stuebben Thornton, has been most understanding and helpful during the long and at times rather painful gestation of this volume.

T.P.T.

WASHINGTON, D.C.

JANUARY 1964

# Contents

## Contents

# THE
# THIRD WORLD
# IN SOVIET
# PERSPECTIVE

*Studies by Soviet Writers*
*on the Developing Areas*

# Introduction

THE view of the developing areas that is presented in this book reflects Soviet attitudes of the early 1960's. Just as American attitudes have changed, so also have those of the Soviets in the years since World War II. In fact, the shift in the Soviet position has been much more abrupt and extreme than in the American. Shortly after the war, the Soviet Union had adopted a rigid and hostile policy toward the outside world, including the countries of what we would now call the "third world." There was no third world for the Soviets then, however—only the "two camps" of communism and non-communism. This period of Soviet history, closely associated with the names of Stalin and Zhdanov, was reflected in the emerging countries by armed Communist rebellion, excoriation of such "bourgeois" leaders as Gandhi and Sukarno, and isolation of communism from the nationalist movement except in China and Vietnam. Soviet writings of the period tended to be stereotyped, dull, vitriolic, and virtually useless either for research or as guidance for any rational policy.[a] The small degree of flexibility that had characterized Communist activities in the early Comintern period and then again during the Popular Front of the 1930's had withered and showed only slight signs of resuscitation.

As Stalin's heirs went about their housecleaning after 1953, however, it was obvious that some sort of *modus vivendi* had to be reached with the newly independent countries if the

a. A mild example is the excerpt by I. I. Potekhin reprinted below (No. 1). For some typically extreme statements, see such articles as I. Lemin, "Plody imperialisticheskogo khozyaynichan'ya v Indii i Pakistane" [The Fruits of Imperialistic Domination in India and Pakistan], *Voprosy Ekonomiki* [Questions of Economics], No. 1 (1952), 73–89, translated in CDSP, IV (No. 11), 26–28; or V. V. Balabushevich, "Novyy etap natsional'no-osvoboditel'noy bor'by narodov Indii" [New Stage of the National Liberation Struggle of the Peoples of India], *ibid.*, No. 8 (1949), 30–48, in CDSP, I (No. 49), 8–10. Probably the best-known source is the book *Crisis of the Colonial System* (Bombay 1951), a translation of *Krizis kolonial'noy sistemy* (Moscow 1949).

1

### The Third World in Soviet Perspective

struggle with the West was to be pursued under optimum conditions. The political acts which marked this readjustment were Khrushchev's and Bulganin's trip to South Asia; the establishment of the spirit of Bandung as the theme of Communist policy in Asia; and the 20th Congress of the Communist Party of the Soviet Union, held in 1956, when the initial phase of de-Stalinization was extended to many phases of Soviet activity, including "orientology." [b]

The form of de-Stalinization in orientology was parallel to that in other fields of endeavor. It consisted of an ostensible reinterpretation of theory in terms of Marxism-Leninism, rather than the Marxism-Leninism-Stalinism (with overwhelming emphasis on Stalinism) that had been enjoined during the late dictator's lifetime. Even with the best of good will, it is difficult to make much use of Marx and Engels in dealing with the developing areas. Although Marx's concept of "oriental despotism" (as a form of society distinct from slavery, feudalism, capitalism, etc.) might offer some potential, the Communists have chosen to neglect it. [c] Soviet writers look rather to Lenin as the guide for their theoretical excursions into interpretation of the world scene, and it is possible to derive a fairly coherent body of doctrine from Leninist concepts.

Lenin had found it necessary to reinterpret Marx in the light of conditions of the early twentieth century. In part, he was attempting to find a formula which could make Marxism immediately relevant in Russia. The answer was the "new type of party," highly disciplined and organized, which at least in theory is the model for all Communist parties today. Of less

b. The "Orient" is a singularly undifferentiated concept in Soviet writings. It has included not only East Asia, but also the Middle East and even Africa. Attempts to foster some differentiation go back at least to Stalin (cf. *Works* [English edn.], vii, 148), but as late as 1957 a leading Soviet figure defined the East as reaching from Morocco to the Pacific (N. A. Mukhitdinov, "Velikiy Oktyabr' i Vostok" [The Great October and the East], SV, No. 5 [1957], 24). In the last few years, however, more serious attempts have been undertaken, symbolic of which was the change of the name of the Institute of Orientology to the Institute of the Peoples of Asia and Africa.

c. The concept is discussed at length by Karl A. Wittfogel in *Oriental Despotism* (New Haven 1957), especially chapter 9. See also p. 190, below.

## Soviet Writers on the Developing Areas

practical importance—but more interesting theoretically—was Lenin's reinterpretation of the nature of capitalism. Marxists of the new century faced problems with which Marx had not dealt—which indeed had not existed in Marx's time. The most significant of these were the great colonial expansion of the European powers and the slow but certain reversal of the trend of impoverishment of the masses which Marx had assumed to be a permanent feature of capitalism. Socialism itself had grown respectable, and national patriotism rather than proletarian internationalism was becoming common among the working classes. The members of the proletariat had acquired a stake in society and a sense of identification with the seemingly powerful expanding empires in which they lived.

Lenin explained these phenomena as results of a new development in capitalism. In *Imperialism—The Highest Stage of Capitalism*,[d] written during World War I, Lenin set forth the theory that imperialism was a further development of capitalism, occasioned by the need for the monopolies in the capitalist countries to find new and more profitable fields for investment of capital. On the one hand, the competition for colonies and the general malaise which imperialism represented were signs of capitalism's imminent demise; yet imperialism had played an important role in temporarily stabilizing the domestic position of the capitalists, who had diverted a small part of their colonial profits to bribing an influential stratum of the working class and diverting it from the business of proletarian revolution. This "workers' aristocracy" could be conveniently blamed for the lack of revolutionary ardor in the European proletariat and the conciliatory approach which Socialists took toward their governments.[e] Inherent in Lenin's theory was the expectation that the uncorrupted proletariat of the advanced

d. Written in 1917, this work is widely available in all languages. For good non-Marxist interpretations of Lenin's theory of imperialism, see Alfred G. Meyer, *Leninism* (Cambridge, Mass., 1957), chapter 11, and Henri Chambre, S.J., *From Karl Marx to Mao Tse-tung* (New York 1963).

e. The authoritative Soviet presentation of economics is the textbook *Politicheskaya Ekonomika* [Political Economics]. The most recent edition (1959) is available in German translation (Berlin 1961), and an earlier edition has appeared in English as *Political Economy: A Textbook* (London 1957).

## The Third World in Soviet Perspective

countries shared a substantial identity of interest with the oppressed colonial peoples: the overthrow of imperialism.[f]

Lenin wrote extensively about the imminent collapse of the colonial system,[g] and the entire analytical apparatus of present-day Soviet theory is drawn from his work. The post-Stalin leadership has clearly lacked the temerity (and perhaps the intellectual acuity) to reexamine Lenin's theories in the light of the changes that have taken place in the intervening half-century. Whether the Soviet interpretation of Lenin is even the "correct" one need not concern us here. (The Chinese, working from the same base, have of course come up with a completely different interpretation.) In general, Soviet policy is based on the more flexible postulates of the Lenin canon, although it has shown certain changes even in the past several years.

Immediately following the Soviet policy shift of the mid-1950's, Soviet writers followed the lead of Khrushchev and wrote with almost unstinted praise of the new states in Asia. This attitude was also extended to the emerging anti-colonial movements in Africa and to Latin American radicals, as Soviet scholarship began to take note of these areas as well. To be sure, the Soviets did not lose sight of the fact that these emerging forces were not Communist and they inserted frequent caveats in their writings. Nevertheless, in the material of this period there is an unmistakable tone of optimism and even credulousness in the treatment of the third world. It represents at least as extreme an overstatement of the case as were the pessimism and suspicion that characterized corresponding American attitudes of the period.

Just as American attitudes began to become more balanced toward the end of the decade, so did those of the Soviets. Initial

f. It is interesting to note that Marx foreshadowed Lenin in this. He believed that the English aristocracy could be overthrown only by separating it from its power base in the Irish countryside. See Marx's letter to Kugelmann of November 28, 1869, in *Marx-Engels Selected Correspondence* (New York 1942), 278; cited in George Lichtheim, *Marxism: A Historical and Critical Study* (New York 1961), 84, note 3.

g. For a selection in English, see V. I. Lenin, *The National Liberation Movement in the East* (Moscow 1957).

## Soviet Writers on the Developing Areas

enthusiasm wore off a bit and Soviet scholars—to a considerably greater extent than the Soviet government—reappraised somewhat the potential which the emerging forces presented for communism.[h] This rectification was not nearly so dramatic as the de-Stalinization, but the tone has shifted perceptibly and a greater selectivity of approach has been attained. To no small extent, this more balanced approach can be attributed to increasing sophistication on the part of the Soviet writers. The radical *volte-face* of 1956 simply shifted the orientation of approach rather than its quality. The intervening years have provided researchers with more opportunities to study source material and even to visit the areas of their interest, and the comparatively relaxed political atmosphere in the Soviet Union has encouraged independent thinking and even open debates on matters of ideological importance—always, of course, within limits of basic orthodoxy.

Thus Soviet orientology was, by the beginning of the 1960's, gravitating toward a middle ground. When the process is viewed in a historical perspective, it would seem that Soviet orientologists may be approaching some sort of a common denominator with their non-Marxist colleagues. Perhaps this is the case, but the operative word in such a proposition must be "approach." The gap between Western and Soviet scholars looms so large as to appear unbridgeable. Analysis by Communist and non-Communist writers proceeds from radically different premises which cannot and perhaps should not be compromised. On the other hand, both groups of scholars have much the same raw material with which to work, even though the selection and treatment of this material vary strikingly.[i] Furthermore, both sides are fully capable of understanding the work of the other and utilizing it in various ways. To do so of

h. Cf. Georg von Stackelberg, "Renewed Attacks on the National Bourgeoisie," *Bulletin of the Institute for the Study of the USSR*, vɪɪɪ (August 1961), 3–9.

i. See, for instances, the articles by Stepanov, Gordon and Fridman, and Avakov and Mirskiy, below. Also, G. Mirskiy, "Tvorcheskiy Marksizm i problemy natsional'no-osvoboditel'nykh revolyutsiy" [Creative Marxism and Problems of National Liberation Revolutions], MEIMO, No. 2 (1963), 63–68; translated in JPRS 19,821.

## The Third World in Soviet Perspective

course requires a familiarity with basic categories of analysis used by the other. It seems probable that the Soviet analyst will have less difficulty in this regard, since the Western premises are much less esoteric than are the Communist and rest more on traditional rules of evidence and logic. (The Soviets would of course deny this.) In order then to deal with Soviet writings on the developing areas, one should begin with at least an outline view of the economic, social, and political theories upon which the Soviet writings are based.

It is the very essence of Marxism that analysis of political and social phenomena should be derived from economic considerations. Since man is an economic animal for the Marxists and derives his significance from the economic role which he plays, the primacy of economics over politics should be automatic. There have of course been frequent debates in Communist circles concerning the primacy of economics or politics,[j] but at least in the developing areas—where economic problems are of such overwhelming importance—one would expect Soviet analysis to be founded on economic bases.

Soviet writers do indeed devote an immense amount of attention to the economic problems of the developing areas. Most of the articles reprinted below are concerned primarily with economics, and the few which are mainly political tend to base their analysis on economic factors. This apparent preoccupation with economics is, however, misleading. Throughout Soviet writing there is an implicit—and frequently explicit —admission that it is politics, not economics, which determines the attitude taken toward economic and social phenomena. Whether the matter under discussion is agricultural reform,[k] the role of the state in the economy,[l] the role of the military,[m]

j. The primacy question has most recently been discussed in G. Glezerman, "V. I. Lenin o vzaimootnoshenii ekonomiki i politiki v stroitel'stve novogo obshchestva" [V. I. Lenin on the Mutual Relationship of Economics and Politics in Constructing the New Society], *Kommunist*, No. 7 (1963), 30–40; translated in JPRS 19,505.

k. Typically expressed in *Agrarnyye otnosheniya v stranakh Vostoka* [Agrarian Relationships in the Countries of the East] (Moscow 1958).

l. See, for instance, *Problemy ekonomiki stran Yugo-Vostochnoy Azii* [Problems of Economics of the Countries of Southeast Asia] (Moscow

6

## Soviet Writers on the Developing Areas

the attitude toward local Communists,[n] or whatever, the criterion applied is not the economic or social effect of a given act, but the presumed political auspices under which the act is performed. With very few exceptions, states that are not friendly to the Soviet Union are regarded as incapable of effective land reform, a rational industrialization policy, etc. Indeed, the degree of this effectiveness is scaled in direct proportion to relative merit ascribed to the given country in the eyes of the Soviet leadership.

Although this approach can be dismissed as cynicism, its roots lie deeper. In Communist eyes, the state is an expression of the power of a given class—bourgeois or proletarian—and this class must inevitably act in its own interests. Since the interests of the bourgeois class are generally "anti-progressive," whatever acts it performs are generally anti-progressive, and their objective content is of only secondary importance. Thus the very successful land policies of Japan or Israel are given much less credit than those of the Asian Communist states or even the halting land reforms planned in Burma or Indonesia. To be sure, Soviet writers do admit that, say, the emphasis on state planning in many non-Communist countries has certain beneficial results and that in many circumstances Communists should support bourgeois reforms on tactical grounds as a step forward. Communist approbation can at best be half-hearted, however, for only a truly socialist (i.e., Communist) government can take measures which by definition are in the interest of the proletariat.

Despite this primacy of what most observers would call political considerations, Soviet writers have developed a fairly elaborate framework for the consideration of both domestic

1958), particularly the chapter by Azovskiy on Burma (p. 47); and *Gosudarstvennyy kapitalizm v stranakh Vostoka* [State Capitalism in the Countries of the East] (Moscow 1960), particularly the chapter on Ceylon by L. G. Ivanov (p. 171).

m. On the military, see Avakov and Mirskiy, p. 291, below.

n. On foreign policy and the position of local Communists, see A. A. Guber, "Distinctive Features of the National Liberation Movement in the Eastern Colonial and Dependent Countries," *International Affairs* (Moscow), No. 3 (1959), 74.

7

*The Third World in Soviet Perspective*
and foreign economic problems of the developing areas.[o] They base their analysis on the colonial past shared by most of the developing areas. Even those areas which were not actual colonies are said to have been semi-colonies—i.e., states whose independence was only a formality. Soviet writers point to the impunity with which the affairs of China, Thailand, or Nicaragua were interfered in by "imperialist" powers such as Great Britain, France, or the United States, and emphasize that most of these semi-colonies' economies were dominated by foreign "monopolies." [p]

The colonies and semi-colonies lacked the sovereign power to regulate their economic life in their own interests. The imperialist countries were interested in the colonial areas only as dumping grounds for cheap manufactures, sources of raw material, and above all as areas where capital, not needed in the metropolitan economy, could be invested to yield "fabulous" profits.[q] Since the various empires comprised individual economic units, there was no attempt to make each component self-sufficient. Given the advanced technology and the often limited resource base of the metropolitan countries, it was inevitable that the colonial areas became "raw-material appendages" of the metropoles.

By emphasizing the colonial past as basic to the economic problems of the developing countries, Soviet writers tend to overlook the ecological factors that provide relative or absolute restrictions on the potentials of many of the new nations. The idea that a country is economically hopeless is rejected by Marxists—an attitude which is undoubtedly popular in some

o. For the most recent authoritative statement, see R. A. Ul'yanovskiy, "Ekonomicheskaya Nezavisimost'—Blizhnaya zadacha osvoboditel'nogo dvizheniya v Azii" [Economic Independence—The Next Task of the Liberation Movement in Asia], *Kommunist*, No. 1 (1962), 96–107; translated in JPRS 12,844.

p. A monopoly in Marxist parlance is more of a "big business" than a matter of exclusive control, as this term is used in the United States. Thus, to the Marxists, both Ford and General Motors are "monopolies."

q. "Profits [in underdeveloped, colonial, and dependent countries] are usually high because capital is scarce, land is relatively inexpensive, wages are low, and raw materials are cheap." *Fundamentals of Marxism-Leninism* (2nd English edn., Moscow 1963), 246.

## Soviet Writers on the Developing Areas

of the more unlikely national entities that have recently appeared on the international scene—and Malthusianism is dogmatically rejected as racism.[r] Socialist economic organization is offered as a means of rapid development [s] and only indirectly is it indicated that ultimately certain countries must specialize in relatively unattractive fields of endeavor. Such specialization would necessarily be left to the period after these countries have entered the international Communist political and economic system.

Whatever development is to be undertaken naturally requires capital, particularly in the form of foreign exchange which can be used to buy developmental goods from the advanced countries that produce them. In most instances, these funds can be obtained only by the sale of raw materials and agricultural commodities on the world market; even light industrial goods cannot be produced competitively in much of the third world. Unfortunately, the prices of agricultural products and raw materials have been declining relative to the prices of the heavy manufactured goods which the developing countries wish to obtain—a phenomenon that in Communist

r. Cf. A. Popov, "Reaktsionnyye teorii narodonaseleniya na sluzhbe kolonializma" [Reactionary Population Theories in the Service of Colonialism], MEIMO, No. 10 (1962), 39–48. About the maximum concession Soviet writers are willing to make is that there may be overpopulation in certain areas of a country (e.g., Java); cf. P. Anan'ev, "Agrarno-krest'yanskiy vopros v Indonezii" [The Agrarian-Peasant Question in Indonesia], MEIMO, No. 7 (1962), 121.

s. There is a rather extensive technical literature on problems of underdevelopment and the role of socialism. See, for instance, B. N. Brodovich, "O tempakh i proportsiyakh rasshirennogo vosproizvodstva v nesotsialisticheskikh stranakh Azii" [On the Tempos and Proportions of Extended Reproduction in the Non-Socialist Countries of Asia], NAIA, No. 6 (1961), 32–46; N. P. Shmelev, "Burzhuaznyye ekonomisti o roli gosudarstvennogo sektora v slaborazvitykh stranakh" [Bourgeois Economists on the Role of the State Sector in the Underdeveloped Countries], MEIMO, No. 4 (1962), 87–91. Shmelev has also written a book on this subject which I have not been able to obtain: Idiologiya imperializma i problemy slaborazvitykh stran [Ideology of Imperialism and the Problems of the Underdeveloped Countries] (Moscow 1962). On a less scholarly—but propagandistically more effective—level, see the discussion on the potential contribution of the Soviet model in Sovremennyy Vostok [Contemporary East], begun by the article of the Indian economist Mahalanobis in No. 9 (1959), 13–15, and continuing through the next several issues.

9

## The Third World in Soviet Perspective

parlance is termed the "price scissors." A pound of coffee, rubber, or tin does not buy as much in the way of machine tools today as it would have ten years ago. Soviet writers press this point with obvious relish, claiming that terms of trade with the Soviet Union are much more favorable. It is thus incumbent on the governments of the emerging nations to achieve genuine freedom by breaking their dependence upon the former metropoles and other capitalist trading partners and orienting their trade to the Communist countries.

The foreign exchange problem is further complicated by the repatriation of profits to investors in the advanced countries. Very substantial sums are involved, and the developing countries would very much like to have these at their own disposal for the purchase of badly needed imports. Expropriation or extensive nationalization of foreign enterprises is rejected by most governments as a course of action, not least of all since this would rapidly dry up the sources of foreign investment capital which continue to be required. The Soviets are naturally unimpressed by any arguments relating to the protection of private property and lend moral support to any countries embarking on nationalization programs.[t] They argue that the loss of new investment will not be a significant matter if the new countries mobilize their own resources and turn to the Soviet Union for aid.

The Soviets criticize Western aid for supporting private enterprise rather than putting resources directly at the disposal of the local governments, as the Soviet aid program does. They also claim that Western aid is generally concentrated in sectors of the economy that do little to promote self-sufficiency and industrialization and that facilitate continued "neo-colonialist" penetration. There is a substantial segment of the international Communist movement—mostly oriented toward China —which urges the developing countries to reject Western aid.[u]

t. Cf. S. I. Tyul'panov, "K voprosu o gosudarstvennom kapitalizme v slaborazvitykh stranakh" [The Question of State Capitalism in the Underdeveloped Countries], *Vestnik L.G.U.* [Herald of the Leningrad State University], Economics, Philosophy and Law Series, No. 1 (1961), 5–22; translated in JPRS 8370.

u. From the extensive literature on foreign aid, the following are of

10

## Soviet Writers on the Developing Areas

The Soviets have not adopted this extreme position, but do claim that the new nations would have little to lose if they were to dispense with aid from the West.

The Soviets have not been faced with demands for aid from a great number of nations and have never really been put to the test of providing aid on a broad scale to compensate for losses of Western investment and aid. If not the bulk, then at least the most spectacular of the Soviet aid projects have been in support of large-scale undertakings, principally in the field of industry. This is described as necessary for redressing the economic imbalance characteristic of the aftermath of colonial rule, and the acquisition of an industrial base is extremely attractive to developing countries. The Soviets believe that by creating industry and its attendant industrial proletariat, the chances for proletarian hegemony of the continuing revolution are enhanced. Furthermore, since the non-Communist world does form a sort of coherent economic unit, it is in the Soviet interest to encourage particularism and autarky as steps toward breaking up the international economic system and reducing the scope of trade. Since loans from the Soviet Union are normally to be repaid in traditional trade goods, the normal flow of trade is reduced all the more.

Clearly the need for capital cannot be solved by reliance on foreign aid or on the proceeds from nationalized industry. Resources for development must be derived mainly from domestic resources. In the developing countries this generally involves restrictions on consumption and increased productivity —specifically in the agrarian sector which, poor as it may be, represents the bulk of available resources.

more than routine interest: R. G. Iskandarov, *K voprosu o pomoshchi slaborazvitym stranam* [The Question of Aid to the Underdeveloped Countries] (Moscow 1960); translated in JPRS 16,141. Also R. A. Ul'yanovskiy, "Imperialisticheskaya politika 'pomoshchi' S.Sh. slaborazvitym stranam Azii" [The Imperialistic Policy of U.S. "Aid" to the Underdeveloped Countries of Asia], NAIA, No. 2 (1962), 39–57; and "Konferentsiya na temu Amerikanskaya 'pomoshch'' stranam Azii" [Conference on the Theme of American "Aid" to the Countries of Asia], MEIMO, No. 1 (1958), 95–134. The Chinese view is presented by Liu Ning-i, "Speech at the WFTU General Council Meeting," *Peking Review*, No. 24 (1960), 12.

## The Third World in Soviet Perspective

The peasantry is not only the main resource of most of the developing countries; if it can be mobilized, its size alone makes it the most important single element of the population. Thus any program which attempts to rationalize and increase agricultural production must also take into account the agricultural producer. For the Communists, the peasantry is of utmost importance in the quest for power and, particularly in Asia, it assumes a role much greater than that of the proletariat. The Communist attitude toward the agrarian question is therefore of crucial importance and has received a great amount of attention in the scholarly literature. The governments in most of the Asian countries, and many in Latin America and Africa, must find means to break up large land holdings that are socially unacceptable and at the same time see that production does not become inefficient. Communist criticism of the land reforms undertaken by non-Communist governments has been sharp and follows the expected pattern of giving greatest credit to those countries that are on the best terms with the Soviet Union.[v]

The Communists concentrate their tactical interest on two particular rural groups—the "poor peasantry" and the "agricultural proletariat." The poor peasantry is not readily defined; generally some arbitrary acreage figure is selected and all peasants with smaller holdings are by definition "poor." This acreage limitation is not universal, but varies from country to country and frequently seems to be selected so that about 40 per cent of the peasantry of a given country falls into the "poor" category. There are similar criteria for middle and rich peasants (occasionally called "kulaks"). The poor peasant has the greatest interest in land redistribution and the rich peasant is the main force opposing it. By agitating for radical land reform, the Communists attempt to mobilize the peasantry by creating a class struggle in the countryside corresponding to the class struggle that is said to exist between the workers and the bourgeois-capitalists in the cities. Land reform by the bourgeois governments—which often are closely tied to the landed interests—are only palliatives undertaken to inhibit the

v. See note k above.

## Soviet Writers on the Developing Areas

development of rural class struggle. Communist writers show little enthusiasm for such reform, although they concede that some small benefit is derived, especially when there is a cooperative movement to embrace the newly entitled peasantry.[w] Only what Ul'yanovskiy terms agrarian reform "from below," [x] executed on the poor peasants' own terms, would provide a satisfactory solution for the Communists. Obviously no government interested in maintaining output and a semblance of law and order could tolerate such a course.

Communist coolness toward bourgeois land reform stems from another important consideration. In Marxist terms, the agrarian relationships of the developing countries are "feudal" or "semi-feudal" in nature—that is, they are precapitalist and are characterized by such features as sharecropping, payment in kind, compulsory labor, and the general lack of a money economy.[y] Bourgeois land reform is designed to bring the agrarian sector only into the capitalist stage, an entire historical era behind the achievement of socialism which the Communists seek. Granted that capitalist development of the countryside promotes class differentiation and would ultimately create a genuine agricultural proletariat (as in the advanced countries); the Communists are not inclined to let history take its course but prefer to prod it.

In Russia, China, and several of the satellites, agriculture was brusquely propelled past the capitalist era by granting "land to the tillers," only to collectivize it immediately into "socialist" forms. Insistence on land reform "from below" and the favor with which the Communists view the precollective cooperative movements indicate that they consider this technique to be generally applicable in the developing countries.[z]

The "poor peasantry" is not a proletarian class in the strict Marxist definition, since it does own land and other means of

w. Even the modest credit which has been given to agrarian reform in the past is now said to be excessive. See the comments by G. Kim in *World Marxist Review*, No. 4 (1962), 75.

x. See Selection No. 10, below.

y. See *Fundamentals*, 385–86.

z. I. Farizov, "Pervyye shagi kooperativnogo dvizheniya" [First Steps of the Cooperative Movement], *Kommunist*, No. 13 (1962), 96–99.

*The Third World in Soviet Perspective*

production. Poor peasants do frequently sharecrop or work as hired labor, however, and the Communists have found it advantageous to make them a sort of "honorary proletariat," although in practice they are well aware of the problems of forcing any peasant into the proletarian mold. In a number of countries, there are large plantations that do employ a sort of agricultural proletariat—wage workers whose entire efforts are consumed in working plantation land. Ceylonese tea, Indonesian rubber, Latin American fruits, and African cocoa are frequently grown on such plantations, and in many instances the landowners are individuals or companies operating from the ex-metropoles or other advanced countries. In such cases, the Communists enjoy the tactical advantage of being able to combine the anti-capitalist slogan with that of anti-imperialism, and substantially avoid the difficulties encountered when attacking domestic interests. The agricultural proletariat is usually too small to be a decisive factor in class struggle, but the Communists believe that, within its limitations, it offers them some of their best opportunities. To the extent that the poor peasantry and the agricultural proletariat can be unified under one leadership, they represent the most powerful group in many of the developing areas.

There are occasional variations in the patterns outlined above and one of them has become a major matter of interest to the Soviets. In much of tropical Africa, agrarian relationships are prefeudal and land is collectively owned. There is little discernible difference between this type of land ownership and the collective farms that Communists advocate. It would take very little beyond ideological baptism to accept the African village as a socialist production form, but there are a number of problems that arise in this connection. These have been dealt with in considerable detail by Soviet writers; [aa] the

aa. See Selection No. 11, below. Also by Potekhin, "On 'African Socialism,'" *International Affairs* (Moscow), No. 1 (1963), 71–79. On the question of communal land holdings in earlier Marxist polemics, see L. Pistrak, "Soviet Views on Africa," *Problems of Communism*, XI (March–April 1962), 24–31. The problem also caused some stir in—of all places—Albania during the guerrilla war there. One Mustafa Jinishi seems to have felt that the Geg system of land tenure was a semi-socialist form.

14

## Soviet Writers on the Developing Areas

problem is closely related to the entire question of classes in African society, which we shall discuss later.

The working class, the keystone of Marx's social analysis, is extremely weak in the countries of the third world. With a very few exceptions, the proletariat simply cannot play a leading role in the revolutionary movements which continue to characterize the development of Asia, Africa, and Latin America. The Soviets attempt to extract the maximum propaganda from whatever successes the labor movement does have, and indeed they have had no little success in organizing workers and exploiting their discontent. They are fully aware, however, that the labor movement is an extremely weak reed.[bb] The workers are especially difficult to organize, because of extensive unemployment. In addition, many are only seasonal workers, almost all have strong ties to the land which inhibit the formation of class consciousness, and industry is on such a small scale that they tend to identify with their employer rather than with their "own" class.[cc]

The Communists expect conditions to improve as industrialization proceeds, especially where liberal socialist governments become increasingly unwilling to restrain Communist organizational activities. This prospect seems to lie rather far in the

For this or other heresies he met an untimely death. Julian Amery, *Sons of the Eagle* (London 1948), 266–67.

bb. Zhukov has clearly stated that Soviet writers tend to "varnish the truth" and attribute too much potential to the workers in the developing areas. Cited in Yu. B. Bromley, "K itogam nauchnoy deyatel'nosti uchrezhdeniy otdeleniya istoricheskikh nauk AN SSSR za 1961 god" [Summary of the Results of Scientific Work Carried out by the Department of History of the USSR Academy of Sciences for 1961], *Voprosy Istorii* [Questions of History], No. 4 (1962), 126; translated in JPRS 13,890.

cc. On the working class, see V. V. Balabushevich, "O nekotorykh osobennostyakh rabochego dvizheniya v stranakh Vostoka no sovremennom etape" [On Some Peculiarities of the Workers' Movement in the Countries of the East at the Present Stage], SV, No. 2 (1959), esp. 51–52. A broader survey appeared in *Kommunist*, No. 6 (1962), 103–11— "Pod"yem rabochego dvizheniya v stranakh Azii i Afriki" [Upsurge of the Workers' Movement in the Countries of Asia and Africa]; translated in JPRS 13,774. Probably the best Marxist work on all classes in the third world—including the proletariat—is by the East German Walter Markov, "Mouvement national et classes sociales dans le Tiers-Monde," *Cahiers Internationaux*, No. 117 (1962); pp. 51–52 have particular relevance for the workers' movement.

15

## The Third World in Soviet Perspective

future, however, and the labor movement plays a generally secondary role in Communist activities. The peasantry and intelligentsia appear to be much more fertile fields for endeavor, and one may suspect that the degree of attention devoted to the labor movement is more a result of piety than of conviction. As early as 1956, the editors of *Sovetskoye Vostokovedeniye* found it necessary to remind their readers that the organization of workers should not be neglected out of enthusiasm for the possibilities of peasant-based revolution.[dd] The intervening years have done but little to stimulate interest in the labor movement; indeed the realization is growing that the workers are still of little political value.

The question of social classes in the developing areas is central to the entire Soviet analysis. The customary division into bourgeois, proletarian, peasant, and intellectual is taken as a starting point, but the nineteenth-century European class distinctions of Marx are today even less applicable in the third world than they are in the advanced countries. In the colonial era, it was generally assumed that the exploiters comprised the colonial power in alliance with the local big and comprador [ee] bourgeoisie and landed classes. The exploited were the peasantry and the very small middle class and workers' class. The indigenous exploiters were closely bound to the colonial system, since it was the colonial power that permitted them to occupy their position and in many cases had provided the comprador and big bourgeoisie with their start up the ladder. These were thus *status quo* forces, obviously not interested in any form of social revolution, and not even interested in the liberation of their countries from colonial rule. The big bourgeoisie was, after all, part of the international bourgeoisie, tied closely into the capitalist system (which Marxists believe to be just as "international" as they would like the proletariat to be). Under the domination of the imperialists and local big bourgeoisie, the normal course of development for the colonies

dd. "Velikaya Oktyabr'skaya Sotsialisticheskaya Revolyutsia i sovremennyy Vostok [The Great October Socialist Revolution and the Contemporary East], SV, No. 5 (1956), 7.

ee. A "comprador" was a native who acted as an agent for the colonial power in dealing with the local population.

would have been the long and arduous road to monopoly capitalism constructed on the American and European model, after which the time might come when revolution—both social and political—would be possible.

A few decades ago, there was little apparent unrest in the colonies and semi-colonies, and the upper classes did tend to identify with the colonial power rather than with the great mass of their compatriots. There arose, however, nationalist movements demanding freedom from foreign domination, whether colonial or semi-colonial. This revolutionary trend rapidly became the all-important fact of life in the third world, rendering the theories of the colonists and Communists equally irrelevant. Lenin no doubt had some grasp of these forces, which were beginning to stir in the latter part of his life, and the Soviet adventure in China was the initial faltering attempt to come to grips with the new opportunities. The term which was to characterize the class behind the national liberation movement—the national bourgeoisie—was already applied to the Kuomintang in the period of Kuomintang-Communist cooperation, and for a few years in the late 1920's communism appeared to see its destiny in the East.

This is not the place to trace the theoretical or practical course which the Comintern and the Soviet leadership took toward this national bourgeoisie.[ff] Suffice it to say that until the death of Stalin the Soviets had just about completely failed to appreciate what was going on in the emerging third world and had met with almost consistent failure in their efforts to inject themselves into it. The great shift in Soviet attitude of the mid-1950's can well be described as a coming-to-terms with the national bourgeoisie, on both the theoretical and the practical political level. Nehru, Sukarno, Nasser, Nkrumah, Houphouët-Boigny—even Perón—were enemies of international communism mainly because the Soviets chose to regard them as such. In most cases, all that was required to alter its role was recognition that the national bourgeoisie was funda-

ff. The early Communist policy toward the colonial areas is discussed at length in Dimitrio Boersner, *The Bolsheviks and the National and Colonial Question* (Geneva 1957).

## The Third World in Soviet Perspective

mentally opposed to imperialism and an acceptable ally of communism. The Soviet policy shift made this recognition and the third world was brought into being almost overnight. Realization of the options that were opening up as a result of the emergence of genuinely independent new states and "national liberation movements" made possible the most fruitful Soviet foreign policy move since the period of the Popular Front and World War II.

The policy readjustment was not without some difficulties, of course—not the least of which was the threatened loss of the hoary bogey of colonialism. Unwilling to lose such a useful symbol entirely, the Soviets fabricated the concept of "neo-colonialism," which admits the political independence of the new nations but denies their economic independence and perpetuates the threat posed by international monopoly capitalism. Neo-colonialism, a movement led by the United States, attempts to reassert the primacy of the imperialist powers by anti-Communism, economic infiltration, and a relatively sophisticated use of force. Standing outside of the "International Socialist System" and still tied into the international system of capital, the national bourgeois states are in constant danger of losing both their political independence and whatever small amount of economic independence they have been able to achieve.

Neo-colonialism has powerful allies within the new nations —an alliance of the big bourgeoisie and the remaining feudal interests in the countryside. In some independent countries, such as the Philippines, the big bourgeoisie is actually in control of the government; in others, such as India, it constantly strives to capture the state machinery and oust the national and patriotic forces. Soviet writers helpfully point out that the only trustworthy allies which the national bourgeoisie has are the local Communists. If their participation is rejected, the outcome of the struggle of national versus big bourgeoisie will hang precariously in the balance.

It is extremely difficult to separate the national and big bourgeoisie analytically, and it is probably impossible to arrive at any satisfactory definition of "national bourgeoisie" at

## Soviet Writers on the Developing Areas

all. The big bourgeoisie is generally said to have made its fortune under colonial auspices,[gg] while the national bourgeoisie fought for independence in order to create a political and economic atmosphere in which it could freely develop. Also, some attempts are made to distinguish between the two groups on the basis of their wealth. Nevertheless, the only useful criteria seem to be class objectives and foreign policy orientation, with the latter, not unexpectedly, being the main factor.

The big bourgeoisie is pro-imperialist, while the national bourgeoisie tends to assume a neutral position in international affairs and to pose opportunities rather than obstacles for Soviet foreign policy. "Neutralism" in the Soviet context of course has very specific meanings. In itself, it is not even a positive phenomenon; determination must first be made as to whose interest is served by a specific neutralist policy.[hh] Also, neutralism with regard to imperialism is not permissible [ii] and by analogy the same holds true with regard to neo-colonialism. If applied strictly, this would mean that a true neutral would have to be consistently opposed to the United States. The Soviets have not yet found it politic to press this point, since their primary interest is a negative one: to ensure that the new nations are not allied with the West and pose no threat to the Soviet Union.

The class objectives of the big bourgeoisie and national bourgeoisie in the domestic economic sphere are described as "state monopoly capitalism" and "state capitalism," respectively. The former is said to be the economic structure characteristic of the Western capitalist nations, where the monopolies have firm control of the state machinery and exploit it for their own ends. "State capitalism," on the other hand, is the

gg. N. Savel'ev, "O natsional'noy burzhuazii v stranakh Yugo-Vostochnoy Azii" [On the National Bourgeoisie in the Countries of Southeast Asia], MEIMO, No. 4 (1961), 40, 42.

hh. Cf. S. I. Tyul'panov, "Problema neytralizma slaborazvitykh stran v svete resheniy XXII s"yezda KPSS" [The Problem of Neutralism of the Underdeveloped Countries in Light of the Decisions of the 22nd Congress of the CPSU], *Vestnik LGU*, Economics, Philosophy and Law Series, No. 4 (1961), esp. p. 17.

ii. S. Viskov, "The Collapse of Colonialism and New Trends in International Relations," *International Affairs* (Moscow), No. 9 (1961), 10.

## The Third World in Soviet Perspective

characteristic economic structure of the national bourgeoisie. The Soviets evince great interest in this model, which in Western terms could be defined as a nationalist and moderately socialist economic policy. They applaud the element of planning that state capitalism introduces into the economy, as well as the nationalization of certain private enterprises (especially those foreign-owned) and the popularization of socialist slogans. State capitalism provides a certain groundwork for the later introduction of "scientific socialism" under Communist guidance and is thus somewhat comparable to the cooperative movement in the agricultural realm, at a much more advanced level.

Soviet writers continually stress that state capitalism is an ambivalent phenomenon. It is, after all, a capitalist system and can just as readily develop into state monopoly capitalism as into socialism, under pressure from the big bourgeoisie and the blandishments of the neo-colonialists. On balance, however, the Soviets probably believe that internal pressures toward radicalism, coupled with the international influence exerted by the Soviet Union,[jj] will generally serve to move state capitalism along the path toward socialism and communism. At a minimum, state capitalism serves to weaken the role and position of the monopolies within the international economic system and reduce the strength of the imperialist and neo-colonialist powers.

The ambivalent nature of state capitalism is a reflection of the dual nature of the national bourgeoisie as a whole, which is progressive insofar as it opposes imperialism, but anti-progressive insofar as it is interested in promoting its own bourgeois-capitalist interests. By supporting the national bourgeoisie, the Communists are restrained from pressing the theme of class struggle, but this is in any event compatible with the national interests of the Soviet Union, which would be more than willing to settle for the national bourgeois bird in hand rather than the proletariat and peasantry in the bush. The sacrifice of local Communist interests has at times been painful, but no more so than many another that Communists have made at

jj. Markov, 59, and Mirskiy, "Tvorcheskiy Marksizm . . . ," 66.

20

the behest of the Soviet leadership. The doctrinal problem of making common cause with the bourgeoisie is also nothing new and is generally passed over with the justification that Communists support only those aspects of the national bourgeois program which are progressive—i.e., anti-imperialist—while reserving the right to oppose the national bourgeoisie on specific issues. The Soviets accept the national bourgeoisie for what it is and, particularly in the past few years, their illusions about it have steadily dwindled. They consider it to be only a transitional class, and attempt to make what use they can of this uneasy ally.

Table I summarizes in very broad terms some of the characteristic differences between the states dominated by the national bourgeoisie and the big bourgeoisie. In addition, it includes the other state forms that comprise the Soviet taxonomy of governments found in the third world.[kk] The few remaining colonies and the countries that are already "socialist" are included only for the sake of filling out the picture, but the other categories are of no little practical and theoretical importance.

The most challenging countries for Communist analysis are those where class analysis breaks down almost completely. Particularly in sub-Saharan Africa the traditional categories are clearly inadequate, and even such an *ad hoc* term as "national bourgeoisie" has little meaning; Mali or the Congo has no significant class which could be designated as bourgeois of any type. Class differentiation has simply not progressed that far because—the Communists would say—the colonial powers did not permit the local populace to engage in the type of enterprise, or enjoy the education, that would produce a capitalist-bourgeois outlook. Even in West Africa, where there were more opportunities, only the beginnings of an indigenous

kk. This taxonomy is based on that given in Chapter 16 of *Fundamentals of Marxism-Leninism* (see p. 49, below). Those who collect taxonomies can find alternate ones in Stalin, *Works* (English edn.), VII, 148; Dobrev in *World Marxist Review*, No. 5 (1962), 68; Avakov and Mirskiy, pp. 293–295 below; and Mirskiy and V. Tyagunenko, "Tendentsii i perspektivy natsional'no-osvoboditel'nykh revolyutsiy" [Tendencies and Perspectives of National Liberation Revolutions], MEIMO, No. 11 (1961), 26.

TABLE 1

Types of States in the Third World

| Dominant Class | State Form | Domestic Economic Structure | Relationship to International Systems | |
|---|---|---|---|---|
| | | | Economic | Political |
| Colonialist (Imperialist) | Colony | Colonial | Imperialist | None |
| Big (Monopoly) Bourgeoisie | Bourgeois Dictatorship | Monopoly Capitalist | Capitalist | Pro-West |
| National Bourgeoisie | Liberal Democracy | State Capitalist | Capitalist | Neutral |
| "Progressive Intelligentsia" | Liberal Democracy | State Capitalist | Independent | Neutral |
| United Front | National Democracy | State Capitalist | Independent | Pro-Bloc |
| Workers and Peasants | People's Democracy, etc. | Socialist | Socialist | In Bloc |

bourgeoisie can be found—not large enough to play a decisive role in national development.

Sub-Saharan Africa is thus noticeably differentiated from the rest of the third world; among significant areas, only in Indonesia do the Soviets appear to feel that the colonial experience produced somewhat analogous results. The agrarian problem in Africa also defies traditional analysis, as we have noted. Agrarian relations have for the most part not entered the feudal phase, so there is little class differentiation in this, the largest sector of African society. There is conveniently an incipient proletariat in some of the African countries, one that grew up not in dialectical opposition to an indigenous bourgeoisie but as a result of imperialist exploitation, which is rapidly being eliminated. The African proletariat is not exactly numerous (except in Southern Africa, where the mines have attracted many laborers), but it is regarded with considerable interest by Soviet writers.[11] The absence of a bourgeoisie and the scanty potential for class conflict in any part of the society pose both problems and opportunities when viewed in the light of Soviet theory.

The doctrinal problems are mainly concerned with the difficulties of establishing socialism without first having passed through capitalism or even, in some cases, feudalism; and with the delineation of African "classes," particularly the elites that have assumed control of most of the emerging African states. In addition, most of these leaders have declared themselves to be socialists or even Marxists, but pursue programs that have little in common with "scientific socialism" as practiced in the USSR.

The opportunities offered are less complicated. The absence of a bourgeoisie—the natural enemy of the proletariat in competition for leadership of the ongoing revolution of modernization—should leave the road to power relatively unobstructed for any Communist group that can muster at least

11. For instance, M. I. Braginskiy, "Sotsial'nyye sdvigi v tropicheskoy Afrike posle vtoroy mirovoy voyny" [Social Changes in Tropical Africa After World War II], *Sovetskaya Etnografiya* [Soviet Ethnography], No. 6 (1960), 31–43. Translated by the Slavic Languages Research Institute; summarized in *Mizan Newsletter*, III (February and June 1961).

## The Third World in Soviet Perspective

some strength and determination. The Africans are particularly sensitive to the problem of neo-colonialism and many of the new leaders are willing to look to Soviet models in their desperate search for forms of development. The Soviets claim that the Soviet Union does offer a pertinent model of development for backward countries in Africa and elsewhere. At the same time, they solve one of their pressing doctrinal problems: the achievement of socialism without first passing through capitalism. This feat was accomplished by the Central Asian Republics and Mongolia under the influence and with the support of socialist development in Russia.[mm] Given the preponderance of Soviet power and influence on the world scene, the Soviets say, countries in the third world can make a similar transition. Indeed, they *must* make it, since it would be impossible to demand that they pass through the agonies of capitalist development and put off to a very indefinite future the attainment of their ambitions. Mongolia or Uzbekistan may seem an odd model for Mali or the Yemen. The Soviets do not see any incongruity, however, and perhaps many Malians or Yemeni do not either.

The other doctrinal questions have not found such ready solutions. The problems of "African socialism" and classes in African society are among the most hotly debated questions of Soviet orientology. I. I. Potekhin has been at the heart of both of these discussions, and problems of everyday politics are clearly at stake.[nn] If African socialism has some validity as a "separate path," the more radical African states can be treated as virtual members of the bloc, or at least as being in a transitional stage of "national democracy."[oo] Similarly Nkrumah,

mm. See M. S. Dzhunusov, *O nekapitalisticheskom puti razvitiya* [On the Non-Capitalist Path of Development] (Moscow 1963). A "scientific conference" was also held recently on this theme in Dushanbe; it was reported in *Pravda*, June 9, 1962, and at greater length by Z. Osmanova in *NAIA*, No. 1 (1963), 237–39.

nn. See note aa above.

oo. The literature on "national democracy" has been summarized by William Shinn, "The National-Democratic State: A Communist Program for the Less-Developed Areas," *World Politics*, xv (April 1963), 377–89. Since then, several additional important pieces have become available. See A. Sobolev, "National Democracy—The Way to Social

## Soviet Writers on the Developing Areas

Modibo Keita, Sékou Touré (in his day), and perhaps other emerging leaders (in theirs) seem to be exceptionally well disposed toward the Soviet Union, and it would be ideologically tidy if a special category could be devised to single them out from the run-of-the-mill national bourgeoisie.

The rubric under which these elites have for the most part been gathered is a type of "progressive intelligentsia," without any clearly elaborated class economic interests. The intelligentsia exists of course throughout the third world, in the form of a "military intelligentsia," a "bureaucratic intelligentsia," or just an intelligentsia which is in the business of politics. Whatever the form, and whether in power or out, the intelligentsia is a major preoccupation of the Communists, who recognize the gap between expectations and possibilities that characterizes the status of these frequently deracinated groups. The Communists note a "leftward migration" of the intelligentsia in its search for fulfillment of individual or national aspirations, and they intend to make communism the means of expression of this "leftness." [pp]

The Communists are of course not without competitors. The intelligentsia—particularly if it has achieved power, but also if its members can be integrated into bourgeois society—can move just as readily toward bourgeois and even imperialist attitudes as it can toward communism. Certain African leaders, for instance, are said to have succumbed to the pressures of domestic reaction, the big bourgeoisie, and feudal landowners —weak as these may be.[qq] Simultaneously, imperialism and especially neo-colonialism continually attempt to seduce and corrupt independent governments. The threat is thus similar to that facing national bourgeois governments, but the Com-

Progress," *World Marxist Review*, No. 2 (1963), 39–48; B. Dimitrov, "Concerning the National-Democratic State," *Filosofska Misul* (Sofia), No. 4 (1962), translated in JPRS 16,179; V. I. Pavlov and I. B. Red'ko, "Gosudarstvo natsional'noy demokratii i perekhod k nekapitalisticheskomy razvitiyu" [The National Democratic State and the Transition to Non-Capitalist Development], NAIA, No. 1 (1963), 29–40; and articles by Richard Lowenthal and Justus M. van der Kroef, "On National Democracy," in *Survey*, No. 47 (1963).

pp. Markov, 55; Sobolev, *passim*.
qq. Mirskiy, "Tvorcheskiy Marksizm . . . ," 65–66.

## The Third World in Soviet Perspective

munists seem to believe that their chances are better here than when dealing with national bourgeois regimes. Indeed, the main practical difference between national bourgeois and "intelligentsia" regimes is probably the much greater optimism with which the Soviets regard the latter.

In competition for the allegiance of the intelligentsia, the Communists seem to fear the liberal ideologies of democratic socialism, trade unionism, and nationalism at least as much as the activities of domestic reaction and neo-colonialism. Probably no group is handled with such singular venom in Soviet writings as are the Democratic Socialists. To some extent this may be a heritage of the bitterness which has been typical of Communist-Socialist relations since World War I, and considerations of orthodoxy versus heresy cannot be overlooked. Yet it is hard to avoid the conclusion that Communists are obsessed with the fear that moderate leftists will seize the leadership of the leftward drift of politics in the developing areas. There is little else which can account for the virtually unparalleled attacks on such progressives as Betancourt or Haya de la Torre, or on the Indian and Indonesian Socialists.[rr]

The Soviets are rather more tolerant of socialism which is not openly anti-Communist and which is not related to the Socialist International. They have accorded guarded recognition to "socialism" in Ghana and Mali—in part no doubt because they do not feel these doctrines to be serious competitors, but also because opposing them would place the Soviet Union in the position of opposing African nationalism. Nationalism and regional supranationalism (the pan-African and pan-Arab movements) are dynamic forces, and the Communists have no intention of repeating their earlier mistakes and isolating themselves from the mainsprings of sentiment in the developing areas. Although nationalism and the "pan" movements pose substantial obstacles to the expansion of Soviet influence, the Communists see no alternative but to work with them as best they can and attempt to utilize them by turning nationalist

rr. See Shul'govskiy, Selection No. 14, below; and Ye. Dement'ev, "Aziatskaya Sotsialisticheskaya Konferentsiya" [The Asiatic Socialist Conference], MEIMO, No. 5 (1958), 133–37.

## Soviet Writers on the Developing Areas

sentiments against the former metropoles and the United States.

The neo-colonialist slogan is to a considerable extent an attempt to capture nationalist sentiment by keeping alive the discords of the past. The newly independent states are portrayed as being in constant and real danger that can be overcome only by rallying all of the progressive forces of the country in a united front. Unity of national purpose—often embodied in the single-party state—is a vital issue, particularly in the politically backward states, and their relative lack of social differentiation facilitates the formation of a united front. Furthermore, these countries, led by insecure elites, tend to feel themselves gravely endangered by neo-colonialism. Although particularly well suited to them, the united front is the slogan not only for the sub-Saharan states; it is the officially enjoined program for Communists in all of the developing areas. Successfully pursued, it provides the Communists with a legitimate political and social role and simultaneously vitiates the threat of anti-communism that has wrought havoc among a number of Communist parties, especially in the Middle East.

The united front is but a way-station, however, for of itself it is not the chosen vehicle for Communist accession to power. The penultimate aim of Soviet policy is to place the united front in power and thereby establish a "state of national democracy," which in turn is the transitional form to people's democracy and socialism—i.e., to the exclusion of all except Communists from positions of real power, and accession to the "International Socialist System." National democracy is a rather vague category [ss] which has never been clearly extensionalized

ss. Dimitrov (JPRS, p. 7) specifically refers to it as a very vague concept. If there ever has been a national democracy, it was Cuba, although only East German writers seem to have made the identification. Neither the Cubans nor the Soviets have confirmed it and, in any event, it was a very short historical period, since Cuba joined the socialist camp not long after the doctrine of national democracy was promulgated. During 1963, a tendency to avoid the use of the name "national democracy" was evident. Thus, although Algeria had been specifically mentioned as a candidate for national democracy, an authoritative article in late 1963 never mentioned the term. V. Kaboshkin and Yu. Shchirovskiy, "Alzhir: Ot natsional'no osvobozhdeniya k sotsial'nomy" [Algeria: From National to Socialist Liberation], *Kommunist*, No. 16 (1963), 110–20. (Trans-

27

## The Third World in Soviet Perspective

and which even in theoretical discussion is highly ambiguous. Its characteristics were first set forth in the 1960 Moscow Declaration, although the term had been used previously. They are broad enough to be declared applicable in practically any national social and economic setting, although progress to national democracy is explicitly envisioned only for relatively backward states. Cuba, Guinea, Ghana, Mali, and Indonesia have been mentioned in this regard; Cuba passed through the stage quite rapidly and the other four have yet to attain it. More countries may be added to the list of prospective national democracies (Burma is a particularly good prospect) [tt] and it would not be surprising to find Guinea expunged, in view of the deterioration of Soviet-Guinean relations in 1962.

Good state relations with the Soviet Union seem to be a prerequisite for nomination as a prospective national democracy; perhaps even the main practical criterion. Officially, a national democracy must free itself from neo-colonialist influence in both domestic and foreign affairs, grant "broad democratic freedoms," and commit itself to a "non-capitalist path of development." These requirements involve an approach to the Soviet Union, the acceptance of domestic communism, substantial rejection of Western influence, and a commitment to something resembling the Soviet developmental model. This is quite a program, obviously, but far from enough to satisfy the Chinese and other "dogmatist" critics of Soviet policy. Success in achieving Communist control via the road of national democracy presupposes the voluntary relinquishment of power by ruling elites. Granted, there is always the possibility of the threat of violence at some stage of the transition and nowhere do the Soviets reject the use of violence in seizure of power in the developing areas. Yet the national democracy in its essence provides for a peaceful transition of power; the Soviet

lated in JPRS 22,368.) The authors do, however, discuss Algeria's future in terms that are unmistakably those of a "national democracy." Also, see below, p. 54.

tt. R. A. Ul'yanovskiy, "Birma no novom puti" [Burma on a New Path], *Pravda,* March 15, 1963; and A. Semyonov and A. Filippov, "Burma's Struggle for a New Way Forward," *International Affairs* (Moscow), No. 5 (1963), 46–50.

literature—official, scholarly, and popular—relegates the possibility of violence firmly to the background, except perhaps in the case of states allied closely with the West.[uu] As is well known, the Chinese reject this approach and their hostility is exemplified by their failure even to recognize that such a category as "national democracy" exists. But for the Soviets, violence—a basic tenet of Marxism-Leninism—is of little interest.[vv] They offer as models the almost bloodless united-front seizure of power in the October Revolution (as distinct from the ensuing civil war) and a means of economic development that can efficiently facilitate the process of modernization.[ww]

Unquestionably, the Soviets have come a long way and have made significant progress in developing new theoretical concepts to define the situation of the third world and their relationship to it. This is by no means an irreversible process; the emergence of a dogmatic leader after Khrushchev could alter the situation rapidly and cause a turn to the hard lines associated with Zhdanov and Mao Tse-tung. Yet it seems unlikely that the Soviets, so far committed to a gradualistic, "revisionist" approach to revolution in the developing areas, will readily alter their position. We must assume that the views held now will remain the basis of Soviet policy for some years to come.

uu. One of the more specific references—and it is vague enough—is in G. Starushenko, "Cherez obshchedemokraticheskiye preobrazovaniya k sotsialisticheskim" [Through General-Democratic Reforms to Socialist], *Kommunist,* No. 13 (1962), 107; translated in CDSP, xiv (No. 41), 15ff.

vv. I have discussed the problem of the resort to violence in *Communism and Revolution,* ed. by C. E. Black and T. P. Thornton (Princeton 1964), chapters 9 and 10.

ww. The Chinese have been quick to rebut the Soviets, claiming that the October revolution was not at all non-violent—"The Proletarian Revolution and Khrushchev's Revisionism—Comment on the Open Letter of the Central Committee of the CPSU (VIII)," *Renmin Ribao,* March 31, 1964. Translation in *Peking Review,* No. 14 (1964).

SELECTION 1

# Stalin's Theory of Colonial Revolution and the National Liberation Movement in Tropical and South Africa *

### BY I. I. POTEKHIN

*DESPITE its adulation of Stalin and dogmatic tone, this article has not been chosen to serve as a typical example of Soviet orientology in the Stalin era. Nor has it been included to raise unwelcome ghosts for the author—now the most prominent Soviet Africanist—although comparison with the tone of his current writing is edifying.[a] In fact, the attitude toward the national bourgeoisie which Potekhin shows in this article is much less hostile than most other writings of the time, and the bulk of the article (not reprinted here) is a remarkably scholarly piece when viewed in the context of 1950. Even the tributes to Stalin are relatively restrained, considering the occasion for which the article was prepared.*

*Stalin took considerable pride in his work on the "national and colonial problem." His first significant theoretical work— undertaken in 1913 at Lenin's direction—was in this area[b] and his first position in the Soviet government was as Com- missar of Nationalities. Although falling far short of the un- orthodox practices and attitudes of the Khrushchev period, Stalin's approach to the colonial and national problem and to the national bourgeoisie allowed for a certain degree of flexi- bility.*

*In the late 1940's—in the period of Zhdanov's ascendancy—*

---

* SOURCE: "Stalinskaya teoriya kolonial'noy revolyutsii i natsional'no-osvoboditel'noye dvizheniye v tropicheskoy i yuzhnoy Afrike," *Sovetskaya Etnografiya* [Soviet Ethnography], No. 1 (1950), 24–40. This report was read at the session of the Learned Council of the Institute of Ethnography dedicated to the Seventieth Birthday of Comrade J. V. Stalin.

a. See Selection No. 11, below.

b. See Isaac Deutscher, *Stalin: A Political Biography* (New York 1960), 117.

# Soviet Writers on the Developing Areas

*little of this flexibility was evident, and it was only after Stalin's death that a rapprochement with the national bourgeoisie and a generally more fruitful policy toward the third world were initiated. It is now apparent in retrospect that even during Stalin's last few years, however, some reappraisal of the sterile Zhdanov line was being undertaken and it is possible that this article by Potekhin was inspired by the faint breeze of a new emerging trend. There is certainly little on the surface that would give credence to such an interpretation, but in comparison to the piercingly strident tone characteristic of most writings of the period, Potekhin's moderation is unmistakable. Whether marking the end of one era or the beginning of another, this excerpt provides a good starting point from which to view the development of Soviet attitudes toward the third world.*

THE second period in the development of the national question begins with the epoch of imperialism.[c] The leading capitalist powers acquire colonies and are converted into colonial empires with many nationalities. Likewise, the national question has grown into a colonial or national-colonial question —i.e., into the question of freeing the peoples of the colonies and dependent countries from imperialist enslavement. While the national question previously was an internal question, it has now become an international one: the national question has bcome part of the overall question of proletarian revolution and the dictatorship of the proletariat.

The opportunist leaders and theoreticians of the Second International did not want to heed this radical change in the development of the national question. It was only Lenin and Stalin who first revealed the connection of the national question with the question of the colonies, who theoretically established this connection and made it the basis of the revolutionary activity of the proletariat.

"Previously, the national question usually became the center of a narrow circle of questions mainly pertaining to the 'cul-

c. The "first period" was characterized by such national movements as those of the Irish, Poles, Hungarians, etc.

tured' nationalities. The Irish, Hungarians, Polish, Finns, Serbs, and certain other nationalities in Europe constituted the group of peoples without civil rights who became the center of interest of the members of the Second International. Tens and hundreds of millions of Asiatic and African peoples, suffering national oppression in its most vulgar and cruel form, were generally left out of consideration. It was decided not to place white and black, 'cultured' and 'uncultured' people on the same plane. . . . We should now consider this duality and halfway policy in the national question as eliminated. Leninism has exposed this flagrant disparity, has destroyed the wall between the whites and the blacks, between European and Asiatics, between 'cultured' and 'uncultured' slaves of imperialism, and has thus connected the national question with the colonial question. Likewise, the national question was turned from a private internal question into a common international question, into a world question of the liberation of the oppressed peoples of dependent countries and colonies from the yoke of imperialism." [1]

J. V. Stalin, the master of materialist dialectics, the coryphaeus of science, has developed a well-ordered and rigorously scientific theory of colonial revolution, as noted in basic outlines by V. I. Lenin. Stalin's theory of colonial revolution proceeds from the fact that the solution of the colonial question, the liberation of oppressed peoples from colonial slavery, is impossible without a proletarian revolution and the overthrow of imperialism. In recent years since the Second World War, the "theory" of the possibility of eliminating the colonial system without destroying the capitalist means of production has gained wide popularity in bourgeois intelligentsia circles in colonial countries. The Nigerian Orizu, in his book *Without Bitterness*, subjects English colonial policy to sharp criticism, demands that Nigeria be given independence, and at the same time supports maintenance of the bases of capitalism. The Indian Ghoshal, in his book *People in the Colonies*, criticizes the imperialist colonial system in its entirety, demands its immediate elimination, and feels that such elimination is pos-

1. J. V. Stalin, *Sochineniya* [Collected Works], VI, 138–39.

sible while capitalism is preserved in the United States, England, and other countries.

It is not difficult to see that the class basis of the "theory" of Orizu and Ghoshal is the interests of the national bourgeoisie in the colonial countries. It would like to obtain independence —i.e., the possibility of independent control of its country— while maintaining inviolable the capitalist means of production and avoiding any radical democratic reforms whatsoever. The theoretical basis of this point of view is Kautsky's concept of imperialism.[d]

As a "classical" definition of imperialism, Ghoshal cites the definition of J. A. Hobson, who, in V. I. Lenin's estimation, took essentially the same point of view as Kautsky. Kautsky separated the politics of imperialism from its economics, and maintained that monoplies in the economy are compatible with non-monopolistic, non-violent, non-predatory forms of political behavior.

V. I. Lenin and J. V. Stalin, proceeding from the scientific theory of imperialism, maintain that the overthrow of capitalism and the annihilation of the colonial system are two aspects of the same problem. J. V. Stalin, at the 10th Party Congress in 1921, stated: "History says that the only means of destroying national injustice, the only means of establishing a regime of brotherly cooperation among the toiling masses of people, both oppressed and unoppressed, is to eliminate capitalism and establish the Soviet structure." [2]

The almost three decades which have passed since then have lent brilliant support to Stalin's position. In the USSR, along with the elimination of capitalism and the construction of socialist society, not only has national oppression in all its forms been eliminated, but in those nations which came under Soviet authority the actual injustice inherited from the old im-

---

d. Karl Kautsky (1854–1938) was the leading theoretician of the Socialist movement in the early twentieth century. Although Lenin originally had had a high regard for Kautsky, he later broke with him and— especially after the Bolshevik seizure of power—the two became implacable enemies. For more on Kautsky's views of imperialism, see p. 316 below, footnote c.

2. Stalin, v, 38.

perialist regime has also been eradicated. As a result of the victory of socialism in our Soviet country, each nation, large and small, feels itself at home; no one oppresses it or suppresses it, and all nations form together a single friendly family which is engaged in the common task of constructing communism. On the other hand, in the countries which still remain under the imperialist system, national-colonial oppression has not weakened one iota in these past thirty years, but has become even more cruel and unbearable. Imperialism cannot exist without some nations being enslaved and oppressed by other nations, the weak ones by the strong ones. The ideology of equality of all races and all nations, the ideology of the friendship of peoples, is foreign to the exploiting classes.

It thus follows, Comrade Stalin teaches, that "the national and colonial questions are inseparable from the question of liberation from the power of capital," that "the nations and colonies which are deprived of their civil rights cannot be liberated without overthrowing the power of capital." [3]

The struggle of the oppressed peoples in the colonies and dependent countries likewise coalesces with the struggle of the proletariat against imperialism in the metropoles of all advanced capitalist countries—for the dictatorship of the proletariat, for socialism. On the other hand, since the colonies are the rear forces,[e] the reserve of imperialism, the proletariat of the advanced capitalist countries cannot attain a durable victory over imperialism without liberating the colonies. The following important position of the Leninist-Stalinist theory of colonial revolution thus arises:

"The interests of the proletarian movements in the developed countries and the national liberation movement in the colonies require unification of these two types of revolutionary movements into a common front against the common enemy, against imperialism." [4] The Communist parties of the metropoles, proceeding from this main position, have always

e. "Rear forces" is a military metaphor, indicating that in terms both of manpower and of resources the colonies lend support to the imperialists in their fight against the revolutionary proletariat of the metropoles.

3. *Ibid.*, v, 56–57.

4. Stalin, vi, 145.

34

rendered and are rendering—especially now, after the Second World War—every kind of aid to the development of the national liberation movement in the colonies. The French Communist Party, for example, rendered and is continuing to render great and invaluable aid to the anti-imperialist movement in the French colonies of Africa.

Nowadays, the national liberation movement of the colonial people is an organic part of the overall anti-imperialist, democratic camp, headed by the Soviet Union. This is obvious even in the example of backward Africa, not to speak of the most developed colonies and dependent countries.

The labor unions of Africa belong to the World Federation of Labor Unions and send their delegates to its congresses. The youth organizations of Africa belong to the World Federation of Democratic Youth. A member of the executive committee of the WFDY, Gey Abdul, is a representative of the African youth. In the last festival of students and democratic youth in Budapest, representatives of African youth organizations participated. The democratic organizations of Africa have taken part in the World Congress of the Partisans of Peace in Paris; African representatives have been included in the permanent committee of the Congress. The vice-president of this committee, Gabriel d'Arbouissier, who visited Moscow during the All-Union Conference of Partisans of Peace, is the secretary-general of the African Democratic Union. African women's organizations are part of the World Democratic Federation of Women. African women participated as guests in the Conference of Asiatic Countries which was held recently in liberated China. "No longer can the African people be separated from the democratic camp," declared the African youth representative to the second WFDY Congress in Budapest.

The next extremely important thesis of Stalin's theory of colonial revolution is the requirement for making a strict separation "between revolution in imperialist countries—in countries which are oppressing other peoples—and revolution in colonial and dependent countries—in countries which are suffering from imperialist oppression by other states. Revolution

35

in imperialist countries is one thing; there the bourgeoisie is the oppressor of other peoples, it is counter-revolutionary at all stages of the revolution, and both the national force and the moment for a struggle for liberation are missing. The revolution in colonial and dependent countries is something else; there the yoke of imperialism of other states is one of the factors of revolution, this yoke cannot but provoke the national bourgeoisie, and the national bourgeoisie to a considerable degree and for a considerable length of time can support the revolutionary movement of its country against imperialism. There the national force and the moment for the fight for liberation are factors of revolution.

"If we do not make this distinction and do not understand this difference, if we identify the revolution in imperialist countries with the revolution in colonial countries, then we are veering off the path of Marxism, off the path of Leninism, and pursuing the path of the followers of the Second International." [5]

From this thesis comes the extremely important principal conclusion concerning the special strategic stage of colonial revolution, the stage of the common national anti-imperialist front, when the national bourgeoisie still supports the revolutionary movement.

This, of course, does not mean that there are no contradictions at this stage between the proletariat—the broad working masses—on one hand, and the national bourgeoisie on the other. The bourgeoisie supports the revolutionary movement of the people only in order to take advantage of the fruits of the revolution and to attain political power in order to subjugate and enslave the masses of its own country. This stage of the common national front is possible only when and where the proletariat has not yet emerged as an independent and decisive force, as the antipode to the national bourgeoisie, where the proletariat is still not in a condition to lead the struggle of the non-proletarian working masses.

In speaking before the students in the Communist University of Workers of the East in 1925, Comrade Stalin pointed

5. *Ibid.*, x, 10–11.

out that "as the revolutionary movement grows, the national bourgeoisie of such countries will become divided into two parts: into a revolutionary part (petty bourgeoisie) and a compromising part (big bourgeoisie), of which the first will continue the revolutionary struggle, and the second will enter into a bloc with imperialism." He warned that the big national bourgeoisie can support the revolutionary movement of its country against imperialism only *at a certain stage and for a certain period,* and that "fearing revolution more than imperialism, and in protecting the interests of its own pocket more than interests of its own country," it in the end will conclude a "bloc with imperialism against the workers and peasants of its own country." [6] Succeeding events have completely supported Comrade Stalin's prediction. The experience of the Chinese Revolution has shown that the common national front was possible only in its first stage, when the revolution was directed mainly against foreign imperialism. The big national bourgeoisie struck a bargain with imperialism when the movement of the workers and peasants developed, and the revolution assumed the character of an agrarian revolution.

Not only the Chinese bourgeoisie, but the big bourgeoisie of India, Indonesia, the Philippines, Egypt, and many other colonies and dependent countries have already betrayed national interests in their own countries and have sided with imperialism.

Comrade Stalin warned, and the past quarter-century has completely confirmed, that complete and final victory of the colonial revolution is possible only when the proletariat has the leading role. The petty-bourgeois nationalist organizations and parties have already shown their incapacity to accomplish the task of national liberation. They tend to limit themselves to constitutional reforms, attaining a formal bourgeois democracy which cannot provide a complete break from the system of imperialism—i.e., factual and not formal independence. Only the working class, which headed the national front of all anti-imperialist forces, is capable of leading a decisive, final struggle for independence and profound demo-

6. *Ibid.,* vii, 148.

*The Third World in Soviet Perspective*

cratic reforms, corresponding to the interests of the popular majority.

The victory of the great October Socialist Revolution in Russia marked the beginning of the crisis in the colonial system of imperialism. It pointed out a new proletarian method of solving the national question, it inspired the oppressed peoples in the colonies and dependent countries, awoke them, stimulated them to struggle. In evaluating the international significance of the October Revolution, Comrade Stalin pointed out in his article, "The International Character of the October Revolution": "The era of revolutions of liberation in the colonies and dependent countries, the era of the awakening of the *proletariat* of these countries, the era of its *hegemony* in the revolution, *has arrived.*" [7]

Such in a most general outline is the theory of colonial revolution developed by Comrade Stalin. It is the guideline for action for the Soviet ethnographer studying the peoples in the colonial and dependent countries. The Soviet ethnographer cannot study the ethnography of the peoples in the colonies apart from the national liberation movement of these peoples. He cannot do this, first of all, because he feels it the duty of the Soviet scientist to use his research to aid the struggle of the forces of progress against the forces of imperialist reaction. He cannot, secondly, because the situation of the class forces in the national liberation movement in backward colonies is the sole criterion for a correct understanding of the complex social processes which are taking place within the society of colonial peoples who have been enslaved by imperialism. . . .

7. *Ibid.*, x, 245.

SELECTION 2

# The National Liberation Movement
## of the Peoples
## Against Imperialism *

Fundamentals of Marxism-Leninism (Osnovy Marksizma-Le-ninizma)—*one of the most important books published in the Soviet Union in past years—attempts to present in a single volume a* summa *of contemporary Communist doctrine. It is intended for use in the higher educational institutions of the USSR, and has also been translated into a number of foreign languages, apparently as a means of providing Communists the world over with a ready reference from which they can derive the currently authoritative line on virtually any problem—philosophic, economic, political—that may confront them. Printings total several million copies so far. The book is admirably suited for use as a classroom text; it presupposes practically no knowledge of Marxism, but still presents its material at a comparatively high intellectual level. The authoritative nature of the* Fundamentals *is underscored by the presence of O. V. Kuusinen—the Old-Bolshevik Central Committee member—as its chief editor. In order to find a work of comparable authority, scope, and intent, one would have to go back at least to Bukharin and Preobrazhenskiy's* ABC of Communism (1919) *or perhaps even Engels'* Anti-Dühring.

*For some reason, Stalin felt it unnecessary (or perhaps unadvisable) to issue a work of similar nature. The* Fundamentals *strives to undo many of the* ad hoc *revisions to which Stalin subjected Marxism, while at the same time canonizing the revisions of the Khrushchev leadership. (The book has of course never been popular in China.) The chapter on the developing areas—printed in excerpt below—is typical. It grossly neglects Marx, slavishly (if selectively) parrots Lenin, ignores Stalin, and presents its subject matter in a manner reflecting the*

* SOURCE: *Fundamentals of Marxism-Leninism* (2nd English edn., Moscow 1963), chapter 16.

39

*The Third World in Soviet Perspective*
*exuberance and relative realism of Khrushchev. Part of the*
*chapter is devoted to an application of Lenin's theory of im-*
*perialism (discussed in greater detail in Chapter 9) to the*
*third world. I have deleted most of this since the matter is*
*adequately covered in my introductory essay. Another ex-*
*tensive section—omitted here for reasons of space—gives a*
*broad survey of the current situation in Asia, Africa, and Latin*
*America. Most valuable for our purposes are those sections*
*that outline the currently valid Soviet theoretical line on the*
*developing areas. These provide a basic orientation for the*
*material that comprises the remainder of this book.*

*Fundamentals is now in its second edition, both in Russian*
*and in English. The first Russian edition appeared in 1959, and*
*the corresponding English translation in 1961. The second*
*Russian edition was signed to the press on August 7, 1962,*
*and its English translation became available in the United*
*States in late 1963. The following excerpts, and all other*
*quotations from the* Fundamentals *in this book, are taken from*
*the second English edition. (A few very minor changes in*
*spelling, capitalization, and the like have been made so that*
*the text will conform in style to the other selections in the*
*present volume.) The first and second editions do not vary*
*greatly. Much of the material of Chapter 16 has been rear-*
*ranged in the new edition, and I have indicated in the foot-*
*notes where some interesting changes were made. In either*
*edition,* Fundamentals of Marxism-Leninism *is indispensable*
*for any serious student of contemporary Marxism.*

### I. Rise of the National Liberation Movement
### and Break-up of the Colonial System

ONLY a few decades ago the colonial rule of the imperialist
powers seemed unshakable. The division of the world into a
handful of privileged, oppressor nations and an overwhelming
majority of oppressed peoples deprived of rights was declared
by the imperialists to be a natural state of affairs, which could
not be changed. The ideologists of colonialism talked of the
racial inferiority of the enslaved peoples and depicted them

as an enormous mass of human beings forever stagnating in apathy and submissive indifference. However, the idea that colonial domination could not be shaken proved an illusion. Life itself refuted the slander about the inferiority of the peoples of the colonial and dependent countries, about their passivity and eternal submissiveness to the imperialists. The crisis of the colonial system began simultaneously with the general crisis of capitalism.[a]

*The Split of the World into Two Systems and the Rise of the National Liberation Movement*

Here too the turning point was the Great October Socialist Revolution. By shaking the very foundations of imperialism it gave a mighty impetus to the national liberation movement in the East, opening up for it prospects of victory over the colonialists. The October Revolution for the first time successfully united in one stream the uprising of the proletariat against the capitalist system and the struggle of the enslaved peoples of tsarist Russia for the overthrow of national-colonial oppression.

The first socialist state became an inexhaustible source of moral and political support for the oppressed peoples of the world. In particular they saw the inspiring example of the Central Asian republics of the Soviet Union, which in a very short period of history passed from colonial backwardness to the all-round flowering of their national economy and culture.

A new stage of the national liberation struggle began as a result of the Second World War. Many countries of the colonial world were drawn into the maelstrom of war; some of them (in Asia and North Africa) themselves became the theater of hostilities. The needs of war economy impelled the imperialist

---

a. The "general crisis of capitalism" is distinguished from the periodic crises (e.g., depressions) which afflict capitalist states. It coincides with the period of imperialism, and is characterized by the inability of the system to maintain its position as the dominant socio-economic order. For further details, see *Fundamentals,* 257ff.

powers to speed up the development of certain industries in their colonial possessions and this led to the rapid growth of the local proletariat.

The emancipatory, anti-fascist character assumed by the Second World War in the course of time, especially after the Soviet Union entered it, evoked a mighty response among all the oppressed peoples. The rise of the political consciousness and organization of the masses was also facilitated by the internal weakness of the Western colonial powers that became evident during the war years.

The most favorable conditions for the development and success of the national liberation movement were created by new alignment of forces in the international arena resulting from the rout of German fascism and Japanese imperialism and from the strengthening of the might of the Soviet Union and the emergence of the people's democracies. The formation of the world system of socialism and the associated weakening of the positions of the imperialist camp made it easier for many countries of Asia and Africa to win their independence. The national liberation struggle has assumed gigantic dimensions and the crisis of colonialism has entered its concluding phase, that of the break-up of the colonial system.

In 1939 the colonialists still dominated almost two-thirds of mankind. After the Second World War, however, the situation radically altered. The colonial empires that were the creation of centuries began to collapse with increasing speed. Between 1945 and 1960 more than 1,500 million people freed themselves from the imperialist yoke and took the path of independent development. In the colonies that still remain there are now not more than 76 million people, less than 3 per cent of the world's population. Thus, the complete elimination of the colonial system is on the way. With its final disappearance, what is perhaps the most shameful page in the annals of capitalism will have been turned over.

The break-up of the system of colonialism is thus a result of the powerful upsurge of the national liberation struggle under favorable international conditions created by the weakening of imperialism and the transformation of socialism into a world force.

The imperialists try in every way to belittle the role and significance of the national liberation movement. For this purpose they insistently spread the myth that the colonial and semi-colonial countries have won their political freedom not as a result of struggle and revolution, but with the aid of the imperialist powers. At the same time attempts are made to picture the long rule of the capitalist monopolies in the colonial countries as a necessary period of "preparing" these countries for independent existence. In this connection a great deal is being said about the "civilizing mission" of capitalism in the colonies.

As a matter of fact, the "mission" of capitalism in the colonies had nothing to do with the interests of their peoples. The imperialists were never concerned with the all-round development of the economy of the colonies or with preparing them for independent existence. All fabrications to this effect are exposed by the simple fact that all the countries that have broken away from imperialist oppression and have become independent are *underdeveloped,* i.e., they are very backward economically, precisely because of foreign domination.

It stands to reason that during the many decades of their rule in the colonies the imperialists have objectively and in spite of themselves done some historically useful work there. Guided by egotistic, mercenary considerations they have objectively and against their will hastened the ripening of the prerequisites for a political and social revolution in Asia. It is precisely in connection with this that Marx referred to the colonialists as "the unconscious tool of history." At the same time, however, he emphasized that the "civilizing" activity of the imperialist bourgeoisie promised the masses neither national nor social liberation. In particular Marx wrote: "All the English bourgeoisie may be forced to do in India will neither emancipate nor materially mend the social condition of the mass of the people, depending not only on the development of the productive powers, but on their appropriation by the

43

people." He furthermore pointed out that the Hindus would never be able to reap the fruits of civilization till they "themselves shall have grown strong enough to throw off the English yoke altogether." [220]

History has confirmed the correctness of Marx's words. It has also demonstrated that from the point of view of the imperialist "civilizers" no people of any colony is ever "ripe" enough or "quite ready" for independent existence till it rises against the rule of the colonialists. The facts testify that the colonialists leave only when forced to do so by the actions of the mass of the people. The colonial peoples *wrest* their independence from the imperialists; they do not get it as a gift.

The liberation of the hundreds of millions of colonial slaves has taken place, of course, in various ways, including armed struggle and methods of political pressure. But whatever the concrete means, the *basis of liberation has always been a struggle of the broad mass of the people. . . .* [b]

*Attitude of the Working Class to Nationalism of Oppressed Nations*

The movement of the peoples for colonial liberation is often waged under the banner of nationalism. In this connection the servitors of imperialism slanderously assert that Communists support the liberation struggle of the colonial peoples only as a matter of tactics; as internationalists they allegedly cannot sympathize with the nationalist aspirations of the peoples of Asia and Africa.

Such allegations are false from start to finish. In making them the advocates of colonialism are merely trying to introduce confusion into the clear question as to who are the friends and who are the enemies of the national liberation movement.

Marxism-Leninism approaches nationalism, as it does all

b. A lengthy discussion of classes in the developing areas—duplicating material contained in the Introduction to this volume—is omitted.

220. K. Marx and F. Engels, *Selected Works* (Moscow 1962), I, 356. (This, and all other footnotes in this selection, are to English-language versions.)

## Soviet Writers on the Developing Areas

social phenomena, from a concrete historical point of view, i.e., from the point of view of the interests of social progress. Lenin repeatedly warned against abstract formulations of the question of nationalism and above all against confusing the nationalism of an oppressor nation with that of an oppressed nation.

The imperialist states, such as the USA, Britain, France, etc., are one thing. Here bourgeois nationalism has become the symbol of national exceptionalism, racial arrogance, and militant chauvinism. It serves the monopoly bourgeoisie to justify enslavement of other nations. To this reactionary colonialist nationalism, Communists, as proletarian internationalists, are indeed irreconcilably hostile.

The nationalism of the peoples of the colonial and dependent countries is another thing. This nationalism, as a rule, reflects the sound democratism of the national liberation movements, the protest of the masses against imperialist oppression, and the striving for national independence and social reforms. Lenin had this in mind when he wrote: "The bourgeois nationalism of *every* oppressed nation has a general democratic content which is directed *against* oppression, and it is this content that we support *unconditionally*." [224]

The nationalism in the countries of contemporary Asia and Africa is, as a general rule, precisely such nationalism. It is a nationalism of oppressed nations struggling against their enslavers and fighting for political and economic independence. It manifests itself in countries where national ties are for the most part only in the process of formation and where the bourgeoisie as a whole is, under certain conditions, still able to play a historically progressive role. Noting this trait of the bourgeoisie, Lenin wrote: "The Western bourgeoisie is in a state of decay; it is already confronted by its grave-digger —the proletariat. In Asia, in contrast, there is *still* a bourgeoisie capable of championing sincere, militant, consistent democracy, a worthy comrade of France's great enlighteners and great leaders of the close of the eighteenth century.

"The principal representative or the principal social sup-

224. V. I. Lenin, *Selected Works* (Moscow 1952), I, pt. 2, 337.

port of this Asian bourgeoisie, which is still capable of fighting in a historically progressive cause, is the peasant." [225]

The nations and national consciousness in the countries of Asia and Africa are being formed in the struggle against imperialism and feudalism; this leads to the awakening of the masses from medieval dormancy, to a struggle against colonialism, backwardness, and reaction. All this imparts to the nationalism of the contemporary East a democratic, progressive content. National consciousness forms the initial stage of anti-imperialist consciousness, particularly for the many millions of peasants.

Marxists-Leninists regard such nationalism as historically justified. They can support it with a clear conscience and they do so without relinquishing an iota of the principles of proletarian internationalism.

Of course, Communists are aware that even the nationalism of an oppressed nation has its reverse side. It usually reflects the ideology and desires of a reactionary top section of exploiters who endeavor to utilize nationalist slogans in their own selfish interests, often at the expense of other nations.

Communists support nationalism only insofar and as long as it serves the cause of winning national freedom and victory over imperialism and feudalism, and awakening in the masses a sense of their own dignity, which the oppressors suppressed and derided. All preaching of racial or national exclusiveness, all attempts to make use of nationalism for reactionary purposes, as an instrument of national egotism and subjugation of other peoples, or for the struggle against the just demands of the masses, cannot meet with the sympathies of Communists.

*Historic Significance of the Break-up of the Colonial System*

Imperialism impedes general human progress not only by suppressing the *working classes* in the developed capitalist countries but also by forcing *whole peoples* into obscurity—the peoples of the colonies and semi-colonies. The powerful

225. V. I. Lenin, *The National-Liberation Movement in the East* (Moscow 1957), 43.

46

upsurge of the national liberation struggle signifies the awakening of half of mankind to active participation in the making of history, participation in deciding the fate of the world. This hastens the advance of progress and vastly extends its scope.

The masses of people in Asia and Africa who have joined the national liberation movement are a powerful factor in the destruction of imperialism, in intensifying all its contradictions. The colonies and dependent countries are still very important for the imperialists. There the monopolies obtain at very low costs the raw materials they require and sell their industrial commodities at exorbitant prices. In the colonies and semi-colonies the imperialists establish their war bases, strongholds, and communications. The national liberation movement undermines and sometimes altogether abolishes these positions of imperialism. Moreover, it transforms the colonial and dependent countries from a reserve of imperialism into allies of the progressive anti-imperialist forces. *Following the formation of the world system of socialism, the break-up of the colonial empires is another crushing blow against imperialism.*

The break-up of the colonial system has an important, favorable influence on the development of international relations. Many of the young national states of Asia and Africa pursue an independent peaceful policy, joining the vast "peace zone." Their anti-war position is one of the reasons why war has ceased to be fatally inevitable. The national liberation movement strengthens the cause of peace also by shattering the unequal, forced forms of relations between countries, promotes closer relations of peoples, and reduces the possibility of war conflicts.

The Program of the CPSU adopted at its 22nd Congress gives due credit to the great international role of the newly independent countries: "The national states become ever more active as an independent force on the world scene; objectively, this force is in the main a *progressive, revolutionary, and anti-imperialist force.* The countries and peoples that are now free from colonial oppression are to play a prominent part in the

*The Third World in Soviet Perspective*
prevention of a new world war—the focal problem of to-day." [226]

The cessation of the rapacious exploitation of the colonial countries and the development of their national economy make it possible to utilize world resources much more fruitfully. This brings closer the time when it will be possible to overcome the glaring difference that now exists in the levels of economic development of the different countries and to secure for all the people on earth a life worthy of human beings. The revival and development of the thousand-year-old culture of the peoples of the East, which has been slighted and subjected to destruction by the colonists for centuries, will at last enrich the culture of the whole world.

The decay of the colonial system is thus a tremendous triumph not only for the peoples who have thrown off the colonial yoke, but also for all progressive humanity.

## II. *Main Achievements of the National Liberation Revolutions in Asia, Africa, and Latin America*

As a result of the diversity in the conditions and forms in which the former colonial countries won their independence, they have found themselves at different stages of political development. This is particularly true of the countries which threw off the yoke of colonialism after the Second World War.

Where the anti-imperialist front was under the leadership of the working class and its Marxist, Communist parties, the revolution did not stop at the bourgeois-democratic stage but developed into a socialist revolution, along the lines of a people's democracy.

Where the movement was headed by the bourgeoisie or bourgeois influences predominated in the anti-imperialist national front, the national bourgeoisie that came to power led society along the path of capitalist development, thus delaying the transition to a higher stage of the revolution.

As a result of the break-up of the colonial system the fol-

226. "Program of the Communist Party of the Soviet Union," in *The Road to Communism* (Moscow 1962), 496.

# Soviet Writers on the Developing Areas

lowing are the principal groups of countries that have now been formed:

1. Countries which, having thrown off the yoke of imperialism, have taken the path of building socialism. This group has broken away not only from the colonial but also from the capitalist system and has joined the socialist camp (the Chinese People's Republic, the Korean People's Democratic Republic, and the Democratic Republic of Vietnam).

2. Countries which have won their political independence and pursue an independent foreign policy, which have freed themselves from imperialist enslavement but remain in the capitalist system of economy (India, Indonesia, Burma, Cambodia, Laos, Ceylon, Iraq, the United Arab Republic, Algeria, Syria, Ghana, Guinea, Mali, Sudan, Tunisia, Morocco, Libya, etc.).[c]

3. Countries which won their independence but immediately allowed it to be greatly limited by entering into fettering economic agreements and joining the aggressive blocs of the imperialist powers (Pakistan, Thailand, the Philippines).

Lastly, some countries continue to be enslaved (colonies in Africa, remnants of the colonial possessions in Asia and Latin America, some island possessions of Britain, Portugal, the USA, and other imperialist powers).

It should be remembered that, apart from the states which have firmly taken the path of building socialism, the other newly independent states are still in process of political formation. After the winning of independence, their social development has not only been greatly accelerated but is taking place under conditions of a sharp struggle of different class forces. The policies of these countries and their position in the world system of states depend on the forces—reactionary or progressive—that gain the upper hand in this struggle. Owing to this the boundaries between the second and third groups of countries are still quite fluid. . . .[d]

c. Laos, Mali, and Algeria were not listed in the corresponding passage of the first edition.

d. At this point the first edition included a laudatory paragraph on Iraq. Thirteen pages on the various countries of the developing areas have been omitted here.

# The Third World in Soviet Perspective

### III. *Immediate Prospects of Historical Development of the Countries Liberated from Colonial Oppression*

One of the basic problems today is that of the paths and prospects of historical development of the countries liberated from the colonial yoke. It affects the fate of many large and small peoples comprising a considerable section of mankind. The question of the direction in which they are going is of vital importance both for these peoples themselves and for the progress of the world as a whole.

The young independent states, the Program of the CPSU points out, belong neither to the system of imperialist states, nor to that of socialist states. But the overwhelming majority of them have not yet broken loose from the network of world capitalist economy although they occupy a special place in it. They are a part of the world that is still exploited by the imperialist monopolies. So long as these countries do not put an end to economic dependence on imperialism, they will play the part of the "world countryside" and remain an object of semi-colonial exploitation.

Clearly, the liberated states cannot simply repeat the usual course of capitalist development that was passed through by the old European states.

Such a repetition cannot happen in our day because both the internal and external conditions for it are absent. It is well known that in the Western countries capitalist industrialization was carried out largely by means of the exploitation of the colonies and other weak states. National capital in the young states of Asia and Africa does not have this possibility; it is not only unable to "conquer" foreign markets and sources of raw materials, it is still forced to wage a hard struggle for existence against the old imperialist plunderers.

The prospect of a "leap" from backwardness by super-exploitation of the working class and ruination of the peasantry, as happened in the countries of "classical" capitalism, is also unreal. The mass of the people will now certainly not tolerate the "classical" capitalist course with its painful primitive

# Soviet Writers on the Developing Areas

accumulation [e] and bitter suffering of the working sections of the people. A certain part is also played by such factors as the general discredit of capitalism in the eyes of the peoples and the growing influence of the example and experience of the socialist countries. . . .[f]

The experience of more than a decade of the independent existence of the main liberated countries has shown that contradictory processes are taking place in their internal life. A deep insight into these processes was given in the report of the Central Committee of the CPSU delivered by N. S. Khrushchev at the 22nd Congress of the Party.

The struggle for political independence, N. S. Khrushchev noted, united all the national forces that suffered under the colonialists and were prompted by common interests. "Now that the time has come to tear up the roots of imperialism and introduce agrarian and other urgent social reforms, the differences in class interests are coming more and more into the open." [229] The demarcation between the forces takes place along the following lines. Wide sections of the working people, and a considerable part of the national bourgeoisie that is interested in a solution of the main tasks of the anti-imperialist, anti-feudal revolution, want to advance farther along the path of consolidating independence and of social and economic reforms. But among the ruling circles of these countries there are also forces which are afraid of further cooperation with the democratic, progressive sections of the nation. They would like to appropriate the fruits of the popular struggle and hinder further progress of the cause of national independence and democracy. These forces pursue a policy of agreement with the imperialists outside their

e. "Primitive accumulation," the beginning of capitalist production, consists of the appearance of a class of wage-earners (proletarians) and the accumulation of wealth in the hands of capitalists. "New-born capital," Marx wrote, "comes dripping from head to foot, from every pore, with blood and dirt." (*Fundamentals*, 212.) See below, p. 98, note g.
f. A discussion of "state capitalism" follows at this point.
229. N. S. Khrushchev, "Report of the Central Committee of the CPSU to the 22nd Party Congress," in *The Road to Communism*, 32.

countries and with the feudalists within them, and resort to dictatorial methods. Where the victory of such a course leads can be seen from the examples of Pakistan, the Philippines, South Korea, and South Vietnam. Degradation of the national economy, the exhausting burden of military expenditure that is connected with participation in the war blocs of the imperialists, and ultimately the threat of complete loss of the independence that had been won—such are its direct consequences.

Thus, two contradictory tendencies are clearly visible in the political life of the liberated countries. In the policy of the governments of the national bourgeoisie this most often finds expression in inconsistency, in an inclination towards unprincipled compromises in deciding major questions of the country's life. Thus, the effort to build up national industries often goes hand in hand with a liberal attitude to foreign capital, which continues to pump out large revenues from the economy of the liberated countries.

The urgent changes required in the social and political spheres are also being carried into effect slowly. In most of the young states feudal and caste privileges have been abolished, the legal status of women has been improved and some bourgeois-democratic reforms have been carried out. But at the same time, democracy still suffers from some essential restrictions, the Communist parties are being persecuted or completely banned. The political activity of the mass of the working people at times meets with severe repression.

In no field, however, does the inconsistency of the national bourgeoisie manifest itself so clearly as in the agrarian problem. Here more than anywhere else it makes concessions to the feudal-landlord elements by sacrificing to them the interests of the many millions of peasants who bore the brunt of colonial oppression. The landlords are often given enormous compensation for the lands taken from them, while considerable masses of peasants continue to suffer bitterly from lack of land, poverty, high taxes, and bondage to usurers. The feudal survivals [g] in agriculture are still a very big obstacle to

g. "Feudal survivals"—e.g. share-cropping, corvée labor, mal-distribution of land. (See *Fundamentals,* 386.)

the creation of a well-developed national economy. In the meantime, the national bourgeoisie in power, although interested in destroying feudal relations, is afraid to encroach on the property of the landlords. As a rule, it prefers to let the landlords retain their large landholdings and only helps them in changing to a capitalist type of enterprise. It is clear that this way of economic development is slow, painful for the people, and takes place mainly at the expense of the interests of the bulk of the peasantry.

A general appraisal of the role of the national bourgeoisie at the present stage was given in the Statement of the Moscow Meeting of Representatives of Communist and Workers' Parties (1960), and in the Program of the CPSU.

"In present conditions," the Statement says, "the national bourgeoisie of the colonial and dependent countries unconnected with imperialist circles is objectively interested in the accomplishment of the principal tasks of anti-imperialist, anti-feudal revolution, and therefore can participate in the revolutionary struggle against imperialism and feudalism. In that sense it is progressive." [230]

At the same time both the Statement and the Program of the CPSU point out the instability of the national bourgeoisie and its tendency to compromise with imperialism and feudalism, which increases as social contradictions become sharper.

Since a considerable section of the national bourgeoisie remains interested in consolidating the political, economic, and cultural independence of their country, there still exists in the young states of Asia and Africa a basis for broad cooperation of all the national and democratic forces—the working class, the peasantry, the progressive circles of the national bourgeoisie, and the national intelligentsia. Under favorable conditions this cooperation can go so far as to include participation of the working classes and their parties in the management of the state. It is this prospect that provides the basis for the idea of a *state of national democracy* as a state that expresses

230. *Program Documents of the Struggle for Peace, Democracy, and Socialism* (Moscow 1961), 66.

53

the interests not of any one class but of a bloc of broad sections of the people.

How Marxists envisage the principal features of such a state is described in the Statement of the Moscow Meeting of Representatives of Communist and Workers' Parties in 1960, elaborated with the participation of delegations from the Communist parties of the Asian, African, and Latin American countries. A state of national democracy is described as "a state which consistently upholds its political and economic independence, fights against imperialism and its military blocs, and against military bases on its territory; a state which fights against the new forms of colonialism and the penetration of imperialist capital; a state which rejects dictatorial and despotic forms of goverment; a state in which the people are assured broad democratic rights and freedoms (freedom of speech, press, assembly, demonstrations, establishment of political parties and public organizations), the opportunity to work for the enactment of an agrarian reform and the realization of other democratic and social changes and for participation in shaping government policy."[231]

It is clear to Communists, and they try to bring it home to the broad masses, that only by the path of non-capitalist development is it possible to put a speedy end to age-old backwardness, to raise the living standards of the whole people, and to consolidate properly the independence of the country. Under present-day conditions, and with the support given by the world system of socialism, non-capitalist development of the liberated countries is a perfectly feasible path.

The choice of one or other path of development, of course, is the internal affair of the people of each country.

#### IV. *Imperialism Is the Chief Enemy of the Liberated Countries and Peoples Struggling for Their Independence*

The imperialists refuse to reconcile themselves to the loss of their colonies. They are searching for ways of saving colonialism. These searches have given rise to numerous theories

231. *Ibid.*, 67–68.

of "neo-colonialism," i.e., a new colonialism which is alleged to be free from all the defects of the past and which reconciles the interests of the oppressed and those of the oppressors. Actually, this new colonialism is nothing but an effort to attain the usual imperialist aims by indirect control of the countries that have achieved liberation, and in this way to make the independence they have won purely formal or to deprive them of it.

In the practice of colonialism, the method of indirect control is not new. The new feature is the attempt to make it the chief instrument of present-day colonialism, since the old methods of direct coercion of the peoples are so discredited that not even the imperialists as a whole dare defend them.

## New Forms of Colonial Policy

In the first place, the colonialists are making every effort to extend the social basis of their rule and to find new military, political, economic, and ideological means of consolidating it. As already mentioned, the feudal and comprador [h] circles have always been the traditional social support of the imperialists. Since these classes depend on antiquated economic relations, their positions have now become much weaker. Besides, they have (with minor exceptions) irremediably compromised themselves in the eyes of the mass of the people. While continuing, wherever possible, to support the feudal lords and the compradors, the imperialists have been looking for other allies mainly among the representatives of the Right wing of the national bourgeoisie most alien to the interests of the people, and also among certain groups of the intelligentsia and reactionary clergy. Relying on the most reactionary circles of the local exploiting classes, they endeavor to set up military despotic regimes wherever possible and to put power in the hands of puppets obedient to the imperialists.

In order to reach a deal with these circles, the imperialists try to intimidate them with the non-existent "Communist menace," bring military and political pressure to bear, and offer them certain financial and economic inducements.

h. See note ee of the Introduction.

## The Third World in Soviet Perspective

The old, "classical" colonial policy started out from the striving to hinder the colonies, insofar as it depended on the imperialists, from developing any, except extractive, industry. In words the inspirers of "neo-colonialism" support industrialization, but by this they mean only the development of the light and mining industries and means of transport and communication, something that cannot essentially endanger the economic positions of the foreign monopolies. At the same time the strivings of the Asian, African, and Latin American countries for real industrialization continue to meet with resistance. There were many cases, for example, when the Western countries refused to supply the young states with industrial equipment, machinery, and machine tools. In the last resort the imperialists establish their own enterprises in these countries, but demand freedom to export their profits and various guarantees against nationalization. The imperialist monopolies generally greatly resent and resist the development of a state-owned sector in the economy of the former colonial and dependent countries.

Aggressive blocs, like SEATO and CENTO, organized on a "mixed" basis, i.e., with the participation of the formally independent states and their previous imperialist oppressors, have become the main military and political form of the new colonialism. Formed under the banner of "anti-communism," these blocs actually aim at opening the gates of the former colonial countries to the military forces of imperialism, establishing political and strategic control over these countries and utilizing them for the struggle against the national liberation movement of neighboring peoples.

In the economic sphere, new forms of enslavement of the liberated countries, such as their inclusion in the "Common Market" system, are coming more and more into the forefront. Through the channels of the "Common Market," the imperialists would like to flood these countries with their surplus goods, whereas it is clear that the nascent industry of the young states of Asia and Africa cannot compete with the industry of the West. At the same time the monopolies want to continue pumping out raw materials and foodstuffs as cheaply as possible from the underdeveloped countries. If the young states were to submit to these plans, it would mean reconciling themselves to the role of agrarian-raw material appendages of the imperialist countries. And in the course of time this would inevitably entail the loss of political independence.

Is there a possibility of averting this danger? Experience shows that there is. Many of the young independent countries are introducing a system of strict state control over foreign trade and currency operations, taking the first steps towards establishing a monopoly of foreign trade. They are also making plans for setting up their own regional trade and economic associations, independent of the capitalist monopolies and counterposed to them.

Of late the ideological bases of colonial policy have also undergone a certain revision. Under present conditions the imperialists have more and more often to refrain from open propaganda of racism and outdated theories of the white man's "superiority." Falling in with the social moods, even the most inveterate imperialists are now not averse to discoursing on the single human family and the right of all peoples to independent existence. Actually, however, the new signboards (for example, that of the "interdependence" of the metropolitan countries and the former colonies) serve as a cover for the old aims of colonial enslavement.

Such "novelties" also include various theories of "collective colonialism," of late repeatedly advocated by American imperialists—in the Congo, for example, where the united front of the old and new colonialists even used the emblem of the United Nations as a screen. This maneuver aims at replacing the rule of individual Western powers in the colonies by their joint exploitation of the colonial countries, invariably with the leading participation of American capital. Of course, the oppressed peoples have no reason to expect any more relief from this than a person could feel on finding out that he was being robbed by a gang rather than a single robber.

In our days the champion of the new colonialism and its principal support on a world scale is American imperialism. Since the Second World War, the United States has noticeably enlarged its dollar empire. In addition to the actual seizure of part of China (Taiwan) and the occupation of a number of Japanese islands in the Pacific, the American monopolies have settled down in South Vietnam and South Korea and have acquired important economic and strategic positions in North Africa and the Middle East.

Nevertheless, until recently American imperialism managed to pose as a champion of "anti-colonialism" and of "liberation" of the oppressed peoples. It won this reputation in the cheapest possible manner, by demagogically criticizing some of the most outrageous actions of the European colonial powers and by offering economic "aid" to the underdeveloped countries. Some short-sighted people did not at once realize that the "anti-colonialism" of the American monopolies was a mere pretense and that they refused to act together with the European colonialists only when they wanted them to be defeated, in the hope of taking their place. As for American economic "aid," its purpose is to chain the countries accepting it to the war chariot of American imperialism. Suffice it to say that, even from the data of a special committee of the American Congress itself, of the total allocations of the USA for foreign states, an average of 7 per cent are for actual economic "aid," and 5 per cent are for technical "aid." The remaining 88 per cent are used directly or indirectly for military purposes. Small wonder that many Asian and African countries, despite their need for capital, have repeatedly declined offers of aid from the USA.

The peoples of the world can see ever more clearly that in our time the United States has become the main *bulwark of modern colonialism,* and without which it would have collapsed much sooner.

Thus, as the Program of the CPSU points out, imperialism remains the chief enemy and the chief obstacle to the solution of the national problems facing the young sovereign states and all dependent countries. *A paramount condition for the solution of national tasks,* the Program stresses, *is a consistent struggle against imperialism. . . .*[1]

i. Two pages excoriating anti-communism are deleted here.

# Soviet Writers on the Developing Areas

## V. The World Socialist System Is a Bulwark of the Peoples in the Struggle Against Colonialism

The successes of the national liberation movement in the East are inseparable from the existence of the socialist states and their irreconcilable attitude to colonialism. This reveals the profound objective connection and community between the anti-imperialist interests of the oppressed peoples and those of the peoples of the socialist system.

The socialist countries are sincere and loyal friends of the peoples fighting for liberation or those who have thrown off the imperialist yoke, and they render them all-round assistance. They stand for the abolition of all forms of colonial oppression and in every way help to consolidate the sovereignty of the states rising on the ruins of the colonial empires. A great contribution to the historic cause of the final liberation of the peoples from the shameful yoke of imperialism was made by the Soviet Union, which was the initiator in the adoption by the United Nations Organization of the Declaration on the granting of independence to all peoples.

In consistently opposing colonialism, the socialist countries pursue no selfish aims. Unlike the USA, they do not seek to take the place of the expelled colonialists and do not look for "spheres of influence." Socialist economy is incompatible with exploitation and oppression. It does not need to export capital because its aim of steadily improving the well-being of the working people requires increasingly greater capital investments inside the country. The socialist states are interested in expanding international trade and economic cooperation, but they are not seeking markets for the sale of surplus goods. Socialist economy does not know any crises of overproduction.

In supporting the national aspirations of the colonial peoples the Soviet Union and the People's Democracies are guided by principles of socialist ideology, which is irreconcilably opposed to all oppression and defends equality of rights and friendship among the peoples. By opposing colonialism, the socialist countries at the same time help to lessen the danger of war. It is well known that during the last 10–12 years the

*The Third World in Soviet Perspective*

attempts to save or restore colonialism were the source of numerous so-called "local" wars. The colonial appetites of imperialism are still one of the causes of international tension.

The postwar years have convincingly demonstrated the role of the socialist states as a powerful factor in restraining the aggression of the imperialists who otherwise would have descended upon the national liberation movement with all their might and would have strangled it.

The significance of the socialist states as an anti-colonial factor is continuously increasing. Firstly, the foreign policy of the socialist countries, firmly based on principle, plays an increasingly direct and decisive role in frustrating the colonialist plans of the imperialists. For example, the socialist countries made a very important contribution to the victory of the Egyptian people over the imperialist aggressors. They also foiled the attack of the colonialists against Syria and later against the young Iraqi Republic. Secondly, the socialist camp is becoming the bulwark of the young national states of the East in their struggle for economic independence. . . .[j]

j. The chapter closes with a brief survey of Soviet and Bloc economic aid to the developing areas.

SELECTION 3

# Introduction to Indonesia [*]

BY A. A. GUBER

*THE volume* Respublika Indoneziya, *of which this essay forms the introduction, is a symposium on contemporary Indonesia—one of many such works on individual countries of the third world to which Soviet specialists on history, politics, agrarian matters, the labor movement, industrialization, etc., contribute articles. The essay is by the dean of Soviet orientalists, the historian A. A. Guber, and was written to provide a background against which the Russian reader can better understand the picture of contemporary Indonesia that is presented in the subsequent chapters of the volume.*

*Indonesia offers a particular challenge to the Soviets. Of all the countries of the third world, few have such close ties to the USSR as does Indonesia; its Communist Party is the largest and probably the strongest outside of the Bloc; and few neutral countries have assumed positions so antagonistic to Western interests. Indonesia is the one Asian country named in Soviet literature as a likely prospect for "national democratic" status, sharing this distinction with the African states of Guinea, Ghana, and Mali.*[a]

*Guber's essay is an excellent and concise presentation of the Soviet view of the colonial background underlying Indonesia's special position—the strength of domestic communism and the weakness of the stabilizing force of the bourgeoisie. Although Guber emphasizes the special conditions of Indonesia in contrast to, say, India or Egypt, his study is in many ways a typical Soviet analysis of colonialism and can,* mutatis mutandis, *be applied to most other colonial areas.*

[*] SOURCE: "Vvedeniye" [Introduction], *Respublika Indoneziya: sbornik stat'ey* [The Republic of Indonesia: A Collection of Articles] (Moscow 1961).

a. See pp. 27–28 above. Although Burma and Ceylon are occasionally mentioned in connection with the status of "national democracy," they are clearly on a "lower" level than Indonesia.

61

## The Third World in Soviet Perspective

THE Indonesian people have followed a glorious and difficult path in the years since the Declaration of Independence, which restored the national sovereignty they had lost as a result of foreign occupation. For more than 350 years, Indonesia suffered the oppression of greedy and cruel European invaders. In the sixteenth century, immediately after the Portuguese arrived in India and Singapore, Indonesia was victimized by their acts of piracy, and soon became the scene of a severe struggle among the European powers who were establishing their colonial empires. Holland, "the model capitalist country of the seventeenth century" which was the first to accomplish a bourgeois revolution, succeeded in emerging victorious in this struggle.

Indonesia became the monopoly outpost of the Netherlands East India Company. The organization of the company, its methods of penetrating formerly independent principalities and subjugating them to its control, and all its activities in Indonesia laid the foundation for a bourgeois colonial system. This system was later "perfected" in the British colonies. During the period of domination by the Netherlands East India Company, the pernicious results of foreign colonial control and exploitation were demonstrated. The powerful feudal principalities which had existed in the Middle Ages and achieved considerable economic and cultural development, whose glory had spread far beyond the archipelago, were destroyed. Proof of this glory lies in the remains of the wonderful monuments, the creations of Indonesian sculptors, and the surviving works of poets and chroniclers.

The unrestricted colonial plunder of the natural resources and the intensification of feudal exploitation of the population for the sake of the insatiable Dutch traders doomed the great masses of people to poverty. They were forced to surrender the products of their labor without payment, to work for nothing to construct forts, city buildings, ports, and roads. In its activities, the Dutch Company depended on the representatives of the feudal class, whom it gradually was able to interest in increasing the exploitation of the people.

The decline of Holland in the eighteenth century, and the

inevitable victory of English industrial capital over the Dutch traders, inevitably undermined the monopolistic domination of the Netherlands East India Company. At the same time, the struggle which had brought the population of the archipelago to despair, the corruption and selfish piratic activities of the workers and agents of the Company, weakened the Dutch from within. In a series of trade wars, England dealt heavy blows to the Dutch colonial empire. In the struggle for hegemony between England and France, Holland, which had been closely tied to France since 1795, lost a significant part of her colonies. Temporarily, all of Indonesia fell into British hands. Here, the farsighted and energetic British official, Stanford Raffles, was the first man in the history of colonial policy to attempt to organize the exploitation of the country according to methods which corresponded to the interests of the British industrial bourgeoisie and gave birth to the free trade system. The brief domination of England (1811 to 1816) was not long enough to exert any decisive influence in changing the methods of exploiting the colony. After Indonesia was returned to Holland, the ruling circles of the latter returned to the old means of exploitation.

In Holland, the voices of those who supported a continuation of Raffles' policy were still too weak to prevent the trade and financial oligarchy that was closely tied to the House of Orange from returning to the time-tested monopolistic methods of exploiting Indonesia through serfdom. A concrete example of these methods was the system of forced cultivation, introduced in the 1830's, which served as the basis of colonial exploitation until the 1870's and disappeared only during the epoch of imperialism.

State ownership of land in all territories controlled by the Dutch authorities constituted the legal basis underlying the state serf system of exploitation of the Indonesian population. By considering the immediate producers to be their tenants (the peasants had traditionally owned the land on the basis of communal land ownership, although in many parts of Java this was already yielding to individual ownership), the Dutch forced them to cultivate products for export (coffee, sugar cane, tobacco, indigo, etc.) on the best lands and followed the system of obligatory labor. All harvested products were subject to delivery to the state warehouses. The produce was initially processed by European enterprises, which were for the most part manned by the same peasants. Forced labor was expanded to include the construction of roads, warehouses, ports, and the transport of cargo.

By plundering the productive forces of Indonesia, and by exploiting the people through serfdom, capitalist development of the metropole proceeded at a rapid pace, large industry appeared, and the industrial bourgeoisie became strong. The colonial market made possible the development of a powerful textile industry and many other branches, and provided an opportunity to compete with the more powerful European countries.

The peculiarities of Dutch colonial policy resulted in the fact that Indonesia, unlike the colonies of other European powers, essentially did not experience a period of exploitation by methods characteristic of industrial capitalism. The system of monopolistic state serf exploitation was replaced, with practically no intermediate period, by the domination and exploitation of monopoly capital, which is characteristic of the transition of capitalism to its ultimate imperialist stage.

When Holland, yielding to the demand of large capital in the cities and the onslaught of foreign powers, began to abolish the system of forced cultivation and opened the colonies to private initiative, monopoly capital soon gained control over the most important plantations, the enterprises for processing agricultural produce, and the mining enterprises.

Dutch subjugation of the principalities beyond Java that were still in fact independent or semi-independent coincided with the completion of the territorial division of the world. Further acquisition of "no man's lands" by the imperialists became impossible and the ever-deepening inter-imperialist struggle raised the problem of redividing colonial booty which had already been secured. Weak in comparison with the so-called "great" imperialist powers, Holland had good reason to fear that her colonies would become the next object of repartition. This forced the Dutch ruling circles to establish their unique "open door" policy, to offer to the capital of all imperialist powers the opportunity to participate freely along with the Dutch in exploiting the wealth and the peoples of Indonesia.

This tactic of Holland, which was forced upon her and which differed in principle from the policy of the powerful colonial powers, made non-Dutch monopoly capital (chiefly English) into a unique co-owner of the Dutch colonies, and led to the widespread and continually increasing subjugation of the Indonesian archipelago to imperialist exploitation.

The development of Indonesia as a Dutch colony in the pre-imperialist and imperialist periods resulted in a number of peculiarities in the formation and relationship of class forces which distinguished Indonesia from many other colonial and dependent countries. Without taking this peculiarity into consideration, one cannot understand either the peculiarities of the national liberation movement of the Indonesian people in the colonial period, or the present struggle of the Republic of Indonesia to strengthen its independence and attain economic self-dependence.

A result of colonial domination was the significant transformation of the classes of the former feudal Indonesian society and the unique formation of new classes. During the three centuries of Dutch rule, the former rulers of the feudal society in Java became public servants, deprived of the land which had served as the basis of their domination. All privileges, titles, and opportunities for the Javanese aristocracy to participate in exploiting their own people were dependent upon participation in the colonial administration.

The relatively high salaries, the various sources of income, and the official grants which were offered by the colonial authorities to the Indonesian public servants provided opportunities to accumulate and appropriate the land of the peasants who had been ruined. A new class of landlords was gradually formed from part of the former aristocracy, and from a number of usurers, market manipulators, and middle-

## The Third World in Soviet Perspective

men. A characteristic of the landlord property ownership was the absence of any kind of large latifundia. The land holdings of such landlords numbered hundreds and thousands of hectares, but they usually consisted of dozens of parcels which were scattered in various regions, even in outlying districts. The peculiar nature of landlord property ownership, along with the general causes which retarded the development of large national capitalist entrepreneurship in agriculture, helped to preserve the enslaving lease system, sharecropping, and precapitalist payment in labor as the basic system for obtaining rent.

Connections with Dutch imperialism and interest in preserving opportunities for exploiting the peasantry made the new landlords the mainstay of foreign domination. It is now these strata that supply the leadership for internal counterrevolution and are the agents of external reaction. It was position and role in the process of social production, and not aristocratic origin, which determined the attitude of the offspring of this class toward the national liberation struggle. Many active fighters against colonial domination, for genuine independence of the homeland, came from the ruined *priaji* —the children of the civil servant system, who could not find work or opportunities for application of their knowledge. At the same time, some representatives of the bourgeoisie who had become semi-feudal landlords, usurers, or agents of foreign monopoly capital became interested in maintaining alien domination and precapitalist survivals, since their well-being and livelihood depended on them.

The Indonesian peasantry was interested in eliminating the feudal relationships. However, the colonists' declarations of state land ownership, the burden of taxes and obligations to the government, the expropriation of the best lands for lease by the government, and of the rural communities by the foreigners caused the struggle of the peasants to be directed primarily against Dutch imperialism. The peasantry emerged as the most active force in the national anti-imperialist revolution.

Favorable objective prerequisites for the revolutionary organization of the peasantry were created by the relatively high percentage of the rural proletariat (chiefly on foreign-owned plantations) and the very great proportion of poor people and semi-proletariat among the peasants of Java, Western Sumatra, and certain other regions, resulting from the rapid stratification of the peasantry during the epoch of imperialism. The national bourgeoisie developed in Indonesia under conditions which were still less favorable than in India, Vietnam, or the Philippines. By the time of the epoch of imperialism in Indonesia, no class of national or even merchant bourgeoisie had been formed. The functions of the middleman and limited possibilities for internal trade were seized by Chinese, Arab, and partly by Indian, capital. In the epoch of imperialism, the competition of large foreign capital, which brought under its control the basic branches of production and the foreign trade of the country, also created almost insurmountable obstacles to the development of a national bourgeoisie. As a result, there was no kind of big bourgeoisie (particularly industrial) in Indonesia during the colonial period. The national industrial bourgeoisie was represented only by the owners of a few semi-primitive shops and enterprises. A stratum of middleman bourgeoisie appeared which, in competition with other more powerful comprador groups (Chinese, Arab), was as closely tied to imperialism as any comprador bourgeoisie.

Owing to the weakness of the Indonesian bourgeoisie, it was unable to establish any important political party which would advance its own bourgeois nationalistic program, or give it any ideological basis. The Indonesian intelligentsia, which expressed the awakening of national consciousness during the first period, was mainly tied to the bureaucratic and aristocratic classes, whose members were the first to gain access to education in Indonesia and abroad. The first national organization, the Budi Utomo (Glorious Endeavor), which was created by it in 1908, was unable to raise itself higher than cultural and educational activities and demands for equality with the Dutch. Soon, however, a considerable inflow of non-aristocratic intellectuals, petty-bourgeois intelligentsia,

67

predetermined the growth of revolutionary democratic ideas in the awakening national movement. This obviously affected the first mass organization, the Sarekat Islam.

In contrast to the national bourgeoisie, the working class first emerged in foreign concerns (transport, docks, mines, large plantations, and related enterprises which processed agricultural products). It was formed fairly rapidly and achieved considerable concentration. In the almost complete absence of large enterprises belonging to national capital, the emerging workers' movement—at first elemental and then organized —joined with peasant activities directed primarily against the imperialists (i.e., the owners of large enterprises and plantations) and against the colonial authorities. The class struggle of the proletariat in the colonial period coincided with its anti-imperialist struggle.

Because of this condition, which differed from that in India, the Philippines, and many other colonial countries, the struggle of the working class did not frighten the national bourgeoisie, who had become interested in the development of the workers' movement directed against the foreign capitalists.

In the absence of any influential bourgeois parties, the organizations of the Indonesian proletariat which appeared during the First World War, and especially after the October Socialist Revolution, were under the influence of revolutionary social-democratic ideas. Along with favorable objective circumstances, the movement was aided by an important subjective factor—the emergence in Indonesia by 1914 of the Social Democratic Union, which was created upon the initiative of representatives of the revolutionary branch of Dutch social democracy (the Tribunists). Before the Great October Revolution, the Social Democratic Union counted only Dutch and Indonesian intellectuals among its still small membership and contained various reformist tendencies along with revolutionary elements. The great work of its revolutionary branch brought tangible results in mass organizations, especially in the Sarekat Islam.

Thus, the peculiarities of the class structure and the relationships of the class forces in Indonesia, particularly in Java, where two-thirds of the total population of the colony was concentrated, created extremely favorable objective conditions for establishing the broadest common national front. They made the Indonesian national bourgeoisie considerably more revolutionary than the national bourgeoisie in other colonies in Southeast Asia. The weakness of the bourgeoisie and its implacable contradictions with foreign monopoly capital promoted the influence of socialist ideas not only among the workers, but among the growing intelligentsia. Under the objectively favorable conditions for the formation of a single national front, even in the early stages of the national liberation struggle, the opportunity appeared for the working class to gain a decisive role in the anti-imperialist national democratic revolution.

All of this appeared clearly during the First World War in the Sarekat Islam. After several years the Muslim Merchants' Union (Sarekat Dagang Islam)—which was formed in 1911 by a group of Javanese merchants and owners of batik shops and set for itself the unpretentious objective of a struggle against oppression by usurers and middlemen—became a broad popular organization. This fact served to demonstrate the severity of the contradictions with imperialism, the awakening of a national consciousness among the masses, and the common interest of the various classes in the struggle for democratic national good.

During the First World War, which greatly worsened the situation of the majority of the Indonesian people, the anti-imperialistic movement grew. In 1916, a congress of the Sarekat Islam declared itself the First National Congress. The Second National Congress, which was held in October 1917, on the eve of the Great October Revolution, demonstrated that the important work done in the Sarekat Islam by the revolutionary social democrats had found suitable soil. The Social Democratic Union at first widely propagandized the ideas of socialism, and familiarized the Indonesian people with the revolutionary struggle in other countries. Because of the Union, the revolutionary events in Russia found a response in Indonesia earlier than in many countries in Asia. In the publications of the Union, the overthrow of tsarism was held up to the Indonesian people as an example of the struggle against imperialism.

At the Second National Congress of the Sarekat Islam, the slogan of the struggle against "shameful" capitalism was unanimously supported, together with an exposé of the colonial system and the Dutch authorities. Under the influence of the Great October Socialist Revolution, the national liberation movement gained even wider scope. The victory of the October Revolution was above all reflected in the delimitation of forces within the Social Democratic Union. It inspired the revolutionary forces and frightened the right socialists of all colors. The latter left the Union in 1917 and established the Indonesian Social Democratic Workers' Party.[b] It had few members, no foundation among the masses, and was an affiliate of the opportunistic Dutch Social Democratic Party. The Social Democratic Union, which had freed itself from the rightists, further extended its work in mass organizations, its activities in the organization of workers' unions, and in the management of strike activities. On the basis of this Union, the Communist Party was formed in 1920. The Communist Party of Indonesia (PKI) was closely connected to the masses. From the first days of its existence, it exerted direct and strong influence on the liberation struggle of the people, and was the first Communist Party in Southeast Asia.

The young PKI was the most influential mass party. The bourgeois and petty bourgeois parties which existed during that period either became essentially cultural and educational organizations (Budi Utomo, Muhamadja, etc.) or united small groups of intelligentsia, reflecting the growth of the national movement in different regions of the country (Pasundan in Western Java, the Union of Sumatrans, the Union of Madurans,

b. It is a commonplace of Communist doctrine that the October Revolution in Russia awakened the revolutionary trends in the colonial areas. Following the Bolshevik seizure of power, the already shaky socialist movements throughout most of Europe split along radical and moderate lines. Many of the radical groupings were subsequently to join the Comintern and become the Communist parties of their respective countries.

etc.). The truly mass organization, the Sarekat Islam, whose membership reached 2.5 million by 1919, was a unique people's organization, a bloc of various classes; national bourgeoisie, the working class, peasants and petty bourgeoisie, and Communists participated in its management along with bourgeois and petty bourgeois representatives—both revolutionary and moderate.

The existence of objective prerequisites for forming a single national front was seen in the unification of Indonesian organizations into the so-called "Radical Concentration," which reflected the growth of the anti-imperialist movement and the profound dissatisfaction with the miserable "reforms" which Holland was forced to carry out after the end of World War I.

Sarekat Islam could have become an authentic organization of the single anti-imperialist front, but the struggle within it between the proletariat and bourgeoisie for control of the national liberation movement became acute. In spite of all Sarekat Islam's economic and political weaknesses and the obvious fact that its goals could be attained only by relying on the broad popular masses, the national bourgeoisie still did not wish to give up its leading role. The national bourgeoisie opposed the ever-increasing influence of the Communist Party over the masses, both within the Sarekat Islam and outside of it, by using religious slogans which had no small effect on the Muslim population of the country.

The Communist Party, after allowing a number of serious errors of a leftist order (underestimation of the national liberation character of the struggle against the Dutch, misunderstanding of the bourgeois-democratic tasks of Indonesian revolution, advancement of a slogan for an immediate socialist revolution, etc.), itself weakened the possibilities for expanding its influence and strengthening a unified national front. In the split which took place in the Sarekat Islam, the emerging section which was controlled by the Communists was first called the Red Sarekat Islam, and later the Sarekat Rakjat. This split, together with the split in the single labor-union center, weakened the national liberation movement, but at the same time it demonstrated the influence of the PKI on the workers, a considerable number of whom had followed the Communists.

Differing from other colonial authorities, the Dutch for the first time permitted the legal existence of a Communist Party and affiliated organizations, counting on a split in the common national movement and isolation of the Communists. They were able to achieve a split, but the imperialists were frightened by the influence which the Communist Party maintained even after that occurred.

The "liberalism" of the imperialists was quickly replaced by a system of persecution and terror. The Communist Party, which had no experience in illegal work, suffered tremendous losses in 1923–1925. A number of draconic laws were introduced against the workers' movement and against revolutionary activity and propaganda. At the same time, the Sarekat Islam, which had become a political party controlled by the Islamic members, substantially lost its foundation among the masses.

Owing to the suppression and downfall of the national liberation movement, an armed uprising led by the Communists broke out in a number of regions in Java in November 1926, and in eastern Sumatra in January 1927. The Dutch imperialists succeeded in drowning the uprising in blood. The PKI and the labor unions, womens' and youth organizations connected with it were disbanded and proscribed. Thousands of patriots were sent without trial or inquiry to a special labor camp in West Irian.

The imperialists were not strong enough to extinguish the national liberation movement or the class struggle of the workers. The majority of the old political parties, including the Sarekat Islam, were afraid to come out with sharp criticism of the colonial order or to conduct work among the masses. However, in 1927, the Nationalist Party (PNI) emerged which was led by a young engineer named Sukarno, who openly supported the task of fighting for complete national independence and for improving the conditions of the popular masses. The  party quickly attained popularity and many patriots joined its ranks, including Communists who had survived arrest and exile.

The party sought and found support among the masses, in whom Sukarno saw the main strength of the national movement. The Dutch authorities did not slow down in their efforts to split the party leadership. Sukarno and a number of his colleagues were arrested in 1929, accused of preparing for an armed uprising, and sentenced to various prison terms. Sukarno was able to convert the defense speech at his trial into a denunciation of imperialism. Imprisoned by the colonialists, he remained the most popular political leader of the national liberation movement.

The Nationalist Party ceased to exist, but was soon resurrected under a new name, the Party of Indonesia (Partindo). While Sukarno was in prison, the party continued to organize the masses under the directorship of Sartono and others. The exceptionally severe consequences of the world economic crisis for Indonesia stimulated new enthusiasm in the anti-imperialist movement. In spite of the anti-labor laws, the strikes not only encompassed various categories of white- and blue-collar workers, but even affected the army. The actions of naval personnel in the uprising on the battleship *De Zeven Provincien,* in spite of its weak organization and the leaders' lack of clear goals, was the first to unite Dutch and Indonesians.

The growth of anti-imperialist tensions in connection with the attempt by the imperialists to find a way out of the crisis at the expense of the colony affected the position of even the moderate bourgeois strata and led to the formation of a number of new bourgeois national parties at the beginning of the 1930's.

In 1932, the Communists were finally able to begin restoring the party organizations in the underground. The growing anti-imperialist movement was led by leftist elements of the national bourgeoisie and the revolutionary petty bourgeoisie, which were connected primarily with Partindo. Sukarno was the recognized leader and ideologist of Partindo and led the party after he left prison.

## The Third World in Soviet Perspective

In the article by O. I. Zabozlayeva,[c] the principles of *Pantja Sila* are described, as they were formulated by Sukarno during the Second World War and the Japanese occupation, and their further theoretical and practical development in the struggle to secure independence is traced. We can see the basic outlines of these principles in the articles and program documents of the Nationalist Party and Partindo, especially in the brochure by Sukarno, *For a Free Indonesia*, written in 1933.

The great revolutionary significance of the brochure can be seen not only in the analysis and exposure of imperialist exploitation, but in the tasks which were set forth to attain independence through a mass struggle to construct a society which "has no aristocracy, no bourgeoisie, no classes, no capitalism."[1]

The appeal contained in the brochure to prohibit the rise of the aristocracy or the bourgeoisie to positions of power in free Indonesia found widespread support among the broad masses of the Indonesian people. Sukarno proceeded from a correct analysis of the historical process as a struggle between the exploited masses and the exploiters, but he did not notice the formation of classes among the Indonesian people. To him, the workers, peasants, and petty bourgeoisie did not represent separate classes who occupied a specific place in the process of social production and had their own class interests. They were all oppressed *marhaeni,* poor people who were opposed by imperialism and its internal reactionary allies.

Sukarno frequently noted the influence of Sun Yat-sen on the formation of his views. The democratic character of his ideas about the possibility of eliminating social inequality and constructing a socialist society doubtlessly brought him close to Sun Yat-sen. However, the historical situation in which Sukarno's ideas were developed differed basically from the period in which the ideas of Sun Yat-sen had evolved. During the epoch of the general crisis of capitalism and the

c. An article that appeared in the symposium to which this piece of Guber's provides the introduction.
1. Sukarno, *Indonesia Accuses* (Russian edn., Moscow 1956), 246.

74

Soviet Writers on the Developing Areas

struggle of the two systems,[d] the Indonesian revolutionary democrats were more inclined to accept socialist ideas. The program of Partindo and the PNI, headed by Sukarno, was the brightest expression of socialism. It was adopted democratically and indissolubly connected with the national liberation struggle. The militant democratic program of Partindo showed opportunities for uniting the true revolutionary patriots, and made it possible for the Communists to operate legally.

Of course, not only the weak national bourgeoisie, but a significant part of the petty bourgeois intelligentsia expected independent Indonesia to be a capitalist country where the bourgeoisie held authority. The interests of different strata of moneyed classes, including those who were striving for complete independence, were expressed by different parties. The majority of these parties, which were under threat of terror, were afraid to criticize imperialism openly or to appeal for a struggle for independence. The Dutch imperialists did not weaken their repression, not only of the Communists, but of all true fighters for independence. In 1933, Sukarno and a number of other political workers were again arrested and exiled. The policy of imperialism only helped to make all national forces aware of the necessity for uniting in the national liberation movement.

The organization Gerakan Rakjat Indonesia (Gerindo), which was established in 1937 by revolutionary representatives of the national bourgeoisie and the consistent fighters for the freedom of the Indonesian people—the Communists—gave expression to the movement of the most decisive and patriotic forces.

On the initiative of Gerindo and a number of other parties and partisan organizations, the GAPI (Indonesian Political Union) appeared, representing a broad national front. Under the conditions at the beginning of World War II and the threat of Fascist aggression, the GAPI protected national in-

d. The reference is to the two international systems of capitalism and "socialism" (i.e., communism).

75

terests and demanded above all self-rule and democratic representative government, and was ready to cooperate with the Dutch authorities in the struggle against fascism.

However, even when the Dutch imperialists were threatened with the loss of their colony, they did not wish to make even the slightest concession to the just national demands of the Indonesian people. The policy of the Dutch imperialists and their more powerful imperialist patrons made it easier for Japan to conquer Indonesia and the other colonies of the Western powers in Southeast Asia.

During the Japanese occupation, there was further progress in consolidating the patriotic forces fighting for independence. The forms for uniting the national forces under conditions of the Japanese occupational regime were to a considerable extent created by the regime. While the Japanese imperialists' propaganda succeeded at the very beginning of the occupation in attracting to their side a portion of the national forces, who naïvely believed that it was possible to liberate themselves from three centuries of colonial oppression by collaborating with the Japanese, these illusions were quickly dispelled. . . .

The necessity for the Japanese imperialists to combine cruel exploitation with political maneuvering in order to satisfy their selfish interests called forth a unique combination of selfless armed resistance and use of legal and semi-legal opportunities. Cadres of Indonesian revolutionaries were tempered by the difficult situation and their aspiration for total independence was strengthened.

The dispersion of the main forces of Japanese imperialism on the Asiatic continent by the Soviet Army and the resulting Japanese surrender created an exceptionally favorable situation for the Indonesian people.[e] The Japanese occupation forces were demobilized. The armed forces of the previous colonial rulers and their imperialist allies could not imme-

e. The Soviets consistently assert that the fall of Japan was due primarily to the Soviet defeat of the Japanese forces in Manchuria in the last days of World War II. The American victories served only to contribute to the weakening of Japan.

diately come to the archipelago. The Indonesian people turned over a new page in their history. . . .[f]

f. This and the previous ellipsis indicate the exclusion of sections in which Guber discusses various articles in the symposium. The material omitted is irrelevant to the course of his argumentation.

# The 20th Congress of the CPSU and Problems of Studying the Contemporary East *

*THE 20th Congress of the Soviet Party, held in 1956, marked in many respects the end of the Stalin era It provided the setting for Khrushchev's "secret" speech on the travails of the previous decades and signaled a general easing of pressures in the Soviet Union and in Eastern Europe. As part of the de-Stalinization program, Soviet orientology was subjected to severe criticism for its shortcomings—many of which can be directly traced to the stultifying influence of Stalinist narrowness and orthodoxy. In effect, the orientalists were being chided for following orders from the previous political leadership. It was obvious to all concerned that this was scarcely a matter of their own choosing, and the "criticism" to which they were exposed was often more a means of signaling a change than of actually calling individuals to task for their misdeeds.*

*The change in line did not result from any particular devotion to truth and scholarship on the part of the Khrushchev leadership. The Soviet government found itself badly out of touch with the emerging areas and realized that measures to improve the situation were urgently required. In addition to the necessary political moves that were already under way, a new body of research and theory was needed. Even more important, a new generation of students had to be familiarized with the politics, history, customs, languages, and other aspects of the emerging countries. The Institute of Orientology (Institut Vostokovedeniya) of the Academy of Sciences of the USSR was to be infused with a new sense of purpose, and the moribund publication Sovetskoye Vostokovedeniye (Soviet Orientology) was to be the journal for disseminating the fruits*

* Source: "XX S"yezd Kommunisticheskoy Partii Sovetskogo Soyuza i zadachi izucheniya sovremennogo Vostoka," SV, No. 1 (1956), 3–12.

## Soviet Writers on the Developing Areas

*of the new efforts as well as the more purely scholarly work on the Orient.*

*The following article—unsigned and therefore authoritative —has thus a double purpose: to castigate the errors of the past and point the way to the future. It emphasizes the importance of recognizing that there are genuine national liberation movements which have achieved power by peaceful means, and it sharply criticizes some of the dogmatic distortions of the Stalin era. It can be taken as the start of the contemporary phase of Soviet research on the third world.*

*The 21st and 22nd Party Congresses have also been commemorated by similar articles, reflecting a judicious mixture of self-satisfaction and self-criticism,[a] and programmatic articles of this type are a regular feature of Soviet scholarly journals. They are often turgid and uninformative, but in view of their authoritative nature they can give valuable clues to shifting trends in research policy.*

*I have substantially abridged this article. The reader is spared the first three pages, highly general and replete with Leninisms. The final pages (except for the last paragraph) have also been dropped. These discuss in detail some of the specific tasks which the Institute and its journal should undertake to raise the level of oriental studies. A more interesting sample of this type of material can be found in the article by Mikhaylov, printed below.*

. . . At the 20th Congress [of the CPSU] the state of ideological work was subjected to thorough criticism. The Congress emphasized that the Central Committee was correct in

a. Communists lay great stress on frequent and intensive criticism as a means of improving all aspects of the movement. An integral part of this is "self-criticism," in which the individual confesses his own faults publicly and promises to improve his performance in the future. In a tactical sense, a modest amount of self-criticism is often used to forestall severe criticism from above or as a means of indicating submission to higher authority which has already made known its displeasure with the victim's past performance. As in the present case, it is often difficult to determine the extent to which self-criticism is only ritualistic. Similar "examinations of conscience" on the occasions of the 21st and 22nd Party Congresses are listed in the bibliographic note at the end of this book.

79

attacking the cult of personality, which had become widespread and was weakening the role of the party and the masses. The Congress pointed to the need to struggle against the remnants of subjectivist-idealist views on the role of personality in history. As was pointed out at the Congress, the stagnation on the ideological front is explained by the fact that scientists have paid little attention in their work to the treasury of Lenin's ideas, as well as by the fact that dogmatism and blind acceptance were widespread and propaganda was out of touch with the practice of Communist construction; as a result, new historical experience has been but weakly tied in with the facts of living reality.

Completely sound and justifiable criticism was made of the Institute of Orientology of the Academy of Sciences of the USSR. A. I. Mikoyan was perfectly right in stating in his address to the 20th Congress: "While the entire East has awakened in our time, this Institute has been napping up to this day. Isn't it about time the Institute raised itself to the level of the needs of our time?"

We cannot reconcile ourselves to the fact that many of the most vital and important problems in studying the East have been either avoided completely or considered from erroneous positions. Dogmatism and blind acceptance are still being encountered in the handling of many economic and historical problems of the contemporary East. Criticism of imperialism, colonialism, and bourgeois ideology has not always rested on convincing examples and facts.

The misunderstanding of the character and seriousness of the contradictions between the forces of imperialism and internal reaction, and the forces of national progress in the non-socialist countries of the East, has been very detrimental to orientology. Our orientologist-economists have occupied themselves chiefly with studying the activity of foreign capital in the national economies of the countries of the East. Sufficient attention has not been paid, however, to analysis of the internal processes; the objective trend toward independent capitalist development, which has been undermining the dominant position of imperialism, has not been given its due

## Soviet Writers on the Developing Areas

evaluation. The development of the world socialist system has been the most important factor undermining the position of foreign financial capital in countries of the East. Thus the countries embarking on the road to independent development need no longer turn to their former oppressors for modern equipment, since the socialist countries can offer them such equipment without setting any political or military conditions.

Since World War II, when a radical change in power relationships occurred on an international scale, dominance of foreign capital in the economies of certain countries of the East has no longer meant that imperialism is necessarily dominant in the political life of these countries. For example, countries such as Indonesia or Saudi Arabia, which have not been liberated from the economic oppression of imperialism, are presently pursuing a sovereign policy.

Underestimation of the objective process of independent economic development in the countries of the East stems from the scholastic idea that the general tendency of capitalism to decay spreads mechanically, even to all the non-socialist countries of the East, and excludes the possibility of them developing their own productive forces. Many orientologists, exaggerating the role of feudal remnants,[b] have not noticed the changes which are coming about in the economies of countries of the East owing to the development of capitalist relationships. The point was reached where a far-fetched, quotation-capped theory was advanced by certain orientologists, regarding the "expansion of feudal exploitation" in the modern Indian village.

Such a dogmatic approach betrays ignorance of Lenin's teaching that during the epoch of imperialism the general tendency toward decay does not exclude the rapid growth of capitalism in individual countries. The facts have shown that as national capitalist enterprise grows in the countries of the East, the contradictions between the local bourgeoisie, and foreign financial capital [c] and feudal land ownership,

b. On "feudal" survivals, see above, p. 52, note g.
c. Financial capital denotes the gradual merging of entrepreneurial and banking interests—e.g., into holding companies—that is said to charac-

81

*The Third World in Soviet Perspective*

become intensified. Inability to comprehend the objective pattern of these economic contradictions was one of the main reasons for the failures of certain orientologists in their attempts to explain the essence of many of the most important political processes.

As O. V. Kuusinen [d] noted in his speech at the 20th Congress of the CPSU, sectarian [e] errors have been present in certain public addresses of Soviet orientologists in recent years, as expressed in the incorrect description and evaluation of the role of the national bourgeoisie of the countries of the East. The Marxist-Leninist thesis is well known that during the general crisis of capitalism the proletariat in colonial and dependent countries—where capitalism is relatively highly developed—can achieve hegemony of the national liberation and anti-feudal revolution. This thesis is brilliantly supported by the great victory of the Chinese people and the peoples of other people's democracies in the East.

From this absolutely correct thesis, however, was drawn the incorrect conclusion that only the leadership of the proletariat can assure victory in the struggle for national independence. Therefore, when India, Burma, Indonesia, Egypt, and certain other Eastern countries where the proletariat—which is the vanguard of the patriotic forces—was not yet able to secure hegemony, achieved sovereignty under the

terize the latter stages of capitalist development. The concept was developed by the Austrian Rudolf Hilferding (1877–1941) and popularized by Lenin in *Imperialism—the Highest Stage of Capitalism* (1917).

d. Otto V. Kuusinen (1881– ), a Finn by birth, is one of the few "old Bolsheviks" still prominent in the hierarchy of the CPSU and is regarded as the most venerable theoretician of contemporary Soviet communism. He is the editor of *Fundamentals of Marxism-Leninism*. There is no small degree of irony in finding Kuusinen as a critic of "sectarianism" in colonial policies. In the Comintern period he was responsible for enunciating some of the most sectarian views of Stalin. See Lazar Pistrak, "Soviet Views on Africa," *Problems of Communism*, xi (March–April 1962), 27, n.14.

e. "Sectarianism" is a sin of an excessively leftist approach to tactical questions, more or less synonymous with "dogmatism." A sectarian approach in the present context would indicate that Communists fail to strike a tactical alliance with non-Communist forces and thereby forfeit the benefits to be gained by infiltrating and dominating a "united" or "popular" front.

leadership of the national bourgeoisie, many orientologists were unable to make a sufficiently objective evaluation of the great significance of this event in the history of the East. Furthermore, in some works this method of gaining sovereignty was considered the "final collusion of the big bourgeoisie with imperialism."

It is known that there is a basic difference, especially in terms of the ultimate goals of the liberation movement, between achieving independence under leadership of the proletariat—which is the sole consistent fighter for national and social liberation—and the attainment of sovereignty under leadership of the national bourgeoisie. This, however, by no means justifies the negative attitude toward many important processes which have been and are now taking place in the countries of the East.

Inability to comprehend the essence of the objective contradictions which exist between the national bourgeoisie and imperialism resulted for a time in the former's position being determined by solely one factor—fear of the class struggle of the masses. Similarly, the dialectical representation of the duality in the nature of the national bourgeoisie was incorrectly replaced by one-sided representation of the national bourgeoisie as a true ally of imperialism in the struggle against the toiling masses of its own country. From such a position the political activity of the national bourgeoisie could be depicted only as a chain of capitulations, betrayals, and demagogic maneuvers. Especially for the past few years, the political line of the bourgeoisie of India and the National Congress, headed by M. K. Gandhi, has been depicted in this fashion.

Of course, Soviet orientologists do not subscribe to the philosophical views of Gandhism. However, this by no means excludes recognition of the outstanding positive role of Gandhi in the history of the struggle of the Indian people. The same type of error was also allowed in evaluating the bourgeois parties and their leaders in the study of Turkey, the Arab countries, Burma, and Indonesia.

Underestimation of the contradictions between the national bourgeoisie and imperialism led to groundless negation of the indisputable fact that, in certain stages of the anti-imperialist struggle, the interests of the bourgeoisie have coincided with the interests of the popular majority. Thus the patriotic demands contained in the program set forth by the bourgeois leaders during their negotiations with the colonists have reflected objectively the interests of the people who rose in the struggle for liberation. The colonists actually retreated and made concessions, not because of the policies of the bourgeois leaders, but because of pressure from the masses.

Meanwhile, certain stages in the history of the attainment of sovereignty by countries of the East have been depicted in our literature on orientology as a series of agreements made between the bourgeoisie and imperialism behind the backs of, and against, the people. The masses have thereby been assigned the role of a powerful but elemental force which only indirectly influences the course of history. Objectively speaking, the authors of such concepts have exaggerated the role of bourgeois leaders and underestimated the historical role of the masses.

Undoubtedly, the programs promoted by the bourgeois leaders were extremely inconsistent and contained selfish class theses which required principled criticism from the standpoint of Marxism-Leninism. For some historians, however, the inconsistency of the national bourgeoisie's program has served as an excuse to brand the entire program as demagoguery, although it did in fact express national demands. Such an approach to the programs of the national bourgeoisie, which were supported by the majority of the people, inevitably led to sectarian self-righteousness.

Sectarian errors were also manifested in lack of clarity about the multitude of forms of the struggle for national liberation in the countries of the East. In particular, the possibility of gaining independence through peaceful means under certain historical conditions was ignored. Neither the peculiar characteristics of certain Eastern countries, nor the decisive change in the relationship of the power of reaction and the power of progress which took place both internationally and within the Eastern countries themselves, were taken into con-

## Soviet Writers on the Developing Areas

sideration. The facts demonstrate that the growth of the authority of the Soviet Union; the enormous strengthening of the entire socialist camp, especially after the formation of the Chinese People's Republic; the defeat of capitalist armies in Korea and Vietnam; the powerful upsurge of solidarity between the workers of the metropoles and the colonial peoples; and, finally, the general upsurge of the national liberation struggle in the East, in which the decisive role belongs to the workers' class and the peasants, have been forcing the colonists in certain cases to flee without unleashing large-scale colonial wars.

Misunderstanding of the character of the contradiction between the forces of national progress and the forces of imperialism has had an adverse effect on the evaluation of a number of measures taken in those countries of the East which have set out on the road to sovereignty. There have been cases of an unobjective disregard of the first modest but important successes of the young states which are with great effort overcoming the terrible heritage of colonialism. Thus the concrete significance of land reforms in India, Egypt, Burma, Syria, and other countries has not been revealed in our literature.

These reforms do not of course satisfy the needs of all levels of the peasantry. They do, however, weaken and even undercut the system of feudal exploitation of the peasants. Measures taken in the field of independent economic and cultural development of those countries which have attained national sovereignty have a progressive significance. The industrialization of these countries, which has just begun, will aid in strengthening their national independence, intensify the economic contradictions between them and imperialism, including the contradictions of the national bourgeoisie, on the one hand, and foreign monopolies and local feudal reaction, on the other.

In evaluating such measures it is necessary to take into consideration the above-mentioned process of establishing national unity in these countries. By relying on this national unity which encompasses the democratic and patriotic forces of all

85

parties, classes, and strata of the population, the peoples of Eastern countries will be able to accomplish their great tasks in the struggle for national freedom, a consistent policy of peace, and attainment of prosperity for the people.

In literature on the East, errors have been made in analyzing Japan's postwar situation. In underestimating Japan's capability for independent economic development and, consequently, the seriousness of U.S.-Japanese contradictions, some writers took the attitude that this nation, which is industrially highly developed and has powerful monopolies, belonged among the semi-colonial countries. Others ignored the progressive elements in such important undertakings as agrarian reform and labor legislation. These measures were carried out in the changed conditions of the Far East after the Second World War under the pressure of the democratic movement which developed in that country.

Notwithstanding historical facts, some studies idealized the policy of tsarism in China and other countries of the East.[f] Idealization of the foreign policy of tsarism, as A. M. Pankratova [g] noted at the 20th Congress of the CPSU, makes it impossible to understand the extent to which the Soviet Union, since the first days of its existence, has been conducting a basically new, peace-loving policy. It is perfectly natural for the peoples of the East to regard the Soviet Union as their constant, true, and sincere defender against the horrors of colonialism, and the warm feeling of friendship of the peoples of the East toward our country has become a powerful factor in strengthening peace throughout the world. . . .

Inspired by the historic decisions of the 20th Congress of the CPSU, Soviet orientologists will devote all of their energy and knowledge toward fulfilling the majestic and most noble

f. A significant aspect of Stalin's policy was the fostering of Russian patriotism, especially during the years of World War II. Stalin did not scruple to exalt the virtues of Tsarist Russia, even though tsarism was not exactly a social system that would normally receive Marxist approbation.

g. Anna M. Pankratova (1897–1957)—Soviet historian, chief editor of the journal *Voprosy Istorii,* and member of the Central Committee of the CPSU.

task of constructing Communist society. They will rally even closer together around the Communist Party and Leninist Central Committee, and in the shortest period of time will eradicate the faults in their work, which has been subjected to just criticism at the 20th Congress of the Communist Party of the Soviet Union.

SELECTION 5

# The Study of Latin America in the Soviet Union *

## BY S. S. MIKHAYLOV

*LATIN American studies have traditionally been among the weakest areas of Soviet "orientology." The continent is remote from the Soviet Union and—until recently at least—the Monroe Doctrine seemed to pose an almost impenetrable barrier to Communist influence. Especially since the rise of Castro, however, Latin America has assumed great importance and Soviet scholars have begun to give serious consideration to its problems.*

*The newly established Latin American Institute of the Academy of Sciences is charged with the task of giving direction to those efforts, and the following article by the Institute's director provides interesting light on the problems and perspectives which he sees from his new position. The article is of considerable interest from the methodological viewpoint: it reveals the general type of work undertaken at the institutes of the Academy and particularly the policy orientation that governs research work in the Soviet Union.*

*The criticisms made by Mikhaylov are not merely formulas to fill the requirement for "Marxist criticism and self-criticism." [a] They point up very real defects, particularly the charge that Soviet scholarship tends to treat Latin America as one big undifferentiated area. Although significant beginnings are being made,[b] the Latin American Institute clearly has its work*

* SOURCE: "Izucheniye Latinskoy Ameriki v Sovetskom Soyuze," *Voprosy Istorii* [Questions of History], No. 4 (1962), 98–106; based on the translation in JPRS 13,890.

a. See above, p. 82, note a.

b. See, for instance, the articles by Shul'govskiy and (to a lesser extent) Grechev in this volume. Good material is also contained in M. V. Danilevich and A. F. Shul'govskiy, eds., *Problemy sovremennoy Latinskoy Ameriki* [Problems of Contemporary Latin America] (Moscow 1959).

## Soviet Writers on the Developing Areas

*cut out for it in achieving the degree of competence required for making significant contributions to policy or scientific research.*

*Several paragraphs that deal with Soviet research on Latin America prior to World War II have been deleted.*

THE history of the Latin American peoples is unique and complicated. Their culture is an extremely interesting one. But today these are not the only considerations which arouse the interest of the entire world in the countries of Latin America. Today Latin America is a struggling continent.

The importance of Latin America is increasing with each day. Not too long ago, the bourgeois press regarded that continent as the most reliable backyard of imperialism. But today Latin America is a new and powerful front in the national liberation movement which is playing an ever greater role in the struggle against the imperialism of the USA—the main stronghold of modern colonialism and world reaction.

The peoples of this continent are now faced with extremely serious and vital problems: the struggle to overcome imperialism and internal reaction, the development of their independent national economies and culture, and the liquidation of poverty and age-old backwardness. Under modern conditions, scientific elucidation of these problems is extremely opportune, since it aids the peoples of Latin America in their struggle to achieve their goals.

A knowledge of the historic past makes it possible to understand correctly many contemporary problems. In this connection, Fidel Castro said: ". . . what was our history, if not a struggle against national and foreign forces which tried to hinder the realization . . . of the just desires of our nation?" [1] The same thing may be said with regard to other countries and peoples of Latin America.

Latin American problems are attracting the attention of scholars the world over. Soviet scientists—historians, geographers, and economists, who are doing everything in their

1. Fidel Castro, *Speeches and Addresses* (Russian edn., Moscow 1960), 247.

*The Third World in Soviet Perspective*
power to contribute to the elucidation of a number of scientific problems important to Latin America from the practical standpoint—are also very interested in the subject.

The efforts of Soviet scientists in the study of Latin American problems are highly valued by progressive Latin American historians interested in the development of their own scholarship. Their attention is drawn not only by the content and scientific qualities of Soviet studies, but also by the progressive methods and traditions of Soviet scholarship. Some of the works of Soviet historians are well known in Latin America. The article by the Soviet scholars M. S. Al'perovich, V. I. Yermolayev, I. R. Lavretskiy, and S. I. Semenov entitled "On the War of Liberation of the Spanish Colonies in America, 1810–1826," published in *Voprosy Istorii*, No. 11 (1956), was translated into Spanish and published in a number of Latin American countries. The objective evaluation of Simon Bolívar presented in this article was of great help to the progressive historians of Latin America in their struggle against the reactionary historical school which distorts the point of view of Marxist-Leninist historiography regarding the most important stages of the national liberation movement in Latin America. The monograph by Soviet historians M. S. Al'perovich and B. T. Rudenko entitled *The Mexican Revolution of 1910–1917 and US Policy* (Moscow 1958) was published in Spanish in Mexico. This book provides documentary proof of the aggressive character of US policy in Mexico during the period of the revolution. The outstanding Mexican historian Canovas wrote in the preface to the Mexican edition of this work that it should be read by every Mexican. Of great interest to Mexicans were the studies carried out on the deciphering of the ancient Maya script by the Soviet ethnographer and linguist Yu. V. Knorozov. Many more examples could be cited to show that the works of Soviet scientists are enjoying recognition and attention in Latin America.

The study of the most important socio-economic and political processes in Latin America allows us to conclude that the development of the Latin American countries is taking place within the framework of general historical laws operat-

## Soviet Writers on the Developing Areas

ing the world over. The laws of socio-economic development discovered by Marxism-Leninism operate with the same force in Latin America as in other regions of the world. But Latin America developed under special historical conditions, so that both the past and present life and struggle of the Latin American peoples bear a unique stamp. One of the chief features of the historical development of Latin America is that in modern and contemporary times the continent has found itself under a foreign yoke which fettered its material and spiritual forces.

It is well known that barely had the peoples of Latin America liberated themselves from Spanish colonialism after a long, heroic struggle when they became saddled with a new form of oppression. One contemporary scholar has correctly noted that the countries of Latin America early in the nineteenth century had won their "banner and coat of arms," but were relegated to economic subjugation in the process of the formation of the imperialist colonial system.[2] This is the chief cause of the general backwardness of Latin America from the economic and socio-political standpoint; it is this historical circumstance that explains the special features of capitalist development and the preservation of feudal and even prefeudal relationships in Latin America.

In this context the necessity for a thorough study of the problems of capitalism (industrial and monopolistic) and feudalism, as well as various forms of prefeudal relationships in Latin America (for example, slavery in Brazil, peonage in a number of other Latin American countries, etc.), becomes quite obvious. Unfortunately, our scientists have not yet made any serious attempts at a complex study of these problems, beyond studies of their separate aspects. Only a deep and comprehensive investigation of these problems will make possible an understanding of the most important phenomena both in the history of Latin America and in its modern class struggle and political life. We are still publishing far too little scholarly material presenting a deep analysis of the economic and political processes now going on in Latin America. The

2. *Problems of Peace and Socialism* (Russian edn.), No. 11 (1961), 19.

backwardness of our social sciences in this regard must be overcome as soon as possible, for life itself demands this. For this reason, it is fitting for us to ask what is the present state of Latin American scholarship in the Soviet Union. Let us take stock of what has already been done and what we must do in the future in this field. The present article represents an attempt to give an approximate answer to these questions which could serve as a point of departure for their further discussion. The need for such a discussion is patent. . . .

In the postwar [i.e., World War II] period, the study of Latin America began to move forward more rapidly. This reflected the increased interest of the Soviet Union in Latin America in connection with the expansion of diplomatic, trade, and cultural relations with the Latin American countries, as well as the fact that in the Soviet Union a certain number of young specialists on Latin America had completed their training in the immediate prewar period. The emergence of the new scholars promoted the more intensive study of Latin America.

After the Great Patriotic War,[c] the training of specialists on Latin America began on a much wider scale, while a number of scientific research and higher educational institutions in both Moscow and outlying areas began to occupy themselves with Latin American topics. Soviet scientific journals opened their pages to the systematic publication of materials on Latin America.

In connection with the new and powerful rise of the national liberation movement in the countries of Latin America, interest in that area and attention to the study of its problems increased to an even greater extent. Following the 20th Congress of the CPSU, which called for the thorough and comprehensive treatment of history from the point of view of creative Marxism, textbooks on modern and contemporary

c. The "Great Patriotic War" is the Soviet term for World War II, although properly speaking it refers only to that part of the war during which the Soviet Union was directly engaged (after June 1941).

history began to include systematic accounts of the problems of Latin American history.

During the following years, the Soviet Union published a large number of interesting articles, symposia, monographs, and reference works on Latin America.[6] Soviet researchers have already done a great deal in this area. This reflected the enormous importance of the resolutions passed by the 20th Congress of the CPSU for all Soviet Latin American scholars and Soviet science at large. After the Party boldly and decisively criticized and condemned the Stalin cult of personality so foreign to Marxism-Leninism, optimum conditions were created for the development of Soviet social sciences, scholarly progress, and the elimination of shortcomings and serious theoretical errors. This also affected the state of writings devoted to Latin America. Soviet specialists put their efforts into high gear, began to make a more thorough approach to the theoretical understanding and analysis of facts, and expanded their range of investigations.

A beneficial effect on this sector of scientific work, particularly as regards the problems involved in the national liberation and workers' movements, was exerted by the well-known resolution of the CPSU Central Committee entitled "On the Tasks of Party Propaganda under Modern Conditions," adopted on January 9, 1960, as well as the documents issued by the Conferences of Representatives of Communist and Workers' Parties held in 1957 and 1960, which constituted

6. M. S. Al'perovich, *Izucheniye istorii Latinskoy Ameriki v Sovetskom Soyuze: Kratkiy obzor* [The Study of Latin American History in the Soviet Union: A Brief Survey], in the symposium *Latinskaya Amerika v proshlom i nastoyaschom* [Latin America Past and Present] (Moscow 1960). Important events in Soviet Latin American studies were the publication of the collective works entitled *Ocherki novoy i noveyshey istorii Meksiki 1810–1945 gg.* [Outlines of Modern and Contemporary Mexican History, 1810–1945] (Moscow 1960), and *Ocherki istorii Argentiny* [Outlines of Argentine History] (Moscow 1961). Recently, Soviet publishing houses have begun to issue more translations of books about Latin America. Also issued were several works by the leaders of Communist and workers' parties in Latin America, as well as individual writings by progressive Latin American scholars.

## The Third World in Soviet Perspective

theoretical weapons for Latin American scholars and provided new prospects and directions for their scientific endeavors.

At the present time, extensive use is made of such effective work methods as scientific conferences and meetings. The preparation and holding of such conferences make it possible to mobilize large collectives of Soviet scientists in various specialties for the solution of various important problems.

A positive role in the development of Soviet Latin American scholarship was played by the scientific conferences and meetings held in 1960 in honor of the 150th anniversary of the wars for independence of the Latin American peoples. The scientific sessions of the History Institute of the Academy of Sciences of the USSR, the World Economics and International Relations Institute of the Academy, and the A. M. Gorky Institute of World Literature of the Academy made a significant contribution to the study of the history, economics, politics, and culture of Latin American countries. It was the first time that Soviet specialists had an opportunity to discuss problems of the past and present of Latin America so broadly and thoroughly.

At a meeting of the History Institute of the Academy of Sciences of the USSR, for example, new light was thrown upon such major themes as the socio-economic background of the 1810–1826 war for independence, its character, and the role of the working masses in this struggle. Serious criticism was directed at reactionary conceptions propounded by bourgeois scholars who attempt to negate the revolutionary character of the war for independence, minimize the role of the popular masses, and exaggerate the role of individual historical figures. For the first time, Soviet historical science posed and exposed the theme of the attitude of Russia and Russian society, especially the Decembrists,[d] toward the war for independence in Latin America.

A significant step forward was taken by Soviet specialists in the study of the problems involved in the modern economic and political development of Latin American countries, at

---

d. The Decembrists were a group of educated Russians who revolted unsuccessfully against Tsar Nicholas I in December 1825.

94

## Soviet Writers on the Developing Areas

the session held by the World Economics and International Relations Institute of the Academy, where thorough analyses were made of such problems as the deployment of class forces in Latin America, the role of the national bourgeoisie at the present time, the question of the necessity for radical agrarian reform, etc.,

One of the important positive aspects of such scientific conferences is the fact that they aid in the theoretical-scientific growth of our young cadres, who are taking an active part in conferences, proposing new ideas, and boldly and originally posing and solving many current problems.[e]

At the present time, owing to the struggle of the Latin American peoples for their national liberation, Latin America is assuming special importance in international life. The positions of imperialism on this continent are becoming ever more precarious. With the victory of the popular revolution in Cuba, a new stage in the national liberation struggle in Latin America has begun. "The 1960's are destined to enter history as the years of the total collapse of the imperialist colonial system," said N. S. Khrushchev at the 22nd CPSU Congress.[7]

It is the duty of Soviet scientists studying Latin America to take due cognizance in their work of the new conditions that have come about in the world situation, reflecting them both in the treatment of their subjects and in the analysis of those phenomena that characterize the present situation in Latin America and its position in the world arena. Some things are already being done along this line.

The History Institute of the Academy of Sciences of the USSR, which recently organized a special section on the

e. Communists lay great stress on the collective approach to scholarship, primarily for ideological reasons. (In Marxist philosophy, man can achieve fulfillment only as part of a social group; individualism is at best suspect.) Grechev's article—printed below—is part of a symposium on the national liberation movement in Latin America, published in MEIMO, Nos. 9 and 10 (1960); a summary of another recent symposium was given by B. Ordynskiy in the same journal, No. 3 (1963), 551–53.

7. N. S. Khrushchev, *Otchet tsentral'nogo komiteta kommunisticheskoy partii Sovetskogo Soyuza XXII s"yezdu partii* [Report of the Central Committee of the CPSU to the 22nd Party Congress] (Moscow 1961), 22.

*The Third World in Soviet Perspective*

history of the Latin American countries, is now planning the publication of several important works. Among these will be the collectively written volumes: *Outlines of Modern and Contemporary Brazilian History, 1500–1945,* a collection of articles entitled *On the 150th Anniversary of the War for Independence in Latin America,* a textbook on contemporary European and American history for university history departments which will include a section on "Latin America, 1939–1961," etc., and Volume X of *The History of the World,* which will include a chapter entitled "The Countries of Latin America During the Years of the Second World War." The prospectus of the Institute includes a whole series of monographs on the history of Latin American countries.

The N. N. Miklukho-Maklay Ethnography Institute of the Academy of Sciences of the USSR is preparing such works as the symposia: *The Contribution of the Indians to the Treasure House of Culture, The Formation and Development of Nations in Latin America,* and a two-volume monograph entitled *Nations of Latin America,* as well as other scientific publications. The Academy of Social Sciences attached to the CPSU Central Committee is planning to publish in 1962 a collective scientific work entitled *The Communist Parties of Latin America in the Struggle for Working Class Unity and a United Anti-imperialist Front.*

The Socio-Economic Literature Publishing House plan for 1962–1963 includes two collective works: *The Economic Problems of Latin America* and *From the Heroic Past of the Latin American Peoples,* as well as a number of monographs on the history of the working class and peasantry of Latin America, US expansionism, the national liberation movement among the Latin American people, etc.

The International Relations Institute Publishing House in 1962 plans to issue collective works on the following themes: *The Economic Cooperation of the USSR with the Countries of Asia, Africa, and Latin America,* as well as *Latin America and International Law*—a brief handbook on the countries of Latin America.

The State Publishing House of Political Literature is preparing a series of popular brochures on the Latin American countries which is to be titled "Latin America Today."

The issuance of these books will to some extent satisfy the need of our country for literature on Latin America. However, as may be seen from plans of scientific research and publishing activities in the field of Latin American studies, there is still much to be done before Soviet Latin American scholars can make up for the time lost when the study of Latin American problems was not accorded enough attention, and can raise scholarly work to a level that will correspond to the increasing needs of life.

Despite the successes of recent years, it is necessary to admit that on the whole the situation as regards Latin American studies still remains unsatisfactory, particularly in the light of those great problems which the 22nd CPSU Congress has posed to Latin American scholars in the Soviet Union as well as to all Soviet scholarship.

The basic fault of the work conducted in the USSR on the history, politics, economics, and culture of the Latin American countries consists in a lack of any clear planning and coordination of research efforts. The choice of themes is not systematic, but arbitrary. The criterion for selection is frequently the private interest or inclinations of the researcher rather than the scientific significance of a given theme. In many cases, the choice of theme is dictated by considerations of availability (or lack) of material. All of this results in a situation in which a number of important problems have not received due consideration. Thus, for example, there is a total lack of studies devoted to the modern political and economic situation in individual Latin American countries and Latin America as a whole. Also quite insufficient is the attention devoted to such important and timely questions as the development of the national liberation and workers' movement, the development of other progressive social movements in Latin America, the analysis of the role and position of the national bourgeoisie and so-called "middle classes" in the national liberation struggle, the exposure of the traitorous activities of social-reformist parties, etc. Few studies are being made of problems having

*The Third World in Soviet Perspective*

to do with the colonialist policy pursued by imperialist powers (first and foremost, the United States) with relation to the Latin American countries—for example, the forms and methods of this policy. Nor are there any analyses available of the contradictions of the imperialist powers whose interests clash in Latin America, the problem of Latin American economic integration, plans for the creation of regional "common markets," the role of state-monopoly capitalism in the Latin American economies, etc. There are no scientific works devoted to the diplomatic, economic, and cultural relations of the Soviet Union with Latin American countries, although the experience available in this field could have long ago been generalized; and in this connection the possibilities and prospects of economic, scientific, technical, and cultural cooperation of the countries of the socialist camp with Latin America could have been explored. It is necessary to focus our studies resolutely on the crucial problems in Latin America, keeping in mind those which have been posed for the social sciences by the new program of our Party. Life itself requires studies devoted to such important current problems as peaceful coexistence and economic competition of two systems,[f] and the disintegration of the colonial system of imperialism. It is necessary to struggle against bourgeois ideology, to expose anti-Communist, reformist, and revisionist theories, as well as new forms and methods of imperialist policy practiced by the US in Latin America, to analyze heretofore neglected problems of unequal exchange, "primary accumulation" in the liberated countries, etc.[g] Of course, the list of problems which have not as yet received sufficient

f. "Two systems"—see above, p. 75, note d.

g. "Unequal exchange"—denoting the disparity of the developing countries' receipts for their raw materials compared with the higher prices they must pay for finished goods. "Primitive" (or "primary") accumulation is the first and extremely painful step required for initiating the "take-off" of capitalism. (See above, p. 51, note e.) "Two simultaneous processes—the appearance of wage-labourers (proletarians) and the accumulation of wealth in the hands of capitalists—were designated by Marx as primitive accumulation. . . . Some of its methods are still being applied today in the colonial and economically underdeveloped countries." (*Fundamentals*, 212.)

98

elucidation or have been completely neglected could be extended.

Nor can one fail to mention as an extremely significant shortcoming of the general studies on Latin America published so far the absence of a differentiated approach to specific Latin American countries. Frequently the specific peculiarities of these countries are not only not brought into relief, but are on the contrary "smoothed out," so to speak, since the study is concerned with generalities and not the specific characteristics of each of these countries.

We do not as yet have any serious studies on the history of a whole series of Latin American nations (Venezuela, Bolivia, Ecuador, Peru, Colombia, Uruguay, etc.). Still unsolved is such an extremely important problem as dividing the history of Latin American countries into periods. In most cases, the themes of historical works are too far removed from recent and current events. Concentration on the distant past is distracting the attention of those few historians specializing in Latin America whom we have in the Soviet Union, from the study of more recent and current problems. In our scientific literature on the problems of Latin America, the great majority of studies are limited to extremely narrow chronological periods. This makes it impossible to cover the development of events on a larger scale and analyze more gradually developing underlying phenomena. Sometimes the absence of such a broad view leads to a situation where the significance of certain phenomena or processes is overestimated and the researcher neglects negative factors, difficulties of struggle, periods of retreat, etc.

Shortcomings in the study of Latin America to a considerable extent have to do with the acute shortage of highly qualified cadres of specialists on that area. The great need for well-trained Latin American scholars, which incidentally is constantly increasing, is far from satisfied either by our higher educational institutions and their graduate programs or by graduate departments of scientific research organizations. We must be aware of the alarming situation as regards the study of the Spanish and Portuguese languages in the colleges and universities. This situation must be corrected—the sooner the better—since training Latin American specialists who have no knowledge of Spanish or Portuguese is practically impossible. It is necessary for the Ministry of Higher and Secondary Specialized Education of the USSR to devote some attention to the expansion of the teaching of these languages in the higher educational institutions. It is likewise desirable to extend the amount of available information on the history and economic geography of the Latin American countries that is presented to students in higher educational institutions and secondary schools. At the present time, they receive very little knowledge about this part of the world, which is beginning to play an ever greater role in international life.

Of great benefit to the comprehensive study of Latin American problems would be the establishment of closer contact between Soviet scholars specializing in Latin America and their colleagues in the socialist countries. Such cooperation could be extremely fruitful.

Also unfortunate is the situation as regards the coordination of Latin American studies among Soviet Latin American scholars themselves. It is to be hoped that the situation will be altered by the recent creation by the Presidium of the Academy of Sciences of the USSR of a number of Scientific Councils on Complex Problems for the purpose of improving the coordination of scientific research. Latin American subjects are covered by two Scientific Councils on Complex Problems: "Economic Competition of Two Systems and the Underdeveloped Nations," and "The History of the National Liberation and Workers' Movements." The latter Council includes a special section on Latin America. The Councils must unify and coordinate the creative efforts of all scientific collectives working on corresponding problems through the organization of joint scientific research and the initiation of public control [h] so as to guide this research and its productiv-

h. So that all endeavors are responsive to the masses' interests and desires, the public at large is supposed to "control" (i.e., watch over and criticize) the arts, science, political performance, etc. In practice, the Communist Party tends to relieve the public of this burdensome duty,

ity. The Scientific Councils are to embody the principle of collective control over scientific research; the role of the scientific community in the organization of research will increase. With regard to problems connected with Latin American studies, the Scientific Council in our opinion must first of all bring up for discussion the most imperative research tasks, evolve plans of scientific work corresponding to the demands of life, and outline measures to eliminate the shortcomings present both in the treatment of problems and in the organization of research efforts. The Scientific Councils, having introduced elements of uniformity and division of labor into Latin American scholarship, will doubtlessly promote the better utilization of the resources of Latin American scholarship in our country and raise the general theoretical level of scientific research.

Following the 22nd CPSU Congress, which adopted the new Party Program for the construction of communism, the tasks of Soviet social scientists have increased immeasurably. Soviet scholars specializing in Latin America are faced with an extremely wide range of activity in which they may expect highly important and interesting themes for scientific research. There are many important and politically acute problems besetting Latin America that must be studied by our historians and economists.

The Latin American Institute of the Academy of Sciences of the USSR, whose mission is to become the center of coordinated research on the problems of contemporary Latin America, should make a considerable contribution to the solution of those problems. The scientific research efforts of this Institute will likewise be useful to state and public organizations maintaining ties with Latin America, and thereby to the development and strengthening of friendly ties between the USSR and the Latin American nations. The Institute will promote better coordination of scientific work on Latin America among Soviet Latin American scholars, establishing creative contact with Latin American scholars in the socialist coun-

although much publicity is given to citizens' complaints (frequently "inspired") about shortcomings in Soviet society.

tries and scientific and cultural organizations in Latin America. An important task of the Institute will be the training of highly qualified scientific cadres in the fields of Latin American politics and economics; this will be aided by establishing a postgraduate program at the Institute and by granting to the Academic Board of the Institute the right to accept for defense, masters' and doctors' theses on problems that come within the scope of interest of the Institute.

One of the first tasks of the Institute is to prepare a number of reference publications for which a great demand is felt at present. In particular, the intention is to issue in cooperation with other institutes and the Soviet Encyclopedia Publishing House a two-volume encyclopedic reference book on the history, politics, economics, and culture of Latin American countries. The Institute's plans likewise include the publication of a collection of articles devoted to the new stage of the national liberation and workers' movements in Latin America, collections of articles on modern Brazil and the successes of socialist construction in Cuba, and many other books.

There can be no doubt that Soviet scholars specializing in Latin America will intensify their efforts and, having taken as the basis of their activity the new CPSU Program and the resolutions of the 22nd Party Congress, will ensure through their joint efforts that Soviet research on the problems of Latin America will constitute a valuable contribution to the development of Soviet social sciences and thus to the common task of the Soviet people and all progressive mankind—the struggle to establish on earth the most advanced, just, and humane order—communism.

# The Problem of Economic Independence *

## BY L. STEPANOV

*L. STEPANOV, G. Mirskiy, and R. Avakov appear to be some of the most promising younger members of the Institute of World Economics and International Relations. Their approach to the economics and politics of the third world differs considerably from that of the older generation which rose to prominence under Stalin. All Soviet research now attempts to rely more on factual presentation than on the empty vituperation of the earlier period, but this rising generation approaches their tasks with more dedication than do their elders.*

*One of Marxism's most hallowed clichés is that the developing countries enjoy political independence, but are still economically dependent. To some extent this proposition is a truism, yet like most such propositions it leaves much unsaid and begs for empirical substantiation. It should by no means be assumed that Stepanov is here investigating the problem of "economic independence" with the objective of establishing whether or not such a phenomenon exists, but by at least attempting to prove empirically that it exists he has come quite a distance from the era when anything more than a reference to Marxist scripture was considered superfluous.*

*Stepanov's article produces no new conclusions or insights and his use of statistics may be open to question; nevertheless, his is a recognizably "scholarly" piece and illustrates well the new spirit in Soviet research on the third world. At the same time, Stepanov obviously accepts Marxist-Leninist economic analysis—on a rather sophisticated level—as the natural analytical framework. It seems likely that this combination of scholarly competence coupled with an internalized (and therefore not overly obtrusive) commitment to Marxism will be characteristic of the generation of scholars who*

* SOURCE: "Problema ekonomicheskoy nezavisimosti," MEIMO, No. 5 (1962), 85–97; based on the translation in JPRS 14,552.

## The Third World in Soviet Perspective

*were born after 1917 and established themselves in the Khrushchev era. These are the writers who will set the tone of writing as long as the Khrushchev policies remain in the ascendant.*[a]

*I have substantially abridged this article. A few paragraphs at the beginning—consisting of empty phrases on the "collapse of the colonial system"—have been deleted as well as several pages at the end. These final pages are rather repetitious and deal with internal economic problems as they affect "economic independence."*

. . . . IN our literature it is customary to judge the economic dependence of underdeveloped countries according to several factors. It should be noted that one-sided agrarian-raw material specialization makes a country's economy extremely dependent on the world capitalist market. More directly, this feature of dependence appears in the limited variety of exports. Another very important factor of economic dependence has been found in the preservation by foreign capital of strong positions in the economic structure of a given underdeveloped country. The plundering to which the "world countryside" has been subjected under the system of a world capitalist economy is also viewed as a manifestation of economic dependence. The mechanism of this plundering consists both in the withdrawal of profits, percentages, and dividends by foreign monopolies, and in the "price scissors"[b] on raw material and industrial goods—that is, in usually unfavorable trading conditions for the underdeveloped countries on the world capitalist market. An acute and especially serious factor has been unequal exchange,[c] which also perpetuates the

a. It is significant that after the crisis in Sino-Soviet relations in early July 1963, Stepanov and Mirskiy were immediately called upon to justify the Soviet policy in the third world and attack the Chinese position. (*Pravda*, July 18, and *Izvestiya*, July 16, respectively.)

b. "Price scissors"—the progressive decline of the prices of raw materials on the world market, both in absolute terms and, especially, in comparison to the rising prices of finished products.

c. "Unequal exchange"—the advanced countries sell their commodities at an inflated value, while buying the products of the underdeveloped countries below their real value. This varies only slightly from the idea

unjust and exploited position of underdeveloped countries in the system of world capitalism.

There are several other indications of economic dependence which are more specific. For example, the participation of an underdeveloped country in the currency zone of one or another imperialist power undoubtedly restricts the economic self-dependence of this country. The inclusion of certain African countries in the "Common Market," or other special economic agreements which the imperialist powers have imposed on countries of Asia, Africa, and Latin America, are regarded as phenomena of the same order. In connection with the broad use of "aid" as a lever in the foreign policy of imperialist govenments, the economic dependence of underdeveloped countries is not infrequently manifested in forced agreements in order to obtain credits and subsidies from the West in exchange for specific concessions. These concessions can be economic as well as political in nature. Finally, the general foreign-policy orientation toward the imperialist West in many cases has economic dependence as its ultimate and deepest cause and basis.

The main task is to determine exactly what should be understood by the term "economic dependence" (or "independence"), and to make clear what the basis is for regarding the position of a country—according to a number of factors—as one of economic dependence (or independence).

In order to explain the essence of the problem, it is advisable to examine the effect of any given factor that is acknowledged as one of the chief indicators of economic dependence, and also to analyze the results of the total effect of all factors.

What effect, for example, does the export of capital have on the position of underdeveloped countries in the world system of capitalist economy?

In the period from 1955 to 1960, American monopolies withdrew $37 million from India in the form of profits.[2] This sum represents a drain on the national wealth of India. Here

of the "price scissors." On the meaning of "value" in Marxist economics, see note d, below.

2. Here and in what follows (including the tables), all data on export

# The Third World in Soviet Perspective

we have evidence of the redistribution of value [d] to the gain of the imperialists. The real damage done to an underdeveloped country by the transfer abroad of profits of foreign companies consists in the fact that the country thus loses part of its fund for capital accumulation and is compelled to proceed at a correspondingly decreased rate of economic growth; in this regard the lost financial resources are quite often in a non-monetary form, which in effect represents a restriction of opportunities to import acutely needed means of production.

TABLE 1

Repatriation of Profits to the United States from American Direct Private Investments in India and the Rise in These Investments Owing to Export of New Capital
(in millions of dollars)

| Year | Withdrawal of Profits | Export of New Capital | Reduction (−) or Increase (+) in Assets of Capital Accumulation for India |
|---|---|---|---|
| 1955 | 11 | −2 | −13 |
| 1956 | 6 | 7 | + 1 |
| 1957 | 6 | 4 | − 2 |
| 1958 | 8 | −2 | −10 |
| 1959 | 5 | 3 | − 2 |
| 1960 | 1 | 13 | +12 |
| 1955–1960 | 37 | 23 | −14 |

We must, however, consider that this damage can be compensated by the inflow of new foreign capital. Thus, in the above-mentioned Indian example, the loss of $37 million in the period indicated was offset by approximately two-thirds through the export of new American capital to this country in the form of direct private investments. (See Table 1.)

In this manner, the loss to India accruing from the export

of American capital are the result of calculations based on statistics published in the August issues of *Survey of Current Business* for the years 1956–1961.

d. The Marxist concept of "value" differs from that accepted by most economists. For Marxists, the value of a commodity is the measure of the average amount of labor needed for its production. Supply and demand are irrelevant and materials of themselves have no "value."

*Soviet Writers on the Developing Areas*

of American capital in the period from 1955 to 1960 amounts to $14 million. Similar calculations relating to the activity of American private capital in Africa show that in this same period the export of capital by the United States into the countries of that continent and the withdrawal of profits have been practically in balance. If we examine this problem in relation to all underdeveloped countries and focus attention on data covering the ten-year period ending with 1960, we see that the total losses of former colonies and semi-colonies amounted to $8.5 billion, representing the difference between the export of private capital by the United States ($4.8 billion) and profits repatriated by American monopolies ($13.3 billion). Consequently, whatever the totals may be for individual countries and for individual years, in this narrow sphere of the world capitalist economy a very substantial redistribution of value has been occurring, to the benefit of the imperialist powers and to the loss of the underdeveloped countries.

The export of capital, however, is only one of the levers of the world capitalist mechanism which act concertedly to deprive the underdeveloped countries of part of their national wealth to the benefit of the highly developed nations. The redistribution of value also occurs through channels of international trade, in the area of the movement of loan capital, because of fluctuations in the rates of exchange, etc. There are many figures that indisputably demonstrate the depth of the economic gulf between the former colonies and semi-colonies, on the one hand, and the developed capitalist states, on the other. Table 2 illustrates one of the particular aspects of this trend.

From the data presented in the table it follows that the developed countries not only use (require) all the new power that they have created, but also absorb an ever-increasing amount of the power being developed at increasing rates in the former colonies and semi-colonies. The drain of national resources from the underdeveloped countries is shown here as a redistribution of value.

Similar statistical calculations for other goods can confirm

## The Third World in Soviet Perspective

### TABLE 2

Share of Underdeveloped and Developed Capitalist Countries in Rise in
Production and Demand for All Forms of Power, 1955–1959
(in per cent) *

| | Production of Power | Demand for Power |
|---|---|---|
| Entire capitalist world | | |
| ( % of increase) | 11.3 | 10.2 |
| Economically developed countries | 29.5 | 72.4 |
| Underdeveloped countries | 70.5 | 27.6 |

\* Prepared from data in the *U.N. Statistical Yearbook, 1960*.

but also can refute this position. For example, the share of
underdeveloped countries in world steel smelting (excluding
the socialist states) amounted in 1958 to 2.8 per cent, whereas
their share in the demand for steel was 14.7 per cent.[3] This
is entirely to be expected, since finished industrial products
tend to be imported by underdeveloped countries. The total
balance of the redistribution of value among countries of the
capitalist world can consequently be expressed only through
cost indices—abstracted from the physical form of material
benefits and services.

### TABLE 3

Dynamics of the National Incomes of Developed and Underdeveloped
Countries and Changes in Their Relative Share in the Total Income of
the Capitalist World (absolute figures in billions of dollars) *

| | 1951 | | 1959 | |
|---|---|---|---|---|
| | Sum of Nat'l Incomes | Share of Sum Total (in %) | Sum of Nat'l Incomes | Share of Sum Total (in %) |
| Group of economically developed countries | 407.5 | 87.6 | 622.6 | 90.3 |
| Group of underdeveloped countries | 57.6 | 12.4 | 66.9 | 9.7 |
| TOTAL | 465.1 | 100.0 | 689.5 | 100.0 |

\* From the *U.N. Statistical Yearbook, 1960*.

Table 3 illustrates the change in the share of underdeveloped countries in the total national income of 19 countries

3. *U.N. Statistical Yearbook, 1960*.

108

# Soviet Writers on the Developing Areas

of Europe, Asia, America, and Australia. Brazil, Colombia, Ecuador, India, Indonesia, Pakistan, the Philippines, Burma, Ceylon, and Thailand are shown as underdeveloped countries. The group of developed countries includes the United States, Canada, England, West Germany, France, Belgium, the Netherlands, Japan, and Australia.

Although Table 3 graphically confirms the tendency toward an increasing economic gap between the underdeveloped countries and the developed countries of the capitalist world, it is not sufficient for an analysis of the problem under study. The data presented on the dynamics of national income do not allow us to judge the role of the mechanism of redistribution of value between countries, since the data also reflect the action of internal factors, such as the level of production attained, the rates of national economic growth, etc. Table 4 presents a more graphic picture of the enrichment of the advanced capitalist states at the expense of the underdeveloped countries.

The data in Table 4 not only show the obvious results of the action of the mechanism of redistribution but also permit us to judge the future consequences of these results. In fact, the progressive absolute and relative reduction in gold reserves

TABLE 4

Gold Reserves and Currency Reserves of the Capitalist World
(absolute figures in millions of dollars) *

| | 1951 | | | |
|---|---|---|---|---|
| | Gold Res. | % of Total | Curr. Res. | % of Total |
| Economically developed countries | 30,909 | 91.1 | 8,342 | 55.5 |
| Underdeveloped countries | 3,031 | 8.9 | 6,693 | 44.5 |
| Entire capitalist world | 33,940 | 100.0 | 15,035 | 100.0 |
| | 1959 | | | |
| | Gold Res. | % of Total | Curr. Res. | % of Total |
| Economically developed countries | 35,061 | 92.6 | 12,869 | 67.6 |
| Underdeveloped countries | 2,804 | 7.4 | 6,156 | 32.4 |
| Entire capitalist world | 37,865 | 100.0 | 19,025 | 100.0 |

* Prepared from data in the *U.N. Statistical Yearbook, 1960.*

*The Third World in Soviet Perspective*

and foreign currency reserves of the underdeveloped countries must inevitably lead them to new losses, and is fraught with the danger of decreased rates of economic growth owing to the narrowing opportunities for paying for the import of needed equipment.

Thus, as in the time of the colonial empires, the objective pattern of the world system of capitalist economy continues to be the pumping of riches from underdeveloped countries into the developed. Here it is important to emphasize the objective inevitability of the conditions that engender the process of extraction of value and allow it to develop. Under such conditions the capitalist developed countries deprive the underdeveloped countries of a significant part of their national resources, thus leaving them powerless to use this part of their own resources for their own interests. As has already been stated, even though plundering of underdeveloped countries by the imperialist powers is correctly viewed as an indication of economic dependence, this does not fully indicate such dependence. First of all, the problem of the underdeveloped countries' lack of freedom to control their own national resources is not thereby settled; and, second, the question of why contemporary capitalism is plundering the "world countryside" to enrich the economically developed countries remains unclarified.

In order to answer this question and to approach an understanding of the true extent of the economic dependence of underdeveloped countries, it is advisable to return to the problem of the export of capital and the withdrawal of profits, but to view it not in the framework of the relations between the United States and underdeveloped countries, as above, but conversely to consider the highly developed capitalist countries as trading partners. (See Table 5.)

As in the aforementioned case of the export of American capital to India and other underdeveloped countries, the consequences for the trading partners of the United States—from the viewpoint of reducing or increasing their resources for accumulation—vary from year to year. On the whole, in the six-year period under examination, redistribution of assets

110

# Soviet Writers on the Developing Areas

## TABLE 5

Repatriation to the United States of Profits from American Direct Private Investments in Countries of Western Europe, Japan, Canada, and Australia, and the Rise in These Investments Owing to Export of New Capital
(in millions of dollars)

| Year | Withdrawal of Profits | Export of New Capital | Reduction (−) or Increase (+) in Assets of Capital Accumulation for U.S. Trading Partners |
|---|---|---|---|
| 1955 | 488 | 519 | + 31 |
| 1956 | 663 | 1,021 | +358 |
| 1957 | 693 | 834 | +141 |
| 1958 | 823 | 632 | −191 |
| 1959 | 757 | 852 | + 95 |
| 1960 | 797 | 1,350 | +553 |
| 1955–1960 | 4,221 | 5,208 | +987 |

was in their favor. This, among other things, is one of the secondary, but all the more remarkable, reasons for the difficulties which the United States in recent years has experienced in its balance of payments.

Redistribution of value among the highly developed capitalist countries goes on continually and is carried out through all the channels of the world capitalist system, through which the national wealth of underdeveloped countries is also drained off. Also important here is the inequality of economic development, expressed particularly in the great rise in national incomes of some highly developed countries as compared with others. Moreover, inasmuch as there is a definite system of international division of labor, bourgeois economists speak of the mutual dependence (of the capitalist states). Based on this, imperialist propaganda widely proclaims the concept of "interdependence" of all countries of the capitalist world. The practical steps taken by the Western powers in the field of foreign economic policy (for example, the formation of the "Common Market," with the inclusion of several African countries) have been achieved under this slogan of "interdependence."

For the highly developed capitalist states, the term "inter-

111

*The Third World in Soviet Perspective*

dependence" can represent only the commonplace that these countries have very extensive mutual trade and other economic relations. "Interdependence" as a characteristic of the relations between underdeveloped and highly developed countries of the capitalist world is nothing more than an attempt to conceal the dependent status of the former and the economic dominance of the latter.

On the basis of what has been said above, we must conclude that economic independence under conditions of capitalism must be understood as an international and internal economic position of a country that would provide it with the freedom to dispose of its own national resources (not in spite of, but rather because of, the action of objective laws of the world capitalist system of economy). On the other hand, the absence of such freedom (here again by virtue of the action of the patterns of world capitalism) must be viewed as a position of economic dependence.

Let us examine the behavior of foreign private capital and various consequences of its activity for underdeveloped and highly developed countries in the world capitalist system. It should be noted that the average level of profit for American direct private investments in underdeveloped countries is 4.3 times greater than the corresponding index for [investment in] highly developed countries. Nonetheless American monopolies repatriate about 80 per cent of the profits obtained in underdeveloped countries and reinvest only one-fifth in the countries of origin. But in highly developed countries up to one-half of the profits of American companies are reinvested. The common phenomenon of the flight of capital from underdeveloped countries has usually been explained politically—fear of nationalization, general instability of conditions, etc. These circumstances, however, are compensated by the increased level of profits. Still to be considered is the economic factor that inhibits foreign companies from reinvesting the greater share of the profits they obtain in the former colonies and semi-colonial territories. This factor is the extremely low national labor productivity, which sharply restricts the oppor-

## Soviet Writers on the Developing Areas

tunity for a rapid expansion of extremely profitable capital investments.

In underdeveloped countries, foreign capital is directed first and foremost into those branches of industry where a sufficiently high productivity of labor is ensured by especially favorable natural conditions. It is particularly for this reason that 56.5 per cent of all American direct private investments in underdeveloped countries are concentrated in the extractive (mainly petroleum) industries. On the other hand, in highly developed states 51.3 per cent of capital investments are in the processing industry (data for 1960). The formation of industrial enterprises in underdeveloped countries does not as a rule promise foreign capital the desired profits, owing to the low labor productivity prevailing in these countries. For example, $780 of newly created value is derived from each worker engaged in construction in Mexico, while in the United States the corresponding figure is $6,237 dollars (data for 1955).[4]

TABLE 6

Labor Productivity in Developed and in Underdeveloped Countries of the Capitalist World *

|  |  | National Labor Productivity Per Capita of Employed Population for the Year Indicated (in dollars) | Labor Productivity in Industry (Value of Products Produced in an Hour) |
| --- | --- | --- | --- |
| Denmark | (1955) | 1,549 | 0.92 |
| New Zealand | (1955) | 3,088 | 1.36 |
| India | (1951) | 198 | 0.37 |
| Nigeria | (1952) | 128 | — |

* Prepared through calculations based upon data from the *Yearbook of National Accounts Statistics, 1959* and *Yearbook of Labor Statistics, 1959.*

Table 6 shows the ratio of levels of labor productivity in developed (Denmark and New Zealand) and underdeveloped (India and Nigeria) countries of the capitalist world.

Denmark and New Zealand have been deliberately in-

4. *Ibid.*, 258.

## The Third World in Soviet Perspective

cluded in the group of highly developed capitalist countries; their economies are markedly oriented toward agriculture, so that they superficially resemble the economies of the underdeveloped countries. However, the highly social and specialized (in terms of branches of industry) labor productivity [e] that exists in these two countries puts them in a quite different position with regard to foreign capital from that of the former colonies and semi-colonies. Here foreign capital finds convenient spheres of activity in all branches of the economy. The foreign monopolies are prepared to reinvest an increased share of their profits and, consequently, to restrict their withdrawals from the country, thus strengthening the position of capital, and of capitalism in general, in these countries, but they do not restrict their general economic growth and do not perpetuate a one-sided structure of the national economy; that is, the consequences of their activity are not at all what they are in underdeveloped countries.

It is obvious that the low level of wages—a factor attracting foreign capital into underdeveloped countries—partially loses its significance if at the same time there also prevails an extremely low labor productivity. On this basis it is easy to understand why the share of the processing industry amounted in 1960 to 15.9 per cent of American direct private investments in underdeveloped countries. Moreover, this means that profit—as a motive force for capital export—and the national interests of the underdeveloped countries inevitably come into conflict. In view of the extremely restricted level of surplus for growth in the economies of the former colonies and semi-colonies, the inflow of capital from outside becomes an unavoidable necessity. Solution of this problem by attracting foreign private capital is inconceivable without creating a more or less "favorable investment climate." And this means, in turn, that the assets obtained in this way are brought to bear not in areas where they are most needed from the point of view of the progress of the national economy,

e. All production is a *social* act, not the result of individual endeavor. Higher social concentration (e.g., mass production, interdependence of specialized branches of industry) increases efficiency.

114

but in areas where foreign monopolies count on obtaining the greatest profit.

The underdeveloped countries are thus restricted in their opportunities to direct foreign capital to the branch of the national economic structure that should be developed. On the contrary, they are forced to consider the interests of foreign monopolies and to grant them concessions to the fullest extent.

The most productive branches of the economic structure of the underdeveloped countries are usually those which in the colonial period had already been developed for the purpose of providing the imperialist states with needed minerals and agricultural raw materials. The capital of foreign monopolies continues to be poured into these branches, thus fortifying the colonial structure of the economies of underdeveloped countries.

However, in not all export branches of the economies of former colonies and semi-colonies has production been placed under the control of foreign capital or concentrated in the hands of large local companies. In the majority of cases, the producers of such goods as cotton, rubber, and cacao are small landowners and tenants. Their labor productivity is also very low, and the slightest fluctuations in the market which bring down the price of their goods are usually sufficient to devastate the small producers, who then join the army of paupers. The underdeveloped country as a whole loses significant assets under unfavorable conditions of world trade, but it is partially compensated for these losses by improvement of market conditions in other years. The ruined direct producers cannot, however, by any means be compensated. Thus to some extent the country loses genuine production resources, as has occurred in Malaya, Indonesia, and Ceylon, where as a result of a drop in world prices for rubber in individual years, rubber plantations were completely abandoned or masses of rubber trees were wiped out.

As has already been noted, the overall development of the economies of underdeveloped countries requires the attraction of capital from abroad. We are speaking, of course, not simply of financial assets but of machines, capital equipment, etc.; i.e., of the means of production—capital in its most productive form. The export of foreign capital to underdeveloped countries is not the only way of solving this problem. Capital equipment can also be obtained through import. For this, however, it is necessary in the first place to expand exports significantly when world prices for the exportable goods are stable and, in the second place, to be able to maximize the use of export earnings to pay for imports of the means of production. In both cases, this is at present difficult for underdeveloped countries to achieve, owing to the low labor productivity in their economies.

The world capitalist market is saturated with most of the goods exported by underdeveloped countries. Diversification of their exports is inconceivable without a sharp increase in labor productivity, for they would have to enter into competition with more highly productive branches of the economies of developed capitalist states. On the other hand, in spite of all the efforts undertaken by many governments of African-Asian countries, the export earnings of underdeveloped countries are expended to a significant degree not on acquiring the needed means of production, but on consumer goods. These could have been successfully produced in the required amount at home, but a good number of the former colonies and semicolonies have incurred acute deficits in them. In the imports of Ghana and the Congo (Leopoldville), for example, foodstuffs and textiles amount to 30 per cent; the share of textile goods comes to 25 per cent of the imports of Uganda, half of whose exports consists of cotton; Egypt spends 17 per cent of its import payments for foodstuffs; one-fourth of the imports of Tunisia and Morocco is foodstuffs and fabrics. The lower labor productivity in agriculture and light industry in this instance limits the opportunities for underdeveloped countries to use national resources in the interest of improving their economies.

Finally, the difference between the levels of labor productivity in developed and underdeveloped countries of the capitalist world is, as is well known, the economic basis of unequal exchange. This effect, which in general has been

116

sufficiently and extensively noted by economists quite far removed from Marxism, has not yet been subjected to a precise and concrete statistical analysis. There are a number of convincing individual examples of the effect of unequal exchange. Also available are general evaluations showing that in the middle of the twentieth century underdeveloped countries, for identical amounts of exported products, obtain only from two-thirds to four-fifths of the value which they received at the beginning of the 1900's.

All aspects of economic backwardness find their general expression in the low level of national labor productivity. . . .

SELECTION 7

# Some of the Problems of the Economic Independence of the Countries of Latin America *

## BY M. GRECHEV

*PROCEEDING from the general type of concept outlined by Stepanov in the preceding article, Grechev attempts here to portray the international economic conditions that affect the development of Latin America. As Soviet writers consistently point out, Latin America presents them with substantially different problems than do the other areas of the third world. Here they are confronted by a situation in which the United States is clearly the only significant opponent. The other Western powers—"imperialist" and "neo-colonialist" in the Soviet terminology—play an insignificant role compared with that of the "Colossus of the North." Although the overwhelming political and economic influence of the United States throughout the Western Hemisphere poses a severe limitation on Soviet capabilities (the Cuban missile crisis of October 1962 demonstrated this most forcefully), the Soviets have an unparalleled opportunity. Latin American anger against imperialism or neo-colonialism is directed at only one target—the "Yankee imperialism" of the United States. Elsewhere in the third world, Soviet propaganda must first establish this identification before it can utilize anti-colonial sentiment as a part of its anti-American campaign.*

*Grechev has thus a much easier task than would a writer who wished to utilize similar material to fan anti-Americanism in, say, India or Ghana. Grechev needs only to fan already existing sentiments, and there are unfortunately enough unsavory chapters in the history of U.S. political and economic dealings to provide him with a factual base. He of course does not*

* SOURCE: "Nekotoryye problemy ekonomicheskoy nezavisimosti stran Latinskoy Ameriki," MEIMO, No. 10 (1960), 74–81.

118

*limit himself to a basis of facts that conscientious North Americans and most Latin Americans would accept; rather, the full Marxist schema is brought to bear, with only a ritualistic acknowledgment that Latin America presents quite different problems for Soviet analysis.*

*There can be little doubt that Mikhaylov's criticism of an "undifferentiated approach" was made with articles such as Grechev's in mind.[a] In his grand view of the continent, Grechev seems to look at Costa Rica or Paraguay, Mexico or Argentina, as little more than statistical variables. The individual trees nowhere stand out from the forest. In all fairness, however, it must be noted that—despite its rather recent date of composition—Grechev's is somewhat of a pioneering article. Individual country studies are only now being made by Soviet scholars, and it will be some time before a differentiated approach can be effectively combined with the broad overview that Grechev has attempted to present.*

THE countries of Latin America, like all economically backward countries which enjoy state sovereignty or independence, are faced with the important and pressing problems of developing their national economies and improving the material conditions and cultural level of the masses of the people.

Solutions to these problems are possible only by eliminating dependence upon foreign imperialism. Economic independence is the central problem for the Latin American countries.

Latin America, which was the first objective of U.S. imperialist expansion, has felt especially heavily the yoke of American imperialism, an imperialism which has converted many underdeveloped areas of the capitalist world into its tributaries. That is why the struggle for economic independence in the Latin American countries, whatever form it has taken, has been directed primarily toward liquidating imperialist domination by the United States.

The USA is the main exporter of capital to Latin America.

a. See Mikhaylov, p. 99, above. Also James M. Daniel, "Latin America," in C. E. Black and T. P. Thornton, eds., *Communism and Revolution* (Princeton 1964), 354ff.

## The Third World in Soviet Perspective

The U.S. share amounts to over 80 per cent of all foreign capital investment and 50 per cent of the foreign trade turnover with countries of this region. Latin America supplies 97 per cent of the antimony imported by the USA, 70 per cent of the copper, 52 per cent of the lead, 62 per cent of the zinc, 47 per cent of the iron ore, 83 per cent of the oil, and so on. Furthermore, over 30 per cent of total imports are through affiliates of American companies.

The USA has subordinated the Latin American countries to its military-political domination. The Organization of American States (OAS), the 1947 Inter-American Defense Pact, bilateral military agreements, military bases, military missions, and the like all serve to further this subordination.

Relying on its economic, political, and military position, the USA interferes in the internal affairs of the Latin American countries and exerts pressure on their foreign policies. The USA frequently uses the votes of the Latin American countries in the United Nations in order to obtain decisions which are advantageous to it.

What is needed in order to overcome economic backwardness and to achieve economic independence is agrarian reform.

Over half of the gainfully employed population in the Latin American countries is engaged in agriculture. Agriculture is widespread. The land resources are used unproductively. Productivity is falling. Technical progress is insignificant. In the period 1938–1958, agricultural production increased 50 per cent, yet the volume of agricultural production per capita is still 6 per cent below the prewar level. The relative share of Latin America in the world's agricultural production has been reduced. The food problem is a very acute one, not only as a result of the reduced per capita production, but also because of the relatively more rapid growth of the urban population. Food exports over the past twenty years have fallen 40 per cent, while food imports have grown 26 per cent. The main reasons for agricultural backwardness are large land

holdings and strong remnants of feudal forms of land ownership and exploitation.

Latin America is an area in which land distribution is extremely unequal. According to the 1950 census, over 50 per
cent of the land taken into account belonged to 1.5 per cent
of the farms, which were over 6,000 hectares each in size. Vast
land holdings are concentrated in the hands of foreign companies. In Venezuela the oil monopolies own almost 7 million
hectares of land. Of the 23 million hectares in the Paraguayan
Chaco, 16 million hectares have been given to foreign companies in the form of concessions. A similar picture can be observed in Argentina and Central America.

The overwhelming majority of the rural population has
been deprived of land. In Ecuador 58 per cent of the peasants
have no land; in Chile, 74.7 per cent; in Venezuela, 72 per
cent; in Colombia, 79 per cent; in Guatemala, 80 per cent; in
Peru, 86 per cent; in Paraguay, 93 per cent.

Over 75 per cent of the land used for agricultural purposes
belongs to people who rent it out. The rental payments can
amount to from 40 to 50 per cent of the total harvest. The
short term of the rent and precapitalist rental forms (payments
in kind),[b] as well as sharecropping and corvée labor, entrench
backwardness in agriculture.

Agrarian reform is the most urgent problem in Latin
America. The giving of land to millions and millions of peasants will expand the internal market sharply, and simultaneously act as a powerful stimulus to the development of
productive forces, both in industry and in agriculture. Radical agrarian reform means the liquidation of the landlord
latifundists, including the land holdings of foreigners, and of
the enslaving rental system, and the establishment of state
aid for peasant enterprises. A reform such as this must bring
about an expansion in lands used, technical progress in agriculture, improvement in the standard of living of the peasantry,
and the elimination of the single-crop system. By liquidating

b. "Precapitalist rental forms" would be payments in labor or in kind,
rather than the purely monetary "capitalist rental form."

the class of powerful landowners, the stronghold of internal reaction, agrarian reform clears the way for democratization of social life.

The agrarian reforms which have been undertaken up to this time in certain Latin American countries (with the exception of Cuba) were not radical. These reforms were designed not to liquidate the landlords completely, but only to place restrictions on them. They did not result in the elimination of feudal exploitation. As a result of agrarian reforms in Mexico, which were begun as long ago as the 1930's, the peasantry received 43 million hectares of land, resulting in some growth in agriculture. Yet even today the agrarian question is not settled in this country. Two million peasants have been deprived of land, while at the same time 75 per cent of the land area is concentrated in the hands of the large landowners.

In Guatemala, as a result of the agrarian reforms which began in 1952–1954,[c] 160,000 peasant families received 400,000 hectares of land. Of this area, 159,000 hectares were obtained (by repurchase) from the United Fruit Company. The puppet regime, set up as a result of the 1954 intervention organized by the United States, in fact restored the old agrarian relationships.

The agrarian reforms in Bolivia after 1952 did not yield any tangible results because of the disorganization and indecision of the democratic forces in the face of reaction. The government proved incapable of helping the peasants who had obtained land.

Reactionary circles in Venezuela are attempting to solve the agrarian question without actual liquidation of large domestic and foreign land holdings, but by the colonizing of state lands.

The most radical agrarian reform is being carried out in Cuba by the revolutionary government of Castro. It is aimed at the elimination of the large holdings by Cuban and foreign owners and the liquidation of feudal methods of exploitation.

c. The years 1953–1954 were, of course, the heyday of the Communist Arbenz regime in Guatemala.

Lands have been transferred to the peasants free of charge. The state is helping the peasants by extending credits under favorable conditions. Agricultural cooperation is being stimulated. The reforms are being carried out by the peasants themselves under the leadership of the people's government.

There is no one in Latin America today who denies the need for agrarian reforms. However, there are diametrically opposed views on what is to be understood thereby. The democratic, progressive forces demand radical measures for expropriating the land of the large landowners, the distribution of such lands among the needy peasants, and the establishment of strict controls over the increase of land holdings. The reactionary circles suggest that the reforms be limited to the distribution of state-owned lands; that the private landowners not be touched. Characteristically, in the discussion of Latin American agrarian reforms appearing on the pages of the bourgeois press in the USA, it is particularly emphasized that agrarian reform, regardless of the form it may take, must not violate the principle of private ownership.

The basis of economic independence is the rapid development of the national economy, and primarily the development of industry. Industrialization is the most important means of overcoming economic backwardness and providing rapid rates of economic development. There have been a number of reasons why industrial development in Latin America over the last two decades has been going on at a faster tempo than in other economically underdeveloped countries. The isolation of Latin America from European markets during the years of the Second World War, the absence at that time of foreign competition, and comparatively high prices for exported raw materials—all these gave impetus to the development of national industry (during the war years, industrial production in Argentina increased 62 per cent; in Chile, 48 per cent; in Mexico, 43 per cent; etc.).[1]

1. It should be noted that the dollar balances which accumulated in the Latin American countries during the war years were considerably depreciated after the war as a result of increases in the prices of imported goods.

## The Third World in Soviet Perspective

In the years right after the war, the Latin American countries profited by the heavy demand for raw materials and food, not only in the European countries which had been destroyed by the war, but also in the USA, where an intensive renewal of fixed capital was going on. The Korean War and the stockpiling of strategic supplies by the United States contributed to continued high prices for raw materials. All this made for a comparatively rapid tempo of industrial development in the Latin American countries in the first decade after the war. Of course, the growth of industrial production occurred mainly in those enterprises which belonged to or were controlled by foreign capital.

Between 1945 and 1958 the volume of industrial production in Latin America more than doubled. In this same period, the extraction of petroleum increased almost three times, the smelting of steel six times, the production of cement 3.5 times. In 1958, extraction of petroleum in the Latin American countries amounted to 176.7 million tons,[d] steel production was 3.5 million tons, the production of electric power was 44 billion kilowatt hours, and the production of cement amounted to 14.5 million tons.

The production of certain types of machinery and equipment for the textile, paper and cellulose, and food industry, as well as of electric, gasoline, and diesel engines, lifting and transportation machinery, construction equipment for road building in particular, railroad cars, and so forth, has been introduced into the largest countries (Argentina, Brazil, Mexico, and in part, Chile). New branches of industry have appeared, including automobiles and tractors, chemicals, shipbuilding, etc.

While in 1940 there were 6.4 million workers employed in industry in the Latin American countries, in 1957 the number of workers had reached 12 million (including workers employed in construction work and in transportation).

Structural changes in the economies of these countries are taking place as a result of industrial development. The position

d. It may be assumed that all tonnage figures given by Soviet writers are in metric tons.

124

of the manufacturing industry is rising. The position of the first subdivision [e] is growing in some countries. Thus, for example, the share of the first subdivision in the total industrial production of Brazil rose from 20 per cent in 1939 to 33 per cent in 1956. Between 1920 and 1957 the number of workers in Brazil increased 7 times, reaching a figure of 2 million, whereas in the same period the population only doubled. The concentration of production and the centralization of capital are increasing in all the large Latin American countries. The largest—Brazil, Argentina, Mexico, Chile—have begun to develop from agrarian to agrarian-industrial countries. However, the present rate of industrial development in the Latin American countries stands in sharp contradiction to the vital need to eliminate backwardness and attain economic independence from foreign monopolies as rapidly as possible. These countries produce only from 9 to 10 per cent of the equipment they use. Four countries (Argentina, Brazil, Mexico, and Chile) provide as much as 70 per cent of the production included in total industrial output. In the period 1945–1958, the gross national product increased 80 per cent, reaching a figure of approximately $54 billion (in 1950 prices), while industrial production itself, in the same period, doubled. Taking into account the population growth, the average annual growth of industrial production per capita of population was between 2 and 3 per cent (and if Venezuela is excluded, the annual growth would be less than 2 per cent).

With rates of economic growth such as these, and because of narrow specialization and conditions where key branches of industry are controlled by foreign capital, it is impossible to expect a rapid overcoming of centuries of backwardness, the achievement of economic independence, and the provision of a high standard of living.

The leaders of the most diverse social circles in Latin America consider industrialization a vital necessity. Even the

e. Marx described the existence of two "departments" or "subdivisions" in industrial production. The first is concerned with the manufacture of producer goods ("production of the means of production"), while the second turns out consumer goods.

125

foreign monopolies, which are not at all interested in industrialization, do not dare at present to come out openly against such a popular idea.

Since they are not vigorous enough to delay the process of industrial development, which has become an objective necessity, the American monopolies, their ideologists, and their statesmen are attempting to give to this development a direction which will be advantageous to the USA. There is talk of being able, with the help of American capital (private and government), to maintain the established, international, capitalistic division of labor and to develop principally light industry, while at the same time maintaining the one-sided dependence of the Latin American countries on the USA. This aim is served, in particular, by the so-called theory of interdependence and a mutually supplementary economy, at the basis of which is the fallacious thesis of comparative costs of production that supposedly define the structure and direction of foreign commerce in the capitalist world.

The rate at which industrialization takes place is of overriding importance in overcoming backwardness and attaining economic independence. The rate of development in turn depends on the level of accumulation of capital and on how effectively it is used, on labor productivity, and on the amount of manpower employed.

According to data furnished by the United Nations' Economic Commission for Latin America, the gross capital investment in this area is, at the present time, approximately $9 to $10 billion a year, or 17 per cent of the gross production (as against 12 per cent before the war). Despite the comparatively high level of accumulation, the average rates of production growth have been small (2–3 per cent). There are a number of reasons for this. We note, first of all, that the gross investments include, in addition to investment in new equipment, investments in the construction of housing, schools, hospitals, roads, communications enterprises, transportation, expenditures for irrigation, land improvement, and other items. Approximately 60 to 70 per cent of the gross investment is spent for these purposes, with only 30 to 40 per cent going for new equipment. On the other hand, the low level of effectiveness with which investments are used explains the slow rates of economic growth. One of the most important indices of the effectiveness of investment is the relation between expenditures on equipment and on construction. Thus, for example, according to data furnished by the Inter-American Economic and Social Council, between 1950 and 1955 this relationship was 3:7 in Argentina, whereas in Brazil, the relationship was 1:1. The result was that in Argentina, with a level of accumulation of 20 per cent, the growth in industrial production was 2 per cent, whereas in Brazil, where the level of accumulation was 15.6 per cent, the growth was 5.5 per cent.

The sources and methods of financing are of exceptionally great significance for industrialization and for ensuring economic independence. For the Latin American countries, where foreign private capital is an important source of financing, this problem is especially pressing.

According to our calculations, investment of foreign capital in the economies of the countries of Latin America during the postwar years averaged $1.2 billion a year. Of this amount, direct private capital investment amounted to $600 million; private loans, $100 million; government loans, $350 million; loans by international financial institutions, $100 million; and "aid" in the form of free subsidies, $50 million (80 per cent of this sum was received from the USA). The share of foreign capital in the gross investment was approximately 12 per cent.

The question of the role of foreign capital investment in financing economic development is actively discussed in bourgeois literature. Imperialist propaganda persistently promotes the thesis that foreign, mostly private, capital has a salutary effect on economic development, and alleges that without foreign capital any considerable development of industry would be generally impossible. *Business Week,* an organ of business circles in the USA, wrote in January 1959 that "American private investments have become world-wide economic generators. They stimulate economic development not only among the developed countries throughout the world, but in the underdeveloped countries as well." This thesis was also

127

*The Third World in Soviet Perspective*

the *leit-motif* advanced by President Eisenhower in the course of his travels in South America in February 1960.

The necessity to attract foreign private capital, particularly in the form of direct capital investment, is usually justified as follows: (1) Under the conditions which prevail in Latin America, where national income is low, the internal accumulations are insufficient, and the possibility of obtaining U.S. government loans is limited, private capital can become a practically unlimited source for the financing of industrial development. (2) The virtue of foreign capital in the form of direct investments, as distinguished from governmental loans, is that there is no need to pay interest or to pay off debts. (3) Taxes levied against the foreign companies are an important source of budgetary revenue. (4) The foreign exchange problem is eased. (5) Foreign capital stimulates the development of productive forces.

Just what is the situation? It is true that foreign capital is an unlimited source of financing? The facts do not confirm this. The average annual growth of foreign private capital in Latin America has in the postwar years been approximately $600 to $700 million, or from 4 to 5 per cent of the gross investments in Latin America. This is explained mainly by the fact that the export of private capital requires the creation of what is known as a favorable investment climate in Latin America, one in which foreign capital would be free of taxes, where there would be unimpeded repatriation of profits with governmental guarantees against nationalization—and, most important of all, the possibility of obtaining great profits. In Latin America the profits on foreign direct capital investments run from 15 to 30 per cent, which is three times higher than profits within the USA.

The claim that taxes paid by American companies really are an important item in budgetary income is unsound. First of all, these taxes cover no more than 5 per cent of the budgetary income of the Latin American countries; secondly, they are but a small part of the huge profits, which amount to approximately $1 billion a year. This is why the argument that foreign private capital in the form of direct investment is more advantageous than government loans, which must be paid off and on which interest must be paid, is absolutely unsound. And here, of course, we must keep in mind that the loans are used effectively.

Equally false is the assertion that foreign private capital eases the foreign exchange problem. Between 1946 and 1958, direct capital investments by the USA in Latin America grew $5.7 billion, of which $4 billion was new investment ($1.7 billion was reinvested). The total profits from all direct American investments in the period indicated amounted to $9.8 billion, of which $7.6 billion was sent to the USA. Thus, the outflow of foreign exchange in the form of transfers of profits exceeded the influx of foreign exchange in the form of new direct investments to the amount of $3.6 billion.

So far as productive forces are concerned, foreign investments cause them to develop in a direction which does not in any way correspond to the interests of the national economy and economic independence. The foreign monopolies invest their capital primarily in the highly profitable extractive industry, causing the development of the economy to take on a one-sided, misshapen character. Of the overall total of American private capital investment in Latin America,[2] the share of such investments in the mining and oil industries increased from 39.5 per cent to 50 per cent in the period 1946–1958. On the other hand, there was a flow of capital away from the less profitable branches of industry. Thus, for example, the share of investment in public utilities dropped from 25.6 per cent to 13.4 per cent in the same period of time.

It is true that in recent years foreign capital is also being invested in the manufacturing industry. The share of American investments in the manufacturing industry increased from 13 per cent in 1946 to 20 per cent in 1958. However, an analysis of these investments reveals that they are mainly in light

2. Of $12.8 billion of American investments in Latin America in 1958, 85 per cent were private, of which some 70 per cent were direct, and only 13 per cent stemmed from government loans.

industry, and only partially in the chemical industry. A total
of 5.3 per cent of the foreign capital was all that went to
machine-building and metallurgy in 1955.

Foreign capital, using the most varied of methods of expansion (branches, affiliates, a system of sharing, mixed companies, and others), has secured control over the key branches
of the economies of the Latin American countries.

Thus, for example, American companies in Brazil control
90 per cent of the petro-chemical, 81 per cent of the meat
slaughtering, and 65 per cent of the pharmaceutical industries,
and 55 per cent of the production of artificial fertilizer. Manganese mining is in the hands of two American companies.
The tobacco industry is controlled by one English firm. Sixty
per cent of all the power produced by the largest electric
power stations is in the hands of two foreign companies.

There are 360 American companies active in Argentina.
They control over 40 per cent of the meat slaughtering industry, 70 per cent of the production of tungsten, 30 per cent of
cement, 90 per cent of zinc, 50 per cent of sulphur, 80 per cent
of the production of electric power, and 50 per cent of the
chemical industry.

In Mexico, 250 American companies control 90 per cent of
the production of zinc, lead, and copper, 50 per cent of gold,
and 60 per cent of silver.

In Venezuela, 140 American companies control 70 per cent
of the extraction and refining of oil.

There are 80 American companies in Chile. They control
95 per cent of the copper mining and 70 per cent of the extraction of nitrates.

In Peru, there are 100 American companies in operation,
controlling 80 per cent of the mining of copper, 70 per cent
of lead and zinc, 50 per cent of silver, and 100 per cent of bismuth.

In Cuba, prior to the victory of the revolution, over 1.5 million hectares of land belonged to American companies, land
which was given over mostly to the planting of sugar cane.
American companies owned 31 sugar mills and controlled
50 per cent of petroleum refining, 95 per cent of the produc-

tion of electric power, and 40 per cent of the railroads. The capital investment of the USA in Cuba was approximately $1 billion. Today a considerable part of these capital investments has passed into the control of the Cuban government.

The United Fruit Company, which is gaining for itself an unfortunate reputation, holds sway in Central America. Over 600,000 acres of the best lands belong to this company. Through its many affiliates, the monopoly controls the production of bananas, sugar, cocoa, and other agricultural (primarily tropical) crops. In addition, the company owns a fleet of 65 ships and its railroad network is over 1,500 miles long. It owns radio stations, a telegraph system, sugar refineries, ports, etc.

The dominance of foreign, primarily American, capital is the main cause of the narrow specialization of the Latin American countries, a specialization which turns them into single-crop, raw-material appendages [f] of the imperialist powers.

The aggressive actions of the USA against revolutionary Cuba can serve as a graphic example of how narrow specialization and one-crop agricultural programs are used by the imperialists to interfere in the internal affairs of a country so as to prevent the attainment of economic independence.

As is known, the production of sugar is the chief source of income for the majority of Cuba's population (sugar comprises 80 per cent of the country's exports). Until recently, half of the annual sugar production (almost 3 million tons) was exported in conformity with a special agreement with the USA.

The ruling circles in the USA decided to take advantage of the established dependence of Cuba on the North American sugar market and to force the Castro government to renounce any revolutionary reforms. At the beginning of July 1960 the government of the USA curtailed the Cuban sugar import quota by one-third, threatening to cut off all imports of Cuban sugar completely. However, this act of economic ag-

f. The underdeveloped areas are regularly called "raw-material appendages"—i.e., areas which are not permitted any significant international economic function beyond providing raw materials for the use of industry in the developed countries.

131

gression was not able to force Cuba to her knees. Now Cuba has friends capable of giving her active economic and political assistance. Cuba's surplus sugar was purchased by the Soviet Union.

The USA has also attempted to use the position of private capital in Cuba to disrupt the mutually advantageous economic agreement between Cuba and the Soviet Union. The fact of the matter is that almost all the oil which is imported by Cuba is processed in three oil refineries (two of the refineries belong to Americans, one to the English). At the demand of their governments, the owners of these refineries refused to process the oil which Cuba obtained from the Soviet Union in exchange for sugar. The foreign monopolies wanted to force Castro's government to renounce its importation of Soviet oil. However, at the beginning of July 1960, Castro's government took over control of the refineries and at the same time put an end to the sabotage of the foreign monopolies.

The export of private capital, under the conditions of competition which exist between the two systems, serves far-reaching political purposes. Speaking at Columbia University on June 2, 1959, Herter's assistant, Dillon, emphasized that the export of private capital is called upon to demonstrate, first, that private "initiative" can do more than the Communist methods of economic progress; and, second, that, by cooperating with local capital, private capital strengthens the position of local capital. He frankly stated that "the problem of exportation of capital is the problem of the struggle with communism." In order to stimulate the export of private capital to the countries of Latin America, the USA passed legislation to reduce the taxes on income from capital investments in the Western Hemisphere (the Foreign Incomes Act of 1954). Special bilateral agreements were concluded by the American government with Colombia, Uruguay, and Haiti, for the purposes of creating a favorable "investment climate" in these countries. The government of the USA also engages in what are known as investment guarantees for the exporters of capital in the event their capital is expropriated, or if difficulties are encountered in converting foreign exchange when repatriating profits, etc. Such agreements were concluded with Bolivia, Colombia, Costa Rica, Ecuador, Guatemala, and other countries. The exportation of private capital is also stimulated by governmental loans made by the USA through the Export-Import Bank, loans and subsidies of various types in the aid programs (the Mutual Security Program, Public Law 480, etc.), and loans and credits by international financial institutions where the USA has decisive influence (the International Bank for Reconstruction and Development, the International Monetary Fund, etc.).

The attitudes of the various social strata in Latin America to foreign capital differ. The democratic forces favor maximum limits and strict control over foreign private capital. There exists, in the majority of the Latin American countries, legislation which in one way or another limits the activities of foreign capital. In many countries, however, these limitations are expressed in a greater or lesser degree of taxation, which is predicated on the interests of the state budget. In some of the countries the legislation stimulates foreign investment (as, for example, in Venezuela and Brazil).

Insofar as foreign governmental loans and credits and aid in the form of subsidies are concerned, progressive circles believe that these must be long-term, bearing low interest rates, and containing the right of payment in the national currency (or with traditional export goods). It goes without saying that the loans and the credits should serve no political purpose whatsoever.[g]

It is no wonder that the pages of the Latin American press carry sharp criticism of the loans which have been made by the Export-Import Bank as well as of the loans which have been made by international financial institutions, in view of the fact that they have been made at high interest rates and with conditions concerning so-called plans for the stabilization of the economy which signify interference in the internal affairs of other countries.

That section of the national bourgeoisie which is to some

g. The credit terms described are approximately those on which the USSR makes its developmental loans.

*The Third World in Soviet Perspective*
extent connected with foreign capital takes an inconsistent
position with regard to the question of foreign investments.
Looking to its own interests, the national bourgeoisie as a
rule supports the attraction of foreign (including private)
capital, although it frequently demands some sort of limitations to safeguard its own interests.

Internal accumulation of capital is the chief source of financing. It occurs in the form of capital investment by the government as a result of budgetary allocations, funds from governmental life insurance corporations, internal governmental loans,
etc., as well as investments made by the private sector. The
relationship between governmental and private investment is,
on the average, 1:3. Government capital investments in Mexico comprise 50 per cent of budgetary expenditures; in Brazil
and Colombia, 25 to 27 per cent; and in Peru, Chile, and Argentina, 17 to 18 per cent.

The advantages of governmental capital investments include the following: (1) they make it possible to carry out
the construction of large industrial installations which are beyond the competence of national private capital; (2) investment can be directed toward those branches and enterprises
which do not attract private investment, but which are necessary in order to achieve all-around development of the national
economy; (3) in the state enterprises it is possible to devote
more of the funds to expanding production and at the same
time improving the workers' conditions; (4) state capitalism
can become an effective means for attracting foreign private
capital.

State capitalism, under the conditions which prevail in
Latin America (the public sector, in particular), plays a generally progressive role. This is especially demonstrated by the
example of Cuba.

The ruling circles in the USA are definitely opposed to state
capitalism, and above all are opposed to the public sector in
the economies of the Latin American countries. They are
afraid that the strengthening of the public sector could
weaken their position and lead to undesirable social changes.

At the same time, foreign capital is attempting to penetrate

*Soviet Writers on the Developing Areas*

the public sector in the Latin American countries, primarily by means of oganizing "mixed companies." In this way foreign capital obtains all the advantages which are given to public enterprises, while the state must assume all the risks.

The Latin American press frequently voices complaints concerning the insufficiency of internal accumulation of capital, which the bourgeois economists ascribe to low national per capita income. However, it is not so much a matter of low national income as of extremely uneven distribution. The broad masses of the people lack the possiblity of making any kind of savings which could be used for accumulation. The local exploiting classes are reluctant to invest their capital in industrial enterprises and prefer to invest this capital in real estate or commerce, to use it for speculative purposes, or to transfer it abroad. Inadequate taxation of the moneyed classes, and the great number of privileges they have, while indirect taxes continue to grow and overburden the ordinary consumers—all this hinders an increase in the level of accumulation.

Of great importance to the economic development of the Latin American countries is the stability of foreign trade. As countries with narrow specializations, they export up to 25 per cent of their gross product.

Foreign trade is the chief source of foreign exchange for the importation of equipment and one of the chief sources of budgetary income. In Venezuela, for example, the export of petroleum provides 97 per cent of the foreign exchange and 78 per cent of the budgetary funds; in Chile, the comparable figures are 50 per cent of the foreign exchange and 33 per cent of the budgetary funds.

The Latin American countries are interested in stability of the prices for those items which they have traditionally exported, and they are also interested in stable markets. However, the instability of the world capitalistic economy and the foreign economic policies of the Western powers, particularly of the USA, adversely affect the Latin American countries. The system of tariffs, quotas, the U.S. policy of dumping—all these have a pernicious effect on the trade and payments

135

balances of the Latin American countries, and lead to the exhaustion of foreign exchange, inflation, etc.

Certain groups of the national bourgeoisie hope to solve the foreign trade problems in their countries by forming a Latin American "common market." This market, according to the plans of its initiators, would lead to the expansion of trade among the countries of Latin America (today this trade is only 9 per cent of the entire foreign trade of the area), to the development of division of labor and of internal markets, and to the acceleration of industrial growth.

Many regard a regional Latin American market as a means of eliminating dependence on the USA. However, today the USA also supports the idea of a regional Latin American market, hoping to use it in the interests of its own monopolies. (American companies with industrial enterprises in the Latin American countries would, if a "common market" were formed, extract all the benefits from the removal of trade and economic barriers.)

The formation of the "common market" is running into great difficulties, since many countries fear the competition not only of the affiliates of the North American monopolies, but also of their own, stronger, Latin American partners. Today there exists only an agreement among five of the Central American countries (Salvador, Nicaragua, Guatemala, Honduras, and Costa Rica) on a "common market," and among seven countries of South America (Argentina, Bolivia, Brazil, Chile, Paraguay, Peru, and Uruguay) on a free trade zone.

Thus, the solution of the problem of economic independence for the Latin American countries means:

(1) Introducing radical agrarian reform to do away with the large landlords and the foreign landowners, the greatest brake on the development of productive forces.

(2) Limiting the sphere of investment by foreign private capital and strict control over its activity even to the point of excluding it completely.

(3) Overcoming narrow specialization, as a result of which the countries of Latin America have found themselves in the

position of agrarian-raw material appendages to the industrially developed capitalist countries.

(4) Overcoming economic and technical backwardness by maximum stimulation of industrial development and industrialization as the basis for high rates of national economic growth.

(5) Establishment of economic and commercial ties, on the basis of equality and mutual advantage, with all the countries of the world, and primarily with the socialist countries.

The problem of economic independence cannot, however, be presented as a purely technical-economic problem. Technical progress and industrial development do not automatically lead to economic independence.

Economic independence is inextricably connected with political independence and democratization of internal political life. One is a prerequisite to the other. Because it is the basis of genuine state independence, economic independence in turn is determined by the degree of political independence.

Contemporary Cuba, which—thanks to the democratization of social life, to nationalization of the property of foreign companies on her territory, and to the conduct of an independent foreign policy—has assured herself of the necessary conditions for unprecedented economic progress, is striking evidence of this fact.

# The Position of the Southeast Asian Countries in the World Capitalist Market *

## BY M. PANKIN

*FOCUSING on the foreign trade of Southeast Asia, Pankin takes still another view of the problems that developing countries face on the world market. Declining demand for and overproduction of certain raw materials and agricultural products have caused serious problems for Southeast Asia as well as for many other areas of the third world. Western economists have been acutely aware of these trends—one blade of the "price scissors"—and the material that Pankin presents is only too familiar.*

*Most interesting, of course, is the author's explanation of why this situation has arisen and how it can be improved. It is not Indonesian mismanagement that has ruined that country's exports, but the machinations of imperialist monopolies. The continuing Indian import crisis can be overcome simply by attacking the monopolies and moving closer to the Soviet Union—the long, arduous path which non-Communist economists foresee need not be traversed. The skeptical should only remember that demand is artificially curtailed in the capitalist countries by the low standard of living imposed upon the masses. Western economists can hardly accept the Soviet explanation of these points (just as the Soviets will not accept that of the West). Sophisticated Asians are also likely to see behind such specious reasoning, but there is no attractive alternative and the naïve must be sorely tempted by the beautiful simplicity of Marxist analysis at this level.*

*Pankin is clearly conversant with the problems of foreign trade and in this article—published in a journal intended for*

* SOURCE: "Polozheniye stran Yugo-Vostochnoy Azii na mirovom kapitalisticheskom rynke," *Vneshnyaya Torgovlya* [Foreign Trade], No. 4 (1961), 11–17.

## Soviet Writers on the Developing Areas

*a specialized readership—his approach is for the most part on the technical level. Specialized as it may be, however, it does not escape the ubiquitous Communist stereotyped analysis.*

THE fall of the colonial system of imperialism has given rise to a whole complex of new social, political, and economic problems. The struggle for national rebirth by the peoples enslaved by imperialism does not end with the establishment of their national state. "After gaining political independence," according to the Statement of the Congress of Representatives of Communist and Workers' Parties,[a] "the people seek an answer to the social problems which are brought about by life, and to questions of strengthening national independence."

The problems of reconstructing the entire system of international economic ties that the young Eastern states inherited from the era of colonial rule are far from the least important of such questions. The solution of this problem is complicated by the fact that the countries of the East, although they have broken away from the colonial regime, still remain branches of the world capitalist economy, whose entire contemporary structure, according to V. I. Lenin, is a system of oppression and financial suffocation of the vast majority of the earth's population, by a small group of imperialist monopolies.

The development experience of the South and Southeast Asian countries is very instructive in this regard. The peoples of this region of the globe clashed decisively with the colonizers before many other peoples did. More than ten years have passed since colonial regimes in India, Indonesia, Burma, and Ceylon collapsed under the blows of the national liberation revolutions and the people in those countries gained the right to existence as independent states. Marked upheavals have occurred in the economic life of these countries. The development of productive forces has accelerated. The foundations for a national industry are being laid. The level of agricultural production has risen. Stable economic ties with the socialist world have been established.

What has changed in their position in the world capitalist

a. The reference is to the 1960 Moscow Conference Declaration.

market, and what have they gained in this respect by achieving governmental independence? When answering these questions, we must keep in mind that in no sector of the colonial economy has the total domination of foreign capital been so conspicuous as in economic relations between the colonies and the outside world. Commodity import and export in Southeast Asian countries prior to liberation were almost completely in the hands of foreign firms. In areas where national [locally owned] companies appeared (in India and Thailand, for example), they eked out a pitiful existence. The regulation of imports and exports had only one purpose—to assure the metropole's capital a privileged position in purchasing raw materials and food, and in disposing of the products of its own industry in the markets of one or another colony in Southeast Asia. As a consequence, only a limited circle of states— among which the metropole occupied a dominating position —had ties with these countries. The tariff borders were especially symbolic. Foreign importers and exporters traded, for example, not *with* India, Indonesia, or Burma, but *within* India, Indonesia, and Burma. They freely bought up raw material and food from the producers and sold their finished products on the domestic market of these countries through their own marketing system.

Thus, the right to represent the countries of Southeast Asia on the foreign market during that period was usurped by the colonizers to the same extent as was the right of general representation in foreign relations. Therefore the contemporary position of the countries of Southeast Asia in the foreign market cannot be evaluated correctly without considering how much the conditions of these countries' access to the world market have changed in the past few years.

The elimination of colonial regimes was the beginning of the end of the uncontrolled domination of foreign capital in the foreign trade of the countries of Southeast Asia. In practically all countries of this region—even in those which became entangled in the net of military and political dependence upon imperialism—a marked weakening of the foreign companies' role in trade between these countries and the

140

*Soviet Writers on the Developing Areas*

world capitalist market is evident. This process has gone especially far in Indonesia. In 1957 the "Big Five" Dutch trading firms still maintained control of up to 80 per cent of all export-import operations. Now the Dutch foreign trading companies have been nationalized and Indonesia has assumed control of foreign trade. In India, according to the latest official data, foreign firms in 1958 controlled only 30 per cent of the export and 17 per cent of the import operations. While before the war foreign firms completely controlled the foreign trade of Burma, their present share is only from 20 to 30 per cent of export-import operations.

The state sector is of decisive significance in ousting foreign capital from the field of foreign trade. State organizations play a leading role in foreign trade in many countries of Southeast Asia at the present time. State organizations account for about nine-tenths of the total turnover of goods in foreign trade in Indonesia; in India and Pakistan, for 40 to 50 per cent; in Burma, for about one-third of imports and two-thirds of exports; in Ceylon, for about 25 per cent of imports.

Experience has shown that concentration of the import and export of goods in the hands of state organizations is the most reliable barrier against penetration of foreign capital into the area of foreign trade. Private national companies often lack the strength to withstand the competition of foreign monopolies, and in some instances they counteract the development of the state sector, willingly allowing the participation of foreign capital in their activities. It is noteworthy, for example, that private Indian firms in recent years have partially yielded their positions in the export and import of a number of important goods to foreign companies. There has been an especially marked increase in the position of foreign firms in private Indian import of metals (from 9.9 per cent in 1956 to 16.8 per cent in 1958), electrical equipment (from 52.4 per cent to 57.9 per cent), and cotton (from 9 to 12 per cent); as well as in private export of cotton (from 17.3 to 22.7 per cent), cotton yarn and fibers (from 6.4 to 8.9 per cent), and jute products (from 29.3 to 31.8 per cent). Symptomatic in this regard is the admission of the Burmese Minister

141

## The Third World in Soviet Perspective

of Trade, U Tin, that even though people of Burmese nationality were given wide access to the import trade after the achievement of independence, "there are very few successful Burmese entrepreneurs at present."

The former one-sided orientation of foreign trade in the countries of Southeast Asia toward the metropole states is now a thing of the past. Table 1, which was compiled from United Nations statistical data, will make it possible to judge the extent of this process.

TABLE 1

The Share of England, the United States, France, and the Netherlands in the Foreign Trade of the Southeast Asian Countries Which Were Their Colonies
(in per cent of total turnover of goods)

|  | 1938 | 1959 |
|---|---|---|
| *England* |  |  |
| In the foreign trade of India | 32.9 | 22.9 |
| Pakistan | — | 18.0 |
| Ceylon | 36.9 | 26.3 |
| *United States* |  |  |
| In the foreign trade of the Philippines | 75.9 | 50.4 |
| *France* |  |  |
| In the foreign trade of Laos | — | 3.8 |
| Cambodia | 50.0 | 30.5 |
| South Vietnam | — | 21.4 |
| *Netherlands* |  |  |
| In the foreign trade of Indonesia | 20.7 | 1.9 |

An opportunity is arising in the countries of this region to exploit market competition and the contradictions among their main imperialist trading-partners, thus guaranteeing for themselves more favorable conditions in their economic ties with the capitalist world.

Finally, in the foreign trade policy of the countries of Southeast Asia, the subordination of foreign trade ties to the solution of vital problems of economic development is becoming better defined. Protectionist measures to preserve national production in combination with measures to stimulate exports, a rigid policy with regard to currency restrictions in the import of non-essential goods into the country, attempts to increase the efficiency of foreign trade operations, and so forth have become characteristic features of this policy. Its results are expressed in these new tendencies, which are characteristic, for example, in the development of imports. Machinery and equipment have become the leading import articles for many countries of the region. India, for example, in the years of the Second Five Year Plan spent $550 million annually for machinery imports. The share of equipment [b] among imports now exceeds 30 per cent, as against 21 per cent in 1951–1952. During the Third Five Year Plan, the average annual volume of Indian equipment imports is supposed to reach $800 million a year. In Ceylon in 1959, 17 per cent of the total value of imports was for equipment, as against 7.5 per cent in 1950; in Burma, the corresponding values are 27 per cent (1956) as against 12 per cent, etc.

It would be premature to overestimate the significance of the changes that have taken place. The former complete domination of the colonizers in the foreign trade of the countries of Southeast Asia has, of course, been seriously undermined. At the same time, the monopoly capital of the developed imperialist states is doing everything to maintain in its own hands this important lever of economic influence—in the final analysis, a lever for plundering the countries of Southeast Asia.

In analyzing the foreign trade of any of the countries of Southeast Asia one can detect many "birthmarks" of the colonial era, and in some cases it is quite difficult to perceive any changes for the better: to this extent the present-day picture reminds us of the days of complete domination by the colonizers. In a number of countries, foreign firms continue to operate on a broad scale in the area of foreign trade. Until recently they held control of almost all foreign trade in oil and petroleum products in the countries of the area. Even in Indonesia, which has progressed farther along the path of liberation from foreign monopolies than have other coun-

b. "Equipment" (*oborudovaniye*) is a frequently used, rather vague term. In the present context it probably differs very little from "machinery." In general, "equipment" is everything needed for heavy industrial production except for products of the metal-working industry (e.g., drill presses but not girders).

## The Third World in Soviet Perspective

tries, the oil companies are still enjoying the privileges of complete currency autonomy. The foreign companies have retained control of the bulk of foreign trade in rubber, tea, tin, sugar, jute, and jute products and certain other goods which determine the status of the countries of the area on the world market. Foreign exchange banks are financing a significant part of foreign trade operations in the countries of the area. The 16 foreign banks operating in India today control more than four-fifths of all foreign trade financing in the country. In the area of sea transport, the monopoly of the largest foreign shipping companies remains firm, and they reap huge profits by servicing the transport of cargo to and from Southeast Asia.

Nevertheless, there is no doubt that the transfer of state authority into the hands of the national governments has, for the first time since they were involved in the system of relationships of the world capitalist market, created for the countries of Southeast Asia the objective possibility of determining independently the character and basic trends in their foreign trade relations. And even though these possibilities are far from being utilized fully, a marked tendency is evident in the countries of the area toward growing independence in developing their economic and trade relations with the outside world.

The most outstanding manifestation of this tendency is their establishment of broader economic ties with the socialist states. Such countries as India, Indonesia, Ceylon, Burma, and Cambodia have embarked on a firm policy of cooperation with the socialist states. How are the trade relationships of the Southeast Asian countries developing on the world capitalist market under these new conditions? What are the basic results of the development of these ties over the last decade? We know that during the postwar period the situation on the world capitalist market has become generally unfavorable for the less developed countries. In the *1958 World Economic Survey* prepared by a U.N. organ, it is noted that "the world trade in raw materials and foodstuffs has decreased in comparison with total world trade"; and this has affected the in-

*Soviet Writers on the Developing Areas*

terests of the economically underdeveloped countries most of all. The countries of Southeast Asia are typical exporters of raw materials and foodstuffs. Between 1955 and 1957, three-fourths of the value of the exports of the countries in the area was accounted for by eight commodities (rubber, oil and petroleum products, tea, rice, coconut palm products, tin, cotton, and jute). As a result, the positions of the countries of Southeast Asia on the world capitalist market have become especially unfavorable. The statistics given in Table 2, which were compiled on the basis of statistical materials of the International Bank of Reconstruction and Development, are especially telling in this regard.

TABLE 2

Share of the Countries of Southeast Asia in World Capitalist Trade [1]
(in per cent)

|  | 1937 | 1950 | 1955 | 1959 |
|---|---|---|---|---|
| *World Export* | | | | |
| Total | 100 | 100 | 100 | 100 |
| Including: | | | | |
| Southeast Asia | 9.2 | 9.0 | 6.8 | 5.8 |
| Near and Middle East | 1.3 | 3.2 | 3.6 | 3.9 |
| Africa | 5.3 | 6.6 | 6.4 | 5.9 |
| Latin America | 8.3 | 13.4 | 10.9 | 9.5 |
| | | | | |
| *World Import* | | | | |
| Total | 100 | 100 | 100 | 100 |
| Including: | | | | |
| Southeast Asia | 5.7 | 7.1 | 6.3 | 5.9 |
| Near and Middle East | 1.1 | 2.4 | 2.6 | 2.8 |
| Africa | 5.7 | 7.3 | 7.1 | 6.9 |
| Latin America | 6.2 | 11.3 | 10.3 | 9.9 |

Two basic conclusions can be drawn from this table. First of all, Southeast Asia constitutes the only group of underdeveloped countries whose share on the world capitalist market is less than it was before the war. In the total world turnover of goods, the share of the Southeast Asian countries was 7.3 per cent in 1937 and had decreased to 5.8 per cent in 1959. Conversely, the share of Latin American countries in world

1. *International Financial Statistics* (October 1960).

145

## The Third World in Soviet Perspective

trade grew in the same period from 7.7 to 9.4 per cent; the share of the Middle and Near East, from 1.2 to 3.3 per cent; and of Africa, from 5.5 to 6.4 per cent. This tendency is characteristic of all Southeast Asian countries. A reduction of the share in world capitalist trade has been noted in India and Pakistan (their total share has gone from 2.7 per cent in 1937 to 1.8 per cent in 1959), in Indonesia (from 1.6 to 0.6 per cent), in Burma (from 0.5 to 0.2 per cent). Only Malaya shows an insignificant increase in its position in the world turnover of goods (0.9 and 1.0 per cent).

Secondly, the tendency toward a drop in the relative position of the countries of the area in world trade has become especially obvious in exports. According to U.N. statistical data, while world exports grew in the 1950–1959 period from $57 to $102 billion (almost 80 per cent), the export earnings in Southeast Asia on the whole increased by only 13 per cent, and after 1955 this growth was only nominal. During the period in question, Pakistan's export earnings were reduced by 34 per cent (from $489 to $321 million); in Indonesia and Malaya, they increased by 9 per cent (from $800 to $872 million and from $1,311 to $1,435 million), respectively; in India, by 13 per cent (from $1,146 to $1,308 million), etc. The export totals from the countries of Southeast Asia to the capitalist market are of special interest. In this case the tendency to stagnate and even to decline is especially apparent. (See Table 3.)

TABLE 3

Development of Exports of Southeast Asia Countries [2]
(in millions of dollars)

|  | 1950 | 1955 | 1958 | 1959 |
|---|---|---|---|---|
| Total | 5,171 | 5,762 | 5,258 | 5,881 |
| Including: | | | | |
| To capitalist countries | 5,027 | 5,590 | 4,960 | 5,455 |

The positions of the countries of Southeast Asia as exporters on the world capitalist market have weakened appreciably over the last decade. During the last eight years,

2. *Direction of International Trade.*

*Soviet Writers on the Developing Areas*

from 1952 to 1959 inclusive, the average annual level of income from exports of the countries of Southeast Asia in trade with the capitalist countries amounted to $5,323 million. The maximum deviation from this average for any year was ±7.0 to 7.5 per cent. In other words, the export trade of the countries of Southeast Asia on the capitalist market has reached an impasse.

What are the causes? We know that the development of exports can be impeded by a deficiency of export resources, or by difficulties in selling export goods. Actually, the countries of Southeast Asia are experiencing difficulties resulting from shortages of different types of goods exported by them. In connection with the growth of domestic consumption, there has been a reduction in Indian export resources of vegetable oils and wool, and of cotton in Pakistan. In Indonesia the export basis for a number of plantation crops has been seriously undermined by the rapacious exploitation of the plantations to the "point of exhaustion" by the Dutch colonists who, in the last stage of their domination, strove to "squeeze" maximum profits out of the holdings that were slipping from their hands.

This, however, is not what determines the development of the export trade of the countries of the area as a whole. The main reason for the unsatisfactory state of exports in the countries of Southeast Asia must be sought in the deterioration of conditions for selling their traditional commodities on the world capitalist market. This appears in various forms.

First, in recent years the largest capitalist states have kept steady or reduced their imports of a number of goods exported from Southeast Asia. The indices in Table 4 give a picture of this. They were calculated on the basis of the customs statistics of the respective countries.

Thus, according to the goods enumerated in this table, the five big importing countries, including the relatively rapidly developing countries of Japan and West Germany, had from 1955 to 1959 increased only their purchase of jute, and at that by a mere 7 per cent. The purchase of other hard fibers

## The Third World in Soviet Perspective

### TABLE 4

Purchase of Certain Goods from Southeast Asia by Imperialist Countries
(in thousands of tons)

|  |  | 1955 | 1957 | 1958 | 1959 |
|---|---|---|---|---|---|
| Raw rubber: | USA | 600 | 510 | 422 | 512 |
|  | England | 279 | 253 | 257 | 180 |
|  | West Germany | 157 | 139 | 134 | 139 |
|  | Netherlands | 18 | 18 | 11 | 11 |
|  | Japan | 95 | 148 | 138 | 172 |
| Tea: | USA | 40 | 39 | 39 | 39 |
|  | England | 199 | 234 | 235 | 202 |
|  | West Germany | 5 | 6 | 6 | 6 |
|  | Netherlands | 7 | 8 | . . . | . . . |
|  | Japan | 2 | 1 | 1 | 1 |
| Rice: | USA | 0 | 0 | 0 | 0 |
|  | England | 55 | 35 | 24 | 22 |
|  | West Germany | 29 | 30 | 37 | 45 |
|  | Netherlands | 104 | 43 | 38 | 32 |
|  | Japan | 277 | 221 | 96 | 102 |
| Copra: | USA | 46 | 54 | 45 | 50 |
|  | England | . . . | . . . | . . . | . . . |
|  | West Germany | 207 | 320 | 235 | 131 |
|  | Netherlands | 99 | 177 | 86 | 49 |
|  | Japan | 51 | 46 | 48 | 55 |
| Jute: | USA | 52 | 60 | 38 | 68 |
|  | England | 132 | 151 | 132 | 150 |
|  | West Germany | 90 | 94 | 77 | 72 |
|  | Netherlands | 11 | 13 | 9 | 11 |
|  | Japan | 31 | 36 | 33 | 38 |
| Jute products: | USA | 359 | 232 | 222 | 268 |
|  | England | 74 | 51 | 56 | 68 |
|  | West Germany | . . . | 97 | 6 | 5 |
|  | Netherlands | . . . | . . . | 1 | 1 |
|  | Japan | . . . | . . . | . . . | . . . |
| Hard fibers except jute: | USA | 46 | 62 | 54 | 52 |
|  | England | 57 | 54 | 43 | 45 |
|  | West Germany | 16 | 20 | 21 | 23 |
|  | Netherlands | 17 | 17 | 11 | 11 |
|  | Japan | 65 | 80 | 71 | 74 |

and tea remained at almost the same level, while other goods
were reduced: raw rubber, by almost 10 per cent; rice and
copra, 30 per cent; jute products, almost 20 per cent. The
comparisons cited are especially illuminating because, after

## Soviet Writers on the Developing Areas

1955, 1959 was the most successful year in terms of the development of exports for the countries of Southeast Asia.

Second, deterioration of market conditions for countries of Southeast Asia on the world capitalist market is evident in the drop of prices on the goods exported by them. The average percentage level of export prices in 1959 (1950 = 100) was, according to data of *International Financial Statistics:* Pakistan—63; Burma—92; Indonesia—94; the Philippines and Thailand—97.

In the economic works of bourgeois authors, it is customary to explain the underdeveloped countries' difficulties in selling their goods on the world capitalist market by a drop in the demand for natural raw materials as a result of technical progress. In a thorough study of the export problems in Southeast Asian countries, U.N. experts have on the whole taken the same point of view, and explained difficulties in selling products on the foreign market by "technical changes" in the consumer countries, by "inelasticity of supply," etc. Moreover, they relate these to a number of factors decisive for the deterioration of the Southeast Asian countries' selling conditions on the capitalist market.[3] At the base of all these arguments lies the unspoken idea that the underdeveloped countries, including the countries of Southeast Asia, are in this case "objectively" the victims of the general progress of mankind, and not of processes which are connected to any particular social system. The theoretical unsoundness of these arguments of the bourgeois economists has already been demonstrated in a special article in this journal.[4] To this we can only add the following.

At the present stage of the general crisis of capitalism, as noted in the Statement of the Congress of Representatives of Communist and Workers' Parties, "the market problem has become unprecedentedly acute." The narrowing of the sphere of imperialist domination, the general increase in the insta-

3. *Economic Survey of Asia and the Far East, 1959* (Bangkok 1960).
4. A. Frumkin, "Burzhuaznyye ekonomisty ob 'uslovivahk torgovli' slaborazvitykh stran" [Bourgeois Economists on "Trade Conditions" of Underdeveloped Countries], *Vneshnyaya Torgovlya*, No. 7 (1960), 29–37.

*The Third World in Soviet Perspective*

bility of the capitalist economy, the unprecedented intensification of the contradictions of capitalism on both a national and an international scale, lie at the basis of this. The collapse of the colonial system and the independent emergence of the former colonies on the world capitalist market have intensified further this market problem.

If we analyze the conditions for disposing of commodities on the capitalist market that have become established for the countries of Southeast Asia in the last decade, we notice that the export goods of many of these countries are encountering growing competition from third countries. As a result, their share in world export of these goods has dropped considerably. The data in Table 5 from the Secretariat of the ECAFE demonstrate this.

TABLE 5

Share of the Countries of Southeast Asia in the Export
of Certain Commodities [5]
(in percentage of the total volume of world export)

|  | 1934–1938 | 1955–1957 |
|---|---|---|
| Raw rubber | 92.8 | 90.8 |
| Cotton | 21.6 | 8.3 |
| Hard fibers (besides jute) | 48.8 | 23.3 |
| Tobacco | 16.4 | 8.9 |
| Coffee | 6.0 | 3.7 |
| Tin | 63.2 | 58.1 |

It would appear that the goods of Southeast Asian countries have been driven off the market by competitors in Latin America (which exports tin, cotton, coffee, manganese ore, mica, hard fibers), Africa (which exports raw rubber, cotton, tobacco, oil seeds, and vegetable oil), and the Near and Middle East (which export cotton, tobacco). In reality, however, it is not the Latin American, African, or Arabian countries of the East that emerge as competitors with the countries of Southeast Asia on the world market, but the monopolies of the large imperialist states that control the basic resources of Bolivian tin, Brazilian coffee and manganese ore, Rhodesian tobacco, and many other commodities.

5. *Economic Survey*, 59.

Such competition between countries of the East that are fighting for economic independence, and monopolies of the imperialist powers that are emerging on the world market, is a new phenomenon in international economic relations. This competition will intensify as the countries of the East free themselves from the control of monopoly capital.

When a monopoly emerges on the market, it does not only attempt to purchase a commodity which is produced in some underdeveloped country. Under modern conditions, the mechanism of commercial bargaining substantially limits its opportunity to obtain a maximum profit. It is important for the monopoly to obtain access to the original source of raw material, where it can reap huge profits either by exploiting the incredibly cheap labor in the mines and on the plantations, or by buying up the products of the small producers for a mere pittance. It is obvious that the greater the scale which the struggle for economic independence assumes or will assume, the less favorable will be the state of economic relations from the point of view of the monopolies, and the more persistently will the monopolies search for new sources of the goods they need in those areas where the conditions still exist for exploitation on the monopolists' terms.

Is this not how we can explain the fact that the countries of Southeast Asia, having been the first to break the chain of colonial slavery, have met with especially fierce competition in selling their traditional goods on the world capitalist market, and that this difficult competitive struggle—as can be seen today—has not yet come out in their favor?

A number of the commodities of the countries of Southeast Asia are being excluded from the capitalist market by the developed imperialist states' own products. An example of such competition is the Japanese exclusion of India from the market for cotton fiber, and the growing supply of American "surplus" grains and cotton to the detriment of the interests of Burma, Thailand, and Pakistan. India is also meeting fierce competition in its attempt to sell the products of its new national industries on the capitalist market.

The progressive deterioration in the export trade of the

countries of Southeast Asia on the world capitalist market is creating even greater obstacles in the path of their economic development. Shortage of means of payment for imports has become one of the most acute economic problems in many countries in this area.

In India during the Third Five Year Plan—according to the most optimistic official estimates—there will not even be a sufficient gain in export income to pay for the current import of machinery, semi-finished products, and raw materials to support the operation of already existing industry. Moreover, India must pay for the import of everything that is needed to realize its plans for capital construction, buy grain to prevent famine, and pay off foreign debts on credits that were obtained previously. India's minimum needs for new foreign credits in this connection have been fixed at $5.5 to 6.0 billion for the 1960/1961–1965/1966 period. Pakistan, according to official estimates, will lack about $1.6 billion for the same period.

The West is counting on the growing dependence of the countries of Southeast Asia on foreign financial aid, and is striving to take advantage of this opportunity to exert new pressure on the governments of those countries and gain concessions from them in matters of domestic and foreign policy.

Under such conditions it is completely natural for there to be an increasing desire in Southeast Asian countries to expand trade and economic ties with the socialist world. The development of these ties is on the upswing. According to U.N. statistical data, exports from Southeast Asian countries to the socialist countries have increased from $172 million in 1955 to $426 million in 1959. Just recently a number of agreements were concluded which will pave the way for further expansion of mutually beneficial trade between the Southeast Asian countries and the socialist countries. According to a Soviet-Indian agreement, the turnover of goods will double in the next three years; and in accordance with a Soviet-Indonesian agreement, it will triple. According to a Sino-Burmese agreement, the Chinese People's Republic will become a big importer of Burmese rice (up to 300,000 tons per annum); this

## Soviet Writers on the Developing Areas

will make it possible to widen considerably the extent of mutually beneficial trade between the two countries.

The policy of the socialist states in the development of trade and economic ties with all countries in Asia, Africa, and Latin America was clearly and succinctly formulated in the historic Statement of the Moscow Congress of Communist and Workers' Parties: "The socialist countries are the sincere and true friends of those peoples who are fighting for liberation or who have already liberated themselves from the imperialist yoke and oppression. They are rendering all possible aid and support to these countries in their development along the road of progress, in creating their own domestic industry, in developing and strengthening their national economy, in training their own cadres. . . ."

The development of economic cooperation with the socialist world will bring new opportunities to the countries of Southeast Asia to achieve full economic independence.

SELECTION 9

# Peculiarities in the Composition and Structure of the Working Class in the Economically Underdeveloped Countries of Asia and Africa (The Example of India and the UAR) *

BY L. A. GORDON AND L. A. FRIDMAN

*THE small numbers of the "proletariat" in the third world present the Communists with a serious ideological problem, but this problem is nothing new to them. The role of the peasantry, petty bourgeoisie, the intelligentsia, and other groups has for decades been of vital concern to Marxists. Although the aura of "proletarianism" remains indispensable to the Communist mystique, workers have not been the revolutionary force that Marx expected them to be.*

*The following article is a serious and ambitious attempt to establish the parameters of the "proletariat" in the developing countries and to distinguish it from the "surrounding" classes and groups which are related to it, but which are not the hardcore proletariat of modern industry. As the authors point out, it would be misleading to group all of this motley agglomeration under the rubric "proletariat," which should, after all, have some meaning beyond simply "working person." At the same time, of course, they emphasize that use must be made of these "surrounding" groups, which clearly have a high degree of usefulness in a revolutionary situation.*

*Gordon and Fridman appear also to be two of the "younger generation" of Soviet writers on the developing areas; their ages and professional approach are comparable to those of Stepanov, Avakov, and Mirskiy. In this article, they have provided the Soviet policy-maker with a much clearer picture of*

* SOURCE: "Osobennosti sostava i struktury rabochego klassa v ekonomicheski slaborazvitykh stranakh Azii i Afriki (na primere Indii i OAR)," NAIA, No. 2 (1963), 3–22.

154

## Soviet Writers on the Developing Areas

*the revolutionary class on which—according to theory—he must place his hopes for Communist revolution. Most other Soviet work in the field is little more than superficial piling-up of meaningless figures on numbers of workers, of strikes, of union membership, etc., with little attempt to differentiate the material in terms of either its ideological or its political significance.*[a]

*The picture drawn by the authors is scarcely optimistic, however, and it would be hard for even the most orthodox Communist to avoid the conclusion that he must look elsewhere than to the proletariat if he desires to establish Communist power in the third world. In other words, he must do what all successful Communist leaders have done in the past—accept the Communist Party as the surrogate of the proletariat and cast about elsewhere for the forces to carry out his revolution.*

THE growth of the workers' movement in the liberated, dependent, and colonial countries—as was noted in the Program of the CPSU—marks the appearance of a new element of the international proletariat in the world arena. The increasing role of the former colonies and semi-colonies is closely connected with those objective changes which originate within the working class itself after the attainment of independence. V. I. Lenin always paid particular attention to the study of the objective premises of the workers' movement and based the strategy and tactics of the proletariat on an exact accounting of the real situation. However, in the years of the cult of Stalin's personality, when "voluntaristic" one-man decisions often affected the sober and comprehensive evaluation of a situation, these principles of Leninism were frequently pushed

a. Such as "Pod"yem rabochego dvizheniya v stranakh Azii i Afriki" [Upsurge of the Workers' Movement in the Lands of Asia and Africa], *Kommunist,* No. 6 (1962), 103–11, translated in JPRS 13,774; and "Kommunisty stran Azii i Afriki—v avangarde bor'by za svobodu i natsional'-nuyu nezavisimost' " [Communists of the Countries of Asia and Africa—in the Forefront of the Struggle for Freedom and National Independence], NAIA, No. 5 (1961), 15–31, translated in JPRS 11,589. These are two of the more interesting pieces.

155

into the background. Regrettably, even to this day there are people who take dogmatic and sectarian positions and try to deviate from the objective factors by substituting various arbitrary constructs for scientific Marxist-Leninist analysis. It is natural that the study of the objective aspect of the workers' movement at the present time is of great significance. A tremendous contribution to the study of this problem was made in the discussion concerning the changes taking place in the structure of the working class that was presented in the journal *Problems of Peace and Socialism* (see Nos. 5, 9, 12 of 1960 and Nos. 4, 5, 6, 9 of 1961). However, the attention of the participants in the discussion was centered on problems concerning the status of the proletariat in Western Europe and America. In addition, the objective premises of the workers' movement in the contemporary Afro-Asian world differ in a number of particulars that require special study. It is understood that such a problem cannot be solved within the framework of one or even several articles. However, the raising of some questions which are connected with these changes, and which originate within the objective situation of the working class of the countries of Asia and Africa, is, in our opinion, of definite interest.

The authors of this article have already had the opportunity to express their considered opinion in connection with one aspect of these changes—the change in the character of exploitation and in the material status of the workers.[1] Here we will attempt to consider the influence of independent development and capitalist industrialization on the structure and composition of the workers' class and the adjoining strata of the army of hired labor. As in the first article, the authors' aim is to clarify some regular patterns which are characteristic of many non-socialist countries of Asia and North Africa, on the basis of the examples of India and the UAR. It should be understood that the specific manifestations of such patterns

1. See L. A. Gordon and L. A. Fridman, "Polozheniya rabochego klassa v ekonomicheski slaborazvitykh stranakh Azii i Afriki (na primere Indii i OAR)" [The Status of the Working Class in the Economically Underdeveloped Countries of Asia and Africa (The Examples of India and the UAR)], NAIA, No. 1 (1962).

## Soviet Writers on the Developing Areas

are not at all the same in these or in other countries. The basic tendencies, however, are in our opinion more or less generally significant.

The use of materials on India and the UAR in this connection is extremely significant. The development of national capitalism in these countries advanced comparatively far, and for that reason the general patterns of its influence upon the proletariat are distinctive. Indian and Egyptian data permit us to some extent to account for the specifics of the most important regions of the Afro-Asian world—the Near East and South Asia.[2]

An understanding of the present changes in the composition and structure of the working class is possible only by taking into account the peculiarities in the building-up of the proletariat under colonial conditions, and its place in the over-all mass of hired workers and semi-proletarians. The most important of these peculiarities are connected with the specific development of capitalism and the peculiar formation of the working class within the framework of the colonial economy.

Colonial exploitation, as is well known, led to the penetration of commodity-monetary relationships [b] into every pore of the national economy, to the mass ruin and impoverishment of the immediate producers—the peasants and the artisans. In the course of the last several decades, this process probably took place faster in many countries of Asia and Africa than it had in Europe during the corresponding stages in the development of capitalism. Yet the same colonial exploitation which accelerated the ruin of the masses retarded capitalistic production, especially in the higher stages connected with big, mechanized industry. Colonialism appeared to be tearing apart, in

b. A "commodity" is a product of labor that is transferred to another person for consumption. Products made for one's own use are not "commodities."

2. Obviously, the conclusions of the present article cannot be related, on the one hand, to the countries of tropical Africa and some countries of Asia where the formation of the proletariat is just beginning, or, on the other hand, to such states as Japan, the South African Republic, and Israel, in which capitalism has already reached a high degree of development.

*The Third World in Soviet Perspective*

time as well as in space, the two aspects of primary accumulation—the formation of masses of people who are deprived of the means of production,[c] and the union of these people with the means of production on the basis of capitalist relationships. Thus were upset the relative proportions of the various aspects of this process that are characteristic of "classical capitalism." Such a breakdown exerted the most significant influence upon the formation of the working class. The "normal" process of the gradual transformation of the immediate producer into a proletarian was distorted. The entire process was extended over several generations and—most importantly—was completed in only a few cases.

Inasmuch as imperialism impeded the development of factory manufacturing, very few of the ruined peasants and artisans became modern workers connected with big, mechanized production. Insofar as the overwhelming masses of former "independent" producers are concerned, they were forced to linger on through the intermediate stages of proletarization and to become not so much capitalist workers as semi-proletarians—semi-paupers. As a result of this, the structure of the army of hired labor in the countries of Asia and Africa assumed a specific colonial character. The nucleus of this army was the workers in the big capitalistic enterprises (factories and plants, railroad, sea and—to a certain extent—river transportation, communications enterprises, plantations, etc.); throughout the colonial period, this nucleus of workers remained relatively small. Even in some of the more developed countries of Asia and Africa at the end of the 1940's and the beginning of the 1950's, the modern proletariat, in the real sense of the word, constituted not more than 5 or 6 per cent of the gainfully employed population. Thus, according to the 1951 census, the gainfully employed population of India exceeded 140 million. At the same time, the country had only 6 or 6.5 million workers in the big enterprises (this includes around 3 million factory

c. Ownership of the means of production is the characteristic of the bourgeois class; the worker has only his own labor power, his own two hands. It should be noted that this rule is in practice not too strictly applied when a definition must be made as to whether this or that person or group is truly "proletarian."

158

## Soviet Writers on the Developing Areas

workers, a little more than 0.5 million miners, around 1 million railroad workers, and more than 1 million plantation workers). In Egypt, according to the 1947 census, the gainfully employed population reached approximately 6.5 million; in the same year, the modern proletariat was approximately 350 or 400 thousand (including 250,000 factory workers and 50,000 or 100,000 transportation and communications workers).[3]

The relatively small size of the modern industrial proletariat[4] in the majority of the colonial and dependent countries was combined with the excessive swelling of the semi-proletarian strata and also with those groups of the working class that are connected with the lower forms of capitalist production.

We can distinguish three large groups from among the mass of workers and semi-proletarians that surround the basic nucleus of the proletariat.

The first of these groups consists of the workers in home and handicraft industries and a considerable part of the formally independent artisans. The majority of the latter nominally maintained ownership of the means of production, but in reality were transformed into semi-proletarians who were subordinated to capital. Such strata of course exist to a cer-

3. *Census of India, 1951* (Delhi 1953), I, pt. 1a, 108; *National Sample Survey*, No. 16 (Delhi 1959), 11, 13, 110 [cited below as NSS]; *Digest of Indian Labor Statistics, 1961* (Delhi 1961), 18–24, 43, 45 [cited below as DILS]; *Indian Labor Year Book, 1960* (New Delhi 1961), 7, 229 [cited below as ILYB]; *Year Book of Labor Statistics, 1961* (Geneva 1961), 14–15 [cited below as YBLS]; *Annuaire Statistique d'Egypte, 1954–55* (Cairo 1957), 224–25; *Tiers-Monde* (Paris), II, No. 6 (April–June 1961), 192–93. Here and below, in characterizing the colonial peculiarities in the composition and structure of the working class of India, we use data for 1950–1951. As is well known, India attained its political independence in 1947. However, by 1951 the changes were still very insignificant in our field of interest. In addition, the use of earlier figures is extremely difficult in view of their incompleteness and lack of comparability with the statistical materials that followed.

4. It should be remembered that here, as well as later, the term "modern [*sovremennyy*] industrial proletariat" is used to designate all workers of big, mainly machine, production (including not only factory [*fabrichnozavodskiy*] workers and miners, but also transportation, communication, and plantation workers, etc.) as distinguished from hired labor in small-scale production.

159

*The Third World in Soviet Perspective*

tain extent in any capitalist society. Nevertheless, under colonial conditions their share (in comparison with the share of the modern industrial proletariat) has noticeably increased, and in countries similar to India and Egypt comprises around 8 to 10 per cent of the gainfully employed population. In India, at the beginning of the 1950's, some 12–13 million people, including 2–2.5 million hired laborers, were engaged in small-scale industrial production (including construction and transport). In Egypt, at the end of the 1940's, there were about 600,000 or 650,000 artisans and home industry workers; half of these were working as hired labor.[5] Another peculiar characteristic of small-scale industrial production in the colonial and dependent countries was that commercial-usurious capital [d] played a greater role than manufacturing-industrial capital. In addition, the development of small-scale industries as adjuncts to the factory (resulting from the inadequacy of the factory itself) had a more or less secondary significance. These conditions brought about a predominance of formally independent owners of small-scale industries, as well as an increase in the "social distance" which divided the hired labor in big and small-scale production. According to the nature of his labor, his living conditions and mode of life, and according to his class-consciousness, the colonial manufacturing worker was frequently engaged in "diffused" production which was entangled in a dense network of medieval traditions and limitations, and, as a result, in many cases he stood closer to the artisans than to the factory proletariat of the modern type. Of course, there were groups among the manufacturing workers which were close to the lower strata of the industrial proletariat. On the whole, however, as was noted by V. I. Lenin, only big, mechanized industry creates a modern proletariat as a "particular class of the population," differing from the peasants and artisans "by its different way of life, different family

d. "Commercial and usurious capital"—i.e., capital invested in commerce and money-lending (as opposed to capital invested in industry).
5. Our estimates, according to materials in NSS, No. 16, 13, 111; No. 43, 3–4; YBLS (1961), 14–15; *Annuaire Statistique d'Egypte, 1954–55*, 224–25.

relations and higher level of needs—material as well as spiritual." [6] Under colonial conditions, the difference between the working masses, engaged in small-scale manufacturing (including hired laborers), and the nucleus of the industrial proletariat was particularly distinct.

The second stratum of the army of hired labor and semi-proletarians which surrounds the industrial proletariat consists of agricultural workers, urban coolies, day laborers, occasional workers, etc. This stratum is the most numerous and distinctive part of the colonial army of hired labor. At the end of the 1940's and the beginning of the 1950's, there were around 30–35 million hired farmhands in the Indian villages (more than 20 per cent of the gainfully employed population). In Egypt in 1947, the number of agricultural workers exceeded 1.4 million (also somewhat more than 20 per cent of the gainfully employed population). [7] The overall number of urban coolies and occasional workers naturally does not lend itself to exact accounting. However, even an approximate estimation shows that the numbers run into hundreds of thousands, and even millions, of people. [8] The hired farm laborers and the coolies were entirely deprived of the means of production under colonial conditions and by and large lived by selling their labor in one form or another. In this sense their status was closer to the living conditions of the "classical" proletariat than to the status of the formally independent artisans. Besides that, the tremendous mass of hired farm laborers and urban coolies in a number of countries of Asia and Africa existed as a special social group, deprived of the means of production in the course of a few generations at most.

6. V. I. Lenin, *Polnoye sobraniye sochineniy* [Complete Collected Works], III, 547. [This reference is to the 5th edn., which began to appear in 1958.]

7. *Agricultural Labor in India: Report on the Second Enquiry, 1956–1957* (Delhi 1960), 48, 59–60 [cited below as ALI]; YBLS (1961), 14–15.

8. In Egypt, for example, according to the data of the census in 1937 and 1947, there were more than 1 or 1.5 million people in the "undetermined professions." See *République Arabe Unie (Région d'Egypte) Annuaire Statistique, 1957 et 1958* (Cairo 1960), 20–21.

## The Third World in Soviet Perspective

It should be noted, however, that the overwhelming bulk of these people engaged in small-scale production. This was particularly true for the agricultural workers, who comprise the majority of the social strata under consideration. In the colonial village, hired labor was used not by the farmer entrepreneurs (who were then practically non-existent), but mainly by the landlords and kulaks, who united capitalist methods of exploitation (according to the advantage of the "manufacturing type") with semi-feudal and sometimes semi-slavery forms of oppression.[e]

The surplus product which was created by the so-called agricultural workers under colonial conditions appeared not so much as surplus value,[f] but in the form of the semi-feudal rent, usurious interest, and merchants' profits. The considerable role which extra-economic compulsion played in the system of exploitation of the hired farmhands is even more strongly underscored by the peculiar social nature of this stratum in the colonial countries. In addition, almost one-half of the hired farmhands retained their own plots of land and the petty economy which created additional conditions for inviting semi-feudal oppression. The status of agricultural workers was also characterized by extreme irregularity of occupation—for example, they were unemployed for about one-half of the normal working time. This exceeds by far the ordinary dimensions of capitalist unemployment.[9] Finally, their entire way of life, their habits, their thousand-year-old traditions

e. It is possible to distinguish among several types of "exploiters" in the rural environment. Landlords (*pomeshchiki*) are of feudal origin and perpetuate feudal land relationships. At the other extreme, the farmer entrepreneurs are thoroughgoing capitalists (like the large-scale American farmers) who employ hired labor for money wages. The kulaks are wealthy farmers who operate on a much smaller scale than do the entrepreneurial farmers.

f. Surplus product is that part of a laborer's output (i.e., value) which is above and beyond the amount needed to sustain him at a subsistence level (necessary product). According to Marx, the capitalist pays the worker only a subsistence wage and appropriates the surplus product for his profit. This surplus product represents the surplus "value" created by the worker.

9. At that, the forced "winter unemployment" cannot play in the East the role that it plays in Europe or North America.

also brought the hired farmhands closer to the peasants than to the proletariat as a class.

Although the wide stratum of agricultural workers in the colonies emerged in the course of the breakdown of feudalism, and although in terms of a number of formal economic indications it was very close to the proletariat, it did not on the whole become a class of capitalist society. Under colonial conditions, this social group transformed itself inevitably into a peculiar transitional stratum, contiguous to the working class, but still not constituting a single entity with it. Servitude, various forms of personal dependence, the humiliation of the caste system, the elements of extra-economic compulsion, and other medieval remnants very strongly influenced the status of the agricultural workers. As the most exploited part of the population of the colonial villages, without any rights, the hired farmhands possessed a number of contradictory characteristics: they were peasants without land, landlords without their own farms, "free workers" deprived of real personal freedom, sellers of their labor who often could not find buyers for their working hands. The general tendency which was transforming the peasant-pauper into a real agricultural proletarian was of course proceeding under colonial conditions. Under conditions of imperialist oppression—artificial preservation of feudal remnants, extremely slow industrialization, and an increase in agrarian overpopulation—transitional social forms came to a standstill, as if they were crystallized, so that a half-step in the direction of capitalism was not later transformed into a full step. Not capital, but the landlord, who was subordinated to imperialist monopolies, remained the main oppressor of the agricultural workers as well as of all other strata of the peasantry. For precisely that reason, the large mass of hired farmhands in the colonies and semi-colonies made up the semi-proletarian part of the peasantry. However, with regard to the agrarian workers of colonial times, it would be more correct to speak not of semi-proletarians, but of a special type of pre-proletarians. They were separated from the real proletarians not only by the presence of property remnants (as is usually the case with the "classical" semi-proletarians—

163

*The Third World in Soviet Perspective*

e.g., the poor peasants and artisans), but also by the semi-feudal forms of exploitation of their labor and common ties with the entire medieval tenor of village life.

The social characteristics of the agricultural workers that separate them from the proletariat were to a certain degree common to the urban coolies and unskilled workers. In the urban centers, personal dependence played a much smaller role, but unemployment was felt even more painfully and it transformed the coolies not even into pre-proletarians or semi-proletarians, but into paupers and lumpen-proletariat.[g]

The third group which was contiguous to the workers' class was composed of hired laborers engaged in commerce, in the service industries, and hired white-collar intellectual workers. In India at the beginning of the 1950's there were around 8 or 9 million hired workers of this type (5 or 6 per cent of the gainfully employed population); in Egypt, 0.6 or 0.7 million people (10 or 11 per cent of the gainfully employed population).[10] This group was extremely diverse. It included many blue- and white-collar workers and people in the professions, who are basically a part of the ruling classes. On the other hand, here were to be found a considerable number of workers who were engaged in commerce, places of entertainment, institutions, etc. The bulk, however, was made up of commercial office employees who had an intermediate status between the contemporary industrial proletariat and the urban middle strata. In colonial times, their status was generally close to the way of life of the latter (see Table 1).

On the whole, the proportion of the various strata of the working class and its adjoining groups in the countries of Asia and Africa differ from that in the developed imperialist states (*YBLS*, Table 1, p. 21).

Under conditions of well-developed capitalism, the industrial nucleus of the proletariat includes the majority of the working class. In the colonies and dependent countries, the

g. The "lumpen-proletariat" are the dregs of society, lacking the dignity, self-control, and self-confidence of the proletariat. They make themselves available to do the work of the bourgeoisie (e.g., as provocateurs or members of Hitler's SS).

10. DILS (1960), 13; NSS, No. 16, 11, 13, 111; YBLS (1961), 14–15.

# Soviet Writers on the Developing Areas

TABLE 1

Structure of the Working Class and the Adjoining Strata in India,
Egypt, the USA, and England at the End of the 1940's and the
Beginning of the 1950's *
(in per cent of the entire gainfully employed population)

| Basic social groups within the working class and its adjoining strata | India 1950/51 | Egypt 1947 | USA 1950 | England 1951 |
|---|---|---|---|---|
| Modern industrial proletariat (including workers engaged in construction, transportation, and plantations); basic nucleus of the working class. | 4–5 | 5–6 | 40–41 | 54–55 |
| Small-scale industry workers, artisans, handicraft workers; home-industry proletariat and artisan semi-proletariat. | 8–9 | 9–10 | 2–3 | 1–2 |
| Hired labor, persons engaged in commerce, services, government, education, public health, etc.; commercial office proletariat and semi-proletariat; intermediate strata. | 5–6 | 10–11 | 36–37 | 33–34 |
| Agricultural workers; agricultural proletariat and pre-proletariat. | 20–25 | 21–22 | 3–4 | 3–4 |
| Entire gainfully employed population (millions of people). | 142.3 | 6.5 | 60.04 | 22.6 |

* Source: The data for India and Egypt were supplied above. For the USA and England, see YBLS (1961), 20–21, 58–59. The present figures serve as a rough guide. Thus in the figures for the USA and England, the industrial proletariat includes all hired laborers in the corresponding branches of industry; in small-scale industry, account has been taken only of the independent producers. This, however, does not change the main proportions of the basic groups of the hired labor army. (In the USA, after the necessary corrections are made, the basic nucleus of the proletariat amounts to 33 per cent. See A. I. Katz, *Polozheniya proletariata S.Sh.A. pri imperializme* [The Status of the Proletariat of the USA under Imperialism] (Moscow 1962), 581.)

*The Third World in Soviet Perspective*
modern industrial proletariat comprises only a comparatively small part of the army of hired labor (in India, 13–14 per cent are working as hired labor; in Egypt, around 14–15 per cent, as against 50–60 per cent in the USA or England). On the other hand, tremendous masses of semi-proletarian (and sometimes pre-proletarian) strata, as well as large groups of people comprising a long ladder of "motley transitional types from proletariat to semi-proletariat," are attached to the working class in the colonies and semi-colonies.[11] The most important peculiarity in the structure of the working class in the colonies and semi-colonies was found in a similar relationship between the nucleus and its surrounding strata.

Colonial conditions left a remarkable imprint not only on the general structure of the army of hired laborers, but also on the composition and structure of its basic nucleus, the modern proletariat which is connected with large-scale production.

Regardless of its small numbers, the industrial proletariat was distinguished by a high degree of concentration in the majority of colonies and semi-colonies. According to data for the period 1933–1943, around 50 per cent of all factory workers in India were concentrated in the biggest enterprises, which had more than 1,000 workers each. In Egypt, the factories and plants which had more than 500 workers each in 1944–1947 employed around 40–45 per cent of the industrial workers.[12] Such a concentration, which sometimes even surpassed the corresponding indices of the developed countries,[13] followed logically from the special conditions of industrial development in the colonies (the creation of big production by

11. V. I. Lenin, *Sochineniya* [Collected Works], xxxi, 55.
12. M. N. Yegorova, "Chislennost' i struktura fabrichnogo proletariata" [Numbers and Structure of Factory Proletariat], in *Ekonimika sovremennoy Indii* [The Economy of Contemporary India] (Moscow 1960), 272; *Annuaire Statistique d'Egypte, 1945–46*, 424–25, 437; Gamal el Din Mohammed Said, *Iqtisadish Misr* [The Economy of Egypt] (Cairo 1951), 225, 227–28.
13. In the USA, 22 per cent of the workers in the manufacturing industries were employed in enterprises with more than 1,000 workers in 1939. See *Monopolisticheskiy kapital S.Sh.A. posle vtoroy mirovoy voyny* [Monopolistic Capital in the USA After the Second World War] (Moscow 1958), 17.

foreign capital and the creation of big enterprises by national capital on Western models, the virtually total impossibility of transforming manual production into factory production, the comparatively low level of mechanization, the extreme cheapness of labor, etc.).

The concentration of the basic elements of the working class in big enterprises considerably increased its potential strength and helped to increase the role which the proletariat played in socio-political life.[14]

Along with production concentration, the territorial concentration of the working class was of great significance. In the prewar years, 60–70 per cent of the Indian proletariat was concentrated in three industrial regions—Bombay, Central Gujarat, and West Bengal. Similarly, around 50 per cent of Egyptian factory workers lived in Cairo, Alexandria, and their environs.[15] The presence of considerable masses of workers in the leading centers in the various countries increased the efficient performance of the proletariat. However, the extreme geographic concentration confined the workers' movement within a comparatively narrow area.

The branch structure of the industrial proletariat of the colonies and semi-colonies did have its peculiarities. Under the conditions of imperialist oppression, only a few branches of industry enjoyed marked development because they were connected mainly with the production, transportation, and initial processing of raw materials, as well as some enterprises of the light and food industries. Naturally, the basic role in the colonies and semi-colonies—as distinguished from the countries of developed capitalism—was played by such elements of the working class as the textile workers, the miners, the railroad workers, and the plantation workers (see Table 2).

There is not only the problem of quantitative correlations.

14. The high concentration is one of the reasons that the Indian proletariat, for example, which was comparatively small in numbers and poorly organized, reached such a level in the strike struggle in the 1920's and 1930's, permitting us to place it as a whole on the same level as the working classes in the USA and England.

15. Yegorova, 268; *Economic Bulletin* (National Bank of Egypt), No. 4 (1957), 340.

TABLE 2

Correlation of the Basic Elements of the Industrial Proletariat
in India, Egypt, the USA, and England *
(in per cent)

| Basic elements of the industrial proletariat | India 1951 | Egypt 1952 | USA 1953 | England 1951 |
|---|---|---|---|---|
| Miners | 10 | 4 | 6 | 8 |
| Railroad workers | 17 | 22 ** | 8 | 5 |
| Metal workers, chemical workers, workers in other branches of heavy industry | 13 | 12 | 48 | 49 |
| Textile workers, workers in the food, tobacco, leather, and other branches of light industry | 38 | 62 | 38 | 38 |
| Plantation workers | 22 | — | — | — |
| All workers taken into account: | | | | |
| per cent | 100 | 100 | 100 | 100 |
| thousands | 5,550 | 343 | 15,727 | 10,207 |

* Source: Our estimates are according to materials in DILS (1961), 18–24, 43, 45; YBLS (1961), 129, 143; *Annual Abstract of Statistics, 1961* (London 1961), 105–8; *Statistical Abstract of the United States, 1959* (Washington 1959); *Ihsa Imahtag el Sana'i, 1952* [Industrial Production Census for 1952] (Cairo 1957), 14–21.

** All transportation workers.

In the colonial period, the small and medium enterprises of a semi-handicraft type were plentiful in those branches of industry which we arbitrarily term "heavy industry." The degree of workers' concentration and also the level of their class consciousness were in this case much lower than in the textile factories, the mines, and the railroads. For that reason, the metal workers, and those other elements of the proletariat which were close to them, were not able to play the vanguard role in the workers' movement of the colonial countries.

A characteristic trait of the industrial proletariat of the Asian and African countries was also its comparative homogeneity with regard to production. In the colonies there was no, or almost no, well-formed stratum of highly qualified work-

168

## Soviet Writers on the Developing Areas

ers. As a rule these functions were carried out by European specialists. As for the local proletarians, they comprised, in their overwhelming majority, a poorly differentiated mass of unskilled and semi-skilled workers. Here, therefore, was one of the reasons for the absence of a workers' aristocracy [h] to oppose the basic groups of the proletariat.

It should not be thought, however, that the working class of the colonies and semi-colonies was homogeneous in all respects. The backwardness of the society, the artificial preservation of the pre-capitalist form of economy, the mode of life and culture, all these helped to preserve within the proletariat many patriarchal, and sometimes purely medieval, partitions. The caste divisions, the language barriers, the dependence on regional associations, and the artificially extended socio-religious differences exerted a great influence on the workers. The complex ethnic composition of the population, the incomplete process of nation-building, the extreme inequality in the socio-economic development of the various regions, and other similar phenomena influenced the composition of the proletariat. Multinational and multitribal aspects were an important peculiarity of the working class in the majority of industrial centers of Asia and Africa. The imperialists tried to use these social and national differences to bring about disunity in the workers' movement.

The question concerning the role of women and children in the ranks of the industrial proletariat of the colonial countries is of very definite interest. In the literature on this subject there exists a deeply rooted idea that the high proportion of these categories is a specific trait of the factory proletariat in the East. This thesis, however, requires major corrections. It is true that during the early stages of the development of big industry in the countries of Asia and Africa (as is always true under capitalism) woman and child labor were widely used.[16] However, in the factory industries of many colonies, a definite

---

h. On "workers' aristocracy," see above, p. 3.

16. At the same time, it should be noted that in Muslim countries religious traditions even during that period prevented the widespread employment of women in the factories.

## The Third World in Soviet Perspective

tendency appeared, during the course of several decades preceding the attainment of independence, toward a relative decrease in the hiring of woman and child labor. Owing to the structure of the labor market, tens and hundreds of thousands of men who were actually ready to work for pennies appeared in the urban centers of Asia and Africa. Naturally, the entrepreneurs preferred under these conditions to hire adult males, whose labor productivity was higher than that of women and children. The gradual development of labor legislation in many of the countries also helped decrease the proportion of women and children in the total number of workers in big industry. The remarkable thing is, however, that in the factories and plants of such a big country as India the number of women decreased to 15 or 20 per cent in the 1920's and 1930's, and to 11 or 12 per cent in the initial years after the Second World War. In Egypt, according to 1947 data, women comprised less than 3 per cent of all hired labor in industry, transportation, and construction.[17] The decrease in the proportion of woman and child labor in big industry did not by any means signify an improvement in the situation of the working people. It did not lead to a decrease in the exploitation of women and children, but transferred it to small-scale industry, to handicrafts, and to commerce, where bondage and oppression assume even worse forms. Thus the peculiarity of colonial conditions consisted in the fact that the marked decrease in the share of women and children in the ranks of the industrial workers corresponded to the increase of their numbers in the composition of artisan and handicraft proletariat and semi-proletariat.

Finally, a very important peculiarity of the industrial proletariat in the colonies was the prolonged preservation of various connections with the village on the part of the workers. This had two basic explanations. First, in the industries of Asia and Africa, workers who had recently left the village

17. Yegorova, 279; *Industrial Labor in India* (Geneva 1938), 41; YBLS (1961), 14–15; see also *Industrial and Commercial Census of Egypt, 1937* (Cairo 1942).

made up a very large group. They had not yet succeeded in breaking entirely away from agriculture; work at the factories was regarded only as a temporary occupation, necessary for the "improvement" of their land holdings. Naturally, all thoughts of this type of worker were directed toward the village. Since the number of such workers in the new industrial centers of Asia and Africa was considerably greater than in the developed countries, this situation considerably strengthened the ties between the working class and the peasantry.

Second, colonial exploitation was forcing a considerable part, and sometimes the greater part, of the experienced and class-conscious workers—proletarians of the second and third generation—to leave their families behind in the village; from which their fathers and grandfathers had been migrants. Here the workers had their own huts and sometimes scraps of land; here their women could acquire some occasional supplementary earnings more easily; here it was easier to maintain oneself on those pennies which a man could put aside for his family from his earnings. As a result of this, the workers who had actually broken away from agriculture for a long time continued to keep close social contact with the village throughout their lives.

The connection of the industrial proletariat with the village means something much more, however, than a simple peculiarity in the way of life. The closeness to the peasantry exerted an immediate influence on the formation of the class consciousness of the workers. It aided the preservation of many peasant prejudices within the ranks of the proletariat and facilitated the penetration of bourgeois influence. But, besides that, the ties with the village increased the influence of the class struggle of the proletariat on the peasantry. Finally, contact with the village left a mark on the tactics of the workers' movement. The unusual length of the mass strikes of the Indian proletariat, in the course of which tens of thousands of people stopped work for several months, is explainable by the fact that many workers could go back to the village and stay there until the end of the strike.

## The Third World in Soviet Perspective

The downfall of imperialist domination, which changed the entire socio-economic situation in the countries of Asia and Africa, leads logically to important improvements in the composition of the working class and its surrounding strata. However, these changes carry with them very special and contradictory characteristics. They are determined not only by the general pattern of capitalist development, but also by the onerous heritage of colonial oppression. Capitalism in the recently liberated countries is incapable, at the present stage of historical development, of dealing with the multimillion masses of pre-proletarians, semi-proletarians, paupers, and other groups which compose, as was indicated above, the majority of the army of hired labor in Asia and Africa. The peculiar structure of the working class and its adjoining strata is for that reason preserved even at the present time, regardless of the important qualitative changes which are taking place inside the various groups of the proletariat and semi-proletariat.

In reality, capitalist industrialization brings about a noticeable growth of the modern industrial proletariat connected with large-scale enterprises in many of the former colonies and semi-colonies. In India, for example, the number of this group of workers rose from about 5 million on the eve of the Second World War to 6 or 7 million at the beginning of the 1950's, and to 8 or 9 million by the end of that decade. In Egypt, in the second half of the 1930's, there were a little over 250,000 workers employed in big capitalistic enterprises. By 1947 this number had increased to 350 or 400 thousand, and by the beginning of the 1960's it had reached 500 or 550 thousand.[18] These figures, which show that the industrial skele-

18. *Ihsa Imahtag el Sana'i, 1952, 1956* [Census of Industrial Production, 1952, 1956] (Cairo 1957, 1959); DILS (1961), 28–35, 43, 45; ILYB (1960), 7, 229; *Indian Economics Year Book, 1961* (Allahabad 1961), 193; NSS, No. 16, 13, 111, and No. 52, 84–86, 145–47; All Indian Congress Committee, *Economic Review* (New Delhi, November 22, 1962), 32; *Economic Bulletin* (National Bank of Egypt), No. 1 (1962), 55; *Tiers-Monde*, No. 6 (April–June 1961), 192–203. In the composition of the industrial proletariat we have included factory workers, workers in the mining industry, the big enterprises, transportation and communications, big construction, and also plantation workers.

ton of the working class in countries like India and Egypt has almost doubled in the course of two decades, are impressive enough by themselves. However, when they are compared with the data given above concerning the size of other groups in the army of hired labor, it becomes obvious that such a growth of the industrial proletariat cannot yet bring about a fundamental change in the correlation between the basic nucleus of the working class and its surrounding strata. It could be maintained, with an extremely high degree of probability, that the situation will remain the same in the near future. A simple calculation will show that with such a structure of the gainfully employed population in general, and of the army of hired labor in particular, which the countries of Asia and Africa inherited from colonial times, the industrial proletariat would have to increase 5 or 10 times in size for its position to reach the indices which are characteristic of the industrially developed countries (see Table 1). One thing is clear, however—capitalist industrialization is incapable of providing such a growth in employment in the course of ten or twenty years. Aside from general limitations on the speed of capitalist accumulation, under contemporary conditions in the Asian and African countries the typically capitalistic and constantly growing gap between the volume of investment and increase in employment is felt particularly intensely. The high level of contemporary technology and the accelerated growth of the organic formation of capital [1] call for an extremely great capital investment in the industries which are now being created in the countries of Asia and Africa. The increase in employment per unit of capital investment was considerably less in the mid-twentieth century than was the case at the time of the industrialization of Western Europe and North America.

On the other hand, the scale of proletarization and pauperization of the masses of workers in Asia and Africa has virtually not decreased in comparison with the colonial period.

i. The organic formation of capital is the relationship between the two aspects of capital—fixed or constant (means of production) and variable (labor). The higher the share of fixed capital, the higher the organic composition.

## The Third World in Soviet Perspective

At the same time, the absence of radical changes in the agrarian system in a situation of "broad" developing capitalism leads to a wholesale growth of the lower forms of capitalism in industry and agriculture. In the course of independent capitalist development, it is natural that the numbers in the various strata which surround the basic nucleus of the working class are not decreased. Thus in India the main part of this "encirclement"—the agricultural workers—numbered some 33 or 34 million in 1956–1957.[19] In Egypt the number of hired farmhands which has been reported in official sources rose from 1.40 million in 1947 to 1.45 or 1.50 million in 1957–1958.[20] In the former colonies, the development of capitalism in agriculture at its present-day level (as distinguished from the situation in the developed countries) does not lead to a decrease in the number of agricultural workers. Even here, of course, rural capitalism brings about some absolute decrease in the demand for labor. However, under the conditions of a tremendous agrarian and urban overpopulation, in which the excessive "saturation" of the labor market makes movement to the cities difficult, this tendency manifests itself for the most part not in a decrease in hired farmhands, but in a decrease in their average employment.

Although the agricultural workers remain the most numerous element of the hired labor army which surrounds the industrial nucleus of the proletariat, the urban strata of this "encirclement" are growing particularly fast in the early stages of industrialization of the countries of Asia and Africa. The accelerated development of large-scale industry is accom-

19. ALI, 59–60. The official statistical publication of the Indian government shows that in 1956–1957 stricter criteria were used for the inclusion of various groups in the numbers of hired farm labor. The comparable figures for 1956–1957 are 13 per cent higher than the data for 1950–1951.

20. Calculated according to *International Labour Review* (Geneva) (November 1960), 441; *Economic Bulletin* . . . , No. 2 (1960), 87. The actual growth in the number of agricultural workers was obviously considerably greater, since the data of the election census of the population for 1957–1958 are somewhat lowered and for that reason are not entirely comparable with the figures of the overall census of the population in 1947.

panied by an extremely rapid growth of smaller branches as "adjuncts to the factories." Even independently, without any connection with the factories, the vitality of the economic cycle after the attainment of independence led to a remarkable increase in employment in small-scale production, services, commerce, etc. The tremendous masses of the excess labor force and its unusual cheapness determine the considerably greater "profitability" of such entrepreneurial activity than is the case under the ordinary conditions of capitalism. Finally, the development of the public sector and the corresponding growth of the bureaucratic apparatus also have resulted in a considerable increase in the amount of hired labor—particularly white-collar employees. Independent economic development is thus accompanied by a rapid growth in artisan-handicrafts and in the commercial office proletariat and semi-proletariat, and also in the intermediate strata of the army of hired labor.

Unfortunately, the statistical materials which reflect this growth are fragmentary and not always comparable. Nevertheless, even estimated data show that, in India, employment in the trades and small-scale production rose from 12 or 13 million to 17 or 18 million (including also around 4 million hired labor) in the course of the last decade. According to the same estimate, the number of hired labor personnel in commerce, services, etc., in present-day India is 9 or 10 million people. In the UAR, the number of artisans and of hired labor in small-scale industry, commerce, services, the state apparatus, education, etc., increased from 1.2 or 1.3 million in 1947 to 1.4 or 1.5 million in 1957–1960.[21] In reality this process moves along even faster, since the nature of small-scale proprietorship and of industry does not lend itself to an accurate statistical accounting. It should not be overlooked that the rapid increase in employment in small-scale production and the services is more characteristic of some countries of Asia and Africa in the early stages of independence than it is of a large-scale capitalist economy.

21. Calculated according to NSS, No. 43, 3–4; YBLS (1961), 14–15; *International Labour Review* (November 1960), 440–41.

## The Third World in Soviet Perspective

Thus, under conditions of independence, the quantitative correlation of the basic groups of the working class and its adjoining strata is preserved as in colonial times (see Table 3).

If the quantitative correlation between the industrial backbone of the working class and the adjoining strata is static for the time being, the social status of the latter, and consequently the moral ties with the industrial proletariat, are undergoing definite qualitative improvements.

To a certain extent, these improvements are connected with the general tendency toward changes in the social structure of contemporary capitalism. In many former colonies as well as in the industrially developed countries, an economic and social rapprochement is taking place between parts of the commercial office employees and the various groups of the intelligentsia on one side, and the skilled industrial workers on the other.[22] The active participation of the large strata of employees in the trade union movement and the struggle of the proletariat through strikes are a reflection of this tendency in political life. Such events as the general strike of government employees in India during the summer of 1960 and the repeated actions of the employees of the Indian banks during the last several years are particularly noteworthy. However, the numbers of the commercial office proletariat and semi-proletariat in the countries of Asia and Africa are not so great that the changes in the social status of these strata could decisively determine the relationship between the nucleus of the working class and its "surroundings."

As distinguished from the condition of developed capitalism, the fate of the multimillion masses of the artisan and handicraft proletariat and semi-proletariat, and also of the agricultural workers, has much greater significance for the former colonies and semi-colonies. The rapid development of capitalism in small-scale industry, discussed above, brings the position of the handicraft workers somewhat closer to the living conditions of the industrial proletariat. This tendency

22. The rapprochement of employees and industrial workers was noted by the majority of participants in the above-mentioned discussion in the journal, *Problems of Peace and Socialism*.

TABLE 3

Number and Composition of the Working Class and its Adjoining Strata
in India and the UAR *
(in millions of people)

| | INDIA | | UAR | |
| --- | --- | --- | --- | --- |
| | 1950–51 | 1959–60 | 1947 | 1957–61 |
| Modern industrial proletariat, *including:* | 6–7 | 8–9 ** | 0.35–0.40 | 0.50–0.55 |
| Workers in factory and mining industries | 3.5 | 4.6–4.7 | 0.30 | 0.40–0.45 |
| Workers in large construction and communal enterprises | 0.5 | 0.8–0.9 | | |
| Workers in large transportation and communication enterprises | 1.0–1.5 | 1.7–1.8 | 0.05–0.10 | 0.10 |
| Plantation workers | 1.2–1.3 | 1.3–1.4 | — | — |
| Workers in small-scale industry, artisans, handicraftsmen; hand-manufacturing proletariat and artisan semi-proletariat, *including:* | 12–13 | 17–18 | 0.60–0.65 | 0.50–0.60 |
| Hired labor | 2.0–2.5 | 3.8–4.0 | 0.30 | — |
| "Independent" proprietors | 10.0–11.0 | 13.0–14.0 | 0.30–0.35 | — |
| Hired labor, persons engaged in commerce, services, personal services, government employment, education, public health, etc.; commercial office proletariat and semi-proletariat; intermediate strata | 8–9 | 9–10 | 0.60–0.70 | 0.85–0.90 |
| Agricultural workers; rural proletariat and semi-proletariat | 30–35 | 33–34 ** | 1.4 | 1.4–1.5 |

* Source: Our calculations are according to the above-mentioned materials which describe the status of the various groups of the working class and its adjoining strata.

** 1956–1957

*The Third World in Soviet Perspective*

is particularly noticeable in the big industrial centers, where small-scale production is developing at the present time in addition to the factories. A greater or smaller overflow of labor from small-scale industry into large-scale industry and vice versa has become a comparatively frequent phenomenon. In addition, the new labor legislation in many countries of Asia and Africa covers a considerable number of small enterprises.[23] This helps even more to obliterate social "boundaries" between the industrial proletariat and part of the handicraft workers. However, the way of life of the majority of artisan-handicraft proletariat and semi-proletariat in the East is still considerably different from the socio-economic status of the basic nucleus of the working class. In the small trades and hand-manufacturing, as was stated before, "the remnants of patriarchal relations and the various forms of personal dependence which in the general framework of the capitalist economy worsen the situation of the working people extremely, humiliating and corrupting them,"[24] are strong. Precisely for that reason, the basic mass of handicraft workers and the majority of the artisans of the countries which are just beginning their fight against economic backwardness comprise, as before, a specific group which is different from the nucleus of the working class.

The changes in the socio-economic nature of the class of agricultural workers—the most numerous element in the army of hired labor in the underdeveloped countries—are of great significance. The development of capitalism in agriculture and also the agrarian reforms which were carried out helped considerably, despite their great limitations, to accelerate the pace of transformation of the village pre-proletariat of colonial times into the agricultural proletariat of the usual capitalist variety. It should be understood, however, that a quantitative analysis of this process is extremely complex and requires special study. Given all the limitations and inaccuracies of the

23. In India, legislation affecting factories includes all enterprises, beginning with workshops that have from 10 to 20 workers. In the UAR, the provisions of the Labor Code are formally applicable to all hired workers, regardless of the size of the enterprise.
24. V. I. Lenin, *Polnoye sobraniye sochineniy*, III, 547.

178

statistical materials, it is very significant that in India, where
the number of hired farmhands is measured by tens of millions, the proportion of landless agricultural workers rose from
50 per cent in 1950–1951 to almost 60 per cent in 1956–1957.
For the same period, the number of farmhands hired for a
term increased (for example, from 10 to 27 per cent) and the
number of those hired by the day decreased correspondingly.[25]
It is significant that in a number of countries of Asia and
Africa, new groups of rural proletariat have begun to form
which are connected with the use of machinery in agriculture.
The number of these groups is not great at present; it is
hardly possible to find any former colony in which the number
of this type of workers would exceed several tens of thousands.
Nevertheless, for some countries (for example, the UAR, where
according to our estimates there are no less than 75–100
thousand rural workers connected with machines)[26] such
figures comprise a fairly significant percentage of the entire
agricultural proletariat.

However, the degree of transformation of the "old" village pre-proletariat into a contemporary agricultural proletariat should not be exaggerated and, what is more, this
tendency should not be taken as an accomplished fact. In
the agriculture of the countries of Asia and Africa, predominantly small land holdings are still developing; they use hardly
any machinery and their position actually is on the level of
handicraft production. Also, it is too early yet to speak of the
full disappearance of the remnants of personal dependence,
bondage, caste humiliation, etc. Moreover, the contradictions
of capitalist development find expression in a way that even
encourages the growth of some patriarchal remnants in the
village. In India, for example, the proportion of payment in
kind to the total sum of earnings of the hired farmhands
has increased (from 30 per cent in 1950–1951 to 40 per cent
in 1956–1957); the debt bondage also rose sharply (in 1950–

25. ALI, 53.
26. It suffices to say that in 1960 more than 27,000 agricultural machines were used in Egypt. See *Economic Bulletin* . . . , No. 1 (1962),
13–45.

1951 some 44 per cent of the hired farmhands had debts, and in 1956–1957 this number was roughly 64 per cent).[27]

The important thing, however, is that even after the removal of the majority of medieval forms of exploitation, the agricultural proletariat, as is shown in the experience of the developed capitalist countries, preserves for a very long time a number of important social differences which put it in a peculiar position with respect to the basic nucleus of the working class. In that connection it is appropriate to remind ourselves that, as V. I. Lenin often noted, "Only a differentiated class—namely, the urban and the factory industrial workers—are in a position to lead all the masses of workers and the exploited." [28] For that reason, even in the developed countries, in evaluating the positions of the class forces in the village V. I. Lenin united the agricultural proletariat with the village semi-proletariat and the poor peasantry, considering it as one of the allies of the urban and industrial proletariat, but not as one of its component parts.[29] It is obvious that for the countries of Asia and Africa, where capitalism in agriculture is still very weak, the necessity of such a differentiation has peculiar moment.

Thus, at the present stage of social development of the former colonies and semi-colonies, the peculiarly complex structure of the working class and its adjoining strata is preserved. Although the degree of homogeneity of the army of hired labor improved after the attainment of independence, the industrial working class still retains basic social differences with respect to the handicraft and agricultural proletariat and, as before, it comprises a minority among all the masses of people who are hired to work.

These considerations, in our opinion, are not only of academic interest. An underestimation of the depths of the real socio-political and socio-economic difference between the modern proletariat, which is connected with large-scale capitalistic ownership on one hand, and with the majority of

27. ALI, 107, 221.
28. V. I. Lenin, *Sochineniya,* xxix, 387.
29. See *ibid.,* xxxi, 130–33.

agricultural and artisan-handicraft workers on the other, will lead to an oversimplified understanding of the problems of formation of the working class in Asia and Africa. An unconditional unification of all elements of the army of hired labor into an entity embracing almost one-half of the gainfully employed population would in reality be an admission that the proletariat has already become the most numerous class of society. Such an approach could produce an incorrect evaluation of the degree of capitalist development and arrangement of the class forces.

By the same token, it would be incorrect to overlook the class nature of the rural proletariat and the handicraft workers, to add them mechanically to the whole mass of working non-proletarians, and to tear them away entirely from the industrial nucleus of the working class. If the simple unification of all strata of the army of hired labor leads to an artificial exaggeration of the objective capabilities of the proletariat, then the reduction of the working class solely to the industrial nucleus seriously decreases its potential strength. The social position of the hired farmhands and the handicraft workers is such that they are capable of accepting the leadership of the proletariat and its party much faster than are the peasantry and the urban middle class. The presence of such special allies (together with the peasantry) increases considerably the capabilities of the proletarian movement.

However, this gigantic revolutionary potential can be transformed into reality only if the contradictory social nature of the agricultural and artisan-handicraft proletariat, which requires special forms of organization and political education, is taken into account. The successful solution of this problem will facilitate the awakening to political life and the struggle among the widest range of the popular masses; it will assure a powerful ally to the proletariat; and through this ally it will widen the influence of the workers' movement among the peasant circles and among the petty bourgeoisie of the city.

The objective conditions of development of the workers' movement in the countries of Asia and Africa are connected also with the important improvements that are taking place in the structure and composition of the modern industrial proletariat. The accelerated development of big industry under conditions of national independence is accompanied not only by the growth in the total number of workers, but also by the formation of new elements of the factory proletariat in the remote regions of the former colonies and semi-colonies. As a result of this, a tendency toward a somewhat more equal territorial distribution of the working class has begun to appear. The example of the growing proportion of the proletariat in South India, where during colonial times there was hardly any modern industry, is demonstrative. While in 1949 there was a concentration of less than 20 per cent of the factory workers in the southern states, in 1959 their number had already surpassed 25 per cent. The same thing happened in the five backward provinces of the UAR (including Aswan, where at the present time a gigantic construction project is going on), which in 1951 had 17 per cent, and in 1961 25 per cent, of all workers engaged in the recorded industry of the country.[30] The distribution of the proletariat in the countries of Asia and Africa still remains, of course, extremely unequal. However, new tendencies are undoubtedly there. Their development will help to widen the area of active class struggle and will involve new strata of the working people in it.

Besides the geographic distribution of the industrial proletariat, its branch structure is changing. The beginning of industrialization in a number of countries of Asia and Africa leads to the rapid development in branches of the first subdivision.[j] The number and position of metal workers, chemists, and other groups of workers of heavy industry are growing; the almost complete lack of these was a characteristic trait of the industrial proletariat in the colonies and semi-colonies (see Table 4).

Especially important are the basic changes in the nature

j. The first subdivision (or department) of industry is that part which turns out producer goods; the second subdivision produces consumer goods.

30. DILS (1960), 14–15, and (1961), 25–26; *Economic Bulletin* . . . , No. 1 (1962), 58, and No. 4 (1957), 340.

# Soviet Writers on the Developing Areas

of the working conditions in metallurgy, machine-building, basic chemistry, and other branches. In place of comparatively small enterprises, where manual labor was a predominant fea-

TABLE 4

Change in the Number of Basic Elements of the Industrial Proletariat in India and the UAR *

| | INDIA | | | | UAR | | | |
| | 1950–51 | | 1959–60 | | 1952 | | 1961 | |
| Basic elements | Thous. | % | Thous. | % | Thous. | % | Thous. | % |
| --- | --- | --- | --- | --- | --- | --- | --- | --- |
| Miners | 549 | 10 | 652 | 10 | 13 | 4 | 15 | 4 |
| Railroad workers | 923 | 17 | 1,160 | 18 | 75 ** | 22 | 100 ** | 20 |
| Metal workers, chemists, workers in other branches of heavy industry | 762 | 13 | 1,147 | 18 | 44 | 12 | 90–100 | 18–20 |
| Textile workers, workers in food, tobacco, leather, and other branches of light industry | 2,104 | 38 | 2,272 | 35 | 214 | 62 | 280–290 | 56–58 |
| Plantation workers | 1,212 | 22 | 1,268 | 19 | — | — | — | — |
| Total included in the calculation | 5,550 | 100 | 6,499 | 100 | 343 | 100 | 495–505 | 100 |

* Source: Our calculations are according to the following materials: DILS (1961), 18–24, 28, 34, 43, 45; *Economic Bulletin* . . . , No. 1 (1962), 55; *Ihsa Imahtag el Sana'i, 1952, 1956* (Cairo 1957, 1959).
  It should be taken into account that figures derived from the official Indian statistics concerning average daily employment decrease the actual number of workers by about 10 per cent. The UAR figures for 1961 are estimates. The percentage correlations which were made by us have been rounded out. Inasmuch as the present table reflects only the basic elements of the industrial proletariat, it is not entirely comparable with Table 3.
  ** All transportation workers.

ture, big plants equipped with modern machinery are appearing. Thousands and sometimes tens of thousands of skilled workers are concentrated in each one of them. In this way, the

183

*The Third World in Soviet Perspective*

objective prerequisites for the transformation of the metal workers and the chemists into one of the forward detachments of the working class in the countries of Asia and Africa are created.

The potential strength of the proletariat in Asia and Africa is also connected with the preservation of that high degree of concentration characteristic of colonial industry. It is true that some of the conditions which encouraged an increased concentration in the past (technological backwardness, low productivity of labor, etc.) are now gradually disappearing. In addition, the introduction of new technology is accompanied by a relative decrease in the demand for labor. However, the development of heavy industry, where the very nature of modern production requires the creation of tremendous plants, neutralizes these factors somewhat. It is significant in this connection that in India, as before, around one-half of the workers are concentrated in big enterprises (with more than 1,000 employees). In the UAR, the concentration of the factory proletariat has apparently increased. In 1961, plants employing more than 500 people accounted for around 50 per cent of the workers (compared with 40 per cent or 45 per cent in the 1940's).[31]

The consequences of the industrialization which has begun are being felt not only in the change in the number and structure of the industrial proletariat, but also in important improvements in its composition. The creation of modern industry, as well as the general upsurge of culture after the liquidation of colonial oppression, logically led to a growth in skill and literacy among the workers. It suffices to say that in the factories and plants of India around the middle of the 1950's, the number of skilled and trained workers had already reached about 43 per cent. In the leading industrial center of Egypt, Alexandria, the skilled and trained workers in those years comprised more than one-fourth of the entire factory proletariat. The data on literacy are similar. A nation-

31. P. Pant and M. Vasudevan, *Occupational Pattern in Manufacturing Industries, India, 1956* (Delhi 1959), 44–46; *Economic Bulletin* . . . , No. 1 (1962), 55; *Ihsa Imahtag el Sana'i, 1956,* 18–27.

184

wide Indian poll showed in 1956 that more than one-half of the urban workers can read and write. Literacy among the urban workers is greater than among the artisans and the peasants. In the biggest cities of the UAR, and in particular in Alexandria, the number of workers who are literate reaches 60 or 70 per cent.[32] The cultural backwardness which was created by colonialism was not, of course, eliminated entirely in the 10 or 15 years of independent development. However, considerable progress in that field cannot be doubted. Such progress favors, on the whole, the growth of class consciousness among the proletariat and facilitates its organization and political education.

It should be noted, however, that along with the general growth of culture within the proletariat that is due to industrialization in the countries of Asia and Africa, a separation of a small group of workers who are highly skilled is taking place. Their wages, especially in the state-owned enterprises, are usually two or three times greater (and sometimes more so) than the wages of the basic mass of workers.[33] It cannot be denied that under certain conditions a stratum of a workers' aristocracy could be formed from among this group of the proletariat.

The growth in the ranks of the industrial proletariat is also accompanied by a noticeable change in its social composition. Under conditions of industrialization, the formation of the basic nucleus of the working class cannot take place exclusively (or even predominantly) as a result of the natural reproduction of the proletariat. The ranks of the industrial workers are joined by the masses of ruined peasants and artisans. Thus, in contemporary India the migrants from the villages and the small towns comprise from 50 to 60 per cent of the hired labor in the big cities where the masses of the industrial working class are concentrated. At that, more than one-third of the gainfully employed population of the Indian

32. Pant and Vasudevan, 54–56; H. el-Saaty and G. K. Hirabayashi, *Industrialization in Alexandria* (S.1., 1959), 83, 123; NSS, No. 34, 56, 111.

33. El-Saaty and Hirabayashi, 108; ILYB (1960), 33–40, 66; *Statistics of Wages and Working Hours, January 1953* (Cairo 1954), 88–100.

cities has lived there less than five years. Among the factory workers of the leading industrial centers of Egypt, the migrants from the villages account for about 40 per cent.[34] It is obvious that as a result of the current acceleration of industrialization, the process of drawing recent peasants, artisans, etc., into industry is moving along faster than before. For that reason, in the early stages of industrialization the proportion of experienced and class-conscious workers who are connected with the traditions of class struggle may temporarily decrease. This factor exerts an especially strong influence upon the new industrial regions and the "young" branches—i.e., where the proletariat sprouts, so to speak, in bare places. The possible consequences of weakening the role of the experienced and class-conscious proletariat in the former colonies and semicolonies are reinforced by the fact that the experienced, class-conscious workers themselves have not yet entirely broken their moral ties with the village, as has already been indicated above. This is understandable, since the situation of a considerable group of workers at present is such that many among them, as before, cannot maintain their families on their meager earnings.

The accelerating pace of accretion in the industrial proletariat of the countries of Asia and Africa exerts great influence on the correlation of the generations within its ranks. It is natural that a great part of the new workers comprises young people. Under conditions in which the average length of labor activity is generally brief, this will lead to an absolute predominance of young people in the composition of the working class. It is worth noting that in India, as well as in the UAR, people who are below the age of 27 comprise from 30 to 40 per cent of the proletariat, while those who are below 37 comprise from 65 to 70 per cent.[35]

The political consequences of improvements in the social and age compositions of the industrial proletariat are obvious. A temporary decrease in the proportion of the experienced,

34. NSS, No. 16, 151, 206–8; el-Saaty and Hirabayashi, 108.
35. NSS, No. 14, 62–63, and No. 34, 102; el-Saaty and Hirabayashi, 66. Data concerning India refer to all hired labor in the cities; data

# Soviet Writers on the Developing Areas

class-conscious proletariat to a certain extent facilitates the penetration of bourgeois influences among the workers. On the other hand, the growing significance of youth helps on the whole to strengthen the combatant, revolutionary spirit of the working class.

In conclusion, such an important phenomenon as the formation and rapid growth, in many countries of Asia and Africa, of the new element of the industrial proletariat—workers who are employed in the enterprises of the state-owned sector—should be noted briefly. In some former colonies and semi-colonies (for example, in the UAR and many other countries of Africa), the state controls enterprises in which the great majority of the modern industrial proletariat is concentrated. However, even in those countries where the state-owned sector embraces a smaller part of industry, the proportion of workers employed therein is most significant. Thus in India, out of 8 or 9 million people who are employed in large-scale capitalist production, more than 2 million are engaged in state-owned enterprises (including around 1.5 million railroad and communication workers and around 0.5 million factory workers).[36] In heavy industry around one-half of all workers are concentrated in the state-owned enterprises. For the time being, it is impossible to make a thorough analysis of the difference in the status of workers employed in the state-owned and privately owned enterprises. It cannot be doubted, however, that the growth of state capitalism accelerates the creation of material prerequisites for the struggle of national democracy and socialism. The creation of large elements of the working class connected with the state-owned sector therefore has great significance. However, one should also not close one's eyes to the other side of the situation. Certain privileges which workers in the state-owned enterprises sometimes obtain, as well as the active and direct interferences of the state in

concerning the UAR refer to all workers in the factory industries in Alexandria.

36. DILS (1961), 45; *Monthly Abstract of Statistics* (New Delhi), No. 9 (1961), 76.

economic life—often directed against individual representatives and even against bourgeois groups—tend to blur the conflicting interests of labor and capital. Nevertheless, as the class-consciousness of the proletariat grows, the broad development of the state-owned sector makes especially clear the necessity for a struggle not only against individual employers, but also against the entire capitalist system.

# Agrarian Reforms in the Countries of the Near and Middle East, India, and Southeast Asia [*]

## BY R. A. UL'YANOVSKIY

*IF the prospects are poor that the proletariat will lead the revolutionary movements in the third world, then the Communists must look elsewhere for the motive force of their movement. Obviously, a prime candidate is the peasantry—not only because of its size, but also because Mao and Ho Chi Minh have shown that it can be used successfully to carry out a Communist power seizure. Given the condition of the peasantry in the developing areas—anywhere from tolerable to outrageously bad, but more often the latter—the Communists must vie with non-Communist forces in promising to improve the peasant's lot.*

*Although there are many difficulties that beset the countryside of the developing areas, certainly one of the main problems is maldistribution of land. Both Marxists and non-Marxists accept the importance of agrarian reform. There is a substantial Soviet literature on the subject;* [a] *one of the most ambitious studies is the lengthy two-part investigation by R. A. Ul'yanovskiy, a leading Soviet orientologist, that appeared in* Narody Azii i Afriki *(Nos. 1 and 2, 1961). Reprinted below are the first part of Ul'yanovskiy's first article (down to the ellipsis) and the second part in its entirety. The bulk of the first article, describing in considerable detail the land reforms of various Asian countries, has been deleted for reasons of space.*

[*]SOURCE: "Agrarnyye reformy v stranakh blizhengo i srednego Vostoka, Indii i Yugo-Vostochnoy Azii," NAIA, No. 2 (1961), 14–30.

a. For a general survey, see *Agrarnyye otnosheniya v stranakh vostoka* [Agrarian Relationships in the Countries of the East] (Moscow 1958).

## The Third World in Soviet Perspective

The principal interest of Ul'yanovskiy's study lies in its attempt to develop a theoretical grounding for the problem in line with classic Marxist doctrine. The author is confronted with a number of difficult problems, for he tacitly admits the irrelevance of Leninist doctrine but still addresses himself to the problem in terms of Lenin's concepts. If his performance it at times tortured, it is nevertheless a very solid exercise in exegesis which manages to remain in touch with reality.

Ul'yanovskiy comes off somewhat better in working with Marx, who at least recognized that conditions in Asia were radically different from those in Western Europe. The author's task would have been much easier, however, had he been able to draw on Marx's concept of "oriental mode of production." For a variety of reasons, this theory has been rejected by the Soviets, even though it continually returns to haunt them. Marx believed that Asiatic society did not fit the slave-feudal-capitalist-socialist pattern of evolution which he posited for Western Europe and America; he thought that there was no "feudalism" in Asia, but rather a system of "oriental despotism" based on the state's control of water resources.[b] This is perhaps a questionable theory, but it is a lot better than anything else Marxists have been able to come up with.

In this and his other writings, Ul'yanovskiy shows a marked lack of enthusiasm for the national bourgeois regimes of Asia and the Middle East. Indeed, he is apparently one of the more conservative Soviet orientologists currently in prominence. The performance of the newly independent governments in the field of agrarian reform has certainly been for the most part quite weak, so that the tone is not completely inappropriate to the subject matter. His discussion of the interrelationships among the peasantry, the Communists ("working class"), and the bourgeois governments is a singularly

b. By keeping this point in mind, the reader will find some of Ul'yanovskiy's ambivalences more understandable. The entire subject is discussed in great detail in K. A. Wittfogel's work, *Oriental Despotism* (New Haven 1957), chapter 9; and George Lichtheim, "Marx and 'the Asiatic Mode of Production,'" in *St. Antony's Papers*, No. 14 (Carbondale, Ill., 1963), 86–112. For Potekhin's difficulties with the same problem, see below, p. 237 and note b; and for more general comments, p. 2, above.

## Soviet Writers on the Developing Areas

*penetrating piece of analysis—one that can be read for profit not only by those who desire to foment Communist revolution, but also by those who would forestall it.*

*Since the exactness of terminology is of exceptional importance in this article, I have used conventional translations, at times at the cost of prose style. Some of the most important of these conventional translations are:* vykup—*purchase;* rabstvo—*slavery;* kabala—*servitude;* pomeshchik—*landlord;* krepostnichestvo—*serfdom;* zemlevladeniye—*land ownership; and* barskaya—*seignorial.*

THE unification of the socialist revolutions in Europe and Asia—which have resulted in the formation of the world socialist system—with the national liberation movements has created a unique historical situation. There are appearing and developing a large group of states which have broken away from the world imperialist system. At the same time, they have not joined the world socialist system. Capitalism has not yet assumed a completely dominant position in the economy of most of these countries, although it is the leading economic order in even the least developed of them. A many-faceted agricultural and socio-economic structure, partially a payment-in-kind but mainly a small-commodity peasant economy, are characteristic of this group of states.

The broad popular masses do not trust capitalism, which they regard as a synonym of colonialism. The progressive forces in these countries correctly recognize the historical limitations and the low efficiency of bourgeois methods of eradicating centuries-old technological and economic backwardness. One of the basic problems of today is the determination of the paths of further development for these countries, the means of solving the socio-economic problems which confront them, and the task of securing peace and protecting their state sovereignty. This has now become the main theme of the struggle of progressive forces in these countries against the forces of internal reaction and imperialism, and serves as a focal point in the struggle of the classes and parties. Among the socio-economic problems which urgently await solution, one of the most basic is the agrarian question.

## The Third World in Soviet Perspective

The attainment of national independence made the radical solution of the land question to the benefit of the peasantry a priority problem. Of course, this could be achieved by eliminating feudal landlord property rights, which would be a major prerequisite for achieving a rapid rate of industrialization and the growth of an internal market in these countries. When the bourgeoisie was confronted with the need to solve this problem, which concerns the entire nation, it continued to display inconsistency and finally inability to solve the matter democratically. In those countries of Asia where the proletariat led the national liberation movement against imperialism and feudalism, the people attained total victory and assured the transition of these countries to the path of socialist construction and the solution not only of the agrarian, but also of the peasant question—i.e., the question of transforming agriculture on the basis of peasant cooperatives. In those Asian countries where the national bourgeoisie led the national liberation movement and where as a result of a common national struggle, national independence was achieved, the tasks of anti-feudal revolution—i.e., the solution of the land question to the benefit of the peasantry—were not fully carried out.

The revolutions which were undertaken after the Second World War by Eastern countries overthrew imperialist domination but did not eliminate the domination of landlord land ownership in the countryside. This dichotomy is the source of the present critical situation in many Eastern countries. The bourgeoisie that led these revolutions succeeded in separating the anti-imperialist movement of the masses from the anti-feudal movement. It was only in China, North Vietnam, and other socialist countries in Asia that these two streams in the mass movement were joined together under the leadership of the working class and the Marxist-Leninist parties.

What, for example, was the political role of Gandhism? It was to direct the revolutionary energy of the working class, the peasantry, the urban paupers—in a word, the broadest masses—primarily in one direction: against British imperialism. Bourgeois nationalism did not give these masses

*Soviet Writers on the Developing Areas*

the opportunity to understand the whole complexity of the situation. It did not allow the peasants, in overthrowing the imperialists, to overthrow the landlords at the same time, and did not allow the workers to overthrow the capitalists.

It is not by accident that all national bourgeois ideologists had a rather well-developed anti-imperialist program, but advanced practically no agrarian program. The revolutions which took place in the countries of Asia after the Second World War were mainly anti-imperialist, and anti-feudal on a much lesser scale. In those places where the national liberation revolutions under the leadership of the working class were truly anti-feudal, there no longer was an agrarian question. In some of these countries there is no longer even a peasant question, since it has been or is being solved on the basis of the socialist cooperative plan.

The national bourgeoisie in a number of countries has succeeded, by establishing first its hegemony in the national liberation movement and then its political power in the country, in rescuing the class of landlords from liquidation "from below." [c] In the final analysis, this is why the national liberation movements in these countries have not been complete. In striving to retain the leading role in the national liberation movement without losing its influence over the masses, the national bourgeoisie—both in the period of the struggle for power and after securing it—constantly tries to isolate the workers' movement from the peasants, the anti-imperialist movement from the anti-feudal, thus depriving the working class of its principal and natural ally, the peasantry. Since the peasantry is the most massive force in the national liberation movement, the participation of the peasantry determines the scope of this movement. Upon coming to power, the national bourgeoisie concluded a bloc of one form or another with

c. The phrases "from below" and "from above" are conscious analogies to the two types of united front that the Communists formed in the 1920's. A united front "from above" was the alliance of Communist groups with other working class groups by means of agreements between the leaderships. A united front "from below" was formed by the Communists' drawing individual workers into the front without the agreement of the non-Communist leaderships.

landlord elements, and over a decade ago embarked on a path of "appeasing" the revolutionary struggle of the peasantry with half-baked reforms and partial concessions. The agrarian reforms which have been instituted "from above" by the ruling circles, without the support of the democratic forces of the peasantry, are aimed at prolonging the isolation of the peasantry from the working class.

In examining the agrarian reforms being carried out in the countries of the East today, we must bear in mind one of Lenin's principal teachings on reform in general: "Any reform, insofar as it is a reform (and not a reactionary or a conservative measure), signifies a certain step or stage for the better. *Any* reform in capitalist society has a *dual* character. The reform is a concession made by the ruling classes in order to restrain, weaken, or stifle the revolutionary struggle, in order to smash the force and energy of the revolutionary classes, to cloud their consciousness, etc." [1]

In considering any question relating to the contemporary East, we must proceed from the Marxist-Leninist position that the East is not a single entity; that there are substantial differences among the countries of the East which have arisen from the uneven economic and political development of these countries. The countries of the East differ from each other in terms of social class structure and composition of ruling circles; in degree of organization and ideological independence of the working masses. There is a substantial difference in the durability of the economic and political positions of imperialism in these countries. The interrelationships of these countries with the socialist states are also not without their differences. Therefore, any conclusion would be incorrect if it were drawn from the study of one or several countries taken as a whole, without regard for local peculiarities, and by generalizing this conclusion to include all countries of the East.

At the same time, the need for a differentiated, concrete approach, based on the study of the characteristics of each country, does not mean that it is impossible to draw some

1. V. I. Lenin, *Sochineniya* [Collected Works], XII, 205–6.

general conclusions for certain principal countries of the East, or for some of its separate regions.

The important thing in this approach of uniting the over-whelming majority of Asian countries when evaluating the state of the present development of their agrarian evolution is that their national liberation movements have not solved the agrarian-peasant question. This question is becoming more than ever one of the main problems of the new stage in the development of the class struggle in these countries.

A brief survey is given below of agrarian reforms and the position of the peasantry in the principal countries of the Near and Middle East, India, and Southeast Asia. . . .

I

The objective necessity for agrarian reforms that are being carried out in the non-socialist countries of Asia should be presented in the light of the solution of the land question and the socialist reconstruction of the countryside in the People's Republic of China, the Mongolian People's Republic, the Democratic People's Republic of Korea, and the Democratic Republic of Vietnam—the four Asiatic people's democracies, which have a total population of more than 700 million. These countries have achieved an uninterrupted rise in productive forces in general, and in agriculture in particular. In determining its political line with respect to the peasantry, the national bourgeoisie of the young independent Asiatic countries has had to consider the great historical significance of the experience of the Asian socialist countries in solving the agrarian question.

The ruling circles of the non-socialist countries must accomplish elementary agrarian reforms, not only because of profound internal factors which are determined by the economic development of the countryside and the class struggle of the peasantry against the landlords, but also because the broad masses of the peasantry in Asia, Africa, and Latin America are aware of the just solution of the land question in the socialist countries of Asia. Even the ruling classes of those countries, where people in positions of authority are closely tied to the imperialist states, are fully aware of this. The agrarian reforms in Turkey, Iran, Pakistan, South Vietnam, the Philippines, and South Korea, which took place after the Second World War and are still taking place to some extent—and which are even more meager and insubstantial than reforms in India, Burma, the UAR, and Iraq— bear witness to the fact that in no country in Asia are the ruling classes able to manage without changing the agrarian order to some extent at least.

Thus agrarian reforms of one kind or another are being effected in almost all non-socialist countries in Asia. In spite of the existing differences in the scales and rates at which they are being carried out, they are all striving, according to their social-class objectives, to guide the countryside along capitalist lines of development. While the peasantry needs radical reforms that will completely abolish ownership of land by landlords, the ruling bourgeois circles of the Asian countries need the half-baked reforms which are at present being realized in order to strengthen their position and to develop capitalism. Since the national bourgeoisie in these countries is weak, it must reckon in its agrarian policy with the increasing size and influence of the industrial and agricultural proletariat. It takes into consideration the growing dissatisfaction of the peasantry and its tendency to revolution, which has increased since the Second World War, and the danger of its unifying with the proletariat.

In essence, when the ruling classes of Asian countries determine their land policy, they proceed from the following: either they will succeed in maintaining their influence over the peasantry, and consequently their authority, or they will lose it and will not be able to keep authority in their own hands. In all Asian countries, the bourgeoisie shares power with the landlords. The bourgeoisie-landlord coalition does not produce any radical land reform on behalf of the peasantry, and the national bourgeoisie—by hoping to satisfy the interests of the peasantry with measures of secondary value— thus attempts to keep the landlord class as its ally against the growing radicalism among the masses of peasants. The national bourgeoisie does not and cannot want to remain in the village in direct confrontation with the peasantry. It feels that it is in no position to handle the tens and hundreds of millions of peasants without the aid of the landlord. If the national bourgeoisie needs the landlord as its ally, the reverse is also true. It is on this basis that these two classes have formed a political coalition directed against the peasantry and the working class.

It is in this fashion that we can explain the constant concern of the national bourgeoisie in carrying out land reforms that are deliberately designed not to eliminate the landlord class completely, but to maintain its foundation. At the same time, these reforms are modernizing the economic role of the landlord in the countryside and are making him into a landlord capitalist. Legislators in Asian countries suppose that such agrarian reforms will enable them to abolish the typical feudal characteristics of the old landowner and give rise to a strong stratum of peasant entrepreneurs, thus pacifying the countryside.

In the majority of the countries under consideration, agrarian reforms limit—and only in some cases do they eliminate—large, privileged, principally parasitic, land ownership, and they only partially affect the usury system. They do not solve the land question to the benefit of the peasantry, since they do not abolish the entire landowner class, do not transfer all land to the immediate producers and, consequently, do not eliminate the virtual or total landlessness of the peasants. Some of the landlords are joining the ranks of the bourgeoisie and are becoming agricultural capitalists.

Reforms, as a rule, have the following objectives: (a) intensification of the development of productive forces of agriculture on a commodity-capitalist [d] basis; (b) purchase and redistribution of a rather significant part of public and landlord property, which is intended to promote peasant land ownership in order to strengthen the prosperous stratum in the village and attract the middle peasant class to the bour-

d. For the Marxist definition of a "commodity," see above, p. 157, note b.

geoisie; (c) partial reduction and regulation of rent; (d) elimination of feudal obligations and extortion; (e) restriction of foreign land ownership; (f) expansion of state agricultural credit; (g) promotion and development of cooperatives; (h) increase in the ability of agriculture to compete on the world market; (i) creation of large and medium landlord-capitalist and farmers' enterprises.

Agrarian reforms have increased the extent of peasant *land ownership* and the legal position of the present owners. The most hated feudal obligations and extortions are being abolished. Conditions for rent and agricultural credit are being made less severe. All types of so-called service cooperative societies are growing rapidly, encompassing tens of millions of wealthy and middle peasant farms. The capitalist elements in the countryside have penetrated and control them. The extent of direct peasant *land tenure* in many countries has remained as before; in others it has increased insignificantly, while in still others it has even decreased owing to the fact that some of the landlords, merchants, and usurers are in the process of transition to private farming; or if they own such a farm, they are expanding it into a medium or a large farm by incorporating the lands which were previously leased to the peasants. In connection with the significant growth of the population, which is not accompanied by a corresponding growth in the area of cultivated lands and the development of industry, the per capita availability of land in the major countries of Asia is decreasing. If we consider that the wealthy strata of the peasantry have considerably increased the area of their land tenure in the same fashion as the capitalist landowners, then we must acknowledge the fact that land hunger among the basic peasant masses has remained unsatisfied. The measures which are being taken against usury have not freed the peasant from this evil. State and cooperative credit has increased considerably, but continues to be inadequate and is available mainly to the wealthy and middle peasant classes, because credit is usually offered against a deposit of land or other guarantees. The lowest classes of the peasantry are practically unable to enjoy this credit.

198

## Soviet Writers on the Developing Areas

The basic mass of the rural population, rural paupers and farm workers, lacks the opportunity to gain rights to land ownership and has received no significant material benefits from land reforms. That part of the peasantry which purchased land has extracted definite benefit from reform. In some countries (India, Burma) this is a considerable part of the population. Repayment installments and increasing indirect taxes apparently absorb somewhat less from the peasant owner than the landowner previously collected from the peasant tenant as land rent.

The landlord who is becoming modernized, the kulak and, to some extent, the wealthy middle peasant appear to be in a more favorable position.[e] Legislation generally helps to transform the old landlord's holdings into a landlord-capitalist farm. Kulak farms are also receiving considerable support, but the benefits extracted by the wealthy kulak elements in the countryside do not satisfy them completely. These classes are to some extent capable of participating in the common peasant struggle to eliminate feudal remnants—especially landlord property rights—since these remnants still survive everywhere to a greater (Iran, Indonesia, Arab countries) or lesser (Turkey, India, Ceylon) extent. In fact, one can currently notice in a number of countries—and in certain regions of others—that the wealthy peasantry is remaining aloof from participation in the peasant movement. This new phenomenon (India, Burma, UAR, and others) is one of the results of reforms that have intensified the split in the peasantry.

Semi-feudal exploitation, especially sharecropping, still exists over vast territories of Asian countries, although in many countries (Turkey, Burma, India) the exploited sharecropper has ceased to be such a central figure in the village as he was from fifteen to twenty-five years ago. The usurer, although he is limited by special legislation, nevertheless continues to be a powerful figure in the village. There has been an increase

e. Kulaks and other rural "classes" are described above, p. 162, note e. A "middle peasant" is simply one who is neither poor nor rich. He is generally a sought-after ally in the Communist drive for power, but is treated much the same as a wealthy peasant after the Communists consolidate their control.

in the movement of monetary capital, accumulated in the village, toward industry, particularly in the processing of agricultural products and raw materials. Capitalist development of agriculture—which accelerated in the period after the Second World War—and postwar agrarian reforms have intensified and deepened the class differentiation of the peasantry. In some countries (India, Burma, Syria), and in certain large regions of others, this sometimes causes the kulak to compromise with landlord elements.

As before, the problem of peasant underemployment—connected with more or less complete unavailability of land—remains the most acute. The partial transition to mechanization on the farms of large and medium entrepreneurs, which leads to some increase in the organic formation of capital,[f] causes a further increase in underemployment and unemployment. The peasants are being driven off the land in many places (Turkey, Iran, India, Pakistan) where landlords and farmers are increasing their role. The flight to the cities of the farming population, especially the youth, has increased.

Thus, the measures which have been taken "from above" by the ruling circles in order to prevent an agrarian uprising have been essentially palliatives. They are incapable of solving the land question to the benefit of the working peasantry. For this reason dissatisfaction with the existing situation is growing among the peasantry, especially the poor and middle peasants and the farm workers.

The accelerated development of commodity-financial and capitalist relationships in the village is resulting to a much greater extent in a breakdown of the old social relationships. This process, which is extremely unhealthy for the masses, is affecting tens and hundreds of millions of people. The war and the postwar national liberation movement in Asia have mobilized great masses of the rural population. Military and social upheavals have torn the population from the customary way of life. In many countries the peasantry has been forced

f. "Organic formation of capital"—see above, p. 173, note i.

on a much larger scale than before to sell not only the product of its labor but its labor power, so that it must seek new sources for a means of existence. Millions of peasants are discontented and dissatisfied. Their interests are varied, contradictory, and for the present inchoate. A trend toward socialism is observable among the advanced section of the peasantry. They are experiencing more and more the influence of socialist reconstruction in the Asian people's democracies. Meanwhile, religious ideology, illusions of brotherhood, equality, and justice, as well as utopian conceptions of a future society, are alive among the peasantry. Bourgeois nationalism cleverly takes advantage of patriarchal beliefs—the ideas of Buddhism, Hinduism, Islam—and supports in every way the illusion of peace between classes. It strives to persuade the peasant to wait patiently for equal distribution of land in the future on the basis of just reforms, and to convince him that it is unnecessary to resort to revolution in order to remove the landowners and usurers.

In the majority of Asian countries, it is at present extremely difficult for the bourgeois or landlord parties to promote openly the idea of capitalist development as a slogan designed to enlist the belief and support of the masses, especially of the millions of working peasants. Therefore the ruling strata advance the nebulous idea of constructing a socialist society of some form or other, often limited to the cooperative system. An active ideological and organizational struggle for the peasantry is developing. The national bourgeoisie is in serious danger of losing its influence among the working peasants, who are dissatisfied with the results of the development of the countryside during the past ten or fifteen years. It is striving to contain them with agrarian reforms and, to an even greater extent, with the deceptions and social demagoguery engendered by these reforms.

The progressive anti-imperialist potentials of the national bourgeoisie have not yet been exhausted. That part of the national bourgeoisie which is not tied to imperialist circles "is objectively interested in carrying out the basic tasks of the

*The Third World in Soviet Perspective*
anti-imperialist, anti-feudal revolution. . . ."[1a] The national
bourgeoisie of the majority of the countries of Asia is continuing to play a progressive role in the struggle against colonialism, in the struggle for political and economic independence, for strengthening the sovereignty of the countries in
question, for peace and disarmament. At the same time the
revolutionary struggle of the working class, the toiling peasantry, and the urban petty bourgeoisie is developing with
great force. There is a steady polarization of the social forces,
a strengthening of the contradictions and the struggle between them. Under these conditions, the bourgeoisie in a
number of sovereign Asian countries is revealing a tendency
toward conciliation with imperialism and feudalism, and the
ruling circles of some Asian countries have open political
and military ties with the aggressive imperialist blocs. Domestic policy in these countries is for the most part reactionary, and their foreign policy is subjugated to the tasks of
preserving the military and political systems of the aggressive blocs. Suppression of the struggle of the masses against
the forces of colonialism and against the military police dictatorship of the dominating classes is the main task in these
countries, where "dictatorial methods of control are combined
with the fiction of parliamentarianism, deprived of its democratic content and reduced to pure formality. Many democratic
organizations are accused of being illegal and are forced to
go underground; thousands of fighters for the cause of the
working class, for the cause of peace, are thrown into prison."[2]

The toiling masses of the city and country demand more
radical domestic reforms, capable of actually improving their
situation. The contradictory process of capitalist development,
the growing speculation, the promotion schemes of the large
industrial and merchant bourgeoisie, the corruption of the
bureaucracy, and the appearance of such afflictions as mass

1a. *Programmnyye dokumenty bor'by za mir, demokratiyu i sotsializm*
[Program Documents of the Struggle for Peace, Democracy and Social-
ism] (Moscow 1961), 66.
2. *Ibid.*, 71.

pauperization, inescapable destitution, hunger, and chronic unemployment engender among the masses feelings of disappointment, dissatisfaction, and opposition to the bourgeois state. The national bourgeoisie is striving to preserve its prestige as a fighter for national independence and to secure for itself the support of the masses. Its reactionary wing is attempting to "present its selfish narrow class interests as the interests of the entire nation. . . ." [3] The disappointment of the popular masses, however, is growing. In some countries a more or less distinct class demarcation has occurred, while in others it is far from established. The solution of the land question assumes primary significance for all non-socialist countries of Asia. "Without profound agrarian reforms, it is impossible to solve the food problem, to remove all medieval remnants which are retarding the development of productive forces in agriculture and in industry." [4]

The experience of history teaches the peoples of Asia that only a union of the working class with the peasantry is capable of becoming the major force which will secure national independence, which will carry out democratic reforms and secure social progress for the entire nation. "This union is called upon to be the basis of a broad national front. The extent of participation of the national bourgeoisie in the struggle for liberation also depends to no small degree on its strength and durability." [5]

The level of development of class consciousness in the peasantry varies greatly not only in different countries, but in different regions within countries and in different strata and groups of the rural population. This depends to a great degree on the political maturity and activity and degree of influence of the Marxist-Leninist parties on the peasant masses. Winning the peasant masses over to the side of the working class, as emphasized in the [1960] Statement of the Congress of Representatives of Communist and Workers' Parties in

3. *Ibid.*, 68.
4. *Ibid.*, 66.
5. *Ibid.*, 66.

*The Third World in Soviet Perspective*

Moscow, has become the most important task, whose successful solution will create conditions for forming an independent, national democratic state.[g]

In studying the agrarian pattern of non-socialist countries of the East, one should not forget the presence of the large foreign sector in their agriculture (mainly plantations). In some countries (India, Ceylon, Malaya, Philippines, Tunisia, Morocco, and others) this sector occupies the key position in the production of tea, crude rubber, coffee, copra, citrus, sugar cane, and spices. Foreign land ownership is the foundation of reactionary class and political relationships. Being organically connected to the monopolies of the world capitalist market, the foreign landowners actively oppose any agrarian reforms, resist nationalization of land and the establishment of maximum norms of land ownership, and attempt to reserve for themselves a special regime of land ownership and tenure. On the plantations, foreign capital always emerges as a partisan of the most cruel relationship toward the workers and coolies and toward the surrounding peasant population. Plundering the riches of the soil, rapaciously exploiting land and water resources, striving to avoid investment of capital in improvement of the plantations, adding the huge profits to reserve funds, exporting profits and superprofits out of the country, appropriating differential rent [h]—these are the characteristic features of the activity of the foreign sector in the agriculture of the non-socialist countries of the East. Any serious agrarian reform cannot but affect foreign land ownership and tenure. In individual countries of Asia (Ceylon, Indonesia, and others) steps are being taken to limit and partially to liquidate the foreign sector in agriculture and transfer it to the control of the state and the cooperatives, but these measures, in spite of their progressive character, do not solve the problem in its entirety. In the majority of Asian countries where the national bourgeoisie has come into power, it dis-

g. The "national democratic state" is discussed above, pp. 27–28.
h. "Differential rent" is of two types: (1) The profit gained from land that is of better quality or more advantageously situated; and (2) the profit gained from increased capital investment in land. For a detailed discussion, see *Fundamentals*, 228–29.

plays its inherent duality and has not nationalized the foreign plantations and land holdings. Future agrarian reforms based upon the peasantry—the agricultural proletariat and the millions of plantation coolies—will inevitably eliminate the foreign sector in agriculture and make the plantations state property.

## II

As the development of capitalism accelerates in the agriculture of the countries of Asia, the struggle of the most revolutionary proletarian and semi-proletarian part of the countryside against capitalist and semi-feudal exploitation, and for revolutionary reform of the agrarian structure on democratic principles, takes on an even greater significance. The proletariat's successful solution of the principal strategic task —the achievement of a durable union with the peasantry and its liberation from the influence of the bourgeoisie and the landlords, as indicated in the Statement of the Congress of Representatives of Communist and Workers' Parties—is the decisive precondition for the transition of the national liberation movement, which generally has an anti-imperialist direction, to a higher level in the struggle for the formation of an independent national democratic state that will pave the way to socialist development.

In analyzing the character of the new socio-economic processes taking place in the agrarian structure of the non-socialist countries of the East, it would be especially incorrect to extend theoretical principles, peculiar to a particular country and a particular historical epoch, to other countries and another historical epoch.

V. I. Lenin demonstrated the possibility of two paths of development of capitalism ("American" and "junker," or "peasant" and "landlord") in Russian agriculture at the end of the nineteenth and beginning of the twentieth century. He fought for a radical solution to the agrarian question exclusively in the interests of the peasantry, through complete abolition of landlord property rights. Even then, sixty years ago, V. I. Lenin noted that neither of these two paths of capitalist development appeared anywhere in Russia in pure form. Both types of agrarian evolution were clearly evident. Lenin pointed out that infinitely varied combinations of elements of one or the other type of capitalist evolution were possible in agriculture.

In considering the question of agrarian reforms and the paths of development of capitalism in the agriculture of the non-socialist countries of contemporary Asia, one cannot depict the bourgeois reforms being carried out there as exclusively "landlord" or "junker" reforms, conducted only in the interests of the feudal class of landowners. Lenin pointed out that the economic base of the Russian agrarian revolution made two basic outcomes possible. Either the old landlord farm that was tightly bound to serfdom would be maintained and gradually converted into a capitalist-junker farm, or it would be destroyed in the course of the revolution and, together with it, all remnants of serfdom—especially large land ownership—would be swept away.

The landlord (junker) path to the solution of the agrarian question necessarily presupposes the preservation of the old landlord farm on a new bourgeois foundation. The landlords slowly shift from feudal-noble farms with all the inherent features of serfdom to new junker landlord-capitalist farms. Landlord farming, conducted with the utilization of serf and semi-serf labor, is the point of departure for this evolution. The landlord serf-owner emerges as the main figure in the junker-capitalist evolution.

We know that the agrarian reform in Russia in 1861 was accompanied by the following: (a) carving up (*otrezki*)—the best peasant lands were given to the landlords; (b) increase in the checkerboarding of peasants' and landlords' land; (c) reservation of the best communal lands for the use of the landlords; (d) strengthening of compulsory peasant labor on the landlord's farm and establishment of a type of serf-like dependence, of so-called part-time compulsory labor; (e) growth of a servitude-serf [*kabal'no-krepostnicheskiy*] lease system.

V. I. Lenin wrote of the peasant reform in Russia in 1861: "the 'great reform' was a serf reform and could not have been otherwise, for it was carried out by the serf-owners. What force caused them to undertake the reform? The force of economic development which was pulling Russia onto the path of capitalism." [6]

The large landlord farm which involved *corvée* labor and existed alongside the farms allotted to the peasants, and which gradually became absorbed by capitalist relationships, historically emerged in Russia as the material and industrial base for the "junker" development of the agrarian structure. In the history of Russia, Prussia, Poland, and the majority of the countries east of the Elbe, capitalization of the landlord farm took place in such a manner that the peasant serfs were gradually replaced by free workers. As a result, there was an intermixture of hired workers and serfs for many decades. The landlords constructed and operated wineries, distilleries, tanneries, linen mills, felting mills, sugar mills, dairy plants, mechanized mills, hulling mills, wool-combing factories, horse farms, cattle-feeding stations, and other enterprises. Thus, by the beginning of the twentieth century in Russia, the landlords not only had huge seignorial lands, which were tilled by hired farm workers and poor peasants, but also organized thousands of large, medium, and small capitalist enterprises. The landlord farm using *corvée* labor was at the base of this evolution—not the parasitic landlord *land ownership* that is found in the countries of Asia, but large or medium *farming enterprises*.

There were 367 million hectares of agricultural lands in Russia by 1913, including 152 million owned by landlords, the government, and the church, and 215 million owned by the peasantry.[7] This means about 150 million hectares (375 million acres) of land belonged to the landlord noblemen, or almost as much arable land as exists in India today with a population of 415 million. The Russian countryside made the transition to capitalism while possessing not only vast unused land resources, but huge areas of land on which the landlord

6. V. I. Lenin, *Sochineniya,* xvii, 95.
7. *Narodnoye khozyaystvo SSSR. Statisticheskiy sbornik* [The National Economy of the USSR. Statistical Handbook] (Moscow 1956), 97.

*The Third World in Soviet Perspective*

had for decades and centuries conducted his own seignorial agricultural enterprises. After the reform of 1861, this to a great extent changed from a compulsory labor system to capitalist farming based on freely hired labor.

Is there anything similar in India and other Asian countries? When the Russian landowner's farm made the transition to capitalism, he did not have to begin this process by driving millions of peasants off the land. He possessed a large area of land which he farmed privately, while the peasants had land allotments. They produced the necessary product on this land, while on the seignorial estate—separated territorially and economically—they produced the surplus product which was appropriated by the landlord.[i]

It is well known that before reforms were carried out, in Turkey, Iran, India, and the countries of Southeast Asia, there was no developed landlord economy which determined the agrarian structure. Nor did one exist in the Arab East. In these countries of the East, there was landlord ownership that encompassed practically all the land in the form of holdings which were no smaller in area than the land holdings in Russia. However, there were no large or medium landlord holdings. These countries did not have the material-production base which the Russian landlords relied upon a century ago when they began their "junker" course of developing capitalism in agriculture. Consequently, there was an enormous concentration of *land ownership* in the hands of the Asian landlords, reaching 80 to 90 per cent or more, but there was almost no concentration of *farming* in their hands. Herein lies the great qualitative difference between the countries of the East and Tsarist Russia.

In this regard, there is great theoretical interest in the publication of comments by K. Marx on the book by Maksim Kovalevskiy, the Russian sociologist who in the 1870's studied feudalism, the agrarian system, and the origin, development, and downfall of communal land ownership in the East.[8] In

i. On "surplus product" and "necessary product," see above, p. 162, note f.

8. See SV, Nos. 3, 4, 5 (1958), and PV, No. 1 (1959); M. M. Kova-

208

## Soviet Writers on the Developing Areas

studying M. M. Kovalevskiy's book, K. Marx wrote: *"On the grounds that one finds in India a 'beneficiary system,' a 're-mission of duties' (the latter, of course, is by no means purely feudal—cf. Rome), and commendation, Kovalevskiy regards this as feudalism in the Western European sense of the word. He forgets, inter alia, about serfdom, an important feature which does not exist in India."* [9]

Serfdom is one of the cruelest and vilest forms of extra-economic pressure connected with exploitation of the peas-antry directly on the proprietor's farm. The absence of this form of extra-economic pressure in India and a number of other Asiatic countries is truly of interest and requires expla-nation. Serfdom, as a specific feature of feudalism, presup-poses private farming by the peasant on one hand, and seigno-rial farming by the landlord on the other.

The greater the role and significance of compulsory labor and, consquently, the higher the development of the public or private feudal seignorial farm, the stronger will be the extra-economic pressure. A historical peculiarity of India and a number of other countries in Asia that has been noted by historians and agrarian specialists is the lack of developed, feudal, large or medium seignorial farms as a factor deter-mining the agrarian system in these countries. This peculiarity is characteristic of the entire period of the Middle Ages in these countries and can be detected before and after Euro-pean penetration. Moreover, the presence of large or medium landlord property rights in these countries, unaccompanied by large or medium landlord land tenure—i.e., an economy not based on serf or semi-serf, voluntary or semi-voluntary, peasant labor—remained characteristic of the situation in these countries right up to the 1940's and 1950's.

The specific forms of private feudal land ownership, since they did not reach the stage of feudal seignorial farms, natu-rally did not require the organization of peasant labor into a

levskiy, *Obshchinnoye zemlevladeniye, prichiny, khod i posledstviya ego razlozheniya* [Communal Land Ownership, the Causes, Course and Con-sequences of Its Decay], Vol. I (Moscow 1879).

9. SV, No. 5 (1958), 12.

serf system on the lands of the landlords. Communal or individual peasant land tenure, or a mixture of both, was accompanied by the appropriation of the surplus product of the immediate producer primarily in the form of rent in kind (appearing in the form of monetary rent in certain periods— for example, in India).

Thus India, like a number of other Asian countries, was characterized chiefly by small peasant agriculture on land belonging to a landlord. This characteristic assumed exceptional significance during the transition in these countries to a simple commodity economy and later to a capitalist one—a transition connected with European colonial penetration. This did not alter the economic structure of land tenure. With the exception of plantation crops, whose production became the monopoly primarily of foreign capital, this form of economic development has remained insignificant in the majority of countries.

The aforementioned historical uniqueness of the material and economic structure of feudalism in India and a number of other Asian countries predetermined the basic difference between these countries' transition to simple commodity and then to capitalist agriculture in the nineteenth and twentieth centuries, and the European pattern, where landlord farming, gradually becoming capitalist, was one of the decisive factors in this transition.

Since the Second World War, as a result of the destruction of colonial domination and the achievement of political independence, large and medium landlord farming is becoming more firmly established under the influence of agrarian reforms. This is resulting in the expulsion of small peasant tenants or landowners from the land (India, Turkey, Iran, UAR, and others). On the other hand, the peasants' struggle to eliminate landlord property rights is becoming more intense. The delayed establishment of a landlord-capitalist agricultural economy is necessarily connected with the alienation of land from millions of immediate producers, and with the deprivation of property or lease rights, to the advantage of the landlord or capitalist farmers. This inevitably has caused an in-

tensification of the class struggle. It is not only elimination of
the surviving rights of a very small minority of large landowners and rent collectors (mainly absentee landlords) that
is a most vital task. This has already been accomplished in a
number of Asiatic countries. The main task is to eliminate *all*
landlord property rights, and *all* landlord farming, *all* foreign
land ownership, and to liquidate the exploitation of the peasantry by merchants and usurers. These demands are contained
in the agrarian programs of the Marxist-Leninist parties, and
the peasantry is rallying to the struggle to accomplish them.
The peasants in Asian countries have not yet achieved any
decisive victories along this path in the struggle for land,
but even the compromising agrarian reforms which are being carried out by the ruling circles in Asian countries are
the result of the peasants' struggle and are, therefore, an
achievement of the peasantry.

Thus the historical peculiarities of the development of feudalism in Asia, which Marx time and again depicted, are appearing in our time. They must be taken into consideration
when studying the pressing problems of the evolution of agriculture in contemporary Asian countries.[10]

When, say, the landlord-entrepreneur in India, Turkey, or
Iran establishes his farm and brings a tractor into the countryside, he frequently begins to drive the peasant tenants
from his land, as he has little or no land that is not rented to
peasants. Here is where a most burdensome operation begins, one which requires great class and political courage.
V. I. Lenin wrote that "Stolypin[j] and the landlords bravely
embarked on a revolutionary course of shattering the old
order in a most ruthless manner, delivering the peasants over

10. This question is treated in more detail in the report by L. S.
Gamayanov and R. A. Ul'yanovskiy at the 25th International Congress
of Orientologists: *Trudy Russkogo sotsiologa M. M. Kovalevskogo "Obshchinnoye zemlevladeniye . . ." i kritika ego K. Marksom* [The Works
of the Russian Sociologist M. M. Kovalevsky, "Communal Land Ownership, . . ." and Criticism of It by K. Marx] (Moscow 1960).

j. P. A. Stolypin (1863–1911) was the Tsarist prime minister following the abortive revolution of 1905. He attempted—with little success
—to rationalize the structure of Russian agriculture.

to the landlords and kulaks for plunder and pillage." [11] Fifty years ago in Tsarist Russia, there were vast areas of free land on which it was possible to develop capitalist-landlord and kulak farming, resorting when necessary to expelling the peasants from their long-established dwellings. Stolypin's policy in Russia was carried out after the defeat of the 1905–1906 revolution. Such a circumstance does not exist at present in any oriental country.

The national liberation struggle and, in many countries, the peasant movement are on the upswing. The bourgeoisie fears for the fate of the landlords, as the latter must commence driving millions of peasants from the land. In spite of this, the national bourgeoisie on the one hand is trying as far as possible to retain the landlord class by partially altering it according to its own image and likeness, while on the other hand it is understandably afraid of accelerating this risky process. Therefore, it strenuously maneuvers and seeks to compromise both with the landlord class and with the peasants, and strives to secure its influence over the peasants and split their ranks. Therefore the ruling circles of the bourgeoisie sometimes have to impose considerable limitations on the rights and authority of the rural landlords, even when it [the bourgeoisie] encounters some resistance from different groups in its own ranks and acute opposition from the landlords.

Such was the case in Kashmir, for example, when the ruling circles abolished landlord property rights and set the maximum limit on possession of land at 22 acres (9 hectares). In another Indian state, the Punjab, the landlords and kulaks have during the past four years obtained more than ten million rupees of state bank credit for the purchase of tractors which they are introducing on the farms. Already more than five thousand tractors are at work in the fields. In connection with this, tens of thousands of peasant tenants were driven off the land in the Punjab. This intensified the class struggle in this very important state and, together with other factors,

11. V. I. Lenin, *Sochineniya*, xiii, 420.

has resulted in the development of a massive peasant movement.

Those who attempt to institute a policy of forcible destruction of the peasantry cannot ignore the fact that the possibilities for carrying out such a policy are limited. The state authorities, under pressure of the peasant movement, were forced to enact legislation to set upper limits on present land holdings and on those newly acquired. This was indisputably a concession to the peasantry. Later, as was mentioned in the press, sabotage of these laws began. Out of 46.7 thousand large landowners in Punjab state, only 22.5 thousand reported that the lands they possessed were above the established maximum. The others tried to disguise their excess land. Of the 450 thousand acres of excess land that were subject to distribution among the peasantry, only 25 thousand acres, or 6 per cent, were officially registered. The landlords divided great areas of land among their relatives or sold them to dummy buyers. In the same state, during the ten- to twelve-year reform period, 485.4 thousand families of tenant peasants purchased the rights to possession of 5,056 thousand acres of land.[12] Such were the contradictory results of the active struggle of the peasantry against the landlords for land and the sabotage of the agrarian reform by the landlords and the bourgeoisie that the latter had themselves instituted. The dual nature of the national bourgeoisie in developing agrarian legislation, in the means chosen for its implementation, and in the goals that they followed, stands out especially clearly in the present situation.

The development of capitalism in the non-socialist countries of Asia has its own characteristic peculiarities. In Asia, as in prerevolutionary Russia, capitalism in rural areas makes its way in the face of many feudal remnants. Russia was an independent country, however, while the Asian countries have just recently been liberated from centuries of colonial or semicolonial dependence. The most substantial difference is that political power in Russia before and after the 1861 re-

12. According to data calculated by the government of Punjab state, in *Link*, January 24, 1960, 25.

form remained in the hands of the landlords in the person of an autocratic monarchy, while political power in India and similar Asian countries already belongs to the national bourgeoisie, who have formed a coalition with the landlords. While in the reformed Russia of the 1860's and 1870's the bourgeois democratic revolution was still far in the future, agrarian reforms in the majority of Asian countries, regardless of how inconsequential they may have been, were the result of an already accomplished national liberation revolution directed primarily against foreign imperialist domination and partly against feudal landlords.

Capitalism as a world system still had long-term prospects of prolonged development and transition to its highest imperialist stage when agrarian reform was being carried out in Russia. The present development of capitalism in the agriculture of Asian countries is taking place under completely different conditions; under conditions of the existence and growth of a powerful world socialist economy, the failure of the colonial system of imperialism, and, on the basis of this, a change in the world balance of power in favor of socialism. The contemporary problem of the paths of development of capitalism in the Asian countryside can be considered only in close connection with the growth of socialist and democratic forces in that area. The historic struggle of the Asian peoples themselves has advanced an alternative to capitalist development of agriculture in Asian countries—a non-capitalist path of development which has proved itself in Central and Southeast Asia and the Far East, under conditions of settled agriculture and nomadic cattle raising.

The economic and political possibilities of carrying out a policy of capitalist agricultural development on the basis of a "Prussian" or "junker" system in contemporary Asia have been greatly curtailed in comparison with possibilities which existed in Russia and Prussia in the nineteenth and the beginning of the twentieth century. This is due to the aggregate of historical and economic peculiarities in the development of Asia in the past, and to the particular historical stage which world capitalism is undergoing today, and which is determining its fate.

## III

The historical experience of the development of the world capitalist economy shows that the direct remnants of feudalism exist side by side with modern capitalism. Monopolies and servitude exist side by side in Western Europe and America. There is developed capitalist industry in the city and virtual servitude in the country. One can find such a combination in fantastic forms all over the Latin American continent. In Europe, where the course of development of capitalism in agriculture was restrained by the remnants of feudalism, the survivals of servitude and serfdom that are employed by monopoly capital are even more significant. One has but to point to the contemporary Southern Italian, Sicilian, Spanish, Portuguese, and Greek countryside, and the rural areas of Eastern Europe prior to the establishment of socialist reforms. Even in the United States of America, the classical country of the "American" path of development of capitalism in agriculture, the higher forms of servitude which have been described not only appear in economic life as a consequence of former negro slavery, but are being reproduced again and again on a broad scale by monopoly capital, which has an interest in such servitude, encompassing both colored and white workers.

Therefore, the principal difference between the "American" and "Prussian" paths of development of capitalism in agriculture, which was of great significance during the period of the young, emerging capitalist system, is being obliterated in the period of the general crisis of capitalism, in the epoch of the transition to socialism. The question of the paths of development of capitalism in the agriculture of agrarian countries no longer has its former importance. This pertains not only to the West but also to the East. The very formulation of the problem of the two paths of development of capitalism in agriculture now requires a different approach.

The embourgeoisement of landlords and their transformation into capitalist entrepreneurs are consequences of the objective inevitable pattern of capitalist development. But the initiator of this process is now the national bourgeoisie, which has attained political power. It strives to maintain the peasants under its influence when it opposes colonialism and imperialism, the large feudals and princes, the absentee landlords and the accompanying feudal injustices suffered by the peasantry. Such is the situation in India, Indonesia, Burma, the UAR, and other countries.

The abolition of all principalities in India is not only an administrative but also a socio-economic reform. The elimination of royal land ownership and the large land holdings of the pashas in Egypt, of the large and medium-size feudal principalities in Indonesia, the nationalization of land in Burma or of mosque properties in Tunisia, as well as the limitation of foreign land ownership in many countries, and even the abolishment of landlord property rights in Japan, are in no way similar to the classical "Prussian" path of development known in the history of Russia and East Europe. These cannot be called serf reforms.

The overt landlord-serfowner method of solving the agrarian question used in Russia a century ago is impossible in the present situation in the countries of the Orient. The national bourgeoisie lacks the power to employ this means and, what is more important, it is not in its interests. Now, the reactionary feudal and semi-feudal elements in many Asian countries are anti-national and pro-imperialist. In striving to secure political domination the national bourgeoisie, in order to preserve its influence over the peasants and—more important —in order to prevent the establishment of a solid union of the proletariat with the peasantry, is forced to undertake agrarian reforms which, without completely abolishing the class of landlords, will considerably limit and sometimes seriously undermine its political and economic power in the rural areas. This aim finds expression primarily in a general and significant limitation or, in exceptional circumstances, abolition of landlord property rights in various regions and an increase in peasant land holdings; in the abolition of the legal privileges of the landlord class; in the attempt to cause a split among the peasantry by forcing its differentiation.

There has been a definite increase in the economic interest of the bourgeoisie in limiting the range of feudal and semi-feudal exploitation of the peasantry, in eliminating this exploitation in many cases, in accelerating the process of capitalist development, in the penetration of capital into agriculture and the processing of agricultural products, in subjugating merchant and usury capital. It is not only these goals that compel the bourgeoisie to undertake reforms, however, even though they constitute the economic basis of these reforms.

Political goals often play a leading role. The national bourgeoisie and its political parties fear the working class, its agrarian reforms, and the activities of the Communists in the countryside. The national bourgeoisie can no longer oppose the Communists on the agrarian question without taking any measures in the countryside, without making any reforms or only those reforms that serve the landlords' interests. This circumstance is forcing the national bourgeoisie to consider the peasants' interests to some extent. The national bourgeoisie knows that it cannot maintain its political authority if it has no influence over the peasantry.

The national bourgeoisie regards the separation and isolation of the peasantry from the working class as its strategic task. The most far-sighted representatives of ruling circles in the Asian countries know that retarded agrarian reforms inevitably result, at a certain stage, in the peasants' no longer being able or willing to put up with a delay in the solution of the agrarian question, and showing signs of rebellion. They begin to seize land on their own. Such phenomena have occurred more than once in the non-socialist countries in Asia over the last seven to ten years. The ruling circles in these countries have succeeded in weakening the peasant movement against the landlords and thus have intensified the contradictions and the struggle among the peasants. The kulaks and some of the wealthy middle peasants have taken advantage of the right to acquire land by purchase. They take advantage of the excellent market prospects which in many countries (India and others) are supported by the process of industrialization. All this allows the ruling circles to maneuver in the land question and postpone its final solution. We should add that the influence of the working class on the peasantry is not yet strong enough to achieve through unified effort a reformation of the ruling class in the country or to force the ruling circles to institute radical reforms in the interests of the peasant "lower classes."

As far as the objectively occurring process of capitalist development is concerned, the representatives of revolutionary democracy, and even some of the moderate representatives of the national bourgeoisie, support the free development of the national economy, unrestrained by semi-feudal landlords or foreign capital. The Communists in Asian countries believe that just such an economic development of the countryside, directed against the landlords and foreign capital, will provide the most favorable conditions for a class struggle for the next stage in the national liberation movement, when the peasants, together with and under the leadership of the working class, will go on to an independent national democratic state.

But is the choice of paths, methods, and forms of developing national capitalism the basic task of the working class and its Marxist-Leninist parties, when bourgeois agrarian reforms have not been completed in, for instance, such countries as India, Egypt, and Indonesia, not to mention Japan? It follows from the whole meaning of the Statement of the Congress of Representatives of Communist and Workers' Parties that the main task of progressive democratic parties is not determining the method of "constructing" national capitalism and choosing the better of the two theoretically possible paths for its development in agriculture in order to eliminate centuries-old backwardness in the country. This task existed sixty or seventy years ago in European countries and in Russia.

"The popular . . . masses are convinced that the best way to eliminate centuries-old backwardness and to improve their living conditions is the path of non-capitalist development. The people can be delivered from exploitation, poverty, and

218

hunger only by following this path. The working class and the broad peasant masses have been called upon to play the major role in solving this basic social issue." [13]

The main question in Asian countries is achieving the union of the working class and the peasantry, leadership over the peasantry, and winning the peasants over to the side of the workers in order to establish a progressive independent national democratic state that will provide the opportunities for serious preparatory work for the transition to a non-capitalist path of development.

More than fifteen years ago the Indian National Congress raised the slogan of the peasant movement, "Land to the tiller!" Objectively speaking, this slogan implies the transfer of land from the landlords to peasant ownership and is consequently the slogan of the radical agrarian revolution, the slogan of the revolutionary democrats.

The National Congress, however, is not a revolutionary democratic, but a bourgeois organization which includes liberal landlord elements. Why did they raise the slogan "Land to the tiller!"—the slogan of the revolutionary democrats? The National Congress had to use this slogan because it was put forward by the peasant unions; otherwise it would not have succeeded in maintaining its influence over the peasants. Subsequently, the National Congress was incapable of carrying out this slogan. The Legislative Assemblies of many states, in which the majority belongs to the Congress Party, in fact prevented its being carried out for more than a decade. The national bourgeoisie will support the radical slogan "Land to the tiller!" to the extent that it needs new social support in the rural areas to secure its political influence among the peasants, and to the extent that it is interested in expanding the domestic market and industrialization. But since it is tied to semi-feudal land ownership and is afraid of abolishing it and thereby establishing a precedent for the general liquidation of bourgeois property, it opposes the honest and consistent carrying out of its own slogan.

13. *Programmnyye dokumenty*, 67.

*The Third World in Soviet Perspective*

The dual nature of the national bourgeoisie is now apparent not only in its relationship to foreign capital and imperialism. Since the national bourgeoisie came into power, its dual nature has become apparent to an even greater extent than before in its policy with respect to the semi-feudal landlords. The instability of the national bourgeoisie in general consists in the fact that "along with its progressive nature, it tends to compromise with imperialism and feudalism." [14] This does not mean that the bourgeoisie carries out reforms exclusively in the interest of the landlords. To think so is not to understand either the bourgeois character or the political significance of the reforms carried out in these countries—to misunderstand the possibility of employing them to the advantage of the peasantry and the working class, against the landlords and the bourgeoisie.

The Marxist-Leninist parties in Asian countries do not support the "American" path of capitalist development as an alternative to the "Prussian" path. The non-capitalist path of development that is being followed in the day-to-day lives of hundreds of millions of peasants in the socialist countries of Asia is historically opposed to any path or form of capitalist development at the present time. Of course, the Communist parties in Eastern countries are fighting for a reduction of land rents and taxes, abolition of usury and feudal extortion, and establishment of a just maximum of land ownership as the starting point in land reform, but not because this will provide the opportunity for the free "American" path of capitalist development. They believe that just as an agrarian revolution from below, directed by the working class, inevitably paves the way for a non-capitalist path of economic development, so will the bourgeois reforms which are being carried out—independent of, or even in spite of, the will of their initiators—make it possible to organize the peasant masses on a broad scale to fight for an agrarian revolution and thereby will aid in its accomplishment.

In India and a number of other Asian countries, the period of purchasing land from the landlords has begun—a period

14. *Ibid.*, 67.

Soviet Writers on the Developing Areas

which is painful to the peasants. This is the period of direct realization of agrarian reform. The bourgeois form of land ownership, which has been known in Asia since the Europeans first penetrated that area and, as K. Marx observed, was virtually a caricature, is now getting an adequate economic foundation.

The parceled peasant and landlord property becomes bourgeois land property as soon as constant and variable capital [k] begins to function on the peasant and landlord farm—i.e., as soon as the kulak-farmer and the capitalist-landlord become established. Prior to this period, land property has a bourgeois form (private, inherited, alienated, put into economic circulation, deprived of any "noble" class status), but it still is not capitalist. The main feature of the majority of Asian countries is that the form of land property became more or less bourgeois a long time ago, when European domination was becoming established, but its content has remained pre-bourgeois. The appearance of constant and variable capital in agriculture in the colonies proceeded at a sluggish rate and capitalization did not so much affect the farm itself, its methods, its mode of production, or its agricultural technology, as it did the forms of land ownership and property—i.e., not the area of material production but the area of economic exchange. The postwar bourgeois reforms which have been carried out by the ruling circles attempt to bring the mode of agricultural production into greater agreement with the form of the ownership. The national bourgeoisie is thus maneuvering busily and is trying to find a compromise between the peasantry and the landlord class.

In connection with this, the peasant farm is increasingly becoming commodity-oriented: the class of agricultural workers is growing; differentiation among the peasantry is becoming deeper; capitalist agricultural productive forces are developing; a new agriculture is becoming established, which is to

k. "Constant capital" and "variable capital" are, respectively, the expenses for "means of production" (plant, raw materials, etc.) and wages. These, together with the surplus value, represent the "value" of commodities produced by the capitalist enterprise.

a considerable extent coming to replace the old. On the basis of all these factors the class struggle in the countryside is growing more intense.

Use of the capitalist land lease as a means of reforming feudal agriculture, which is so typical of Europe, previously found no extensive development in India or other Asian countries, although now it has increased markedly. The British latifundia could not obstruct the growth of farmer capitalism. The latter circumvented the former through extensive development of the capitalist land lease. The Russian latifundia, which were the basis of feudal remnants, strongly impeded the growth of peasant capitalism. With the passage of time they became the source of landlord-capitalist agricultural development, and peasant capitalism did not succeed in breaking them up. Peasant capitalism, which surged forward after the 1861 reform, gave rise to Stolypin's reform, a second set of bourgeois agrarian laws for the benefit of the capitalist agricultural entrepreneur. The reform was carried out in Russia not during the old feudal aristocratic monarchy, but during the bourgeois landlord's monarchy of 1907–1910, after the 1905–1906 revolution had been suppressed. The Russian landlords' latifundia were abolished and distributed for the peasantry by the proletarian socialist revolution of 1917. Victory of the British method of circumventing the latifundia by means of the capitalist lease is historically improbable in the Eastern countries. This would require expelling all peasants from their land and converting them into a proletariat. Capitalism in Asia also does not have the historical time needed for achieving victory by following the paths of Prussian or Stolypin reforms. The historical possibility of totally abolishing feudal remnants and instituting agrarian reforms in the interests of all peasants, under leadership of the working class, is becoming more imminent.

The essence of the class struggle that is taking place in the contemporary Asian countryside objectively consists not in the choice of one of two paths of capitalist development, but in the struggle between the capitalist and non-capitalist paths of development that reflects the struggle between two world systems. It is in this connection that all democratic and progressive forces in the Eastern countries, in conformity with the concrete situation in each of them, and in consideration of the national and historical peculiarities in the rural agrarian system, are waging an all-out struggle for realization of the agrarian reforms which have already been proclaimed. Organizing the peasantry, they are preparing it for truly radical agrarian reforms that will destroy all remnants of feudalism and clear the path for the free development of the rural areas on a completely new foundation.

# Land Relationships in the Countries of Africa *

## BY I. I. POTEKHIN

*IN the years since his article in praise of Stalin, Potekhin has risen to a position of great importance among Soviet scholars who deal with the third world. In the freer atmosphere of the Khrushchev era he has been able to travel abroad, make use of a broader range of data, and explore Marxist-Leninist theoretical problems that would have been forbidden in earlier years. In many ways, his development is typical of the change that has taken place in Soviet orientology over the past decade or so.*

*Potekhin reflects the general Soviet preoccupation with the enigmatic problems presented by the emerging forces in Africa —forces that require new categories of analysis if they are to be understood and exploited by Soviet policy. As he indicates, his article on agrarian relationships in Africa is more of a guide for further research than a definitive exploration of the subject; nevertheless, he does present a rather thorough exposition of the main problems and prospects. The role of the agrarian question is inevitably crucial in a continent where nearly all of the population is tied to the land. Its solution is basic to the entire question of the further development of Africa, particularly the establishment of a socialist society, whether on the Soviet or some other model.*

*Marxist writers are preoccupied with the question of the classes in African society, particularly in the primitive, almost undifferentiated, communal villages characteristic of much of the continent. Other articles by Potekhin explore other ramifications of the problem and outline the points at issue.[a] The*

*Source: "Pozemel'nyye otnosheniya v stranakh Afriki," NAIA, No. 3 (1962), 16–31.

a. For instance, "On 'African Socialism,'" International Affairs (Moscow), No. 1 (1963), 71–79.

*Soviet Writers on the Developing Areas*
one presented here provides the basis for a scientific (in the
Marxist sense) definition of the problem and its implica-
tions.

THE basic sphere of material production in all countries on
the African continent is agriculture. It is common knowledge
that all African countries except the Republic of South Africa
belong to the underdeveloped agrarian countries. It is impossible to define accurately the share of agricultural production in
the total annual output, since subsistence farming is predominant in these countries and there are practically no
statistical data available on this area of economics. In the
statistical tables that are available on this question, the position
of agricultural production is, as a rule, purposely lowered.
Data on the distribution of the population between the city
and the country can give some idea of the position of agriculture in the economics of African countries. Although a
considerable shift of the population from rural areas to the
cities has taken place during the last two decades, the rural
population in the various countries nevertheless constitutes
from 67 per cent (Egypt, 1957) to 96 per cent (Togo, 1956);
only in the Republic of South Africa is the urban population
approximately half (46.6 per cent, 1951) of the total population.[1]

The peasantry makes up the mass of direct producers in the
agriculture of African countries. The position of large capitalist
production in agricultural production is not high, and belongs
chiefly either to foreign companies or to European settlers.
Class differentiation of the peasantry in the great majority of
African countries is still scarcely noticeable. The agricultural
workers who have broken their connection with the land—the
proletarians—are not numerous. Land relationships are consequently directly related to the vital interests of the overwhelming majority of the population.

All African countries that have achieved political independence are confronted by the immediate problem of reconstruc-

1. United Nations, *Economic Survey of Africa Since 1950* (New York
1959), 14.

225

*The Third World in Soviet Perspective*
tion and the development of agriculture. The speed with which
this problem is solved depends to a great extent on the existing
land relationships, which can either hinder or help the development of agricultural production. Reconstruction and development of agriculture are organically related to the common task
of eliminating economic backwardness and economic dependence. Therefore, the question of providing the direct producer
(the peasant) with land, and the question of forms of land
ownership and land tenure, deserve the most careful study and
present extremely difficult problems. A complex interlacing of
different types of land ownership (public, communal, private)
and of land tenure is characteristic of Africa. The existing
literature does not provide an answer to many questions. The
present article is, therefore, only a first attempt to make general statements from the available material; it is a guideline
for research rather than its result.

## I

The question of providing the direct producer with land
has two different aspects. V. I. Lenin described the two types
of land monopolies as "The monopoly of land ownership based
on property rights, and the monopoly of farming on a given
piece of land."[2] The second type of monopoly means that all
of the land is occupied by farms, that the organization of new
farms or expansion of the area of the existing farms is impossible owing to the absence of free, unoccupied land. This type
of monopoly requires special study according to the specific
region involved. We will limit ourselves here only to general
observations.

If we take the African continent as a whole, the average
population density is eight persons per square kilometer. In
comparison with Europe this is not much; in France, for example, the population density is 80, and in England greater
than 200 per square kilometer. Average density, however, is
meaningless with respect to Africa. Egypt is an outstanding
example: the population density computed with respect to the

2. V. I. Lenin, *Sochineniya* [Collected Works], v, 104–5.

entire territory is 25 per square kilometer, while in the zone of the cultivated oasis it exceeds 700.

In Morocco, the agricultural reserves, including forests, pastures, and alfalfa land, occupy 48 per cent of the entire territory of the country; the remaining 52 per cent is still unsuitable for farming.[3] Farm lands in Algeria amount to 47 million hectares, roughly 20 per cent of the territory of the country, including 39 million hectares of meadows and pastures. Not more than 3 per cent of all the land in the country is cultivated.[4] In Libya only 15 million hectares of the total area of 175 million are considered productive lands, and only about half a million hectares can be used for cultivation at present.[5]

A study of the literature on this question reveals great confusion of such concepts as agricultural lands and agricultural resources, cultivated lands and lands suitable for cultivation; thus the statistical data on this question that are encountered in the literature demand a critical attitude, comparison, and checking. Great areas of the continent are covered by deserts, are boggy, or consist of impenetrable tropical forests. Considerable areas of many tropical countries are so infested with the tsetse fly that they are unsuitable for human habitation. In certain regions of Africa the limitations on land suitable for use are acute, but in most countries there is no dearth of such land. The areas under cultivation in tropical Africa amount to only a small per cent of the total land. We must also take into consideration the following conditions. Certain lands which are unsuitable for agriculture today may be made suitable tomorrow. For example, construction of the Aswan Dam, which is being accomplished with Soviet aid, will make it possible suddenly to increase the area of cultivated land in the UAR by

3. F. Joly, A. Ayache, J. Fardel, and L. Suech, *Geografiya Marokko* [Geography of Morocco] (Moscow 1951), 120.
4. N. A. Kravets, *Alzhir* [Algeria] (Appendix to the map "Algeria") (Moscow 1960), 2.
5. United Nations, Technical Assistance Administration, *A General Economic Appraisal of Libya*, prepared by John Lindberg (New York 1952), 1, 9.

*The Third World in Soviet Perspective*

one-third. Almost everywhere in tropical Africa a field rotation system predominates under which a considerable land area cannot be used for cultivation for many years; transition to a rational crop rotation system will make it possible to increase considerably the areas under cultivation.

The African peasantry suffers not so much from insufficiency of suitable land as from colonial enslavement and its remnants, which are far from eliminated in those countries that have already regained their state sovereignty. One of the manifestations of colonialism is inequality in the rights of land ownership. Here we come to another type of land monopoly—"the monopoly of land ownership based on property rights," which is the essence of land relationships.

## II

The colonization of Africa by European imperialist powers was accompanied by land expropriations, robbery of land from the African peasantry for the sake of the European settlers, miners, and plantation companies. The extent of land expropriations in various countries was determined by geographical and socio-economic factors, the nature of colonization, and the degree of resistance by the indigenous population. The peasantry of those countries which were converted into immigrant colonies suffered the most. This includes South Africa and, to a lesser degree, the English colonies in Central and Eastern Africa, the Portuguese colonies, and French colonies in North Africa.

In the Republic of South Africa, the European population (2.9 million people) amounts to about one-fifth of the total population (13.9 million in 1956). About one-fifth of the gainfully employed European population is engaged in agriculture (including lumber and fishing). Among the Europeans engaged in agricultural production we can find landowners, tenant farmers, farmhands with allotted land, and proletarians. A huge concentration of land in the hands of a small group of large landowners is typical of European land ownership; according to the data for 1947, 6 per cent of the landowners, each having more than 3,000 morgens,[6] owned 43 per cent of all land belonging to the Europeans. In addition there are many farmers with a small amount of land or no land at all.

The European colonists have occupied almost all the land, either by force or by deception. When the Union of South Africa was established (1910), only 7.83 per cent of all land in the country—the so-called reservations—was made available to the indigenous African population. At the present time, as a result of the transfer of part of the colonial reserve lands (the so-called "Crown lands") to the African peasants, and certain other measures, this percentage has risen to 12.[7] Huge masses of peasants were completely deprived of land; others, driven into the reservations, have been suffering from severe lack of land.

At the present time, the African peasantry in the Republic of South Africa is divided into four groups, according to the character of the land relationships. The first group comprises peasants on the reservations, in the vast majority of which communal land ownership is maintained (about half of the total population). The second group are peasants outside the reservations, on lands which are their collective or private property (about 6 per cent of the total rural African population). The third group are the peasants who live on the lands of missionary stations, on Crown lands, and on lands privately owned by Europeans, on which the owners themselves do no farming. These peasants lease land for monetary payment (about 5 per cent of the total African population). The fourth group are the peasants who live on farms and plantations belonging to Europeans. These as a rule are large capitalist farms, where the relationships of the capitalist hiring system are interwoven with the contract (*otrabochnyy*) labor system and pure compulsory labor. The typical figure on these farms is

6. A morgen equals 0.85 hectares (2.1 acres).
7. A. B. Davidson, "Apartkheyd—sistema rasovogo poraboshcheniya" [Apartheid—System of Race Enslavement], in the collection of articles, *Rasovaya diskriminatsiya v stranakh Afriki* [Race Discrimination in the African Countries] (Moscow 1960), 36;*Official Year Book of the Union of South Africa and Basutoland, Bechuanaland Protectorate and Swaziland, No. 2, 1948* (Pretoria 1950), 848.

the African hired hand with a land allotment. This group of Africans amounts to about 40 per cent of the total African rural population.[8]

Southern Rhodesia was supposed to become a settlers' colony like the Republic of South Africa, but there was no very large influx of settlers, so that the present population of European origin amounts to only 7.8 per cent of the total population (178 thousand out of 2,481 thousand in 1956). About 13 per cent of the gainfully employed European population is engaged in farming; there is no information available on its class composition. It is known that 7.7 per cent of European landowners control 52 per cent of the entire land area taken over by the Europeans. The average size of the land holdings of this group is more than 16,000 hectares. According to certain indirect indices, one may assume that poor farmers exist side by side with the owners of large capitalist farms.[9]

Lands of all categories that are allotted to the indigenous population of Southern Rhodesia amount to a little more than half of the total land area of the country. It is impossible to define statistically the extent to which the African peasants have been provided with land. It is necessary to consider first of all the farming value of the land. According to a report by the South Rhodesian investigator, B. Y. Mnyanda, the reservations "are absolutely unsuitable for purposes of settlement and providing food to the local inhabitants, since they lack water and productive lands and the soil is rocky and sandy." [10] The best lands have been taken by the Europeans. We must also take into account the fact that the majority of African peasants are still practicing the field rotation system of agriculture, which requires a great deal of land. African peasants are un-

8. For more details on agrarian relationships in the Union of South Africa, see I. I. Potekhin, *Formirovaniye natsional'noy obshchnosti yuzhnoafrikanskikh Bantu* [Formation of the National Community of the South African Bantu] (Moscow 1955), 122–38.

9. L. D. Yablochkov, "Korennoye naseleniye Britanskoy Tsentral'noy Afriki" [The Indigenous Population of British Central Africa], in *Afrikanskiy etnograficheskiy sbornik* [Ethnographic Handbook of Africa], II (Moscow 1958), 116.

10. B. Y. Mnyanda, *In Search of Truth* (Bombay 1954), 65, quoted in Yablochkov, 128.

Soviet Writers on the Developing Areas

able to feed themselves and their families on the lands available to them. The mass exodus into the cities and mining centers testifies to this. More than 200,000 Africans are working
on farms and plantations which belong to the Europeans. The
majority of Africans are living as hired hands with allotted
land.

Eloquent testimony concerning the African peasantry of
Southern Rhodesia has been published by United Nations
economists who have been studying the enlargement of the
exchange economy in tropical Africa: 38 per cent of the monetary income of the peasants is earned away from their own
farms.[11]

Thus two-thirds of the land in Southern Rhodesia, including the best land, has been taken by the Europeans. The bulk
of this land is concentrated in the hands of a small group of
extremely powerful landowners; only 3 per cent of the European privately owned lands is under cultivation. The lands
taken from the Africans are becoming deserted, the Africans
are suffering from a severe lack of land, and they are forced
to work for the European capitalists in order to eat.

Another region of the African continent where mass land
expropriations occurred is the Maghreb countries—Algeria,
Morocco, and Tunisia. The peasantry of Algeria, where
2,700,000 hectares of the best land belong to the European
companies and colonists, has suffered especially severely.[12]
The indigenous population is suffering from a severe lack of
land, and a significant number of Algerians have no land at all.
As early as 1946, as the colonial administration admits, about
one-half million families had no land. By 1956, the number of
landless peasant households grew to 625,000, about one-third
of the total indigenous population of the country. The landless peasants work on enterprises belonging to Europeans and
constitute a huge army of unemployed, some of whom emigrate
to France in search of work.

The French imperialists have justified their unwillingness

11. United Nations, *Enlargement of the Exchange Economy in Tropical Africa* (New York 1954), 26.
12. Larbi Buhali, "Algeria Belongs to the Algerians," *Problems of
Peace and Socialism* (Russian edn.), No. 2 (1958), 64.

231

*The Third World in Soviet Perspective*

to grant the Algerians the right to national self-determination by claiming that this would deliver a blow to the interests of the French colonists and landowners. It is known, however, that nine-tenths of the land taken from the Algerian peasants is concentrated in the hands of a small group of large landowners who have from 50 to 100 or more hectares; certain European estates reach from 3,000 to 5,000 hectares; and in certain farms belonging to the Europeans, up to 2,000 farm laborers are employed. Consequently, the problem here does not concern the interests of the colonists in general, but the interests of the large landowners.[13]

In Morocco, 1,000,000 hectares—one-fifteenth of all land suitable for cultivation—belonged to foreigners at the time of the Declaration of Independence and, considering only cultivated lands, the foreign share amounted to one-eighth. These are the best lands of the coastal regions, which belong mainly to large landowners (900 landowners possessed more than 300 hectares each; they owned 60 per cent of all the land taken by the Europeans).[14] In Tunisia in 1949, 25 per cent of all cultivable land belonged to the foreigners (760,000 out of 3,800,000 hectares).[15] In Libya, Italian colonists in 1949 owned 224,000 hectares of tillable land.[16] There is very little land suitable for agriculture in Libya, as 98 per cent of its territory is desert. The basic occupation of the population is cattle raising. At the present state of irrigation, agriculture is possible only on the coast and is mainly under the control of Italian colonists.

In tropical Africa, geographical conditions are less favorable for European settlers. Very little or none of the permanent European population is engaged in agriculture in these countries. An exception to this is Kenya, where the high moun-

13. *Polozheniye sel'skogo khozyaystva i krest'yantsva v koloniyakh i drugikh slaborazvitykh stranakh* [The Situation in Agriculture and the Peasantry in the Colonies and Other Underdeveloped Countries] (Moscow 1958), 80–82, 137–39.
14. A. Ayache, *Marokko, itogi odnoy kolonizatsii* [Morocco, Results of One Colonization] (Moscow 1958), 182.
15. N. A. Ivanov, *Sovremennyy Tunis* [Contemporary Tunisia] (Moscow 1959), 41.
16. United Nations, Technical Assistance Administration . . . , 10.

tainous region was extremely attractive to the European population. According to 1954 data, 46,000 Europeans were living in Kenya. Of the total land reserves, only 7 per cent belonged to the European colonists and companies, but one must bear in mind that a significant part of the territory of Kenya is totally unsuitable for human settlement. The lands which now belong to the Europeans are concentrated in the high mountainous region. The majority of the peasantry has become landless. The European landowners in Kenya are as a rule large farmers and plantation owners, who exploit the labor of the landless African peasants. There are a few extremely large estates (of 100,000 hectares or more each) that belong to plantation companies and private individuals.[17]

In the former Belgian Congo, 20,000,000 hectares of land, amounting to 9 per cent of the total territory, belongs to European colonists and companies. But these 20,000,000 hectares include the lands of the large agricultural concessions, where African peasants continue to live and farm as they did before. It is difficult to establish the amount of land which was expropriated for the Europeans. According to data for 1955, 2,865,000 hectares were used in agriculture, and 399,000 hectares—or 14 per cent—belonged to European companies and colonists.[18]

The extent of the European land ownership in the Portuguese colonies (Angola and Mozambique) is not clear. There are large European concessions, farms, and plantations. A significant number of African peasants have been deprived of land, although it is impossible to determine the actual extent to which this has occurred. There is no colony where there has not been land expropriation for the colonists, and there is no place where the African peasants have not been driven off their traditional lands. In certain colonies all lands were declared the property of the respective imperialist power.

17. For details on the land expropriations in Kenya, see R. N. Ismage-lova, "Narody Kenii v usloviyakh kolonial'nogo rezhima" [The Peoples of Kenya Under the Conditions of Colonial Rule], in *Afrikanskiy Etnograficheskiy Sbornik*, I (Moscow 1956), 118–219.

18. V. A. Martynov, *Kongo pod gnetom imperializma* [The Congo Under the Yoke of Imperialism] (Moscow 1959), 10.

## The Third World in Soviet Perspective

This gave the colonial powers a "legal" basis for expropriating any land at any time. In many colonies, however, especially in western Africa, the extent of land expropriation was very insignificant and did not result in any marked deprivation of land on the part of the peasants.

### III

Another type of land ownership is private feudal land ownership. Church and monastery lands are included here, since the conditions of direct producers' tenure on them do not differ essentially from the conditions of tenure on the landlords' holdings. In many regions of Africa, the relationships between European landowners and African peasants are very close to feudal relationships or even identical with them, but we have placed this category in the first type of land ownership. Here we are considering only lands that belong to African landowners. The region of distribution of this type of land holding comprises the Maghreb countries, Libya, Egypt, Ethiopia, and Uganda.

Before land reform was instituted in Egypt (1949 data) there were 2,706,000 Egyptian and 3.8 thousand foreign landowners. The latter owned 233,000 feddans (1 feddan = 0.42 hectares), or less than 3 per cent of the total land resources of the country. The mosque land amounted to 592,000 feddans, or 7 per cent of the total land resources. Of the total number of Egyptian landowners, 1,950,000—or 72 per cent—had less than one feddan of land each; only 15 per cent of all land resources belonged to them. The bulk of the land belonged to the landlords; among them were landowners who had more than 2,000 hectares each. The land-poor peasants who rented land from the landlord or worked on their estates were subjected to the most cruel exploitation, and became beggars.[19]

In Morocco, one-fourth of all cultivated land belongs to the large landowners who possess several hundreds or even thou-

19. A. Ayru, *Fellakhi Egipta* [Fellahin of Egypt] (Moscow 1954), 34–35.

sands of hectares,[20] while the landless peasant sharecroppers and farm workers constitute more than half the rural population (data for 1952).[21] In Algeria, the indigenous population possesses 7,672,000 hectares. Of these, 24 per cent belongs to small landowners (the average size of their holdings is 4.7 hectares), who constitute 74 per cent of the total number of landowners, while 21 per cent belongs to landowners who have on the average 282 hectares and together constitute only 1 per cent of all landowners.[22]

One cannot establish the general dimensions of the landlords' holdings in Tunisia. There are landlords owning from four to five thousand hectares. Before independence was declared, 1,600,000 hectares of land belonged to Moslem religious institutions (the so-called *qabus* lands).[23] On the eve of World War II, in a rural population of 1.8 million, more than a million were landless peasants and farm workers.[24] In 1956, 80 per cent of the peasants had no land.[25]

Ethiopia is a country with a large, feudal land-ownership system. There are no agrarian statistics for Ethiopia, so it is impossible to express the land relationships by any quantitative values. In theory, all of the land is the emperor's property, while in fact a large part of it belongs to feudal aristocrats and monasteries.

In Buganda, feudal land ownership was established by the English colonists. In 1900 they made a protectorate agreement with the Kabaka, the feudal ruler of Buganda. According to this agreement, the Kabaka obtained 100,000 hectares of land as his own property; his mother, 4,000 hectares; four princes, 2,000

20. Ayache, 364.
21. N. S. Lutskaya, *Marokko vnov' obretayet nezavisimost'* [Morocco Regains Her Independence] (Moscow 1958), 42.
22. *Cahiers Internationaux*, No. 64 (1954), 48.
23. *La Tunisie en travail* (Publication du secrétariat d'état à l'information du gouvernement Tunisien) (1960), 80. N. A. Ivanov's book, *Sovremennyy Tunis*, gives another figure for the Mosque lands—700,000 hectares (p. 43).
24. Ivanov, 45.
25. R. A. Ul'yanovskiy, "Agrarnyye reformy v stranakh Azii" [Agrarian Reforms in Asian Countries], PV, No. 1 (1961), 16.

## The Third World in Soviet Perspective

hectares each; and his remaining relatives together obtained about 25,000 hectares. The ministers and deputies of the Kabaka obtained large estates as personal property and as temporary holdings. Now 230 large landowners have in their possession almost three-fourths of all land resources in the country. The majority of the peasants have been deprived of land rights and have become tenants.[26] There is much in common between the European and the African private feudal types of land ownership; in both cases the direct producer is deprived of the right to land ownership and gives the landowner part of his labor, in money or in kind, for the right to use the land. There are substantial differences between these types of land ownership. Their origins are different. European land ownership was a direct result of the establishment of a colonial regime. The ownership of land by landlords arose before the period of colonization (except in Buganda) as a result of the elemental historical development of the particular society. It is connected with colonialism only insofar as the colonial authorities granted rights and privileges to the landowners over the masses of people exploited by them, and the landowners in turn served as the social support of the colonists. European land ownership is basically bourgeois, while the native landlords' ownership of land is feudal. They also differ in means of elimination. European land ownership can be eliminated through the victory of an anti-imperialist revolution, in which local landlords sometimes participate. The elimination of land possession by local landlords depends on an anti-feudal revolution.

### IV

The third type of land ownership is state feudal land ownership. Its most characteristic feature is the coincidence of rent with taxes, when the direct producer pays no rent except taxes.[27] It is very difficult to define the regions of distribution of this type of ownership, owing to the presence of a multiplicity of transitional forms from communal land owner-

26. *Narody Afriki* [Peoples of Africa] (Moscow 1954), 446.
27. See K. Marx, *Kapital* (Russian edn., 1955), III, 804.

Soviet Writers on the Developing Areas

ship to feudal, and from state to private land ownership.[b] The most typical example of state feudal land ownership is found in the Muslim emirates in Northern Nigeria. The English colonists considered Nigeria a model of the policy of "indirect rule." Before the colonial regime was established, several feudal principalities existed there. The majority of them offered the English colonists no resistance. The feudal sovereigns willingly accepted English protection and the British government guaranteed to defend their rights and privileges. A political union was established between English imperialism and the African feudalists in order to exploit the masses jointly. Where feudal states had not yet been formed, the feudal princes and tribal leaders became the control channels of English colonial policy and an integral part of the English colonial administration. In accordance with English colonial legislation, they were called "native authorities." The Governor General of Nigeria, Lugard, who created the system of indirect rule in Nigeria, stated: "There are not two categories of rulers—British and native—working separately or together; there is only one government, in which the native authorities have specifically designated duties and a recognized status equal to the British civil servants."[28]

There existed 119 "native authorities" in Northern Nigeria before independence was declared. One of them had two and a half million subjects (Kano Emirate); others had only a few thousand each. Let us take the Kano Emirate as an example. The emir stood at the head of the emirate. In theory, the emir was elected, but, in the first place, only members of the ruling family (eldest son, brother, etc.) were eligible for candidacy to the post; and, secondly, the members of the electoral college were appointed by the emir himself with the approval of the British Resident. In essence, he is a hereditary feudal sovereign. The emirate was divided into 24 districts; the heads

b. "State feudalism" is a Leninist euphemism for the "oriental mode of production." (See above, pp. 2 and 190, note b; and Wittfogel, 394.) The sort of thing Potekhin is describing fits rather well into the "oriental" pattern, but he is of course not able to discuss it in Marx's terms.

28. From R. L. Buell, *The Native Problem in Africa*, i (New York [1928]), 688.

of the district were appointed by the emir: in 1951, 13 of them were members of the emir's family.[29] The emir had all the attributes of state authority: police, courts, prisons, and a budget. In relation to his subjects, he was the sovereign ruler; in relation to the British governor, he was a puppet who unquestioningly carried out British orders.

Until the colonial regime was established, the emir was considered the supreme owner of all land. The cultivated lands were under the hereditary control of the direct producers—the peasants. The free land, of which there was much, was owned by the emir himself or by the smaller feudals and vassals subordinate to him. The peasants were obligated to pay the emir a tax called an *ushur*, or tithe. The tax system included other requisitions in addition to the tithe. This was a rent-tax.

When England established its colonial regime, she proclaimed all lands in Northern Nigeria the property of the English Crown, but continued the emir's rights and privileges connected with the land. As before, he owned the land and collected a rent-tax, but now he had to share it with the English authorities, allocating from one-fourth to one-half of his revenue as income for the central colonial budget. From the economic and legal point of view, this meant that English imperialism became the feudal owner of all the land, a suzerain, and the emir its vassal—i.e., the British imperialists became co-participants in a typically feudal form of exploitation.

A similar system was formed in Western Nigeria, in Barotseland (Northern Rhodesia),[30] and in certain French colonies of tropical Africa (Upper Volta, the northern region of the Cameroons). As has already been pointed out, it is very difficult to define by region the distribution of this type of land

29. In 1951, the year when the book by Lord Hailey, *Native Administration in the British African Colonies,* Part III (London), was published. The description of the emirate was taken from this.

30. On feudal relationships in Barotseland, see I. A. Svanidze, "Sel'-skoye khozyaystvo i pozemel'nyye otnosheniya u naroda barotse" [Agriculture and Land Relationships Among the Barots], *Sovetskaya Etnografiya* [Soviet Ethnography], No. 5 (1961).

ownership. With certain limitations, we can include all lands whose direct management has been transferred to the tribal leaders by the colonial powers.

The level of socio-economic development of the peoples of tropical and southern Africa in the precolonial period is far from completely explained. The specific characteristics of the historical development of the African peoples (the slave trade and so forth) engendered certain peculiar forms of transition from a preclass to a class society that are still not completely clear.[c] Attempts to apply European concepts familiar to us do not yield reliable results. It is necessary to do considerable research on the precolonial period in the history of individual peoples and countries, since the absence of an accurate picture of the level of socio-economic development of the peoples of Africa deprives the researcher of the opportunity to understand correctly the influence of the colonial regime on the development of land relationships.

As a rule, we can assume that, with the permission and under the patronage of colonial authorities, the tribal leaders (whether traditional or appointed is not particularly relevant in this case) had in fact at their disposal the land which had not been expropriated for the use of the Europeans. The forms and methods of exercising the leaders' authority over the land were extremely varied, and differed not only from one colony to another, but according to the various regions and tribes in a single colony. In spite of this great variety, it can generally be said that the tribal leaders utilized their authority over the land to enrich themselves and exploit their fellow tribesmen. In addition to collecting the tax established by the colonial authorities, they sometimes obtained a feudal rent in labor, in kind, or in money; in other cases, the tax was the sole form of rent. In all cases the colonial powers participated in dividing the feudal tribute taken from the peasants—i.e., they assumed

c. In Marxist terms, primitive societies, with no systems of ownership of private property, have no classes. Classes exist only in exploiting societies (slavery, feudalism, capitalism) and will disappear again when private property becomes anachronistic and ceases under the conditions of complete communism.

the role of the feudal landowner; from this standpoint, it is
irrelevant whether or not the land was formally declared the
property of a colonial power.

V

In almost all African countries (Egypt is probably the only
exception), communal land ownership continues to prevail.
Communal land ownership does not itself determine the mode
of production in agriculture, since it exists in the primitive
communal structure, in slave-owning and feudal societies, and
even in the initial stages of capitalism. For the capitalist mode
of production, however, it is not communal but private bourgeois land ownership which is characteristic. "The forms in
which the emerging capitalist mode of production finds land
property," K. Marx noted in *Das Kapital*, "does not correspond
to this mode. The corresponding form is first created by capitalism itself through subjugation of agriculture to capital; in this
manner, feudal land property, clan property, and small peasant
property, together with the agricultural communes, are converted into an economic form corresponding to this mode of
production, no matter how their legal forms may vary." [31]
   The fate of African communal agriculture depends upon
which path of development the countries of Africa will follow
—capitalist or non-capitalist. The mere presence of communal
agriculture does not solve this problem, although the degree
of preservation or decomposition of agricultural communal relationships can exert a substantial influence on this solution.
Karl Marx wrote that the dualism of the rural commune—the
collective ownership of land and private production on it—
"allows an alternative: either the proprietary principle will
gain the upper hand over the collective principle, or the latter
will gain the upper hand over the former." [32]
   If we examine the tendency in the development of African
peasant farming on communal land during the last decade, we
can reach a specific conclusion: the proprietary principle has

31. K. Marx, *Kapital*, III, 630.
32. K. Marx, F. Engels, *Sochineniya* [Collected Works] (Russian
edn.), XXVII, 695.

## Soviet Writers on the Developing Areas

gained the upper hand over the collective principle. This is demonstrated by the growth of social differentiation among the peasantry and the appearance of capitalist elements, in the development of mortgages and rent, and the involvement of land in commodity exchange. What is important, however, is something else: how far has this decomposition of the peasantry and the separation of land ownership from land use gone? It is difficult to answer this question, owing to the imperfection or the total lack of statistics, not only on Africa as a whole, but also on the individual countries. Therefore, the bases for judgment are irregular, partially chance data and indirect indices.

Commodity [d] and monetary relationships have deeply penetrated the African countryside. Here we must take into account the following circumstances. First of all, the mean annual monetary income per capita is still extremely low in the countryside. According to the calculations of United Nations economists for the beginning of the 1950's, even in the Gold Coast, where the commodity and monetary relationships have developed to a greater extent than in any other country of tropical Africa, it was still only $45; [33] if an average family consists of five people, this amounts to $225 per year per family. The earnings of a farm worker on enterprises belonging to the colonial authorities in 1953 to 1954 varied from 4s 3d to 4s 9d a day,[34] which amounts to about £70, or $200 a year. The average peasant family had a monetary income equal to the earnings of a farmhand. This average income does not include property differentiation. It is obvious that the monetary income of the absolute majority of the peasants (without considering the goods produced and consumed on the farm) is considerably less than the earnings of a farmhand.

Secondly, we must consider the uneven development of the commodity and monetary relationships among the countries. According to the same calculations by the United Nations

d. For the definition of "commodity," see above, p. 157, note b.
33. United Nations, *Enlargement of the Exchange Economy*, 26.
34. Gold Coast Government, *Report of the Ministry of Labour for the Year 1953–1954* (Accra 1955), 25.

241

economists, the average annual monetary income of the peasants in the countries of French Equatorial Africa amounted to only $6, to $8 in Kenya, and to $9 in Tanganyika. Thus great masses of the African peasantry are still hardly affected by the development of commodity and monetary relationships.

Finally, in analyzing the monetary incomes of the African peasantry, we must make a strict distinction between income from selling one's own agricultural produce and income from side earnings—i.e., money which is brought back from seasonal work in the cities. Here we encounter surprising facts. According to the same United Nations economists' calculations, 95 per cent of the monetary income of the peasants in Northern Rhodesia was from these seasonal earnings;[35] the earnings of seasonal workers in Southern Rhodesia was 78 per cent of the peasants' monetary income, 73 per cent in Kenya, 55 per cent in the Belgian Congo, etc. The growth of monetary incomes in the African countryside, therefore, cannot be considered an index of the development of commodity relationships on the peasant farm. The farm can remain on a subsistence economy, but in the family there may be money which has been earned on the side.

There is no doubt that in the African rural commune there is a stratum of planters and rich peasants who are farming on capitalist terms. It is these who control the bulk of commodity production. It is scarcely possible to speak of the African peasantry as a homogeneous mass without class differentiations. Such a peasantry no longer exists in Africa. Nevertheless, it is indisputable that the economy of the mass of peasants in the majority of African countries still remains basically self-sufficient and that the great majority are small peasants, for whom a beggarly, half-starved existence is typical.

The development of commodity and monetary relationships and the appearance of capitalist elements cannot but be reflected in the norms of land ownership, but the basic break

35. This figure agrees with the official evaluation of the distribution of national income in Northern Rhodesia for 1959: the monetary income of the peasants from the sale of agricultural products amounted to 5.3 per cent. *National Accounts of the Federation of Rhodesia and Nyasaland, 1954–1959* (Salisbury 1960).

in the communal order has not yet occurred; the bulk of the land still remains the collective property of the peasant commune.

There is a great variety of land tenure patterns in the communes. This variety is determined by a number of geographic and social factors: population density, the nature of the crops that are cultivated, the degree of preservation of family relationships, the degree of development of commodity, monetary, and capitalist relationships, and so forth.

In many regions the "free" form of land tenure is retained in which peasants can till any parcel of land after soliciting permission from the village elder or the eldest member of the family unit. Here there is still not the differentiation or redistribution of land allotments that is characteristic of classical communal land tenure. Not too long ago such a pattern was characteristic of the majority of tropical African areas. The break-up of this pattern was in some cases caused by an increase in population density; in some cases, by the introduction of perennial export crops; in others, by both.

Typical communal patterns with a regular redistribution of land allotments are rarely encountered. In heavily populated regions the communal authorities regulate the distribution of cultivated land in one way or another, but there are no periodically redistributed allotments. It seems that the community lands are redistributed at specific time intervals only in Ethiopia. In the majority of the countries there is a direct transition from a "free" form of land tenure to conversion of cultivated sections into hereditary holdings.

Perennial crops, which have become widespread during the last decades, play a significant role in this transition. The planting of perennial crops (cocoa, coffee, and others) has naturally converted the sections of the land devoted to them into hereditary holdings. This is one of the many ways of converting communal land into private property. According to customary law, the owner of such a section uses it throughout his life and hands it down to his heirs, but he cannot sell it. He can, however, sell the trees which he has grown on his section of land. Here the economic element of the arrange-

243

ment comes into contradiction with the law and gradually undermines it. Another way of converting communal land into private property is the development of suburban farming. This, as a rule, is intensive farming; sections of land are fertilized and cultivated annually. Here the provisions of customary law are powerless before the economic laws of capitalism: these sections of lands are bought and sold. Many different limitations are still maintained: almost always the permission of the village elders, the eldest of the family group, and sometimes the agreement of all kinsmen is required; in many regions it is forbidden to sell the land to non-members of the communal group. The ruling group in the tribe opposes the purchase and sale of the lands, which would undermine the economic basis of its domination over the tribal members. The colonial legislation did not recognize any land transactions involving communal land until very recently. It is only in recent years that the colonial authorities have considered it necessary to make some concessions to the capitalist stratum of the African countryside.

## VI

In several countries, private peasant land ownership has already spread widely. In Egypt this is the predominant form of land ownership. In the Maghreb countries, in Ethiopia and in the northern part of the Sudan, there are a large number of peasants who own land under rights of private ownership. There is private peasant land ownership in the countries of tropical and south Africa. The courses of development of private peasant land ownership vary. In the Republic of South Africa, before the land law was passed in 1913, the African peasants had the right to buy land from the Boers and British landowners—i.e., essentially to buy back the land which was taken away from them by the colonists. A certain number of Africans took advantage of this right and now these lands amount to about 5 per cent of the available land in the country. Land is sold to African peasants in Southern Rhodesia, Nyasaland, and Kenya. By 1930 a law was issued in Southern Rhodesia (the Land Apportionment Act, No. 30 of 1930;

*Soviet Writers on the Developing Areas*
amended in 1941 and 1959), according to which a special
amount of land was apportioned (about 2,000,000 hectares)
for sale to the Africans. By the end of 1950, the Africans had
purchased 2,637 sections, averaging 88 hectares in size.[36] In
1955 African owners who possessed sections of land outside
of the reservations numbered about 5,000, each owning about
70 hectares of land. This, however, is still not complete ownership.

Another way of forming private peasant land ownership is
the forceful violation of the commune by the colonial authorities. In some reservations in the Republic of South Africa,
all arable land was divided into very small sections and transferred to peasant ownership under specific conditions. The
forceful violation of the commune is occurring at present in
Southern Rhodesia and Kenya. In 1951 a law was issued in
Southern Rhodesia (Native Land Husbandry Act of 1951), according to which the parcels of land on the reservations must
gradually be allotted to those who till them.[37] These are
countries where there are European colonists and where, consequently, mass deprivation of the peasants' land has occurred.
The colonial authorities have actively interfered in the land
relationships in order to alleviate somewhat the acute agrarian
crisis. In those countries where there was no mass dispossession
of the African peasantry from the land—and this means the
majority of the countries—the colonial authorities hardly interfered in the land affairs of the indigenous population. In these
countries, however, attempts were also made to transfer land
from communal to private ownership.

In the French colonies a registration system was established
by a 1906 law: the peasant could obtain a certificate (*matri-
cule*) for the section of land he tilled and thus make it his
own property, but few people wished to take advantage of this
right.[38] Private peasant ownership of land has been introduced in the irrigated lands of the upper delta of the Niger
River, where the French government organization, *Office du*

36. Lord Hailey, *An African Survey* (London 1957), 779–80.
37. *Ibid.*, 780–81.
38. See *Narody Afriki*, 309.

245

*Niger*,[39] was in control. This organization has now been nationalized by the government of the Republic of Mali. Similar attempts were made by the Belgian authorities in the Congo, where the so-called *paysannat* system was introduced. On January 1, 1955, 135,000 sections of land were distributed to the Congolese peasants.[40]

It should be noted that the peasant ownership of land was almost nowhere complete ownership, as the colonial authorities used various means to limit the disposal of land transferred to African peasant ownership. The objectives of the colonial authorities were well defined: to intensify peasant farming, increase the production of raw materials while keeping the peasant in check, inhibit the free development of capitalist relationships, and not allow the old precapitalist relationships to be broken.

Private peasant land ownership is found in all African countries. It is impossible to determine its extent, although we can positively assert that this type of land ownership has not yet become significantly widespread.

### VII

Such in general outline is the extremely variegated and complex picture of land relationships in African countries. In practice it is even more complex. In nearly every country, along with the peasants who use the communal land, there are peasants who are complete landowners, part landowners, lessees of public lands, lessees of privately owned lands, sharecroppers, farm workers with allotted land. Land relationships are incredibly confused and must be decisively cleared up.

The multitude of forms of land ownership naturally predetermines the variety of means of solving the land question—i.e., the content of agrarian reforms. The most feasible solution of the agrarian question for the Republic of South Africa was formulated in the Charter of Freedom adopted by the Congress of the Peoples of South Africa in June 1955: "The land must be distributed among those who cultivate it."

39. Lord Hailey, 798.
40. For more details, see Martynov, 104–5, and Lord Hailey, 799–800.

## Soviet Writers on the Developing Areas

This applies to Southern Rhodesia, Kenya, and in general all countries where large-scale European land ownership exists. Imperialist propaganda is attempting to convince public opinion that such a solution of the problem will affect the interests of the entire European population of those countries. Actually it affects the interests of only a small group of large landowners. The slogan advanced by the Congress of the Peoples of South Africa is completely in line with the interests of the working sector of the population of European origin.

Progressive forces on the African continent are supporting the elimination of private feudal land ownership and the transfer of landlords' lands to the peasants who are the direct producers. The governments of many African states have already initiated this. In Egypt the first law on agrarian reform was issued in 1952. According to this law, the landowner could have no more than 200 feddans. Any surplus above this maximum was purchased by the government and was put into a fund for distribution among the landless and land-poor peasants. Two hundred feddans (84 hectares) of irrigated land is a considerable amount, considering that the landless peasants were receiving from 2 to 5 feddans. The Agrarian Reform Law of 1952 did not eliminate landlord land ownership; it was called a law for restricting land ownership. In addition, purchase money became a heavy burden on the peasantry.[41] In 1961 the government of the UAR took a further step in this direction: the maximum size of the land holding was established at 100 feddans. The purchase money was reduced.[42] This substantially alleviated the condition of the peasantry and undermined the landlords' land ownership, which, however, still persists.

In Tunisia a number of measures have been taken which are aimed at alleviating land hunger. After the overthrow of the monarchy, the large land holdings of the beys and certain feudals who had cooperated with the colonizers were confiscated. As in Egypt, a landholding maximum (50 hectares)

41. See D. Warriner, *Zemel'nyye reformy v stranakh Blizhnego Vostoka, Egipet, Siriya, Iran* [Land Reforms in the Countries of the Near East, Egypt, Syria, Iran] (Moscow 1958).
42. See *Pravda*, August 15, 1961.

*The Third World in Soviet Perspective*

was established and surplus land was subjected to nationalization. The mosque lands were eliminated; the government became responsible for maintenance of religious institutions through the state budget. The government of Tunisia is gradually buying up the lands of the French colonists.[43]

As yet, no substantial agrarian reforms are being undertaken in Morocco. The estates of the traitors who collaborated with the colonists were confiscated, and a certain number of landless peasants obtained land. A law was adopted for returning to the Moroccan peasants 40,000 hectares of land which belonged to French landowners. Projects are under way for developing new lands, and this will, to some extent, alleviate land hunger.[44] Little has been done toward reforming agrarian relationships in Ethiopia. In 1947 a progressive land tax was introduced, varying according to the size and productivity of the land sections. Certain feudal landlords were forced to transfer part of their uncultivated land to the state. Small sections of public lands were allocated to those who took an active part in the war of liberation against the Italian colonists. A certain part of the peasants are migrating from the central provinces into Kaffa province (the coffee plantation region), where they are receiving sections of land in hereditary tenure.

Land reforms in various countries are taking place in various ways, but nowhere are they complete. Even in Egypt, where land reform is most consistent, land holdings of 100 feddans are maintained by the landlords, while a significant number of peasants either have no land at all or possess sections of less than one feddan. In the interest of developing productive forces, a radical restructuring of land relationships and a determined elimination of the medieval feudal land ownership system are required. "It is necessary," V. I. Lenin said, "to clear the land of all this medieval trash."[45]

43. See *La Tunisie en travail*, 87; *Pravda*, March 20, 1958, November 17, 1959.
44. See *Pravda*, March 3, 1958; *Izvestiya*, March 3, 1958; *Novoye Vremya* [New Times], No. 36 (1959).
45. V. I. Lenin, *Sochineniya*, xiii, 389.

## Soviet Writers on the Developing Areas

In those countries where state feudal land ownership exists, the solution of the agrarian question coincides, in the opinion of progressive forces, with the problem of democratization of the social and state system. The rent tax, which has gone into the treasury of the emirs, sultans, and other feudal leaders, must go into the budget of a democratically elected government to be used, not for the upkeep of a feudal aristocracy, but to increase the people's welfare. In certain countries— for example, Nigeria—the people have already begun moving toward such a solution. But this is not all. State feudal land ownership is generally combined with the private land ownership of the feudal leaders; as the supreme possessor of all state land, any feudal leader has a rather significant amount of land as his own private property. Democratization of the state system must, as progressive African public opinion maintains, be accompanied by nationalization of the personal possessions of the feudal lords and elimination of the middleman in the collection of rent.

What can be the fate of communal land ownership? The following solutions are possible: maintenance of the communal land ownership system or a transition to private peasant ownership. Bourgeois economists insist on the second solution, elimination of the land commune and transfer of the land to the private ownership of the peasants. Thus the economic mission of the International Bank for Reconstruction and Development, which worked in Tanganyika in 1959 and 1960, supported elimination of the commune and even worked out recommendations on how to accomplish the transfer from communal land ownership to private peasant land ownership.

Such a solution to the question is in line with the interests of capitalist development which the bourgeois economists are defending. For the majority of the peasants, such a path signifies dispossession and final ruin. Even the above-mentioned economic mission does not conceal the fact that the transition to private land ownership will involve, "in the final analysis, concentration of land in the hands of the

wealthy, and the emergence of a landless class." [46] This path
leads to rapid and profound class differentiation of the peasantry, the emergence of rich farmers, and the conversion of the
basic mass of the peasantry into landless farmhands.

Many state and political officials of Africa have come out
in favor of preserving communal land ownership, and oppose the introduction of private land ownership. Sékou Touré,
at a meeting with representatives of the press in Moscow on
November 21, 1959, said: "The land is the property of the
nation. . . . In our country the right exists to exploit the
land but no longer does the right exist to own the land, which
is the national property." [47] Kwane Nkrumah, at the First
Conference of the Peoples of Africa in 1958, said: "In the vast
rural areas of Africa, the people maintain communal land
ownership. . . . These characteristic features still predominate in African society, and on this basis, we must bring to life
a more modern, socialist society."

The peasant agrarian commune is not a necessary prerequisite to the socialist path of development, but under
certain conditions the maintenance of communal land ownership can facilitate making the peasant farms into cooperatives
and thus aid the transition to socialism. In many countries of
Africa, however, the land commune at the present time serves
as a cover for semi-feudal exploitation of the peasantry by
the aristocratic leaders who are their kinsmen. Thus many
members of the national liberation movement feel that, for the
peasant community to play a progressive role, it must be freed
of all medieval remnants. Control of communal affairs and the
allocation of land must be in the hands of the commune, in
the hands of democratic self-government.

The governments of the young African states have not yet
determined their own attitude toward the communal question. There is still no appropriate legislation. The only exception is the Republic of Guinea, whose government has for-

46. *The Economic Development of Tanganyika*, Report of a Mission
Organized by the International Bank for Reconstruction and Development (Baltimore 1961), 95.
47. Sékou Touré, *Independent Guinea: Articles and Speeches* (Russian edn., Moscow 1960), 168.

bidden all land transactions. The future will tell what solutions the governments of other states will adopt.

Agrarian reform programs differ in various countries. In spite of the variety of programs, the goal is the same—to eliminate the old land relationships, which are basically medieval, to adapt them to new conditions and new tasks. As the basis of land reforms, the progressive forces in the African countries are making demands for a solution of the basic historical task—elimination of the backwardness caused by colonialism—as soon as possible.

SELECTION 12

# Some Problems of the Establishment of National States in the Independent African Countries *

## BY YU. A. YUDIN

*IN all of the ex-colonial areas, one of the greatest obstacles facing the Soviet Union is the persistent influence of Western political models. Although the Soviet Union has not been tarred by the brush of imperialism (Hungary and Uzbekistan are very far away from the Congo), it also does not have the history of contact and influence that the former metropoles— and even the United States—enjoy. These persisting influences must be broken if the Soviets are to make headway in infiltrating the third world.*

*Perhaps the weakest link in this pattern of Western influence is Black Africa, where the Western economic and political presence was spread rather thin and lasted for only a relatively short time. The Africans now seem to be particularly intent on finding new ways to express their "African personality," and although the Soviets cannot but look askance at some of these attempts—such as "African socialism," "African unity," or non-Communist single-party systems—they seem to be willing to endorse them as means of reducing the residual Western influence.*

*Yudin's article fits well into this approach. His entire argumentation is derived from radical African spokesmen and he heartily endorses their anti-imperialist allegations—in which Africans take second place to nobody, Russians included. He avoids homilies on stability and responsibility—rarely absent from Western writings—and thereby flatters the Africans, who understandably resent being told that they lack the maturity*

---

* SOURCE: "Nekotoryye problemy stanovleniya natsional'noy gosudarstvennosti v nezavisimykh stranakh Afriki," *Sovetskoye Gosudarstvo i Pravo* [Soviet State and Law], No. 2 (1961), 35–47.

## Soviet Writers on the Developing Areas

to develop their own governmental systems or to govern themselves effectively at all. There is an almost complete absence of Marxist theorizing (which is anyway hardly applicable to Africa) and only at the end and somewhat parenthetically does Yudin refer to the possibility of Africa developing along the lines of the Soviet "national democracy" model.

In the absence of any significant Communist parties in Black Africa, the Soviets have placed their bets on African radicalism, which may not show much inclination toward Soviet-style communism but does provide a vehicle for the undermining of the positions of the Western powers. The Soviets are not unreservedly in favor of African unity, but, as revealed in this article, they are willing to support the idea as propounded by the African radicals. In particular, they recognize that the many problems and instabilities arising from the often arbitrary political boundaries of Africa provide a fertile field for exploiting anti-imperialist sentiments. It is an inexpensive and potentially powerful tool for tarnishing still further the image of the former metropoles and undercutting the precarious structures that the colonial powers left behind in Africa.

ONE of the most important characteristics of the contemporary era is the stormy disintegration of the colonial system of imperialism. In the fifteen postwar years, about forty new sovereign states have appeared in Asia and Africa. A front of active struggle for full national liberation has opened in Latin America. "The fall of the system of colonial slavery under the attack of the national liberation movement," the Statement of the Conference of the Representatives of Communist and Workers' Parties points out, "is second in its historical significance only to the formation of the world socialist system." [1]

The time is approaching when the shameful colonial system will be completely eliminated. The successes of the national liberation movement in Africa are testimony of this. In 1960 alone, seventeen national states of African peoples

1. *Pravda*, December 6, 1960. [The reference is to the 1960 Moscow Statement—TPT.]

253

## The Third World in Soviet Perspective

arose on the ruins of colonial empires. Three-fourths of the population of the huge continent—about 180 million people—were liberated from colonial slavery.

The achievement of political independence by the African peoples and the establishment of national states in place of the former colonies are the result of the victory of the national liberation revolution which is now spreading on the African continent. The essence of this revolution is the transfer of power from the hands of the colonial imperialist bourgeoisie to the hands of national forces in the colonies. The forms of this transfer and the paths to independence are determined by the concrete conditions in each country. Whatever these forms may be, peaceful or violent, political independence is won through the lengthy and persistent struggle of colonial peoples, and in no way as a result of the voluntary relinquishment of rule by the colonizers.

The existence of the world socialist system and the weakening of the positions of imperialism gave the peoples of the colonies new opportunities for achieving independence. As the experience of a number of countries (Ghana, Guinea, Nigeria, *et al.*) shows, the African peoples can now attain political independence by peaceful, constitutional means. But this in no way excludes other paths for achieving independence. "Since the colonizers themselves are not giving up their positions," N. S. Khrushchev noted, "the peoples of the enslaved countries are rising to the struggle to throw the colonizers out of their countries. If necessary, they do not stop short of winning their freedom and independence with weapons in their hands." [2] Algeria—where the people are already in the seventh year of a just liberation war against the French colonizers—is not the only example of this. Heroic pages of the national liberation movement of the last decade are: the uprising of the Malgasy people in 1947, the armed struggle of the Tunisian and Moroccan peoples in 1953–1954, the liberation war of the Kenyans in 1952–1955, and the uprising of the people of Nyasaland in 1959. At the opening of the Second All-African Peoples' Conference in January 1960, Tunisian

2. *Ibid.*, October 21, 1960.

254

## Soviet Writers on the Developing Areas

President H. Bourguiba said, "All paths leading to it [free-dom] are justified because the choice does not always depend on Africans: one country travels a tortuous path through a series of stages, and another attains independence by force of arms; one path of struggle is just as good as another." [3]

In contemporary conditions, the imperialist powers have set themselves two basic aims: first, by all means to attempt to hold back the process of disintegration of colonial empires in Africa; and second, to keep the leadership of the transition of the African people from colonial slavery to independence in their own hands in order to maintain their political and economic positions in the liberated countries. In other words, clutching the old forms of colonial rule, imperialists "strive desperately to preserve colonial exploitation of the former colonies by new methods and in new forms." [4] This is why they so violently oppose the demand of colonial peoples for the rapid granting of independence that was raised in the Declaration on the Granting of Independence to Colonial Countries and Peoples, adopted in December 1960 by the 15th session of the UN General Assembly. This demand deals a crushing blow to the plans of the colonizers, who are counting on preparing their colonies for independence in such a fashion as "to devitalize and undermine the national sovereignty of the liberated countries, to distort the sense of the self-deter-mination of nations, to bind them with new forms of colonial rule under the guise of so-called 'interdependence,' to place their puppets in power in these countries, to bribe part of the bourgeoisie, and to utilize the poisonous weapon of national hatred in order to weaken the forces of the young weak states." [5]

Their proposals to stretch out over many years the period for granting independence to the colonies are allegedly moti-vated by the unpreparedness of the peoples for self-rule, by the necessity of training a national cadre, etc. The colonizers

3. *All-African Peoples' Conference, Tunis, 25th–30th January 1960* (Accra 1960), 12.
4. *Pravda,* December 6, 1960.
5. *Ibid.*

*The Third World in Soviet Perspective*

need this "theory of maturity" because they "make it the ideological basis for the recurrent slogans by which they attempt to justify keeping the colonies under their heel." [6] The article published in the journal of the English colonizers, *New Commonwealth*, is typical. Drawing "lessons" from the events in the Congo, the journal writes: "The error of the Belgians was not that they granted independence to the Congolese (this is something that all Africans are demanding and will receive in time), but that they were never prepared for it. . . . When the Belgians capitulated before the first roll of the thunder of dissatisfaction, *they transfered responsibility to a people which had hardly begun to understand what it means.*" [7]

By "readiness of the people of a colony for independence" the colonizers understand primarily the presence of prepared political forces to which they could transfer power and which would ensure the preservation of the political and economic positions of the former colonial power after independence. But for this they need to keep the "preparation" for independence in their control. As the well-known English colonial bureaucrat A. Cohen wrote, it is necessary "by means of keen foresight to attempt to direct the energies of the nationalists into constructive channels and to secure their cooperation in a program of steady but not precipitate political progress." [8] This "progress" found expression in the numerous versions of colonial constitutions which the English and French colonies successively received in the postwar period. The fundamental direction of the constitutional development was a gradual broadening of suffrage, an increase in the number of African representatives in the legislatures and executive organs, and an extension of their jurisdiction, while the decisive authority was maintained in the hands of colonial bureaucrats.[9]

6. Sékou Touré, *Independent Guinea: Articles and Speeches* (Russian edn., Moscow 1960), 53.

7. *New Commonwealth* (September 1960), 557; my italics.

8. Andrew Cohen, *British Policy in Changing Africa* (Evanston 1959), 61.

9. On the constitutional reforms, see *Sovetskoye Gosudarstvo i Pravo*, No. 6 (1959), 112–23.

## Soviet Writers on the Developing Areas

The colonizers did not make political concessions voluntarily, but under pressure of the struggle of the popular masses in the colonial countries. The significance of the victories achieved has always corresponded to the strength of the national liberation movement. The whole history of the national liberation struggle in Nigeria, Ghana, Guinea, and other countries which have received independence testifies to this. In the course of this struggle, national legislative and executive organs were formed in the colonies. However, under the colonial regime the people could not establish their national statehood according to their own freely expressed will and desire.

One should keep in mind that wherever national statehood of the African peoples existed prior to the coming of the colonizers, it was completely destroyed and was replaced by a system of colonial administration that in a number of cases (for example, in some of the English colonies) included the so-called "native" authorities (tribal chiefs, emirs, sultans, and various "native councils"). This system, which received the name of indirect rule, had of course nothing in common with "natural native democracy," as the colonizers have attempted to assert.

In the postwar period, when the colonial powers were forced to make political concessions under the onslaught of the national liberation movement, they began to establish in their colonies a system of state-legal institutions on the "Western European model." In the English colonies this system was built according to the image and likeness of the English system; in the French colonies, according to the French. The introduction of the institutions of "Western European democracy" is explained by the social reorientation of the colonizers; where they formerly depended primarily on the tribal, feudal nobility, now they attempt to make that part of the growing bourgeoisie which is aspiring to cooperate with them into the social support of their rule.

New political forms are also needed by the colonizers because, while the colonial regime still exists, they are attempting to create a "political heritage" that will determine

## The Third World in Soviet Perspective

the direction of the development of national statehood even after the colonies achieve independence. Thus the American jurist, L. Cowan, in his work on the local administrative organs in West Africa, makes the surprising admission: "For better or worse, West Africa will never be able to free itself completely from the political heritage of the period of European control. Even without the colonial powers, the local African institutions must adapt themselves to the requirements of life in the twentieth century or disappear. *However, it in no way follows that the results of this adaptation will necessarily be Western democratic forms.*" [10]

The imperialists are attempting not only to transfer the "ideals of Western democracy" to African soil, but also forcibly to bind the liberated countries with political forms that would facilitate the preservation of the new states' political and economic dependence on the former colonial powers. In some cases these states have been bound to the status of a dominion by the conditions of granting independence under the flag of "interdependence" (Ghana by the constitution of 1957 and Nigeria by the constitution of 1960); others to the status of a member of a community (the former colonies of French West and Equatorial Africa, with the exception of Guinea and Madagascar).[11]

Applying their cherished principle of "divide and rule," the imperialists are carrying out a policy of "Balkanization" of the African continent—by carving up their colonial possessions into as many tiny states as possible, or binding the larger colonies by the principle of a federative state structure.

The French example is characteristic in this respect. The *loi-cadre* of 1956 and then the constitution of 1958 divided

10. L. G. Cowan, *Local Government in West Africa* (New York 1953), 279; italics added.
11. Para. 86 of the French Constitution, as interpreted by law No. 60–525, provides that a member-state of the community can become independent by means of agreements without thereby losing its membership in the community. These agreements limit crucially the sovereignty of the new states. See, for example, the agreements between the government of the Republic of France and the Malgasy Republic (*Journal Officiel de la République Française, Lois et Décrets*, July 19, 1960, 6607).

the two large colonies of French West and French Equatorial Africa into twelve parts, each of which first was given internal autonomy and then, in 1960, independence (with the exception of Guinea, which attained independence in September 1958). This was done, as Sékou Touré has shown, in order to "perpetuate colonization in a form less obvious, but just as real. In the final analysis, this is being done to continue exploitation of the population and riches of Africa, which will become more accessible, thanks to the very fact of fractionization." [12] In fact, many of these new states have neither the human nor the material resources for independent economic development (for example, the population of the Republic of Gabon is 450,000 and that of the Republic of Congo [Brazzaville], 750,000). Such dwarf states are easier for the former colonial powers to keep in political and economic dependence. The essence of the policy of "Balkanization" was graphically illustrated by the president of the Republic of Ghana, Kwame Nkrumah: "Colonialism invented the system of indirect rule. The essence of this system was that the chiefs nominally exercised control while in reality the colonial power controlled them behind the scene. The creation of states of this type [i.e., Balkanized] is nothing but the development of this discredited theory of indirect rule." [13]

An example of the utilization of the poisoned weapon of national hatred is the policy of England in relation to Nigeria. In 1946, Nigeria was artificially divided into three regions— Northern, Western, and Eastern. The subsequent constitutions of 1951 and 1954, and changes introduced in 1957 and 1959, strengthened and reinforced this split.[14] The establishment of the colonial federation followed a fully defined political goal —to undermine the unity of the national liberation movement by introducing into it the spirit of regional and tribal separatism. "The majority of the English political authors and leaders," the Nigerian Akinyede wrote, "began to propagandize

12. Touré, 48.
13. Ghana, *Parliamentary Debates, Official Report*, xx, No. 17 (1960), col. 637.
14. On the development of the federation, G. B. Akinyede, *The Political and Constitutional Problems of Nigeria* (Lagos 1957).

*The Third World in Soviet Perspective*

the idea of regionalism and separation as soon as the strength
of the unity of Nigeria began to represent a source of danger
and threaten English rule in the country." [15]

To a considerable extent the colonizers succeeded in attaining their goal. By exploiting the contradictions among the three
political parties created in the new regions, they postponed
the grant of independence to Nigeria for a number of years.
The elections of 1959 showed that the influence of the political
parties was almost exactly distributed according to the three
regions (the Northern Region—the Northern Peoples' Congress; the Eastern Region—the National Council of Nigeria
and the Cameroons; and the Western Region—the Action
Group).[16] At all the constitutional congresses (1953, 1957, and
1958) the English stubbornly insisted upon the principle of
federalism, and in the new constitution of independent Nigeria
this principle is reinforced by corresponding constitutional
guarantees.[17] In the report of the constitutional conference of
1958, it is stated that "inasmuch as the unity of the federal
structure is one of interdependence, no single unit, including
the federation, can change its constitution by a method conflicting with the general interests of Nigeria as a whole." [18]
The 1960 constitution accordingly provided a complex system
for changing the articles pertaining to the federal structure. A
law for changing these articles must be adopted by a two-
thirds majority in each of the two houses of the federal parliament, and also by a simple majority in both houses of the
regional parliaments of at least two of the regions.

Is federation in Nigeria perhaps a means of solving the nationality problem, as its proponents declare? The national
composition of Nigeria is indeed extremely complex. However,
the division of Nigeria into three regions was carried out absolutely artificially and arbitrarily. Even the supporters of
federation consider that "the existing regions were established

15. *Ibid.*, 29.
16. On the results of the 1959 elections, see *Sovremennyy Vostok*
[Contemporary East], No. 4 (1960), 54.
17. *The Nigeria (Constitution) Order in Council*, No. 1652, 1960.
18. *Report by the Resumed Nigerian Constitutional Conference, 1958*
(London 1958), 29.

## Soviet Writers on the Developing Areas

without considering ethnic factors" and that "there is no justification for this arbitrary grouping."[19]

In this article we are not deciding the question whether Nigeria should be a federation, as some Nigerian political leaders propose, or a unitary state with administrative divisions taking into consideration the national composition of the population, as others propose. We wish only to emphasize that the federation, in the form in which it was established by the colonizers, was forced upon independent Nigeria.

The English government also attempted to carry out an analogous operation in relation to Ghana. In 1954, with the direct assistance of the colonizers, a movement began in that country (then the Gold Coast colony) for the establishment of a federation which united all parties opposed to the ruling National Party.[20] The political aim of this movement was the very same as in Nigeria.

In his autobiography, Kwame Nkrumah wrote: "In the colonial countries where imperialism achieved success in dividing the nationalist movement according to tribes, the anti-imperialist struggle was significantly weakened and the basic aims of the nationalist movement—unity and independence—were sacrificed on the altar of tribalism."[21] Attempting to use the separatist movement for their own aims, the English government leaders insisted upon new elections in 1956 and placed two conditions on the granting of independence: that a significant majority of voters favor the granting of independence in the very near future and agree to a constitution which not only would answer their desires but would be operative. The

19. Obafemi Awolowo, *Path to Nigerian Freedom* (London 1947), 53.
20. The English colony was divided into three parts: the Gold Coast colony proper, and the Ashanti and Northern Territories protectorates. This division reflected the successive stages of the country's seizure by the English colonizers. The proponents of federalism proposed to preserve this division, converting each of the three parts into a separate state and later to unite them in a federation. For more details on these plans, see I. I. Potekhin, "Novoye Afrikanskoye gosudarstvo" [A New African State], *Sovetskaya Etnografiya* [Soviet Ethnography], No. 2 (1957).
21. *Ghana: The Autobiography of Kwame Nkrumah* (Edinburgh 1959), 177–78.

colonizers obviously figured that the existence of the separatist movement in the country would keep the National Party from winning the elections. This plan was substantially thwarted, although the National Party was forced to make concessions to the federalists. The 1957 constitution provided for a broad decentralization—the establishment of five regions with regional electoral assemblies possessing considerable powers.[22] This decentralization was reinforced by appropriate constitutional guarantees. Thus, Paragraph 32 provided that a law for the elimination of a provincial assembly, or the suspension of its activity or the reduction of its powers, must be adopted by the votes of two-thirds of all members of the National Assembly and approved by two-thirds of the provincial assemblies—i.e., by four out of five.

Speaking of the 1957 constitution, Kwame Nkrumah often noted that it was "imposed on the people by the imperial power. We had no choice but to accept it."[23]

Events in the Republic of the Congo demonstrate especially clearly the aim followed by the colonizers in imposing the principle of federalism on colonies that receive their independence. The establishing of the puppet states of Kasai and Katanga and the various plans for the organization of a "free federation" (e.g., states in which the central government is deprived of real power)—all this was designed to facilitate the preservation of the political and economic rule of the imperialists in the Congo. "The proposal to establish a free federation in the Congo is only an attempt, by those who were not able to break Katanga away from the Congo Republic, to achieve the Balkanization of the country by the back door."[24]

One must note, however, that in some cases the colonizers are uniting their colonies. A typical example in this respect is the establishment in 1953 of the colonial Federation of Rhodesia and Nyasaland.[25] The unification of territories differing in

22. *The Ghana (Constitution) Order in Council*, No. 227, 1957.
23. *Proceedings of the Constituent Assembly*, First Sitting, March 14, 1960, col. 2.
24. Ghana, *Parliamentary Debates, Official Report*, xx, No. 17 (1960), col. 645.
25. For more details, see Yu. A. Yudin, *Federatsiya Rodezii i N'yasa-*

ethnic composition and political and economic situation aimed at placing the African peoples of Northern Rhodesia and Nyasaland under control of the European minority of Southern Rhodesia, who had established a dictatorship of colonial fascism. The African peoples of the protectorates are thereby deprived of the right of self-determination and formation of their own national states. The former prime minister of Southern Rhodesia, Huggins, cynically declared: "We do not want our grandsons to have as their neighbors a state . . . in which there is no European guidance." [26] Thus, whether federation is used as a means for dividing up colonial possessions or as a means for their unification, its essence does not change. The basic aim remains the same—the strengthening of rule by the colonizers in one form or another.

The artificially drawn borders between the new states are the consequence of "Balkanization," the legacy of the colonial period. These borders separate related nationalities, break them up in parts, and can, as the colonizers hope, serve as a source of conflicts and friction between African states.

By resorting to these maneuvers and attempting to impose alien political forms on the independent states, the colonizers expect that the African peoples will not succeed in completely freeing themselves from the "political legacy" left to them. However, as the experience of nation-building in the independent countries shows, these calculations are groundless. Of course, the process of the formation of national statehood is proceeding in difficult circumstances. It is influenced both by the intrigues of the imperialists, who are attempting to replace the "classical" forms of colonial rule with neo-colonialism, and by the resistance of domestic reactionaries.

In a number of the new states, the national bourgeoisie which has come to power in alliance with feudal elements is attempting to direct the development of national statehood along the path shown by the colonizers. In a number of states,

*lenda—novaya forma kolonial'nogo upravleniya* [The Federation of Rhodesia and Nyasaland—a New Form of Colonial Administration] (Moscow 1960).

26. *Public Law* (Spring 1960), 21.

## The Third World in Soviet Perspective

it is liquidating even those few norms of bourgeois democracy which had been won by the workers while they were still in conditions of colonial slavery, and is attempting to establish dictatorial and despotic regimes.

Nevertheless, the peoples of the independent countries have already achieved significant successes in building their national states and in strengthening their unity. It is especially important that the development of national statehood in some of these countries is proceeding not along the path of adapting Western European institutions and forms, but along the path of establishing such state legal institutions and such forms as correspond to the interests of the African peoples.

It is characteristic that in these countries public life has been rendered democratic, and the people have been granted broad democratic rights [a] which give them a chance to participate in the determination of state policy. At the same time the governments of these countries are adopting forceful measures against all reactionary elements that are attempting to disrupt the country's unity and favor cooperation with the imperialists.

From the point of view of the colonizers, such a retreat from "Western democracy" is a digression from democracy in general. In English and American literature there recently appeared many articles devoted to the theme: "Will Western democracy survive on the African continent?" The authors of these articles accuse the government leaders of the new states of betraying "the ideals of Western democracy." Thus, an editorial in *The Times* remarked that "in Ghana and in Guinea, a situation has developed in which politicians, reared in the democratic traditions of England and France . . . have to a considerable degree converted the democratic forms inherited

a. The term "broad democratic rights" is interpreted rather narrowly. In practice, the requirement is fulfilled as long as local Communists are not being extensively persecuted—that is, either where there are none or where they are allowed to operate fairly freely. "Democratic rights" need not be extended to groups of which the Communists do not approve. Thus "broad democratic rights" exist in Ghana, but not in the United States.

*Soviet Writers on the Developing Areas*

from the colonists into semi-authoritarian forms in order to attain their own ends." [27]

The Chief Minister of Tanganyika, Nyerere, answered such criticism very well: "Too often those who have doubts about African democracy limit their presentation of it to particular democratic institutions and forms which developed in individual countries and are characteristic of them. . . . For these critics an organized and officially recognized opposition has become almost the essence of democracy."

An example of the freeing of independent states from political forms imposed on them is the constitutional development of Ghana. The 1957 constitution was worked out and adopted not by the parliament of Ghana, but by the English government in the form of an Order in Council. The English Queen was recognized as head of the new state and represented by a governor-general. The system of organs of state power and administration, their interrelations and types of activity, were naturally drawn from the English model. Three years later, Ghana adopted a republican constitution.[28] In the government's White Paper on the projected constitution, it is pointed out that it "is not drawn from the constitution of any other country." [29] Introducing the proposed constitution for the government at the constitutional convention, Minister Ofori–Atta similarly remarked that "the constitution conforms to the way of life and to the psychology of our people and at the same time preserves their democratic rights." [30]

It is characteristic that the opposition, which unites all of the country's reactionary elements, opposed both the method of adopting the constitution (approval of its basic propositions by a plebiscite) and the change from monarchy to republic. One of the deputies from the Union Party pathetically cried

27. *The Times* (London), September 17, 1960.
28. For the text of the constitution, see *Ghana Gazette*, August 18, 1960.
29. *Government Proposals for a Republican Constitution*, White Paper No. 1/60 (Accra 1960).
30. *Proceedings of the Constituent Assembly*, Fifth Sitting, June 13, 1960, col. 164.

## The Third World in Soviet Perspective
out in Parliament, "Does not this smell of a revolution by the Parliament against Ghana's Queen? If this is a revolution, then do we have the right to revolt against our Queen?" [31]

The new constitution of the Republic of Ghana is distinguished by great originality (especially in determining the method of choosing the president, his powers, and the relationships between the government and the National Assembly). However, we shall discuss here only a few of its features, especially those that are also characteristic for the constitutions of a number of other countries.

One of the basic principles of the new constitution is the principle of unity—the country's unity and the unity of all African peoples. This principle has an especially great significance. As has already been noted, the imperialists are doing everything they can to weaken the new states and to interfere with their uniting in a struggle against neo-colonialism.

In the first place, the new constitution proclaims Ghana a unitary republic (Art. 4) and thus deals a blow to the reactionary elements which are still attempting to undermine the country's unity. In the White Paper it is emphasized that "the government asks the people to show by their vote for the proposed constitution that they believe in the unity of Ghana and reject any form of federalism." [32] Second, the constitution speaks of the aspiration of the people of Ghana to facilitate the formation of a Union of African States. Thus Art. 2 states: "Being firmly convinced of the early rejection of sovereignty in favor of a union of African states and territories, the people hereby transfer to Parliament the right to give up the sovereignty of Ghana or of any of its parts."

Thus, the constitution of Ghana counters the neo-colonialist policy of "Balkanization" of the African continent with one of unity. We find an analogous situation in the constitution of the Republic of Guinea. The preamble to the constitution speaks of the desire "to do everything for the achievement and strengthening of the unity and independence of the African

31. Ghana, *Parliamentary Debates, Official Report,* xviii, No. 1 (1960), col. 29.
32. *Government Proposals for a Republican Constitution,* 4.

homeland." In this connection, one should note the interpretation which the Guinean leaders give to the majority-rule system of voting in the National Assembly, chosen by a single national list. Thus Sékou Touré in his talk "On the Nature and Spirit of the Constitution" noted: "In the name of the republic, in correspondence with the demands for the unity of the people and the aspiration to give an all-governmental character to the activities of each, we have adopted a majority-rule voting system." [33] At the same time, the constitution also speaks of the unity of all independent African states. The preamble to the constitution proclaims that the government of Guinea unconditionally supports any policy directed toward the establishment of a United States of Africa and, in accordance with this, Art. 34 provides for the partial or complete repudiation of sovereignty in the interests of accomplishing African unity.

These constitutional provisions have been transformed into reality. In May 1959, Kwame Nkrumah and Sékou Touré signed a projected Declaration of the Basic Principles of a Union of Independent African States.[34] The Declaration provides that countries entering the Union will preserve their political structure and that the question of partial or full repudiation of sovereignty by members of the Union will be decided jointly. Members of the Union must coordinate their activities in foreign policy, and in questions of economics, culture, and defense. The treaty of the Union of Ghana and Guinea is already in force, establishing a special confederate relation between the two states.[35]

The idea of a Union of African States was supported both by the First (1958) and by the Second (1960) All-African Peoples' Conferences and found its expression in the adoption of special resolutions "On Borders and Federations" and "Concerning the Unity of Africa." Of course, many difficulties of a political, economic, and ideological nature stand in the path of establishing such a union. The colonizers took great pains

33. Touré, 105.

34. See *West Africa*, May 9, 1959, 447.

35. In November 1960 the Republic of Mali joined the union. As an example of the development of confederate relations, see the "Casablanca Charter."

*The Third World in Soviet Perspective*

to separate the African peoples and to sow distrust and mutual suspicion. In place of African unity they proposed the "unity" of the African peoples with the former metropoles, and, instead of a Union of African States, various plans for the establishment of Eurafrica. However, the idea of the unity of all African peoples is firmly imprinted in their consciousness. This idea is exerting an ever-greater influence on the development of national statehood in the independent countries.[36]

One of the most important and most difficult problems facing the young states is the problem of establishing a new national state apparatus. The independent African states have inherited an administrative apparatus created by the colonizers and adapted to the latter's needs. The basic task of this apparatus was to support and strengthen colonial rule. This determined its role, structure, forms and methods of activity and the composition of its cadre. All power was in the hands of the governors, who were designated by the colonial ministry of the metropole and answerable only to it. The governor molded the apparatus of the colonial administration and determined its policies. It mattered little that in a number of colonies, in the years just before independence, there were established governments and legislative organs, most or even all of whose members were Africans. "The civil service, the police, justice, defense, foreign relations—all were in the hands of the governor," wrote Kwame Nkrumah of the situation which existed in the Gold Coast colony.[37] The governments and the representative organs had only advisory functions.

36. In 1960 there was created, for example, the Union of the Republics of Central Africa, composed of three republics: Congo, Chad, and the Central African Republic. In 1959, four autonomous republics—Ivory Coast, Dahomey, Niger, and Upper Volta—formed an economic union, the *Conseil de l'Entente*. After receiving independence in 1960, the independent states which were members of the *Conseil de l'Entente* united in a political union, the constitution of which is being worked out at the present time. One should note that the French colonizers are using all means to oppose the uniting of their former colonies; witness, in particular, the plot against the Mali Federation (Senegal and [ex-French] Sudan). In September 1960, as a result of the colonizers' intrigues, the Mali Federation ceased to exist. For details on the constitutional development of the Association, see Maurice Bourjol, "La Communauté 'renouvée' . . . et dépassée," *Democratie nouvelle* (September 1960).
37. Nkrumah, 122.

# Soviet Writers on the Developing Areas

All of these organs were powerless to make any changes, since the apparatus of colonial administration consisted, as before, almost exclusively of European bureaucrats. Thus, in 1949, in the colonial administration of the Gold Coast only 10 per cent of the positions above that of a clerk were occupied by Africans, while in 1956, immediately before independence, the figure was 59 per cent.[38] In other colonies, there either were no Africans at all (for example, the Belgian Congo)[39] or their number did not exceed a few dozen (in the French colony of the Ivory Coast in 1958 there were 20 Africans holding high administrative and technical positions).[40]

As A. Franklin, the Director for Togolization of cadres in the Republic of Togo, pointed out, in the period of French trusteeship only one Togolese per year was sent to an administrative school in France. In thirty-one years, Togo was provided with 30 administrative workers.[41] This is how the colonizers carried out "Africanization" of the cadre of the state apparatus. It was an apparatus of a foreign power, an apparatus of cruel political oppression and of the economic exploitation of the colonies' population.

With the attainment of independence by the colonies, the role of the state apparatus changed basically. "Henceforth," said Sékou Touré at a meeting of administrative workers of Kankan province, "all government institutions in their structure, aims, and activities will become that which they should be—servants of the people, and effective means for rapid and harmonious development." [42] However, for this it is necessary first of all to staff the government apparatus with a cadre of nationals.

The solution of this most difficult problem is complicated by the illiteracy of the colonial population, a consequence of the

38. A. L. Adu, "Problems of Government in Emergent African States," *Revue Internationale des Sciences Administratives*, xxvi, No. 1 (1960), 64.
39. In his speech at the 15th Session of the UN General Assembly, Kwame Nkrumah remarked that "high posts in the army, police and government apparatus were exclusively the patrimony of the Belgians" (*Pravda*, September 25, 1960).
40. See *American Political Science Review*, No. 2 (1960), 398.
41. See *Sovremennyy Vostok*, No. 3 (1960), 22.
42. Sékou Touré, *L'action politique du Parti Démocratique de Guinée et la lutte pour l'émancipation africaine* (Paris 1959), 237.

"civilizing mission" of the colonizers. It is sufficient to state that in 1957, in all the colonies of former French West Africa, only 13 per cent of the children of school age attended school, and in individual colonies this percentage was even lower (thus, in Guinea only 10 per cent of the children of school age attended school; in the [French] Sudan, 8 per cent; and in Dahomey, 7 per cent).[43] The situation with regard to the preparation of specialists in the various fields of economics and culture was even worse. Thus, at the time of Ghana's proclamation of independence in 1957, there were 1,300 people with a higher education;[44] in Nigeria, in the 1959/60 school year there were 5,813 students out of a population of 35 million;[45] and in the Belgian Congo, only 14 Africans had higher education.

In the early period, the independent African states were for this reason forced to retain some of the old foreign bureaucrats in their apparatus. Thus, in 1959 in Ghana, 27 per cent of the higher officials were foreigners.[46] On July 1, 1959, there were 14 Africans with the rank of captain in command posts in the Ghanaian army and not a single colonel, major-general, etc.,[47] and this almost four years after independence! And in countries which received their independence only in 1960, the positions of the old bureaucracy and of foreign specialists are even firmer.

Such a situation creates great difficulties for the governments of the young states. How can they count on the "loyalty" of foreign bureaucrats raised in the traditions of colonial rule and closely tied to their former masters? The governments of the young states understand this very well. As Kwame Nkrumah wrote: "After the political revolution, whether peaceful or non-peaceful, a new government should, upon coming to power, immediately remove from government service all the former leaders. My own experience taught me that if this is not done, the revolutionary government risks defeat."[48]

43. See *American Political Science Review*, No. 2 (1960), 400.
44. *Ibid.*, 393.
45. See *The Times*, September 29, 1960.
46. See Adu, 64.
47. Ghana, *Parliamentary Debates, Official Report*, xv (1959), col. 95.
48. Nkrumah, 122.

## Soviet Writers on the Developing Areas

The former colonial powers are attempting by all means to maintain the old colonial bureaucracy under the guise of rendering "technical and administrative assistance" to the young states. In this connection the plan of the English government announced to Parliament in July 1960 is extremely interesting. According to this plan, the English government intends to conclude agreements with colonial governments for a ten-year period to pay supplemental salaries to the employees of the colonial administration so that they will not leave the service. These agreements would remain in force even after the attainment of independence by the colonies. They propose to spend for this aim £10-20 million. A significant evaluation of this plan is given in the journal *New Commonwealth:* "To the degree that this gives each new country the chance to begin its existence with a healthy administration, a well-organized economy well-disposed toward the former colonial power, and with a strong feeling of cooperation, such an expenditure is a good investment."[49]

Similar agreements were signed by France with certain of its former colonies. These agreements provide not only for French financing of a part of the expenditures for the maintenance of the state apparatus, but also for keeping the armed forces and diplomatic corps of these countries under French control.[50]

Despite all these devices of the colonizers, the struggle of the African peoples for genuine liberation from all forms of colonial dependence, and in particular from such a form as the preservation of the old colonial bureaucracy in the independent states, intensifies with each passing day.[51] In this respect one should emphasize that the tempo of liquidation of the old administrative apparatus is directly dependent on the depth of the revolutionary process in each country. It is sufficient to compare, for example, the situation in Guinea, where the revolution, according to Sékou Touré, bore a national char-

49. *New Commonwealth* (September 1960), 559.
50. See, e.g., the French agreements with the republics of Congo and Chad and the Central African Republic (*Journal Officiel*, July 29, 1960, 7041).
51. For more details, see V. Larin, "Kolonizatory khvatayutsya za solominku" [The Colonizers Are Clutching at Straws], *Izvestiya*, November 14, 1960.

*The Third World in Soviet Perspective*

acter,[52] with the situation in the majority of the former French colonies or in the Federation of Nigeria. In the first case, the old colonial apparatus was completely destroyed and replaced by a new one; in the second case, key positions in the state apparatus, as formerly, were occupied by French and English bureaucrats.

The young states are adopting energetic measures for the preparation of national cadres—the expansion of the system of public education and of higher learning, the establishment of special administrative schools, etc.

The Soviet Union is rendering great assistance in the preparation of national cadres of specialists for the state apparatus and for various fields of economics and culture in the independent African countries. Vivid proof of this is the establishment of the Peoples' Friendship University.[b] At its opening ceremonies, N. S. Khrushchev said: "In opening the Peoples' Friendship University we have only one hope—to assist other countries in the preparation of highly qualified cadres. This is especially important for those countries which for a long time were subjected to heavy colonial oppression and which, through the colonizers' fault, were economically and culturally backward and do not have their own national cadre of specialists." [53]

A particular problem of the establishment of a new state apparatus in the African states is the problem of the so-called traditional authorities. We have already shown that the colonizers included several "native" political institutions in the colonial administrative apparatus in order to consolidate their rule. However, these institutions were deprived of their democratic basis and transformed into a simple appendage of the apparatus of colonial oppression. The essence was the same, whether this was the system of indirect rule characteristic of the English colonies, or the system of direct rule characteristic of the French possessions in Africa.

Tribal chiefs, their assistants, and members of "native coun-

b. Often known as Patrice Lumumba University. Established exclusively for the education and training of students in the USSR from the developing areas.

52. Touré, *Independent Guinea*, 8.
53. *Pravda*, November 18, 1960.

cils" were paid bureaucrats of the colonial administration, selected and replaced by the governor of the colony and answerable to him. By their social position these bureaucrats were representatives of the tribal-feudal nobility—the most reactionary and conservative part of African society. This is why the colonizers, while introducing representative institutions on the "West European" model into their colonies, at the same time continue to support and preserve the "traditional authorities" who have lost their prestige in the eyes of the African people.

The conflict between the revolutionary forces of the national liberation movement and this reactionary element arose even during the colonial regime. In some countries, even before the proclamation of independence, the new government succeeded in liquidating the "traditional authorities"—Guinea—or in significantly limiting their influence—Ghana. In other countries —Nigeria and the majority of the former French colonies—the new states received their constitutions as a "political legacy" from the colonial regime. Thus, the new constitution of Nigeria fully preserves in the structure of the state apparatus such an organ as the House of Chiefs, which functions in each of three regions as a second chamber in the regional parliament. The constitution also guarantees the rights and privileges of the tribal chiefs, emirs, and sultans, whose authority is especially significant in the Northern Region of Nigeria.

In the republican constitution of 1960, Ghana also proclaimed that the "institution of chiefs in Ghana must be guaranteed and preserved" and section VII of the constitution is devoted to the Houses of Chiefs that are established in each province. However, the laws adopted after Ghana's independence (1958–1960) in fact deprived the chiefs of real power, against the protests of the Union Party, whose social support they constitute.

The problem of the chiefs was resolved most radically in Guinea, where on December 31, 1957, a decree was adopted that eliminated cantonal chiefs throughout the country and replaced them by elected representative organs.[54] The elimina-

54. For details, see *Guinée, prélude à l'indépendance* (Paris 1958) and also the article by J. Sure-Canale, "Likvidatsiya instituta kantonal'nykh

273

tion of the institution of chiefs and the limitation of their authority are important conditions for the further democratization of the national state apparatus. An example of this is the Republic of Guinea, where "the people and only the people make all decisions concerning the country's fate." [55]

One of the characteristics of the new apparatus of the independent African states consists in the great place that is beginning to be occupied by organs of direct rule over the economic life of the country. Their appearance is explained by the ever-growing role of the new states in the development and control of the national economy. This question is a theme for special research. Here we emphasize only the trend in the development of the state apparatus of the new African states, which is most clearly seen in the examples of the Republic of Guinea and the Republic of Ghana. The establishment of planning organs, organs for controlling domestic and foreign trade, and the various kinds of public corporations testifies to changes not only in the structure of the government apparatus of these states, but also in its role. The new apparatus is becoming the most important instrument for rebuilding the backward economy left the young states as a legacy of the "civilized" colonizers—an instrument in the struggle for the attainment of full economic independence.

The peoples of the African countries who have won independence in recent years are still taking only the first steps in the building of their national states. Which path of development they will choose—capitalist or non-capitalist—is their internal affair. In the contemporary historical circumstance, favorable international and domestic conditions are being created for the formation of independent national democratic states in many countries, including the liberated countries of Africa.

The thesis on the possibility of establishing a national demo-

vozhdey v Gvineye" [The Liquidation of the Institution of Cantonal Chiefs in Guinea], *Sovremennyy Vostok*, No. 11 (1959), 29–32.

55. Sékou Touré, "Gvineya na novom puti" [Guinea on a New Path], *Pravda*, November 28, 1959.

cratic state,[c] the exhaustive description of this state, and the evaluation of the various social forces participating in the national democratic front that are contained in the Statement of the Conference of the Representatives of Communist and Workers' Parties give the African peoples a clear perspective on the development of their national statehood.

c. On the "national democratic state," see above, pp. 27–28.

SELECTION 13

# Class Structure
# in the Underdeveloped Countries *

## BY R. AVAKOV AND G. MIRSKIY

*THE foundations of Marxist thought lie in economics, but the most vital part of the doctrine is its class analysis. Classes are the reflection of economic factors, and as collectivities of people they provide the motive force of historical change. Marxists emphasize again and again the imperative necessity of understanding the "correlation of class forces" in each country as a prerequisite for properly estimating revolutionary potential.*

*We have already mentioned Avakov and Mirskiy as examples of the younger, more dynamic school of Soviet scholars. (See the prefatory note to Selection 6, above.) In this article—scholastic in methodology but almost revolutionary in intent—they attempt to find a basis for analyzing class forces in the third world as a means of establishing just what the prospects of communism are in these vital areas.*

*Avakov and Mirskiy come up with very few specific answers, since their article is more a methodological than a substantive study. (It is really doubtful that the Marxist framework even permits meaningful answers to these questions, since it was designed to analyze societies of a completely different type.) They do, however, level a sharp attack against a number of traditional Soviet views about the third world—at times explicitly, more often by indirection. In particular, they are attempting to overcome the use of purely political criteria as bases for value judgments about various classes, and to find the explanation of class behavior in economic factors.*

*Obviously they are not able to break through the limitations of Marxist analysis nor, probably, would they want to. Never-*

---

* SOURCE: "O klassovoy strukture v slaborazvitykh stranakh," MEIMO, No. 4 (1962), 68–82; based on the translation in JPRS 14,607.

*theless, they are attempting to start anew by considering the class structure of the third world in terms of "objective" criteria. Very few studies show as clearly as this one the progress that has been made in the post-Stalin era. The distance between Western scholarship and work of this type is still great and the doctrinal gap perhaps unbridgeable, yet the direction Avakov and Mirskiy have taken is undoubtedly the right one.*

THE question of the ways of achieving socio-economic and political development in the underdeveloped countries of Asia, Africa, and Latin America is a question of classes, of their interrelationship in the complex process of societal development, and of the class struggle centering around the problems these countries face. In the final analysis, the choice of a path depends on which class becomes the leading force of society and then succeeds in attracting the masses; and what is the alignment of the class and political forces inside a country. Therefore, the question of the class structure of society in the underdeveloped countries—of the shifts in the power relationships among the various classes and strata of the population, of the interrelationships between the principal classes of these countries—is of primary importance in examining the prospects of the national liberation revolution, the fate of the nationally independent countries of Asia, Africa, and Latin America, and the paths of their further development.

In the contemporary era, which is characterized by the onward rush of time and the global nature of world communications, factors of an external, international character naturally exert a particularly great influence on the class struggle in the underdeveloped countries in selecting the paths of their societal development. It is of decisive importance that at present the principal substance, principal trend, and principal features of the historical development of mankind are determined by the world socialist system—by forces struggling against imperialism and for the socialist transformation of society.

The class structure of society in the underdeveloped countries of Asia, Africa, and Latin America is extremely complex. It bears the imprint of various eras. These classes were formed

## The Third World in Soviet Perspective

under special historical conditions; for various reasons the socio-economic systems developed in a deformed way; many of these countries knew neither a developed slave-owning structure of society, nor developed feudalism, nor, even less, the higher stage of development of capitalist relationships. The process of the rise of one formation and its subsequent replacement by another, more progressive, socio-economic structure did not evolve in these countries in such tempestuous forms as in Europe; the new production relationships displaced the old ones much less intensively. As a result, socio-economic relationships—varying in their historical importance and nature—sedimented, as it were, into superimposed strata that have been "coexisting" for centuries and changing very slowly.[a]

The era of colonial rule played an especially conservative and reactionary role in all this. The establishment of colonial regimes in economically underdeveloped countries interrupted the natural path of their socio-economic development. The European bourgeoisie invaded a society that staggered under the burden of prefeudal relationships. Feudal relationships had not succeeded in becoming a completely dominant force in these societies and often were still in an embryonic stage. They became a deterrent to social progress, since with the victory of the bourgeois revolutions in Europe, capitalism began to determine world development as a whole.

The European bourgeoisie by no means went into overseas countries in order to implant there the prevailing capitalist production relationships. It preserved the precapitalist and prefeudal relationships everywhere, utilizing them to enslave these countries, and it developed capitalism only within definite limits. Nevertheless, in one way or another, capitalist relationships, despite foreign rule, slowly penetrated the enslaved countries of Asia, Africa, and Latin America. New

a. The stages of social development as viewed by Marxists have been written about widely—see, for instance, *Fundamentals*, chapter 4. Each of these stages (slavery, feudalism, capitalism, etc.) is determined by its "mode of production." The mode of production in turn reflects the "productive forces" available (technology, people, resources) and the "production relationships," which determine on what basis people work together (essentially, a question of who owns the means of production).

278

# Soviet Writers on the Developing Areas

classes—the proletariat and local bourgeoisie—began to arise in these countries and gradually these classes transformed themselves into an active political force. The process of their development progressed sluggishly, however, in painful and arduous forms.

In the countries of Asia, Africa, and Latin America, the difficult historical conditions could not but affect the class structure of society, the specific features of the formation of classes and their social composition. In contrast to the highly developed capitalist countries, the process of class formation is still not completed. The class structure of society is characterized by an unusually motley and mosaic-like pattern, by the presence of numerous classes and social groups. While in the United States and capitalist Europe the monopolist bourgeoisie and the proletariat, the upper rural bourgeoisie and the peasantry, are explicit and distinct class antipodes, in the underdeveloped countries the picture is much more complex. The barriers between the classes there are not as sharply outlined, and the polarization of class forces has not reached the degree characteristic of the highly developed capitalist countries. Extreme heterogeneity, many social strata, and fluidity of class composition—these features are inherent in the classes in the underdeveloped countries.

The class structures of the countries of Asia, Africa, and Latin America have not only many similarities but also a number of essential differences. Therefore it is necessary in an analysis to ascertain the specific features of each country, in addition to indicating the general laws inherent in the class structure of the population of all underdeveloped countries as a whole.

A comprehensive and concrete analysis of the class structure of society in the countries of Asia, Africa, and Latin America is greatly complicated by the inadequacy of relevant statistical materials. In many countries social statistics are either lacking or are very confusing. In Table 1, shown below, which was composed from the data of the International Labor Office, an attempt is made to depict the class structure of the population of the countries of Asia, Africa, and Latin America on the

TABLE 1

Structure of the Working Population (Excluding Europeans) of 18
Countries of Asia, Africa, and Latin America, According to Branch of
Economy and Category of Occupation
(in thousands of persons)

| Category of Occupation | Branch of Economy | | | |
|---|---|---|---|---|
| | *Agriculture Forestry, Hunting and Fishing* | *Mining Industry* | *Manufacturing Industry* | *Construction* |
| | 1 | 2 | 3 | 4 |
| *Southeast Asia* | | | | |
| 1. Self-employed persons | 69,539 | 134 | 7,379 | 830 |
| 2. Hired employees | 26,614 | 541 | 4,425 | 853 |
| 3. Unpaid working family members, etc. | 8,594 | 10 | 283 | 8 |
| TOTAL | 104,747 | 685 | 12,087 | 1,691 |
| *North Africa* | | | | |
| 1. Self-employed persons | 4,535 | 2 | 389 | 39 |
| 2. Hired employees | 2,549 | 55 | 595 | 241 |
| 3. Unpaid working family members, etc. | 2,602 | 0 | 51 | 4 |
| TOTAL | 9,686 | 57 | 1,035 | 284 |
| *Latin America* | | | | |
| 1. Self-employed persons | 5,638 | 34 | 1,157 | 152 |
| 2. Hired employees | 5,141 | 370 | 3,010 | 881 |
| 3. Unpaid working family members, etc. | 2,410 | 15 | 201 | 31 |
| TOTAL | 13,189 | 419 | 4,368 | 1,064 |
| *As a Whole* | | | | |
| 1. Self-employed persons | 79,702 [b] | 170 | 8,925 | 1,021 |
| 2. Hired employees | 34,304 | 966 | 8,030 | 1,975 |
| 3. Unpaid working family members, etc. | 13,606 | 25 | 535 | 43 |
| GRAND TOTAL | 127,612 [b] | 1,161 | 17,490 | 3,039 |

b. These are the figures given by the authors. It will be noted that all
are 10,000 too small. The reason for the discrepancy is unclear.

| Electricity, Gas, Water Supply | Trade, Banks, Insurance, Real Estate Transactions | Transport, Warehousing Operations, Communications | Services | Miscellaneous | Total | In per cent |
|---|---|---|---|---|---|---|
| 5 | 6 | 7 | 8 | 9 | 10 | 11 |
| 223 | 6,545 | 853 | 4,925 | 647 | 91,075 | 62.3 |
| 317 | 1,704 | 1,776 | 8,864 | 249 | 45,343 | 31.0 |
| 1 | 352 | 10 | 74 | 491 | 9,823 | 6.7 |
| 541 | 8,601 | 2,639 | 13,863 | 1,387 | 146,241 | 100.00 |
| 6 | 644 | 68 | 203 | 16 | 5,902 | 42.4 |
| 21 | 203 | 430 | 835 | 342 | 5,271 | 37.8 |
| 1 | 63 | 9 | 20 | 6 | 2,756 | 19.8 |
| 28 | 910 | 507 | 1,058 | 364 | 13,929 | 100.00 |
| 10 | 1,411 | 166 | 495 | 126 | 9,189 | 31.9 |
| 137 | 1,108 | 897 | 3,922 | 695 | 16,161 | 56.1 |
| 2 | 136 | 19 | 86 | 549 | 3,449 | 12.0 |
| 149 | 2,655 | 1,082 | 4,503 | 1,370 | 28,799 | 100.00 |
| 239 | 8,600 | 1,087 | 5,623 | 789 | 106,156 [b] | 56.2 |
| 475 | 3,015 | 3,103 | 13,621 | 1,286 | 66,775 | 35.3 |
| 4 | 551 | 38 | 180 | 1,046 | 16,028 | 8.5 |
| 718 | 12,166 | 4,228 | 19,424. | 3,121 | 188,959 [b] | 100.00 |

## The Third World in Soviet Perspective

basis of a generalization of data from 18 countries. Several comments should be made concerning this table.

First, with a few exceptions, the data on individual countries pertain to the first half of the 1950's. Naturally, the subsequent changes in their class structure are not considered here. Of the countries included in the table, the greatest changes took place in Cuba; certain changes are characteristic of the UAR (Egypt). In the other countries, although their population has since increased considerably, the respective share of each class in the working population has remained relatively stable.

Second, the countries included in the table represent three regions of the economically underdeveloped world: Southeast Asia (India, Pakistan, Malaya, the Philippines, Thailand), North Africa (Egypt, Algeria, Tunisia, Morocco, Libya), and Latin America (Argentina, Mexico, Chile, Colombia, Venezuela, Bolivia, Ecuador, Cuba). Although the lack of appropriate data prevented including such large countries as Indonesia, Brazil, and certain others in the table, the data on the countries included reflect on the whole the class structure of society in the regions named. The conclusions of the table cannot be applied to Africa south of the Sahara, because the class structure of the population of this region differs fundamentally from North Africa, and even more so from Asia and Latin America. The class structure of the African states south of the Sahara requires separate study.

Third, statistics of the International Labor Office—instead of being classified according to an explicit principle of distinct population strata belonging to definite classes—were based on obscure criteria [c] which blur the real picture. As a result, population groups differing in their class composition are found in the same column. It is possible to make a rather clear distinction between rural and urban classes. In agriculture the category of self-employed persons includes feudalists and landlords, the big rural bourgeoisie, small and medium

c. The criteria are probably not "obscure" to a Western researcher. A Marxist, of course, has his own set of criteria, since he views society in quite a different way.

282

landowners, as well as tenant farmers who work land independently. In industry this category includes industrialists, bankers, businessmen, small entrepreneurs, and artisans. On the other hand, in a number of cases managers and administrators of companies, who incontestably belong in the bourgeoisie, are figured together with blue- and white-collar workers as employees. In agriculture, the category of employees includes agricultural laborers as well as peasants who work under feudal conditions for big landowners. The third category also includes persons whose class position differs. They are primarily the unpaid members of the families of small landholding peasants and small entrepreneurs.

In the light of these comments, and with the addition of further material on individual countries, a number of conclusions can be drawn regarding the population structure of the countries of Asia, Africa, and Latin America as a whole. Agriculture accounts for two-thirds of the working population of these three regions taken together. In Southeast Asia the proportion of rural population is the highest—three-fourths. The bulk of the working rural population, about 60 per cent, consists of persons who work land independently. In Southeast Asia this category accounts for 66 per cent; in North Africa, 46 per cent; and in Latin America, 43 per cent. An overwhelming majority of the persons who work land independently are small landholding peasants and tenant farmers. The proportion of these strata of peasantry is particularly high in Southeast Asia. For example, according to data from 1954 and 1955, small landholders (up to five acres) and landless peasants accounted for about three-fourths of all farms in India.

Feudal relationships have survived to the greatest extent in Southeast Asia. Although in the postwar years the development of capitalist relationships in the countryside has accelerated there, the structure of the rural population still bears in many ways, if not predominantly, a feudal imprint. This can also be seen from the fact that the agricultural employees in the countries of this region altogether account for 25.3 per cent of its rural population. In this connection, an overwhelming part of the rural population included in the column "Employees" con-

*The Third World in Soviet Perspective*

sists not of agricultural workers but of peasants who lease land on feudal terms.

Capitalist relationships reached their highest development in the agriculture of Latin America, where "employees" account for about 39 per cent of the rural working population. The feudal land-leasing system there is relatively less widespread than in Southeast Asia, and the proportion of agricultural workers is higher. The structure of the rural population of North Africa occupies an intermediate place between the two other regions.

A sizable part of the agricultural population of these regions and, incidentally, of any underdeveloped country consists of unpaid working family members—the so-called "family helpers" who account for 10 to 11 per cent of all rural population engaged in agriculture. This is an index of the relative agrarian overpopulation which has reached a large scale in the countries of Asia, Africa, and Latin America. The "family helpers" constitute an enormous reservoir supplementing the army of the rural lumpen-proletariat [d] and agricultural proletariat.

Even this general survey reveals the backwardness of the class structure of the rural population of underdeveloped countries. The class composition of the local countryside differs somewhat from the conventional class structure in the developed capitalist countries. Likewise, essential differences exist among the underdeveloped countries themselves.

Let us take, as an illustration, the peasantry in the highly developed countries of capitalist Europe, in the countries of Southeast Asia, and in the African countries south of the Sahara (excluding the Union of South Africa). In the first case, capitalist relationships predominate in agriculture as a whole, while in the second case the countryside is characterized by the intertwining of the most varied forms of precapitalist and capitalist relationships. In most of the African countries, the peasantry lives under patriarchal-communal [e] conditions, knowing neither

d. On "lumpen-proletariat," see above, p. 164, note g.

e. The primitive communal system is the first stage in social development, reached just after man emerges from the level of an animal. It is characterized by an absence of private property and low levels of "pro-

# Soviet Writers on the Developing Areas

feudal nor capitalist forms of land ownership. In the African countries, in contrast to many other underdeveloped countries, feudalists and rural bourgeoisie are, with rare exceptions, absent as classes. In the African countryside the collectivist spirit is strong and private-property impulses are alien to an overwhelming part of the peasantry. Accordingly, the agrarian problem is different in different countries.

Similarly, the class structure of the urban population of the countries of Asia, Africa, and Latin America is complex. About one-third of the self-employed population is concentrated in the cities, 63 per cent of the urban population being occupied in the sphere of material production, as well as in trade, banking, and insurance. Of special interest is a comparison of the numbers of the employees and self-employed in the sphere of material production (excluding agriculture). In Latin America the ratio between these two categories is 2.2:1; in North Africa, 1.3:1; and in Asia, 0.6:1. This demonstrates that in the Asian countries the proportion of small production and small trade is far higher than in the two other regions. In other words, the concentration of the proletariat is weaker in Asia. The data on the mining industry are especially indicative: in Asia there are four employees for every entrepreneur; in Latin America, 11; and in North Africa, 22 or 23. In the manufacturing industry, and especially in trade, in the Asian countries there are many fewer employees than entrepreneurs. Thus, compared with North Africa and Latin America, in these countries the capitalist relationships are relatively less developed not only in rural areas but also in towns.

In nearly every underdeveloped country of Asia, North Africa, and Latin America, a national bourgeoisie has been formed and with each year it is expanding its business activities. In most African countries south of the Sahara, the national bourgeoisie does not exist as a developed class. This does not mean that capitalist relationships are completely absent there. In the cities these relationships have arisen and are developing, and a few African entrepreneurs and businessmen do exist.

ductive forces." For further discussion on the topic, see Selection 11, above.

## The Third World in Soviet Perspective

But private national capital [f] is still extremely weak. A different situation prevails with regard to the African proletariat. Even though the working class in a number of countries is still small and weak, it is growing everywhere. This, together with the fact that in many African countries there is practically no urban or rural bourgeoisie or feudal class, is of tremendous importance to the fate of Africa.

What is the composition of the main classes of society in Asia, Africa, and Latin America?

*The Proletariat.* The data on the number of members in the total working class of the countries of Asia, Africa, and North America, and on its individual subclasses, are contradictory. On the whole, the most numerous category is the agricultural proletariat. The principal feature of this subclass of the working class is that the process of the separation of agricultural workers from the principal means of production—land—has not attained any large scale.[g] The most common type of worker employed in agriculture is the worker with a plot of land. This is primarily true for the countries of Southeast Asia and North Africa, in whose agriculture hired labor occurs predominantly in the precapitalist and semi-capitalist forms. The sharecrop system, universally encountered in these regions, is nothing but a transitional form leading to the capitalist leasing system.

The agriculture of Latin America is characterized to a much greater degree by the use of hired labor in its pure form. A major role in the formation of the agricultural proletariat and its class awareness is played by the numerically small stratum of plantation workers.

In the largest underdeveloped countries an industrial proletariat has evolved and developed as an active political force. Of the total number of blue- and white-collar workers, industry accounts for about 35 per cent in India; in Pakistan, more than 25 per cent; in Iraq, about 40 per cent; in Iran, about 20 per cent; in Thailand, more than 25 per cent; in Ceylon, 20 per

f. "National capital" indicates indigenous capital, rather than that brought in by foreign investors.

g. A proletarian is, by definition, one who owns no means of production.

cent; in Morocco, 60 per cent; in Ghana, more than 20 per cent; in Algeria, more than 35 per cent; and in Tunisia, 63 per cent. In a majority of the African countries south of the Sahara, the proportion of industrial workers is much lower. For example, in Tanganyika and Guinea it is 7 per cent of the total number of blue- and white-collar workers; in Kenya, 9.5 per cent; and in the Congo (Leopoldville), 10 per cent, etc.

The weakness of the industrially employed proletariat is its dispersion among numerous small enterprises.[h] The level of concentration of the proletariat, the principal factor determining its role in the socio-political development of a country, is still extremely low. This pertains especially to the enterprises belonging to local capital. The highest degree of concentration of the proletariat is in the mining industry and in other branches of industry owned by foreign monopolies. Another feature adversely affecting the growth of the class awareness of the proletariat in the underdeveloped countries is the small number of members in the stratum of cadre workers. A large part of the working class of these countries consists of former peasants who have not completely severed their ties to the land, and who from time to time return to the countryside. This is a cause of the rather widespread penetration of petty-bourgeois ideology among the ranks of the workers. Lastly, precapitalist and semi-capitalist forms of exploitation of hired labor are practiced not only in agriculture but often in industry and trade as well.

*The Peasantry.* The largest stratum of the peasantry consists of small landholders, and the most widespread forms of exploitation are feudal and semi-capitalist. An exception is the majority of the countries of Black Africa where, as noted previously, patriarchal-communal relationships dominate the countryside.

Let us take as an example the class structure of the Algerian rural population, which can be broken down into the following strata: the rural semi-proletariat, which includes a considerable

h. The modern industrial proletariat is highly concentrated geographically. This enables it to take united action, be effectively propagandized, and develop class-consciousness. See, for instance, p. 167, note 14, above.

## The Third World in Soviet Perspective

section of *khammās* sharecroppers; the agricultural proletariat; the small, medium, and big rural bourgeoisie; the large feudal landowners. According to the 1950–1951 census, there were from 500,000 to 600,000 peasant farms in the country. Of these about 70 per cent were small farms. They belong to the poor and destitute peasantry, the stratum of rural semi-proletariat. The stratum of sharecroppers, the *khamāmisa*, who have leased land on semi-feudal terms, constitute part (approximately one-third) of the peasantry which owns a small amount of land. The small rural bourgeoisie accounted for up to 25 per cent of all farms; the top stratum of the rural population, for about 4 per cent. The agricultural proletariat numbered from 100,000, to 150,000 persons. The social picture of the Algerian countryside would be incomplete without noting that approximately 1.5 million men and women work in agriculture as unpaid members of peasant families.

India is a country with an exceptionally intricate rural class structure and equally tangled and interwoven forms of land ownership and exploitation of the peasantry. The agrarian and peasant problem in this country has been the subject of quite a few studies in our literature, and it is not our aim to discuss it. We would merely like to note that so far technical-economic rather than socio-political analysis has predominated in many of these studies. At present it is of exceptional importance to focus attention on the socio-political aspect of the agrarian-peasantry problem in India and the other economically underdeveloped countries. For example, agrarian specialists consider it a progressive phenomenon that implementation of agrarian reform has resulted in some acceleration of the development of capitalist relationships in the Indian countryside. Does this mean that India's agriculture has slowly but surely chosen the path of capitalism? Is further expansion of the base of capitalism in the Indian countryside progressive under present-day conditions?[i] It is not sufficient to criticize reforms

i. The traditional Marxist view is that class differentiation is necessary to stimulate class conflict. (See above, p. 12.) Both here and in Ul'yanov-skiy's article (No. 10, above) it is indicated that this development may not be necessary in present-day conditions.

negatively and to limit oneself—as many are doing—to the general statement that the Indian (and not only the Indian) peasantry needs radical agrarian reform. The question is: just what concrete radical reform does it desire?

While noting the complexity of the structure of the peasantry in underdeveloped countries, it is necessary to stress a correct observation that is of great significance in analyzing the prospects for a national liberation revolution: the stratum of peasants who own little or no land is, above all, the most natural ally of the proletariat. In the present era, the most favorable possibilities for an alliance between the working class and the peasantry do not necessarily arise in areas where the degree of the class differentiation of the peasants is higher or where more developed relationships of production predominate in the countryside.

*The Bourgeoisie.* In Marxist-Leninist literature, the bourgeoisie of the underdeveloped countries of Asia, Africa, and Latin America is usually divided into national and pro-imperialist. It should be noted that such a division reflects the principal feature of the historical development of this bourgeoisie, which evolved under colonial conditions, under conditions of the rule of foreign capital.

In the different countries, both the national and the pro-imperialist bourgeoisie consist of various strata. What strata are specifically included in each of these two groups of the bourgeoisie? Is there a general economic criterion which would make it possible to differentiate clearly between them? Here one should keep in mind that the national and pro-imperialist groups of the bourgeoisie do not constitute stagnant, stable groups separated from one another by a "Chinese Wall." It should not be forgotten that these groups belong in one and the same exploiting class and that a process of interpenetration is proceeding between them. Therefore, the division itself is largely arbitrary.

In our opinion, the principal criterion which should underlie an analysis of the social structure of the bourgeoisie of the underdeveloped countries and an evaluation of the two groups is their relationship to the national economy. The question is:

where the basic economic activity of one stratum of the bourgeoisie or another is concentrated, what is the degree of its connections with the public sector of the economy and the domestic market, and what is its objective economic interest in developing the national economy and shattering the influence of foreign capital?

The relationship of the bourgeoisie of the underdeveloped countries to the national economy depends to a definite extent on the branch of the economy in which its capital is invested, and on the scale of this capital.

From the standpoint of the various branches in which capital is invested, the bourgeoisie of the countries of Asia, Africa, and Latin America consists of the following basic strata: (a) the industrial bourgeoisie, whose capital is invested primarily in the light, food, and certain other branches of the manufacturing industry; (b) the trading bourgeoisie, which has ties with both the domestic market and foreign trade; (c) the banking bourgeoisie, which is engaged in money-lending operations in industry, commerce, and transport; (d) the usurer bourgeoisie, which is engaged mostly in land speculation and in lending the peasants money at exorbitant rates; (e) the stratum of bourgeoisie whose capital is invested mostly in agricultural production. According to the scale of capital, these strata are broken down into small, medium, and big bourgeoisie. An exception is the banking bourgeoisie stratum, which consists of medium and big bankers.

Depending on the country and the historical and economic conditions of its development, different strata of the bourgeoisie play a predominant role. In a number of underdeveloped countries some of these strata are missing, or even the bourgeoisie itself is lacking as a class. The banking and industrial bourgeoisie is developed in only a few of these countries.

In itself, the fact that the capital of one stratum of the bourgeoisie or another is invested in industry or, say, commerce provides no foundation for classifying the entire stratum as part of either of the two groups of the bourgeoisie—national or pro-imperialist. In the same way, it is not possible to make such a distinction according to the scale of capital. It cannot, for example, be said that the entire small and medium bourgeoisie is national, while the entire large bourgeoisie is pro-imperialist. In certain countries a part of the small and medium bourgeoisie is closely linked to the activities of foreign monopolies, and its profits depend on these monopolies' retention of control over the spheres of the economy concerned.

Nevertheless, only a thorough and detailed analysis of the composition of the bourgeoisie according to its engagement in various branches of the economy and according to the scale of capital can provide a foundation for clarifying the relationship between specific bourgeois strata and the national production, their ties to the national sector of production and to foreign capital, and the degree of dependence of their income on the activity of imperialist monopolies. A study of the class structure of the bourgeoisie makes possible a correct political evaluation of its various strata. The question here is: which strata of the bourgeoisie of the underdeveloped countries do or may act in the national liberation movement as an anti-imperialist force, and under what conditions; and what is the degree of their revolutionary possibilities on the one hand, and which strata adhere to a pro-imperialist orientation on the other?

The intelligentsia of the underdeveloped countries merit special attention. Since under the conditions of colonial rule the general level of political development of the proletariat as well as of the bourgeoisie was always far below that of the industrially developed countries, these intelligentsia, mainly of bourgeois and landlord origin, have from the very beginning played a prominent role in the national liberation movement. In a majority of cases, the cadres of the activists of the political parties consist of professionals and white-collar workers, lawyers, physicians, teachers, engineers, municipal employees, and students—these are the people who, together with small businessmen, form the backbone of nationalist parties and groups. To these should be added the officer class, which in most of the underdeveloped countries comes from petty-bourgeois strata. It is this fairly numerous and politically

*The Third World in Soviet Perspective*

conscious category of people that is the bearer of nationalist ideology. Some of them switch to positions of protecting the interests of workers and join the nucleus of Marxist parties. A majority of the representatives of the intelligentsia express the interests of the developing class of the national bourgeoisie.

*The Feudalists.* As a result of the collapse of colonial regimes, the economic and political positions of the feudal class in the countries of Asia, Africa, and Latin America have been seriously weakened. Although agrarian reforms have been of a halfway and inconsistent nature, their implementation has led to a definite restriction of the influence of the feudalists, and to a certain dislodging of feudal and prefeudal relationships and acceleration of the development of capitalism in the countryside. On the whole, however, this class is still a major force and continues to be a support of imperialism. In certain countries it holds the reins not only of economic but also of political rule. The feudalists represent the most reactionary part of the population of these countries, and the struggle against them is one of the central problems of the developing national liberation revolutions. However, this general appraisal alone cannot suffice. It would be incorrect, for example, to apply the same yardstick to the feudal class in Afghanistan and in Thailand. It must also be recognized that in certain countries (e.g., Morocco) some of the feudalists participated in the struggle for national independence. On the whole, however, these differences manifest themselves only with regard to the foreign policy of the liberated countries. Moreover, the known progressive orientation of the foreign policy of certain countries is to be explained not by the preservation of progressive traits by the ruling feudal class but by historical and international reasons. In all other respects, the feudal class is everywhere a deterrent to the socio-economic and political development of the underdeveloped countries.

Also, the known evolution of the feudalists as a class should not be ignored. The external feudal shell sometimes hides new, bourgeois contents. With increasing frequency, the feudal land-lords resort to methods of capitalist exploitation, "accustom"

*Soviet Writers on the Developing Areas*

themselves to capitalist modes of production by becoming entrepreneurs and investing capital in industry. The type of "bourgeoisified" feudalist is a fairly widespread phenomenon in the underdeveloped countries.

For an analysis of the class structure of society, and, to a still greater extent, of the alignment of class forces, a differentiated approach is especially necessary. What is true for one country—say, India—is hardly or not at all applicable not only to the countries of such regions as Latin America and Africa, but also often to the countries of Southeast Asia. This does not mean, however, that there are no common patterns of behavior and common features in the development and structure of the bourgeoisie of the underdeveloped countries.

According to the level of class development and the interrelationship of the class and political forces holding the reins of power, the following groups of underdeveloped countries can be differentiated:

(1) The group of countries with the relatively most highly developed capitalist relationships and classes, in which the national bourgeoisie characteristically holds power. This group may include such countries as India, Burma, Ceylon, Syria, Lebanon, Tunisia, Brazil, and Mexico. In some of these countries—for example, in India—there has evolved a stratum of big bourgeoisie with monopolist tendencies.

(2) The group of countries in which capitalist relationships are less developed and the national bourgeoisie is weaker. In these countries power is held by the national bourgeoisie; sometimes it shares power with a part of the feudal class which had participated in the national liberation movement and follows a neutralist policy. These countries are Iraq, Morocco, Nigeria, Somalia, Sudan, Cambodia, etc. The countries of both these groups actively struggle for economic independence.

(3) In the third group of countries, which may be said to contain the Philippines, Turkey, Malaya, Thailand, Pakistan, and many Latin American countries, power is held by the pro-imperialist bourgeoisie or by a coalition of this wing of the bourgeoisie and the reactionary feudal-landlord class. The

political independence of these countries is of a largely formal nature. Therefore, their peoples face the task of achieving not only economic but also true political independence.

Of course, definite differences exist in the class structure of the population of these countries. For example, the Philippines are the closest to the first group of countries in the degree of development of capitalist relationships and formation of the bourgeoisie and proletariat. However, the alignment of class forces in this country has grown so complicated that power was seized by the pro-imperialist wing of the Philippine bourgeoisie.

(4) A special group of countries is constituted by Ghana, Guinea, and Mali. The class structure of society in these countries is characterized by the fact that capitalist relationships there exist in a rudimentary state, a national bourgeoisie is virtually or totally absent and, while a feudal class does not exist, a proletarian class is evolving. The correlation of class and political forces in these countries has so evolved that an ever-increasing weight is being acquired by forces favoring the non-capitalist path of development. From this standpoint, Indonesia also could be included in this group. However, the class structure of the Indonesian society differs substantially from that of Ghana, Guinea, and Mali. Although in Indonesia the national bourgeoisie did evolve as a class, it would be incorrect to say that all power in the country is entirely concentrated in its hands. The working class of Indonesia exerts a growing influence on the economic and political orientation of the country—it actively struggles against the domestic reaction that attempts to divert the country from its anti-imperialist path.[j]

(5) The class structure of the fifth group of countries, in which can be included the former French colonies in West and Equatorial Africa, the Malagasy Republic, and also the Congo (Leopoldville), etc., displays on the whole many features similar to the preceding group. However, aside from the

j. These are, of course, the four potential national democracies. (See above, p. 28.) The authors are obviously uncomfortable about the inclusion of Indonesia, but there is not much they can do about it.

Congo, Tanganyika, and Senegal, in nearly all these countries the proletariat is very weak and has barely started to evolve as a class. The main difference, in comparison to Ghana, Guinea, and Mali, is that the political influence of imperialism is very strong and power is held by circles which largely pattern their policies on those of imperialism.

(6) The sixth group includes such countries as Nepal, Yemen, Saudi Arabia, Ethiopia, Afghanistan, and others whose class structure is characterized by the presence of a more or less developed feudal class, small numbers of the proletariat, an exceptionally low level of development of capitalism, and almost no bourgeoisie. There power is held by the feudal class. However, for reasons of a historical and international nature, the foreign-policy orientation of these countries is in general linked with the countries pursuing a neutralist policy.

This division of countries into groups is largely arbitrary. These groups do not represent anything fixed and stable. In the course of the socio-economic and political development of the underdeveloped countries, the composition of these groups naturally will change. It can be disputed whether the above division encompasses all the underdeveloped countries; in what group the UAR should be included; where to include such small countries as the princedoms [emirates] of the Arabian peninsula or the "banana republics" of Latin America; whether the inclusion of a given country in one group or another is justified, etc. But the need for such a division is evident. It is dictated by the consideration that the underdeveloped countries, from the standpoint of their class structure (and not only from this standpoint), do not represent a single homogeneous whole with a common fixed pattern of development. While it is true that the class struggle in these countries tends to develop around common basic problems, it is also true that this struggle develops according to the alignment of the class and political forces inside a country on the one hand, and international factors on the other. So the approach to the solution of these problems differs in different countries. Without a differentiated approach to surveying the class structure of society in the sovereign countries of Asia, Africa, and Latin America, it is

## The Third World in Soviet Perspective

impossible to evaluate correctly the alignment of class and political forces in these countries at the present stage of development of the national liberation revolutions.

There is no doubt that in India, for example, the national bourgeoisie is indeed the ruling class. The policy of the government fundamentally coincides with the interests of this class, which is extremely wealthy, numerous, and has traditions and experience in the political guidance of the masses through the National Congress Party. Of course, the Indian bourgeoisie (or at any rate many of its strata) is closely linked to land ownership. The role of landlords, especially the capitalist landlords, cannot be underestimated, but the greatest influence on government is exercised by the industrial bourgeoisie. Power also belongs to the bourgeoisie in Burma, Ceylon, the Philippines, Syria, Lebanon, and Tunisia.

Here too the differences are of course notable. The foreign and also domestic policies of the bourgeoisie differ in different countries. In certain of these countries which belong in the colonialists' blocs (the Philippines, Pakistan) the foreign-policy orientation of the ruling circles is largely to be explained not only—and perhaps also not so much—by socio-economic factors as by circumstances of a historical nature (in Pakistan enmity toward India and the endeavor to win the support of both the West and the Moslem world; the long-time American rule in the Philippines, etc.). On the other hand, of course, the pro-imperialist position of the ruling elite exerts a retarding effect on the socio-economic development of a country.

In a number of countries the national bourgeoisie manages and directs the machinery of government. But, in Indonesia, for example, the bourgeoisie, which never was as strong and influential as in India, failed to monopolize state power. The nearly 2 million-strong Communist Party, which enjoys enormous prestige among the masses, indubitably influences the policies of the government. Moreover, political struggle in Indonesia has been evolving in such a manner that the most reactionary part of the bourgeoisie, the part linked to imperialism and feudal interests, was either crushed (the separatists) or isolated (Masjumi). The left wing of the bourgeoisie, which in this struggle leaned on the support of the progressive forces of the people, could not but move farther to the left as a result of such an alliance, and the bourgeoisie as a class turned out to be schism-ridden and weakened. These and other circumstances led to the fact that in present-day Indonesia there is no single class which could hold all power in the country. The country is going through a transition period: as Comrade Aidit [k] noted, liberal democracy (that is, bourgeois democracy) is a relic of the past but the conditions for a people's democracy are not yet ripe.

In the UAR extremely radical reforms were recently introduced. Decree No. 117 of 1961 provides for the nationalization of all banks and insurance companies in the country. It is difficult to imagine that the bourgeoisie would exclude itself from such a lucrative sphere of activity as banking and insurance. Pursuant to Decree No. 118, the share of the state in the 91 largest enterprises should be at least 50 per cent. A law has been promulgated that in 159 companies no shareholder may hold shares worth more than 10,000 Egyptian pounds, as well as a new tax law decreeing that persons with an annual income of £10,000 or more have to pay a tax of 90 per cent to the state. If we also consider the nationalization of the "Misr" concern and the move against such large groups as Farghaly, Abboud, and the Greeks, and if we recall that recently the property of about 700 capitalists has been sequestered, the salaries of company directors have been restricted, and several dozen of the wealthiest persons arrested, it is to be concluded that state power in the UAR is used to restrict and weaken the influence of the wealthiest and strongest strata of society.

Indisputably, these measures do not in themselves transcend the framework of state capitalism. The social base of the regime remains narrow, and the popular masses, as before, are

k. D. N. Aidit is the First Secretary of the Communist Party of Indonesia, responsible for building the party from its low point of the early 1950's to its present formidable position.

## The Third World in Soviet Perspective

not allowed to participate in deciding the country's fate. Nevertheless, this narrow base is not a base of bourgeois or, even less, feudal rule.

V. I. Lenin emphasized the inevitability of a difference in the nature of revolutions in the East. In the UAR, power is held solidly in the hands of a group of officers deriving from petty-bourgeois strata. Since 1952, their policies have objectively been contributing to an independent capitalist development of the country. Until very recently, little has been done to shatter the old social structure of the state and accomplish radical reforms. But life teaches a great deal. Cooperation with the world socialist system is playing a tremendous and truly invaluable role in the underdeveloped countries.

The leading group in the UAR, as well as in Iraq, Indonesia, and many African countries, cannot be directly identified with the interests of any single class. Of course, the government of India, too, has to consider the interests not only of the bourgeoisie but also of other classes. On the other hand, the Indian bourgeoisie has incomparably more opportunities to influence its government than do the Indonesian and Egyptian bourgeoisie.

While in such countries as Pakistan, Turkey, and Morocco power is held by a bloc of the bourgeoisie and landowners, and in Iran by landowners, in Ghana, Guinea, and Mali the government consists of representatives of a radical intelligentsia which is hostile toward imperialism. Under normal conditions this intelligentsia would inevitably have become the voice of the interests of the emerging bourgeoisie. At present the conditions are not normal, because of the unique situation caused by the struggle of two systems. The camp of socialism exerts a powerful and growing influence on the entire course of world events, and in the countries existing during the transition stage, the petty-bourgeois intelligentsia does not necessarily have to become a champion of the capitalist path of development.

Thus, the differences between the underdeveloped countries stem not only from the vast differences in their economic situation and make-up, but also from the varying alignments of class forces.

The national bourgeoisie which holds the power or influences government policy manifests in every case a natural striving toward economic independence. The national capitalists dream of reaching the level of the financial magnates in the developed capitalist countries and of occupying a position of equality in the family of the international financial oligarchy. The relations of the national bourgeoisie with foreign monopoly capital are relations of struggle and cooperation. The course toward independent capitalist development is being combined in many countries (India, Morocco, etc.) with the attempt to avoid any resolute measures against foreign capital. The policy of compromise is a half-hearted, irresolute form of eliminating foreign private capital, whose importance to the economy of these countries is decreasing, though very slowly.

In the relatively higher-developed countries considered here (e.g., India) an extremely intricate mutual intertwining of the interests of domestic and foreign capital is occurring. While developing its own industry and displacing foreign capital, a part of the national bourgeoisie nevertheless tries to gain support from foreign capital by organizing mixed stock companies. It depends on British, American, Japanese, West German, and other companies for deliveries of raw material and equipment and the marketing of finished products. The Indian bourgeoisie is intricately linked to foreign capital.

The problem of foreign capital is one of the most complicated. The creation of a developed modern economy requires large capital investments, and no underdeveloped country can get by on its own resources alone. There are only two foreign sources: cooperation with the socialist camp, and the attraction of private and state capital from the countries of the capitalist system. Although for some individual countries it appears possible to base their program of economic construction almost exclusively on their own resources and Soviet aid, in a majority of cases the countries that chose the path of eliminating backwardness still attract foreign capital (in one form or another—on a greater or smaller scale).

Judging from various data, in the next few years monopoly capital intends to intensify its pressure and penetration into many African countries where at present there is virtually no industry. This undoubtedly entails a grave danger to the newly won independence of these countries. If the monopolies are allowed not only to retain their present positions in the extractive industry but also to control the creation of the manufacturing industry, they will obtain influence over the young states that will later on be much harder to eliminate. The monopolies could make the young national bourgeoisie dependent on them and subordinate to them; they will encourage the "Philippine" type of development.

Does this all signify an intensification of the trend toward smoothing out, toward assuaging, the contradictions between the national bourgeoisie and imperialism? On the contrary! Parallel to the growth of cooperation and the strengthening of the bonds between the top stratum of the national bourgeoisie and the monopolist capital of Western powers and Japan, the contradictions between the bulk of the bourgeoisie and imperialism will become more intense.

The economic interests of the national bourgeoisie are opposed to the interests of imperialism. It was noted previously that the bourgeoisie everywhere strives toward independent capitalist development, and it is precisely this development that is being hampered by imperialism. At first glance this is paradoxical: after all, the greatest chance for capitalism in its struggle against socialism lies in turning the "uncommitted" countries, this entire "third world," toward the capitalist path. However, imperialism cannot exist without colonial or semi-colonial exploitation in one form or another, and this means that it is in its interest to keep the exploited countries in the position of the "world countryside"; [1] that is, to preserve that very underdeveloped status whose elimination is of concern to all nationalist forces, including the bourgeoisie. Hence the

1. For "world countryside," see above, p. 131, note f.

prospects for an exacerbation of the struggle between the national bourgeoisie and imperialism.

Although the underdeveloped countries can, under the leadership of the national bourgeoisie, manage to extricate themselves from being agrarian and raw-material appendages of imperialism and to a certain extent win economic independence, they cannot solve completely the growing problem of eliminating their traditional backwardness. Every year the contrast between what the people need and what they can achieve under the leadership of the bourgeoisie is becoming stronger. Undoubtedly a part of the bourgeoisie will seek a way out through rapproachement with imperialism and appeasement; nevertheless, another large part of the bourgeoisie can be drawn by the maelstrom of events into an active struggle against imperialism.

As noted in the Program of the CPSU, the anti-imperialist potential of the national bourgeoisie is not exhausted and it can participate in a national front. By the same token, this emphasizes the harmfulness and inadmissibility of a leftist "skipping of a stage." [m] A majority of the underdeveloped countries in practice now face the problems of a national, anti-imperialist, anti-feudal revolution, a revolution that is in the stage of growth, but far from completed. Therefore, the democratic forces are looking for ways, means, and forms of collaborating with it [the national bourgeoisie] within the framework of a common national, anti-imperialist front.

Attempts to deny the anti-imperialist role of the bourgeoisie started long ago, in the 1920's. To a great extent they were related to the erroneous views of Stalin regarding the prospects for the development of the national liberation movement. In 1925, in his speech "On the Political Tasks of the University of the Peoples of the East," Stalin declared, referring to countries like India: "The fire should be concentrated on the compromis-

m. The condemnation of "skipping a stage" is not meant with regard to a society's passing from feudalism to socialism by "skipping" capitalism. In the present context, it is a criticism of the Chinese, whom the Russians charge with urging direct transition to proletarian (Communist) domination of revolutionary movements without first progressing through the stage of cooperation with the national bourgeoisie.

ing nationalist bourgeoisie" (J. V. Stalin, *Sochineniya* [Works], VII, 148). Further on, he directly set for the proletariat of the colonies and dependent countries the task of "forming a national revolutionary bloc of workers, peasants, and the revolutionary intelligentsia against the bloc of the compromising national bourgeoisie and imperialism" (*ibid.*, 149). By the "compromising" bourgeoisie he meant the [Indian] National Congress.

The decisions of the Sixth Congress of the Comintern,[n] which were clearly influenced by this dictum, noted that "the national bourgeoisie is not a force struggling against imperialism." But the subsequent course of events refuted such an approach to the problem. In India no schism of the bourgeoisie took place, and the National Congress headed the struggle for political independence. The national bourgeoisie also has led the anti-imperialist struggle in Burma, Indonesia, Ceylon, Syria, Egypt, Tunisia, and other countries, although this struggle has not always been waged consistently.

It is known that after Stalin's death, on the initiative of the Central Committee of the CPSU, incorrect appraisals of the most prominent leaders of the anti-imperialist national bourgeoisie were discarded, but by then considerable damage had been caused to the international Communist movement. It is sufficient to mention the events in Iran in 1953, when the People's Party at the critical moment actually struggled on two fronts—against imperialism and against Mossadegh.[o]

The leftist-sectarian approach signifies essentially a denial of the path of national democracy, a path which in the Party

n. The Sixth Congress of the Comintern, held in 1928, propounded some of Stalin's most doctrinaire views. It came just after Chiang Kai-shek had turned on the Chinese Communists, and reflected Stalin's disillusionment with the national bourgeoisie. The Congress was also noteworthy for its complete failure to appreciate the danger of fascism, thus helping Hitler to power in Germany by concentrating Communist fire on the Socialists rather than on the Nazis.

o. On Mossadegh and the Iranian Communists, see Manfred Halpern's chapter on "The Middle East and North Africa" in Black and Thornton, eds., *Communism and Revolution*, 316–19.

Program and in the unanimously adopted Statement of the 1960 Conference of the Representatives of Communist and Workers' Parties is considered as the form of state regime that suits best the conditions currently prevailing in many under-developed countries. The national democratic state, as shown by its very name, can arise because the present stage of the in-ternational revolutionary movement in Asia and Africa, taken as a whole, is at a national democratic stage. This state, based on an alliance of the proletariat and peasantry, with the partic-ipation of the bourgeoisie, is conceived as a weapon for com-pleting the bourgeois-democratic, national liberation, anti-imperialist, and anti-feudal revolution. In the course of its implementation and completion under the distinctive condi-tions of a national democratic state, this revolution will tran-scend the framework of a bourgeois revolution. Just as the bourgeoisie itself, having initiated the revolution, cannot bring it to an end and participation by more radically disposed social forces is needed, so the revolution itself, after its completion, will prove to be broader and deeper than it seemed at first. A thorough examination of all the tasks facing the national demo-cratic state, as enumerated in the Statement of the 1960 Con-ference of the Representatives of Communist and Workers' Parties, makes it clear that their fulfillment will lay the foun-dation for a non-capitalist path of development. On the other hand, along with the fulfillment of the tasks of the national democratic revolution, the center of gravity will inevitably shift toward the more radical popular elements (precisely because they will be the motive power of the most radical transforma-tions), and therefore the class core of the state will shift to the left. The hegemony of the proletariat will then turn out to be a natural result as well as a prerequisite of the entire course of the socio-political development of the national democratic state, which is historically called upon to be the tool of the transition of the underveloped countries to the non-capitalist path of development.

In an analysis of the possibilities for the development of na-tional democracy, special importance attaches to the need to investigate concretely the class forces in a given country. Life poses to us responsible tasks of scientific elaboration of the problems that are of tremendous importance to the entire future of mankind. The 22nd Party Congress has created exceptionally favorable opportunities for fruitful work in this direction.

SELECTION 14

# Imperialism and the Ideology of National Reformism in Latin America *

## BY A. SHUL'GOVSKIY

*ONE of the most difficult problems confronting the Soviets in the third world is competition from other left-of-center groups. The flow of history is supposed to take care of reactionary, capitalist, bourgeois forces, and although these are of great concern, Soviet writers find no particular difficulty in fitting them into the proper historical niche. Communism grew out of the international workers' movement, in which unity was believed to be the prerequisite of progress, and when the movement split during World War I, bitterness among the factions was extreme. The Communists lost in that contest, and even today the European Socialists and their colleagues in Asia (especially in India and Indonesia) are subjected to constant Communist attack— bitter not only because the Socialists are "heretics" rather than natural enemies, but also because the Communists fear them as rivals for the leadership of radical discontent.*

*In Latin America, a similar role is played by such moderate left-wing groups as the Acción Democratica in Venezuela or the APRA of Peru, led by Betancourt and Haya de la Torre respectively. The attacks on these men—typically enunciated in this article by Shul'govskiy—are far more intense than those directed against such dictators as Stroessner or Duvalier or—in his time —Batista. The progressive leaders, who claim to offer Latin America a path to the future that can satisfy the need for radical reforms without falling prey to Communist rule, are just as much under attack from the right as from the Communist left. They are in a position uncomfortably reminiscent of that of the German Socialists, who were destroyed by the joint pressure of Communists and Nazis in the 1930's.*

* SOURCE: "Imperializm i idiologiya natsional-reformizma v Latinskoy Amerike," MEIMO, No. 8 (1961), 45–59.

305

## The Third World in Soviet Perspective

*The Soviets claim that they will not again fall into the trap of helping the extreme right by sabotaging the Socialists, and their position is not uncompromisingly hostile in Europe. In the developing countries, however, they frequently appear to ignore the lessons of history, or else believe that they can be more effective in fomenting and exploiting discontent under a rightist dictatorship than under a progressive government dedicated to the improvement of its people's lot.*

THE upsurge of the national liberation movement in Latin America has caused an intensification of the ideological struggle —a clash of various theories and concepts regarding the paths of development for Latin American countries. In attempting to maintain their economic and political positions in this area, American monopolistic circles have recently stepped up their fight against the national liberation and revolutionary movements. Whereas previously their main efforts were directed toward establishing and giving total support to dictatorial regimes, ever since the overthrow of dictatorships in many countries and the victory of the Cuban Revolution they have been attempting to employ more refined approaches as well. In particular, the American ruling circles are widely employing economic and political means to attain their goals, and are striving to convince Latin American peoples of the desire of the United States to promote "democracy" in Latin America and economic progress.

Recently American propaganda has proclaimed widely the "new program" of the Kennedy Administration for Latin America. This program was set forth in the President's message to Congress on March 14, 1961,[1] and carried the celebrated title, "Alliance for Progress." Although it emphasizes the need for a radical change in the U.S. approach to Latin America, it is essentially directed toward isolating revolutionary Cuba from other Latin American countries. It advocates use of "evolutionary," "democratic" reforms to oppose the revolutionary Cuban methods of the national liberation struggle which are gaining increasing popularity among the masses in Latin America. In

1. *New York Times*, March 15, 1961.

brief, behind these new words are hidden the same old attempts of U.S. monopolist circles to bend all their efforts to prevent the independent development of Latin America.

It is therefore not accidental that American imperialism seeks and finds support among the national reformist circles of certain countries in Latin America, and uses every possible means to encourage them to attack the Communist movement and Marxist-Leninist theory. Rather influential groups within a number of such Latin American political parties as the People's Aprista Party (Peru), Democratic Action (Venezuela), Nationalist Revolutionary Movement (Bolivia), National Liberation (Costa Rica), the Febrerist Party (Paraguay), the Guatemalan Revolutionary Party, the Popular Democratic Party (Puerto Rico), and certain others support the so-called "national reform" platform.[2]

The national reformists defend the theory of the role of American monopoly capital as "positive" for their countries, and the theory of the absence of "radical" contradictions between the national liberation movement and imperialism. Very often they don the costumes of "revolutionaries" and arm themselves with the slogans of liberation popular among the masses, having first emasculated the revolutionary, anti-imperialist content of these slogans.

The social basis of national reformism consists chiefly of certain strata of the petty bourgeoisie, representatives of the middle classes of the population who have to some degree experienced the influence of American monopoly capital. This basis is extremely insecure and is growing narrower every year owing to the incessant growth of revolutionary tension among the middle classes in Latin America. It is indisputable that radical changes are already taking place in Latin America among the

---

2. Only national reformism, which is a unique phenomenon of petty bourgeois reformism under Latin American conditions, is considered in this article. For a number of historical reasons, reformism of the European variety of social democracy has not attained wide diffusion in the ranks of the Socialist parties of Latin America (they are most influential in Chile, Argentina, and Uruguay). The leftist forces in the Socialist parties are now offering more decisvie opposition to American imperialism, and support solidarity with the Cuban revolution.

*The Third World in Soviet Perspective*

petty bourgeoisie, students, and intelligentsia, who are becoming more inclined to cooperate with the working class. This tendency toward a change in the position of the middle classes is creating new opportunities for further development of an anti-imperialist revolution in Latin America. The victorious experience of the Cuban Revolution—the first in the Western Hemisphere to provide a practical example of how it is possible to put an end, once and for all, to dependence upon American monopolies—is exerting a tremendous influence on this process. The national reformists are able to rely only upon the ruling sector of the middle classes, which tends toward compromise with reaction and imperialism.

Already in the 1920's, when the danger of reformism to the liberation movement was just becoming apparent, Latin American Marxists emphasized the need to reveal the social causes of the appearance of reformism, to expose its roots and demonstrate the role of imperialism in the propagation of reformist ideas. The founder of the Communist Party of Peru, José Carlos Mariátegui, gave a clear picture of the attitude of certain petty bourgeois circles in Latin America toward American capital, a picture which even today basically retains its significance. He noted in particular that in the economically underdeveloped countries of Latin America, "the creation of large enterprises, although they cruelly exploit their local servants, nevertheless always means higher wages for that class and therefore encounters a favorable attitude on the part of the representatives of the middle class. American firms offer higher pay, the possibility for advancement, and liberation from keen competition for work within the state apparatus, where prospects are open only to clever opportunity-seekers. This factor acts as a decisive force on the consciousness of the petty bourgeoisie, who are searching for, or already enjoy, some position." [3] In depicting the social roots of reformism another Latin American Marxist, the founder of the Communist Party of Cuba, Julio Antonio Mella, noted that one of the determining factors of this phenomenon is the

3. *El movimiento revolucionário latinoamericano* (Buenos Aires 1929), 151.

308

attempt on the part of the petty bourgeois elements to "earn enough to live on in a bourgeois society." [4] In the draft of the political theses of the Central Committee of the Communist Party of Venezuela, published at the end of 1960 for the 3rd Party Congress, special mention was made of the social basis of national reformism: "In view of their economic position, certain upper levels of the petty bourgeoisie are inclined to deal with the bourgeoisie and support its compromise with imperialism." [5]

The recent increased activity of the Latin American reformists is explained to no small degree by their attempt to "coexist" peacefully with the local compromising monopoly capitalists and the oligarchy, and to share state power with them. Reformist elements who participate to some degree in the control of the government (in Venezuela, for example) "have forgotten" their loud proclamations and appear as passionate defenders of so-called "representative democracy," which in fact is nothing but a camouflaged form of rule by the privileged classes and imperialism. In this manner the ruling elite of the national reformists is ever more closely tied to the compromising monopoly capitalists and actually expresses and defends the latter's interests.

It is typical that a number of present-day leaders of reformism have undergone training in certain international economic and social organizations that are under U.S. influence. The bourgeois theories of "peaceful integration," the different versions of technocratic conceptions, and the theories of "interdependence" have exerted great influence on Latin American reformists. Their "concepts" are an eclectic mixture of certain idealist bourgeois theories which are interwoven with various falsified Marxist ideas sophistically removed from their general context. In speaking of the struggle against the reformists, Julio Antonio Mella emphatically stated: "We are fighting them because their points of view contradict the actual situation in America, are unfruitful, reactionary, and utopian." [6]

4. *Amauta* (June–July 1930), 48.
5. *Tribuna popular* (Venezuela), November 4, 1960.
6. *Amauta* (August–September 1930), 26.

## The Third World in Soviet Perspective

At the basis of the national reform concept lies the thesis of the "special" role of imperialism in Latin America. One of the most pretentious ideologists of national reformism, the leader of the Peruvian Aprista Party, Haya de la Torre, is attempting to assume the role of subverter of Marxist-Leninist teachings on imperialism. He defends the relativist point of view, affirming that while imperialism is the highest and ultimate stage of capitalism for the highly developed capitalist countries, it is the "first or lowest stage of capitalism" for the economically underdeveloped countries of Latin America.[7] This contention is derived from the fact that the penetration of imperialism into Latin American countries "stimulates economic growth" and imperialism in these countries therefore plays the same role that European capitalism did in the period of the collapse of feudalism and the industrial development of European countries.[8]

Laying claim to a so-called sociological basis for his "discovery," Haya de la Torre advances an idealistic, relativistic theory of historical "space-time," artificially dividing the history of human society into self-contained zones and regions which are allegedly governed by laws applicable only locally.[9] In order to create this system, Haya de la Torre emasculates the social-economic content of the concept of imperialism.

7. Haya de la Torre, *Treinto años de aprismo* (Mexico-Buenos Aires 1956), 145–46.
8. *Ibid.*, 151.
9. It is not the purpose of this article to include a detailed description of this theory, which is an eclectic jumble of the ideas of Spengler, Toynbee, certain elements of Hegelianism, and a mechanical transferring of Einstein's theory of relativity to social phenomena. We note in passing that even many of those who share Haya de la Torre's theories of imperialism are skeptical of his "philosophical" theory. This "philosophy" of the leader of the Apristas was subjected to scathing Marxist criticism in a book by the leader of the Uruguayan Communist Party, Rodney Arismendi, *La filosofía del marxismo y el señor Haya de la Torre. Sobre una gran mistificación teórica* (Buenos Aires 1946). The Cuban newspaper *Noticias de Hoy* (February 28, 1961), in an article entitled "Haya de la Torre, the Secret Enemy of the Revolution," says that the Aprista leader is an old enemy of the Latin American revolutionary movement and that at the present time American imperialists are using him in their campaign against Cuba.

Imperialism, he affirms, signifies the inevitable expansion of the more highly industrially developed countries into the economically underdeveloped areas and countries. In the process, imperialism creates the most highly developed technological sector of the economy and helps to destroy the outmoded forms of production. Hence the conclusion: imperialism apparently plays a "progressive" role in Latin America, and represents a necessary stage in the development of Latin American countries.[10] The entire line of reasoning of the Aprista ideologists is called upon to prove that there are in fact no forces in Latin America capable of transforming the backward, semi-feudal, socio-economic structure without the "revolutionizing" aid of American capital.

The attempt of Haya de la Torre and other national reform theorists to prove the inapplicability of Lenin's theory of imperialism to Latin America is worthless, a sophistic distortion of the objective processes of the development of Latin American countries. It goes without saying that the penetration of monopoly capital into Latin American countries actually does bring about some development of capitalist relationships, some industrial growth, and increases employment in certain branches of the economy. But the entire matter centers around the degree to which, and especially the purpose for which, foreign capital does this.

Let us take, for example, the Venezuelan petroleum industry, which is dominated by foreign monopolies. It cannot be denied that its development has exerted a definite influence in undermining the old, semi-feudal relationships in the country. But this "progressive" role of the petroleum industry, the undermining of semi-feudal relationships, is performed only to the extent that is convenient and necessary for the imperialist companies to intensify the extraction of oil, the rapacious exploitation of the natural riches of the country. The petroleum monopolies get along "peacefully" with the landlord-latifundists, from whom they rent a large amount of land. For this reason, the petroleum sector in the Venezuelan economy

10. Haya de la Torre, 125, 143–44ff.

## The Third World in Soviet Perspective

has not only failed to bring about a decisive destruction of the old relationships, but has even "immortalized" the decay of the backward economic structure of the country.

In the postwar period, as can be seen from Table 1, foreign monopolies have strengthened their penetration of the Latin American manufacturing industry and are establishing subsidiaries, while at the same time not hesitating to strengthen their positions in the extractive industry, the sphere in which they traditionally invest their capital.

TABLE 1

Distribution of Direct Capital Investment of the USA in Latin America
According to Branches of Production
(in millions of dollars)

|  | 1940 | 1946 | 1950 | 1959 |
|---|---|---|---|---|
| All direct capital investments | 2,706 | 3,046 | 4,735 | 8,218 |
| of which |  |  |  |  |
| Mining industry | 507 | 506 | 628 | 1,258 |
| Oil industry | 516 | 697 | 1,408 | 2,963 |
| Manufacturing industry | 210 | 399 | 780 | 1,405 |
| Public utilities | 960 | 920 | 1,041 | 1,101 |
| Agriculture | 359 | 407 | 520 | * |
| Trade | 81 | 72 | 243 | 641 |
| Other branches | 73 | 45 | 115 | 850 |

* Data for 1959 are missing, included in other branches. Calculated from "U.S. Investments in the Latin American Economy" (Washington 1957), 111; *Survey of Current Business* (September 1960), 20.

Foreign enterprises usually are provided with modern equipment and have considerable productive capacity. According to recent available data, the production of American companies amounted to 10 per cent of the total gross product of Latin American countries.[11] A considerable part of this goes to the American companies engaged in the extractive industry and is exported out of Latin America. American companies account for about one-third of all Latin American exports.[12] The bulk of the products of the manufacturing industry remains in Latin America, but this is by no means a "favor" to

11. *Survey of Current Business* (September 1960), 22.
12. *Ibid.*

## Soviet Writers on the Developing Areas

Latin American countries. The increasing tendency of monopoly capital to construct its own enterprises in Latin America is explained primarily by the fact that the U.S. monopolies strive to avoid the customs barriers that have been established in some Latin American countries, to become more solidly entrenched in the Latin American markets, and to camouflage their competition with national industry.

The American magazine, *Survey of Current Business,* wrote that American companies in the manufacturing industries are most active in the economically more highly developed countries of Latin America (Argentina, Brazil, Mexico), allegedly for the purpose of satisfying the demand of the "growing local markets." [13] Behind these words, which appear innocent at first glance, is hidden the ugly picture of the ruthless competition of the American monopolies, undermining the national manufacturing industry which could, under favorable conditions, secure an internal market for its own products.

The ideologists of American monopoly capital, together with the national reformists, maintain that American enterprises constitute an organic part of the economic structure of Latin American countries, as if the distinction between national and foreign enterprises had been erased—the Latin Americans do not mind, as long as there is work. The imperialists and national reformists also like to refer to the fact that American enterprises help to introduce modern equipment and the latest methods of production into Latin American countries. In truth, however, foreign enterprises hinder the development of the productive forces of Latin American countries. This cannot but lead to further intensification of the contradiction between the national interests of the people of Latin America and the imperialist plans of foreign monopolies. An objective manifestation of these contradictions is the intensification of the struggle of Latin American countries for economic independence.

To counterbalance the struggle for economic liberation, which they reject as allegedly not corresponding to "Latin

13. *Ibid.* (January 1957), 8.

## The Third World in Soviet Perspective

American reality," the national reformists advance the thesis of the "mutual interest" of the United States and Latin America. According to their ideas, Latin America requires American capital, just as the United States critically needs Latin America as a source of raw materials. From this they draw the conclusion that Latin America is confronted with the task of the overall development, and particularly the "industrialization," of the "traditional" branches of its economy to satisfy the demands of its "Northern neighbor." [14]

In unmasking such fantasies of the reformists, Rodney Arismendi [a] writes: "And this is the essence of pan-Americanism, one of the manifestations of the reality of world capitalism during the epoch of imperialism! Morgan and Rockefeller stand for the same thing, but on the other side. True, they are less confused than Haya de la Torre, who speaks of 'empire-less democratic inter-Americanism,' but in effect they come up with the same idea." [15]

The facts of the pernicious effects of American monopolies on the economy of Latin America are so apparent, and the cases of open interference by the ruling circles of the United States in the internal affairs of the Latin American countries are so numerous, that the national reformists cannot pass over this question in silence. They advance the thesis of the dual character of imperialism. On the one hand, Haya de la Torre maintains, imperialism is progressive and on the other it contains a hidden threat. But this threat arises only when political imperialism is joined with economic imperialism. According to Haya de la Torre, it is thus necessary to combat political imperialism and separate it from economic imperialism. The latter, by renouncing any policy of usurpation, can create the basis for cooperation between the U.S. and Latin America. He has put into general use the perplexing formula: "Democratic inter-Americanism without imperialism."

The national reformists are ready to acknowledge the need

a. Rodney Arismendi is the head of the Uruguayan Communist Party and the leading Latin American theoretician.
14. Haya de la Torre, 161–62.
15. *Problems of Peace and Socialism* (Russian edn.), No. 6 (1959), 34.

*Soviet Writers on the Developing Areas*

for an anti-imperialist struggle, but they are fighting for a special kind of anti-imperialism—one which they call "constructive." It is directed only against political imperialism, and seeks not to "disunite Latin America from the U.S.," but to "unite" them.[16] It is precisely for the purpose of confirming these "theoretical" ideas that the reformists strongly advance the concept of "interdependence," supporting it with geopolitical arguments.[17]

One of the most active representatives of Latin American reformism is the leader of the Popular Democratic Party of Puerto Rico, Luis Muñoz Marin. In an article published in the magazine *Combate* (published in Costa Rica under management of Haya de la Torre, Betancourt, and Figueres), he maintains that the countries of the Western Hemisphere have become so "interdependent" that they must unite closely with the United States for the sake of economic development, and that the "antiquated" concepts of national sovereignty must be rejected.[18] Betancourt, the leader of the Venezuelan reformists, maintains an essentially identical point of view. He contends that "troubled times" will come to Latin American countries if they base their politics on the idea of absolute sovereignty.

The national reformists offer alluring prospects to the people of Latin America for the elimination of imperialism, removal of contradictions, and hopes for "harmonious" cooperation

16. Haya de la Torre, 163, 190, 191.
17. Promotion of the theory of "interdependence" is generally characteristic of the bourgeois reformist concepts under modern conditions. The peculiarity of Latin American national reformism is that it uses geopolitics extensively in attempting to justify its thesis of the "impossibility" of a national liberation struggle in Latin America such as the people of colonial and independent countries throughout the world are waging.
18. *Combate* (January–February 1960), 9. American monopolist circles are forcibly using for their own purposes Luis Muñoz Marin and his Popular Democratic Party, which is headed by a middle-class bureaucratic leadership. Marin pretends to the role of "intermediary" between the nationalist movement in Latin America and the USA. The "free associated state" (such is the name of the colonial regime imposed on the Puerto Rican people by the ruling circles of the USA) is promoted by Haya de la Torre and other reformists as a model of "new," "democratic" inter-American relations.

## The Third World in Soviet Perspective

with the U.S. monopoly capitalists. Such points of view were subjected to scathing criticism by V. I. Lenin during the First World War when he pointed out how reactionary was Kautsky's ultra-imperialist theory.[b] Exposing the theoretical "revelations" of Kautsky, who separated imperialist policy from its economic base, V. I. Lenin characterized the theory of ultra-imperialism in the following manner: "There is a blunting and concealment of the most basic contradictions of the latest stage of capitalism instead of a disclosure of their profundity. We are getting bourgeois reformism instead of Marxism." [19] In bringing to light the profound contradictions of imperialism, V. I. Lenin demonstrated that the objective course of social development refuted the ultra-imperialist theory.

By "interdependence," the national reformists are attempting to prove that imperialism is disappearing and that "cooperation" between the countries of the Western Hemisphere is coming to replace it. In truth, the countries of the Western Hemisphere are now in a state of "interdependence" under the aegis of American imperialism. But there are powerful forces of national liberation coming into operation—Cuba is a prime example—which are undermining this "interdependence" and opposing it with a struggle to strengthen national sovereignty and achieve economic liberation. In the light of the profound changes taking place in the world and at a time when there is a powerful upsurge in the national liberation struggle of Latin American peoples, the attempts of the epigoni of Kautsky from the national reformist camp

b. Karl Kautsky suggested that ultimately imperialist conflicts would be resolved by the creation of a world-wide capitalist superstate. The Communists have firmly rejected this theory. (See *Fundamentals of Marxism-Leninism*, 247–48.) Kautsky's theory is placed in perspective in Alfred G. Meyer's *Leninism* (Cambridge, Mass., 1957), 249. The Chinese, in their anti-Soviet campaign, have accused the "modern revisionists" of subscribing to the Kautskian heresy. See the *Renmin Ribao* article of September 24, 1963, by Ho Wei, translated as "Chinese Comment on Lenin's Criticism of Kautsky's 'Super-Imperialism,' " in JPRS 21,645.

19. V. I. Lenin, *Sochineniya* [Collected Works], II, 257.

to apply a new "ultra-imperialist concept" to Latin America are truly pitiful.

One of the central ideas in the theories of national reformism concerns the benevolent role of U.S. companies in increasing employment in Latin America, in improving the life of the peoples of Latin America, and in the overall economic progress of Latin American countries. Thus Betancourt, in one of his speeches (November 1958), announced that through negotiations with foreign companies the petroleum workers could improve their living conditions, and that the government was receiving from these companies the necessary means for industrial development.

National reformists reply to criticism of their views by saying that they have not stopped being anti-imperialists; rather, it is the foreign companies that have stopped being imperialist.[20] The facts, however, refute these demagogic fabrications. The insignificant improvement of the position of the workers in the Venezuelan oil industry, to which the reformists like to allude, is the result of the long, selfless struggle of these workers, who dared to extract some concessions from the foreign monopolies. The imperialist companies, however, are being compensated for their "losses" a hundredfold. Over a relatively short period of time the number of petroleum workers in Venezuela has decreased appreciably (61,000 in 1948, 45,000 in 1957) while the amount of oil extracted has increased considerably.[21] The ruthless increase in work and intensified exploitation of the workers are flagrant. The presence of a reserve army of unemployed in the petroleum regions gives the monopolies an additional effective means to "put the workers who make 'excessive' demands in their place." [22] As a result,

20. See, e.g., *La Nación* (Bolivia), December 16, 1958.
21. *Tribuna popular*, November 4, 1960.
22. It is characteristic that the oil companies, which were forced in a collective agreement of February 1960 to make certain concessions to the oil workers, categorically refused to include in the agreement one of the main demands of the workers—a guarantee of employment and discontinuation of dismissal of workers.

317

the profits of the oil companies grow constantly. One of the largest American companies, Creole Petroleum, in 1959 alone increased its profits by 20.7 per cent over 1958.[23] As a rule, the profits of the oil companies generally exceed 30 per cent of the invested capital.

For years foreign companies have acted in many ways to deter the preparation of national cadres of specialists. It is characteristic that in the oil industry of Venezuela only 10 per cent of the engineering and technical personnel are Venezuelans. They are paid considerably less than the foreign specialists and they are required to know the English language.[24] The issue of the local workers' position in the oil industry has even become a subject of discussion in the Venezuelan Congress. Many deputies have demanded the immediate establishment of a state oil company which would allow Venezuelan specialists to work in the interests of their own people, and not become "second-rate" people working in foreign companies.[25]

One of the favorite themes of the national reformist theoreticians is the argument about the benevolent role of United States aid to Latin American countries. What is the genuine role of this "aid"? Let us take Bolivia as an example. It is this country which the national reformist ideologists adduce as a convincing example that allegedly supports their theory of the "philanthropic" role of American "aid" to Latin America. Thus, in one of the articles in the magazine *Combate*, it is maintained that American "aid" will make it possible to create a class of small landowners, stimulate the formation of a "middle class," and lead to a "spiritual renaissance" of the toiling masses.[26] The actual result of this "aid" would be to undermine the social achievements of the Bolivian people,

23. *Tribuna popular*, August 22, 1960.
24. The American magazine *World Petroleum* called for an increase in the contingent of Venezuelan lower and middle-level employees—"white-collar proletarians"—to create the impression of a "national character" of the oil industry in Venezuela. It emphasized, however, that the upper managerial positions must be retained in the hands of "qualified foreign specialists." *World Petroleum*, No. 7 (1957), 93.
25. *El Nacional* (Venezuela), August 21, 1959.
26. *Combate*, No. 9 (1960), 77.

*Soviet Writers on the Developing Areas*

sabotage the struggle of Bolivia for economic independence, and impose rapacious capitalist methods of exploitation. The American advisor Eder has proposed a plan for "stabilizing" the economy that is clearly intended to undermine the national sector and to stimulate the activity of American monopolies in Bolivia. Acceptance of this "aid" has led to a sharp deterioration in the situation of Bolivian workers.

The activity of U.S. monopolies which is promoted through the so-called "Inter-American Agricultural Service" is also leading to the same kind of results. It establishes organizations which compete with government institutions and promotes a policy which contradicts the interests of the people. The "Inter-American Agricultural Service," while called upon to cooperate with the Bolivian peasantry, in fact aids the large capitalist enterprises and ignores the needs of the peasant communities. It has taken over the state "mechanization service" which was designated to help the peasants with agricultural equipment. At present, the "mechanization service" is "aiding" only those who can pay quickly and on time. As a result, only the large agricultural capitalists receive any benefits.[27]

The national reformists try to justify such a situation by referring to it as the price of the "industrial revolution" which allegedly is taking place in Bolivia with the aid of American capital. They specifically claim that the Bolivian intelligentsia is now being offered excellent opportunities for "total employment" and for a "leading role," owing to the technical and economic progress in their country. Gradually, as a result of this "progress" Bolivians will replace the foreigners and occupy the leading positions in all spheres—such is the leitmotiv of their assertions.

Another fact is readily apparent: the reformists are attempting to set the middle strata of the population, the intelligentsia, against the working class, the toilers, and declare that the middle strata must take the leadership into their own hands; otherwise they risk the possibility of losing every-

27. *El Sol,* March 11, 1960.

thing, if the proletarians accede to power.[28] Meanwhile, the reformists declare that it is necessary to give full encouragement to the development of capitalism with the aid of foreign capital, making full use of its possibilities for the economic development of the country.

But this is exactly where the petty bourgeois essence of the reformist theory, with its fetish-worship of machinery, its technocratic tendencies, and its fatalist-objectivist approach to reality, becomes distinctly apparent. By leaning on the national reformists, American monopoly capital is trying to strengthen its positions in Latin America; it does not intend to concede them to the Latin Americans. It goes without saying that a small group of the Latin American population, including certain of the ruling members of the petty bourgeoisie, is obtaining specific benefits from such "collaboration" with American capital, while the overwhelming majority of the population is suffering terribly from monopolist exploitation.

In attempting to tie together the loose ends of their theoretical constructs, the national reformists set forth the concept of the so-called anti-imperialist state,[29] which they claim can basically change the interrelationship between foreign capital and Latin American countries. These are big words, but there is nothing revolutionary or anti-imperialist in this theory. Paradoxical as it may sound, the reformists, in advancing the theory of an "anti-imperialist state," are mainly anxious to create "favorable conditions" for foreign capital. According to them, the "anti-imperialist state" should eliminate the pernicious effects of political imperialism without, however, coming out against economic imperialism.

According to Haya de la Torre's assertions, foreign capital, lacking "reliable guarantees," suffers from its own type of "inferiority complex" and therefore resorts to illegal methods,

28. *La Nación*, March 3, December 12, and December 20, 1958.
29. Haya de la Torre proposed the term "anti-imperialist state." National reformist theoreticians of other countries usually do not use this terminology, but the essence of their ideas is the same.

## Soviet Writers on the Developing Areas

not infrequently turning for help to Latin American dictators.[30] He emphasizes that "We urgently need foreign capital, and one of our most revolutionary ideas is to offer foreign capital the right to a voice in controlling the national economy." [31]

While the peoples of Latin American countries are struggling against the domination of foreign capital, the reformists are feverishly searching for a loophole to maintain the positions of the imperialist monopolies. Haya de la Torre advances the theory of establishing in the Latin American countries (in addition to the legislative, executive, and judicial branches), a fourth branch: an "economic congress," in which representatives of foreign capital would participate as equal members along with the representatives of "labor," "state," and "capital." [32]

The reformists claim that the economic congress, as one of the mainsprings of the anti-imperialist state, is in a position to eliminate "political imperialism," the contradictions between national interests of Latin American peoples and foreign capital, and open up "unlimited" opportunities for progress in Latin America. Thus reformist "anti-imperialism" turns out to be only an attempt at state "regulation" of the positions of foreign capital, which is recognized as an "equal" partner in the economy of the Latin American countries. It is not surprising that the real anti-imperialist struggle provokes the undisguised antagonism of the reformists.

They fiercely oppose the nationalization of property belonging to the imperialist monopolies. Nationalization is one form of radical solution of the contradictions between im-

30. Haya de la Torre is quiet about the active participation of American monopolist circles in the establishment of military dictatorships in Latin America. For him, the main guilty party is the Latin American people themselves, who do not know how to bring about domestic order. Turning for help to the military dictatorships, foreign capital acts completely "logically," as it has no other guarantees for protection of its interests; such a conclusion is actually drawn by Haya de la Torre when he comes out as an advocate of foreign capital (*Seminario Peruano*, March 27, 1957, 14).
31. *La Nación*, December 16, 1958.
32. *Combate* (January–February 1960), 24.

## The Third World in Soviet Perspective

perialism and the Latin American peoples. The successes of the nationalization policy in Cuba have demonstrated what great positive results a people can obtain if they follow the path of a resolute struggle against any form of dependence on the American monopolies.

One of the most common reformist arguments concerning the impossibility of nationalization is the theory of interdependence. Nationalization is declared to be an unrealistic, anti-historical act which would destroy already established peaceful economic relationships. Thus, for example, Betancourt writes that since Venezuela has become a world petroleum source, it cannot isolate itself from international economic connections. Interdependence, Betancourt concludes, makes nationalization of the petroleum industry in Venezuela impossible.[33] He is struggling for a "harmonious" collaboration of Venezuela with foreign capital.

In opposing nationalization, the reformists set forth the possibility of painlessly obtaining substantial concessions from foreign monopolies with the aid of state authority, thus accomplishing "nationalization" without deprivation of property rights. In Venezuela, for example, the idea of converting the Venezuelan state into a "partner" of foreign companies to exploit oil is widely propagandized. But how can one talk of such a "partnership" if all levers of control over the oil industry are in the hands of foreign companies, and the "participation" of the Venezuelan state merely amounts to taxing the extraction of oil? The oil companies themselves determine the amount of taxes they must pay Venezuela, and operate on the world market free of control. The oil companies in foreign hands not only fail to play the role of unique accumulator of the capital necessary for the economic development of the country (as the national reformists maintain), but, conversely, are becoming an even greater deterrent to national progress, a type of "state within a state," and are pumping riches out of the country on a huge scale. In 1957 alone, the profits from the petroleum companies in Venezuela amounted to 55.7 per

33. Romulo Betancourt, *Venezuela, política y petroleo* (Mexico 1956), 741.

322

## Soviet Writers on the Developing Areas

cent of total profits obtained by American monopolies in Latin America.[34]

The example of Bolivia is no less convincing. The reformists maintain that the "anti-imperialist state" has hardly been established, and is already successfully conducting a policy of "collaboration" with American monopolies. In determining the principle by which the government exercises control, the Bolivian government newspaper *La Nación* wrote that "national liberation" could be achieved in Bolivia by state support of the balance between the "public" and "private" property sectors.[35] In reality, the term "private property sector" refers to the American monopolies.

How is this "collaboration" put into practice? During recent years the Bolivian government has widely granted oil concessions. In the Bolivian oil industry, American companies "coexist" with the state oil enterprise. American oil companies are gradually expanding their sphere of influence and are continually taking over new oil lands. They are striving to undermine the positions of the state company in order to impose private ownership on the oil industry. One of the leaders of the government company, Romero Loza, has stated that within the company property "there is great oil wealth, but it cannot be exploited owing to the lack of capital." He emphasized that it is impossible to obtain the necessary means because of foreign interference.[36]

The "regulated" capitalist development in Bolivia has resulted in an even greater strengthening of the positions of American capital and has acted as an additional brake on socio-economic reforms. The reformist theoreticians and politicians are attempting to combine a fatalistic acknowledgment of the inevitability of penetration of American capital into Latin American countries with a voluntaristic sermon on the policy of an "anti-imperialist state." Such an unnatural combination will inevitably lead to deplorable results.

34. Universidad Central, *Boletín Informativo* (Venezuela), March 10, 1960.
35. *La Nación*, December 16, 1958.
36. *Unidad* (Bolivia), February 25, 1960.

323

## The Third World in Soviet Perspective

The national reformists also maintain that nationalization is unwise, and allege that it would move the Latin American countries backwards, since the most "advanced" sector in the economy would be underminded through nationalization. Basing their theory on the fetish-worship of machinery, and ignoring the problems of socio-economic development in Latin America, the national reformists substitute an abstract, purely quantitative conception of the growth of production for the problem of nationalization. Thus one of the most active members of Latin American reformism, the leader of the Costa Rican National Liberation Party, José Figueres, maintains that nationalization has lost its significance, and that for purposes of development it is now more important to increase production and justly distribute and accumulate capital.[37] Figueres criticizes the "dogmatic" approach of the United States to the forms of private property. He does this, however, in order to provide a basis for his theory of the necessity for "organic coexistence" of American monopolies with the "anti-imperialist state," which exerts general control over the national economy in the interests of "international unity." There is nothing in Figueres' "theory" which is anti-imperialist or undermines the positions of foreign monopolies. Figueres' attacks on the "dogma of private property" are alternated with criticism of the "dogmas of public property."[38] Such a search for "balance" naturally leads him to the conclusion that it is not the form of property which is important, but the principles of interrelationships between Latin American countries and the United States.

It is not surprising that such "subversive theories" do not alarm the American monopolies. In April 1960, the second Inter-American Congress for the Defense of Democracy and Freedom was held in Caracas. At this congress, along with Adolf Berle (former U.S. Assistant Secretary of State, present special ambassador of President Kennedy, and one of the ideologists of monopoly capitalism), Figueres spoke in regard to joint proposals and recommendations. In these proposals much

37. *Combate* (July–August 1960), 9.
38. *Ibid.*

324

was said about the need for strengthening American aid for the economic development of the Latin American countries in order to eliminate the gap between the underdeveloped and the industrialized nations. But the authors of the proposals tried to convince the participants of the congress that foreign capital, introduced organically into the economic structure of Latin American countries and having become "national," would be a still more effective factor in their progress. Everything was profusely garnished with recommendations that foreign capital express an understanding of the interests of Latin American countries, play a "social" function in developing these countries, and so forth.[39] One need not guess what "contribution" Berle or Figueres made in these proposals. One thing is clear: both the representatives of the American monopolies and the Latin American national reformists readily subscribe to these recommendations.

The popular masses of the Latin American countries are coming to realize even more the inconsistency of the theory and practice of national reformism, which attempts to adapt itself to American imperialism and rejects the struggle for economic independence. Important new processes are occurring among those petty bourgeois classes whose support is most sought after by the reformists. The changes which have occurred in the attitudes of a significant part of the Cuban middle classes have exerted a telling influence on the positions of the middle classes in other Latin American countries as well. In the persistent ideological struggle, the advanced forces of the Cuban people have defeated the right compromising wing of the petty bourgeoisie, which had attempted to paralyze the revolutionary movement and to impede the anti-imperialist policy of nationalization and the creation of an independent economy. At present even broader strata of the petty bourgeoisie and intelligentsia are becoming convinced that only in a free independent Cuba do they have full opportunities for utilizing their creative forces and knowledge.

One of the central problems confronting Cuba is growth of

39. *Ibid.* (July–August 1960), 11–12.

*The Third World in Soviet Perspective*

production, increasing the productivity of labor. "Cuba has begun the battle to increase the productivity of labor, and the victory of the revolution on the economic front depends to a considerable degree on accomplishing this task," stated the Cuban newspaper *Noticias de Hoy*.[40] It is not difficult to notice how this task, set forth by the revolutionary forces, differs from the formally similar slogan of such reformist ideologists as Figueres!

The Cuban example and the spread of the national liberation movement have exerted an increasing influence on the struggle against the ideology of reformism in other Latin American countries as well, and have led to even greater polarization of social forces. A split took place in the ranks of the Acción Democratica party in Venezuela. The leftist groups of the party withdrew from it and in 1960 organized a new political organization called the Revolutionary Movement of the Revolutionary Left (Movimiento de la Izquierda Revolucionaria). The new party opposes the reformist ideology of the Acción Democratica leadership, works together with the Communists, and promotes the anti-imperialist program of radical socio-economic reforms in the country.

"Proceeding from the basic propositions of the program," the new party's newspaper, *Izquierda*, states, "we must acknowledge that in Venezuela no opportunity for revolution can exist without a clear and explicit position on nationalization of the Venezuelan petroleum industry. All attempts to avoid furthering this program, which is vitally important for the future of our country, are manifestations of the capitulatory theories of economic and geographic fatalism, and represent defenses of the theory of 'capitalism as a partner' which is expressed most repulsively by the existence of the Puerto Rican Commonwealth."[41] It is characteristic that this Revolutionary Movement of the Left proclaims recognition of the leading role of the working class. The new party is waging a persistent struggle against the right, capitulatory elements in the liberation movement.

40. *Noticias de Hoy*, August 14, 1960.
41. *Izquierda*, June 24, 1960.

326

## Soviet Writers on the Developing Areas

The struggle against reformism is being intensified in such countries as Peru and Costa Rica, where the leftist forces in the ranks of the Aprista and the National Liberation parties are opposing the compromising, reformist policy of their leaders. True, many progressive personalities of the Aprista Party, who have established their own political organization, the Insurgent APRA, have not freed themselves of illusions with regard to Haya de la Torre and consider him the "anti-imperialist" leader of Latin America. Nevertheless, it is difficult to overestimate the opposition to reformism in the ranks of the Aprista Party and, as the Peruvian Communist newspaper *Unidad* noted, the changes which are taking place in the Aprista Party are a "sign of the times," appropriate to the tasks of the anti-imperialist revolution in Peru. *Unidad* writes, "We extend our hands to the democratic forces in the Aprista Party in the hope that we shall move together along the difficult path of the liberation movement." [42]

No less significant changes are taking place in the Costa Rican National Liberation Party, where the left wing is gaining strength. A direct stimulus to the activity of the leftist elements was the anti-imperialist strike (December 1959–January 1960) of the agricultural workers on the United Fruit Company plantations. During those days many representatives of the National Liberation Party, overcoming the fierce resistance of the right leadership, established broad collaboration with Communists and other democratic forces. The unified front of patriotic forces was the deciding factor in the victory of the anti-imperialist strike. The experience of the struggle convinced many members of the National Action Party [sic] of the treacherous, capitulatory policy of the right reformist elements, who intimidated the people with the threat of American intervention in attempting to hinder the development of the strike. At the beginning of 1960, one of the most ardent anti-Communists, the lackey of imperialism, Gonzalo Facio, was expelled from the party. The Venezuelan newspaper *Tribuna Popular* emphasized that the expulsion of Facio, who was an ally of Figueres, would deliver a heavy

42. *Unidad*, November 7, 1959.

327

## The Third World in Soviet Perspective

blow to the latter's position and foment an ideological struggle in the ranks of the party.[43]

The ideological struggle in Bolivia deserves exceptional attention. In this country, the artificiality and inconsistency of the reformists' "theories" about the necessity for the existence of a "special" capitalist stage of development, which would be stimulated by American monopoly capital, are especially obvious. The growing dissatisfaction of the popular masses, including the petty bourgeoisie, was shown by the split in the ruling party, the Movimiento Nacionalista Revolucionario, whose ranks the right reformist elements have deserted to form their own party, the Movimiento Nacionalista Revolucionario Auténtico. The results of the 1960 presidential elections bear witness to the increasing dissatisfaction of the great mass of people with the policy of the reformists. In the elections, strength was gained by those forces which supported limitations on the activity of American monopolies in the country and the development of an independent economy. It is typical that at this time there was especially strong criticism of American "aid," which was undermining the national economy of the country. "The people voted for revolution, not for reformism," the Venezuelan newspaper *Izquierda* wrote concerning the election results.[44]

The decisive battle of the advanced forces of Bolivian society still lies ahead. Illusions regarding American aid are still rather strong within the country: certain strata of the population are still under the influence of reformism. However, in our view it is necessary to emphasize an important fact which is pertinent in some degree to the other Latin American countries as well. In Bolivia, there is a growing realization of the impossibility of gaining success in the construction of an independent, free country by following the path of capitalist development. On the basis of their experience, the Bolivian people have become convinced of what American "capitalist progress" is bringing to the working people. It is not by accident that there is growing in this country an interest

43. *Tribuna popular*, February 26, 1960.
44. *Izquierda*, June 24, 1960.

328

in socialism which is indissolubly connected with the spread of Marxist ideas and the truth about the Soviet Union and the other countries of the world socialist system that are helping to reveal the true nature of the reformist ideas about "industrial revolution," "technical progress," and American "aid." That is why the Bolivian working people have received with great enthusiasm news of the Soviet Union's readiness to aid Bolivia in constructing tin refineries and developing the national oil industry. Speaking at a mass meeting, the leader of the miners of the Twentieth Century Mine, Federico Escobar, said, "We do not want to receive tips from the Americans, because they are pursuing goals which are alien to us. The Yankees want to enslave us even further. Therefore, we say: 'Long live the unselfish aid of the Soviet Union!'"

"The popular masses are convinced that the best way to overcome centuries-old backwardness and improve their living conditions is to follow the non-capitalist path of development. Only by following this path will the people be able to avoid exploitation, poverty, and starvation. The working class and the great masses of the peasantry have been called upon to play the most important role in solving this basic social question," states the [Moscow] Declaration of the Congress of Representatives of Communist and Workers' Parties.[45] The situation in Latin America completely supports these conclusions.

The progressive, revolutionary forces in Latin America will in the near future face an even more intense ideological struggle with reformism. We must not forget that at the same time as the national revolutionary wing gains strength in the revolutionary movement, the reformists are acting feverishly to unify their forces. Thus, in August 1960 in Lima, the capital of Peru, a conference was held in which the Aprista and Febrerist parties participated, as well as the Democratic Action, National Liberation, and National Revolutionary Movement parties. It is characteristic that, on all principal issues, the

45. *Programmnyye dokumenty bor'by za mir, demokratiyu i sotsializm* [Program Documents on the Struggle for Peace, Democracy and Socialism] (Moscow 1961), 67.

conference accepted a resolution clearly in the spirit of the "conception" of Haya de la Torre and the other reformist ideologists.

Of course, the leading elite of the parties which met in Lima could not completely ignore the frame of mind of the popular masses of Latin America, and the resolutions of the conference contained some criticism directed toward the United States. But here, completely in the spirit of the reformist "constructive anti-imperialism," we are plainly given to understand that the contradictions between the USA and Latin America can be completely eliminated—that an era of "inter-American democratic interrelationships" can come about. At the same time, the resolutions of the conference were characterized by violent anti-communism and hatred of socialist countries.[46] It is not a struggle with imperialism, but the struggle against the revolutionary ideology, against Marxism-Leninism, which is the "last word" of the Latin America reformists. In 1960, the national reformist leaders established in Costa Rica the so-called "International Institute of Political Education," which is charged with preparing cadres to combat the "Communist ideology."

This institute is directed by José Figueres and Haya de la Torre. Harry Kantor, the reactionary American sociologist, has been invited to be one of the directors of the Institute.

As we can see, the national reformists have not abandoned their attempts to subjugate the national liberation movement to their influence, to distort its true purposes and tasks. However, we can already say that the revolutionary ideology and practice of the national liberation struggle are dealing painful blows to reformism and exposing its theoretical and practical inconsistencies—its inability to solve the basic issues in Latin America as it is today.

The Latin American Conference on the Defense of National Sovereignty, for Independent Economic Development and Peace, which was held in March 1961, is a convincing refutation of the ideas propagated by the national reformists regarding "attenuation" of the anti-imperialist struggle in Latin

46. *Noticiero obrero interamericano,* No. 40 (September 1960).

America and the coming of the era of "interdependence." In the declaration unanimously accepted by the conference it is stated: "The main force which is impeding progress in Latin America is North American imperialism. Its close alliance with the oligarchy in our countries and the pernicious results of its economic and cultural penetration are the main reasons for the overall backwardness which characterizes the present situation in Latin America. The most important and vital prerequisite for any plan of development in our countries is to bring about the downfall of imperialism." [47]

The declaration bears witness to the great successes achieved by the national liberation movement in Latin America in unifying its forces and in determining its common tasks in the anti-imperialist struggle.

No reformist devices or sophisms can hold back the historically inevitable process of political, economic, and social liberation of the peoples of Latin America.

47. *Problems of Peace and Socialism* (Russian edn.), No. 5 (1961), 48.

# Abbreviations Used in the References

Throughout the text and in the bibliography that follows, these abbreviations have been used:

CDSP—*Current Digest of the Soviet Press*

CPSU—Communist Party of the Soviet Union

JPRS—Joint Publications Research Service

MEIMO—*Mirovaya Ekonomika i Mezhdunarodnyye Otnosheniya*

NAIA—*Narody Azii i Afriki*

PV—*Problemy Vostokovedeniya*

SV—*Sovetskoye Vostokovedeniye*

# Bibliographical Note

A BOOK which hopes to stimulate the reader's further interest must necessarily include some bibliography. The chief bibliographical references have for the most part been included in my footnotes, especially those to the Introduction. The lists that follow here are meant to supplement these.

The great bulk of the material that provides an understanding of the Soviet view of the third world is of course available only in Russian. There is, however, a certain amount of this material available in English—probably enough to keep the reader abreast of at least the general outlines of Soviet thinking. Listed below are (I) the major Russian-language sources containing relevant material, as well as (II) a list of material available in English translation, including Soviet English-language sources. In addition, I have provided three brief, more specialized lists: (III.A) a selection of articles written by Russians, in which they appraise their own efforts and problems in the field of orientology; (III.B) a list of articles by Western writers who have surveyed the same field in some depth; and (IV) a list of recent Soviet symposia on the third world.

These bibliographical listings make no claim to completeness; particularly, the listing of material available in English represents only those articles that I have been able to discover. In view of the poor state of indexing of this material, it must be assumed that there is much that I have missed. Also, I have not attempted to include every item that I have found, since many are of little or no interest.

## I. *Russian-Language Sources*

The principal journal for the publication of material on the developing areas is *Mirovaya Ekonomika i Mezhdunarodnyye Otnosheniya* [World Economics and International Relations]. It is the only significant source for writings on Latin America, and in general tends to print articles oriented toward current

## The Third World in Soviet Perspective

economic and political problems. More long-range and historical material on Asia and Africa is contained in *Narody Azii i Afriki* [Peoples of Asia and Africa]. This journal has gone through two previous incarnations—from 1959 through 1960 it was called *Problemy Vostokovedeniya* [Problems of Orientology], and from 1955 through 1958 it was *Sovetskoye Vostokovedeniye* [Soviet Orientology]. Prior to 1955, the journal containing the most relevant material was *Voprosy Ekonomiki* [Questions of Economics]. Although *Voprosy Ekonomiki* still exists, it tends now to be chiefly limited to theoretical economic matters, eschewing the political content of its earlier years. Other journals worth consulting are *Voprosy Istorii* [Questions of History], *Sovetskoye Gosudarstvo i Pravo* [Soviet State and Law] (especially before 1955), and the *Vestnik Leningradskogo Gosudarstvennogo Universiteta* [Herald of the Leningrad State University]. The pickings from this group tend, however, to be somewhat lean. Rather "popular" coverage of the developing areas is provided by the periodical *Aziya i Afrika Segodnya* [Asia and Africa Today], which until 1961 was known as *Sovremennyy Vostok* [The Contemporary East].

Comprehensive bibliographic coverage of this periodical material, as well as of the considerable number of books, monographs, and pamphlets published by the Soviets, must be pieced together from various sources. Earlier material (1950–1959) is covered in the German publication, *Literatur über Entwicklungsländer* (Hanover 1961). Material through 1954 is indexed in *Sovetskoye Gosudarstvo i Pravo*. The annual bibliography of the *Journal of Asian Studies* is good for material on Asia. Articles from the relevant journals are listed in the series *Soviet Periodical Abstracts* (until 1962, *Selective Soviet Annotated Bibliographies*): *Asia, Africa and Latin America*, published by the Slavic Languages Research Institute of White Plains, N.Y. A work has been announced for publication by the University of Southern California Press in late 1963 that should be valuable in dealing with nonperiodical literature. It is Peter A. Berton, Gene Overstreet,

## Soviet Writers on the Developing Areas

and Alvin Rubenstein, *Soviet Works on South and Southeast Asia, 1946–1960*.

Voluminous coverage (some 1,000–1,500 items per month) is given in the Soviet listing, *Novaya Sovetskaya i inostrannaya literatura po stranam zarubezhnogo Vostoka* [New Soviet and Foreign Literature on the Countries of the Non-Soviet East]. This excellent bibliography, covering all of Asia and Africa, apparently began to appear in 1959. Unfortunately, it is available in only a few American libraries. The Soviet Academy of Sciences has also produced a series of bibliographies on Japan, India, and Southeast Asia. These are, respectively, *Bibliografiya Yaponii* (Moscow 1960), *Bibliografiya Indii* (Moscow 1959), *Bibliografiya Yugo-Vostochnoy Azii* (Moscow 1960). A bibliography on Africa was reportedly published in 1962, but I have not been able to locate it. Although voluminous, these Soviet bibliographies are far from complete and material that is no longer politically acceptable has not been listed.

Some additional bibliographic sources are listed in Section III, below.

### II. *Material Available in English Translation*

There are two English-language Soviet periodicals which regularly publish material on the developing areas. These are *New Times* (translation of *Novoye Vremya*) and *International Affairs* (translation of *Mezhdunarodnaya Zhizn'*)—the latter not to be confused with the British periodical of the same name. Neither of these Soviet journals is a "scholarly" periodical, but *International Affairs* does occasionally print matters of some theoretical interest. In addition, *Problems of Peace and Socialism* (also known as the *World Marxist Review*), the organ of the international Communist movement published in Prague, frequently has worthwhile contributions. Most of these, however, are by non-Soviet authors.

The most useful source of translated material is the output of the Joint Publications Research Service of the Department of Commerce, which unfortunately is not indexed except for the rather unrevealing survey given in the U.S. Government

## The Third World in Soviet Perspective

Printing Office's *Monthly List* (indexed monthly and annually).
Only occasionally are pertinent articles translated by the *Current Digest of the Soviet Press*, and *Problems of Economics* (published by the International Arts and Sciences Press, New York).

An indispensable tool is provided by the publications of the Central Asian Research Institute (London). This group publishes the *Central Asian Review*, the *Mizan Newsletter*, and the *Yuva Newsletter*. These three review and occasionally reprint (in condensed version) the most important Soviet work on South Asia, Africa and the Middle East, and Southeast Asia respectively. Materials printed in these three journals are *not* listed below; the interested reader should consult them for the area with which he is concerned. There appears to be no corresponding coverage of Latin America.

The material in translation is listed in categories: the first covers general works relevant for more than one geographical area; the remaining three list material on Asia, Africa and the Middle East, and Latin America.

### A. General

Akopyan, G., "O roli i kharaktere natsional'noy burzhuazii stran Vostoka" [On the Role and Character of the National Bourgeoisie in the Countries of the East], MEIMO, No. 6 (1962), 100–3; translated in JPRS 14,870.

Andreasyan, R., and A. El'yanov, "Monotovarnaya spetsializatsiya i ekonomicheskaya nezavisimost'" [Single-Commodity Specialization and Economic Independence], MEIMO, No. 6 (1962), 85–97; translated in JPRS 14,870.

Bragina, Ye., "Planirovaniye—metod razvitiya natsional'noy ekonomiki" [Planning—Method of Development of the National Economy], *Kommunist*, No. 13 (1962), 99–101; translated in CDSP, xiv (No. 41), 12–14.

Brutents, A., "Antinauchnyye kontseptsii i opravdaniye kolonializma" [Pseudo-scientific Concepts and Attempts to Justify Colonialism], MEIMO, No. 11 (1960), 40–48; German translation in *Sowjetwissenschaft* (Gesellschaftswissenschaftliche Reihe), No. 2 (1961), 203ff.

## Soviet Writers on the Developing Areas

Iskandrov, R. G., "K voprosu o pomoschi slaborazvitym stranam" [On the Problem of Aid to Underdeveloped Countries] (Moscow 1960); translated in JPRS 16,141.

Lemin, I. M., "Ekonomicheskaya sushchnost' sovremennogo kapitalizma" [Economic Nature of Contemporary Capitalism], PV, No. 4 (1959), 8–25; German translation in Sowjetwissenschaft (Gesellschaftswissenschaftliche Reihe), No. 2 (1961), 153ff.

———, "Politicheskoye soderzhaniye sovremennogo kolonializma" [Political Content of Contemporary Colonialism], PV, No. 1 (1960), 30–43; German translation in ibid., No. 2 (1961), 173ff.

Mirskiy, G., and L. Stepanov, Aziya i Afrika na rubezhe dvukh epokh [Asia and Africa on the Threshold of Two Epochs]; translation published by Foreign Languages Publishing House (Moscow n.d.) under the title Asia and Africa: A New Era.

Rymalov, V., Ekonomicheskoye sotrudnichestvo SSSR so slaborazvytami stranami [Economic Cooperation of the USSR with the Underdeveloped Countries]; English translation published by Foreign Languages Publishing House (Moscow n.d.).

Shmelev, N., "Burzhuaznyye ekonomisty o roli gosudarstvennogo sektora v slaborazvitykh stranakh" [Bourgeois Economists on the Role of the State Sector in the Underdeveloped Countries], MEIMO, No. 4 (1962), 87–92; translated in JPRS 14,607.

Skorov, G., "Krusheniye kolonialnoy sistemy" [The Breakdown of the Colonial System], MEIMO, No. 3 (1961), 3–18; translated in JPRS 8,407.

———, "Nekotoryye ekonomicheskiye voprosy raspada kolonialnoy sistemy" [Some Economic Questions of the Collapse of the Colonial System], MEIMO, No. 4 (1958), 48–64; German translation in Sowjetwissenschaft (Gesellschaftswissenschaftliche Reihe), No. 8 (1958), 997ff.

Sokolov, I., "Glavnaya problema sovremennosti" [The Principal Problem of the Present Age], MEIMO, No. 2 (1963), 15–26; translated in JPRS 19,821.

## The Third World in Soviet Perspective

Starushenko, G., "Sotsializm i natsional'no-osvoboditel'noye dvizheniye" [Socialism and the National Liberation Movement], MEIMO, No. 2 (1963); translated in JPRS 19, 821.

Tyagunenko, V., "Osnovyye strukturnyye sdvigi v ekonomike slaborazvitykh stran" [Basic Structural Changes in the Economy of the Underdeveloped Countries], MEIMO, No. 3 (1960), 56–70; translated in *Problems of Economics* (New York), III (December 1960), 52–64.

Ul'rikh, O., "O gosudarstvennoy ekonomicheskoy politike v slaborazvitykh stranakh" [On State Economic Policy in the Underdeveloped Areas], MEIMO, No. 4 (1962), 95–98; translated in JPRS 14,607.

Zhukov, Ye. M., *et al.*, "O kharaktere i osobennostyakh narodnoy demokratii v stranakh vostoka" [On the Character and Peculiarities of People's Democracy in the Countries of the East], *Vestnik AN SSSR*, Seriya istoriya i filosofiya [Herald of the Academy of Sciences of the USSR, History and Philosophy Series], XI (January 1952), 80–87; translated in CDSP, IV (No. 20), 3.

### B. *Asia*

Berzina, M. Ya., and S. I. Bruk, *Naseleniya Indonezii, Malayi i Filippin* [The Population of Indonesia, Malaya and the Philippines] (Moscow 1962); pages 1–93 are translated in JPRS 19,799.

Fituni, L., "Problemy planirovaniya v suverennykh slaborazvitykh stranakh Azii" [Problems of Planning in the Sovereign Underdeveloped Countries of Asia], MEIMO, No. 6 (1962), 97–100; translated in JPRS 14,870.

Lavrent'ev, A., "Peremeny v strane Bandunga" [Changes in the Country of Bandung], *Aziya i Afrika Segodnya*, No. 3 (1961), 3–5; condensed translation in CDSP, XIII (No. 19), 7–9.

Pankin, M., "Znacheniye ekonomicheskikh svyazey c SSSR dlya razvitiya stran Yugo-Vostochnoy Azii" [Importance of Economic Ties with the USSR for the Development of Southeast Asia], *Vneshnyaya Torgovlya*, No. 6 (1960);

Soviet Writers on the Developing Areas
translated in *Problems of Economics* (New York), III (August 1960), 27–33.

*Politika S.Sh.A. i strany Yugo-Vostochnoy Azii, Indiya, Birma, Indoneziya* [The Policy of the USA and the Countries of Southeast Asia, India, Burma and Indonesia] (Moscow 1961); translated in JPRS 15,145.

Rostovskiy, S. N., *Rabocheye i natsional'no-osvoboditel'noye dvizheniye v stranakh Yugo-Vostochnoy Azii, posle Vtoroy Mirovoy Voyny* [The Workers' and National Liberation Movement in the Countries of Southeast Asia, after World War II] (Moscow 1959); German translations of the sections on Burma and Malaya are available in *Indonesien, Burma und Malaya im Kampf um Unabhängigkeit und Demokratie* (Berlin 1961). The section on Indonesia in the German edition is a translation of D. N. Aidit's report to the Sixth Congress of the Indonesian Communist Party.

Shaposhnikova, L., "V indiyskoy derevne Pochamlalli" [In the Indian Village of Pochamlalli], *Sovremennyy Vostok*, No. 2 (1961), 25–27; translation in CDSP, XIII (No. 19), 1–2, under the title "India: Bhave and Land Reform."

Simoniya, N. A., *Naseleniye kitayskoy natsional'nosti v stranakh Yugo-Vostochnoy Azii* (Moscow 1959); translated as *The Overseas Chinese in Southeast Asia—A Russian Study* (Ithaca, N.Y., 1961).

## C. Africa and the Middle East

*Des Africanistes russes parlent de l'Afrique*, special issue of *Présence Africaine* (Paris 1960). Contains articles by Potekhin, Orlova, Yablochkov, Ismayilova, Shprit, and a bibliography.

Braginskiy, M. I., "Sotsial'nyye sdvigi v tropicheskoy Afrike posle Vtoroy Mirovoy Voyny" [Social Changes in Tropical Africa After the Second World War], *Sovetskaya Etnografiya*, No. 6 (1960), 31–43. Translation available ($2.00) from Slavic Languages Research Institute, 1 Seymour Place, White Plains, N.Y.; also in *Mizan Newsletter*, III (February and June 1961).

Etinger, R., "Novyye manevry imperializma v osvobodivsihkh-

## The Third World in Soviet Perspective

sya stranakh Afriki" [New Maneuvers of Imperialism in the Liberated Countries of Africa], *MEIMO*, No. 4 (1962), 92–95; translated in JPRS 14,607.

Gavrilov, N. I., *O kooperativnom dvizhenii v stranakh tropicheskoy Afriki* [On the Cooperative Movement in the Countries of Tropical Africa] (Moscow 1962).

Lutskiy, V. B., "Iyul'skaya revolyutsia 1952 goda v Egipte" [The Revolution of July 1952 in Egypt], *SV*, No. 2 (1957), 31–48; partial translation in Walter Laqueur, ed., *The Middle East in Transition* (New York 1958), 496–502.

Potekhin, I. I., *Afrika 1956–61* (Moscow 1961); translated in JPRS 14,232.

——, *Afrika smotrit v budushcheye* [Africa Looks to the Future] (Moscow 1960). This pamphlet is said to have been translated into both French and English, but I have been unable to locate the translations. A substantial partial translation is available in a supplement to *Mizan Newsletter*, No. 4 (1961).

——, *Problems of the Economic Independence of Africa* (Moscow 1962); translation of *Problemy ekonomicheskoy nezavisimosti Afriki.*

——, "Panafrikanizm i bor'ba dvukh idiologiy" [Panafricanism and the Struggle of the Two Ideologies], *Kommunist*, No. 1 (1964), 104–113. Translated in JPRS 23,263.

Sivolobov, A. M., *Natsional'no-osvoboditel'noye dvizheniye v Afrike* [The National Liberation Movement in Africa] (Moscow 1961). Partial coverage is given in *Mizan Newsletter*, III (June 1961), 15; a full translation is found in JPRS 10,683.

Tyagunenko, V. L., *Likvidatsiye monotovarnoy struktury ekonomiki—odna iz predposylok samostoyatel'nosti* [The Liquidation of the Single-Commodity Structure of the Economy —One of the Prerequisites of Independence] (Moscow 1962); translated into French and published in the Soviet Union (French title and date unknown).

Usov, G., "Natsional'naya burzhuaziya i osvoboditel'noye dvizheniye v Vostochnoy Afrike" [The National Bourgeoisie and the Liberation Movement in East Africa], *MEIMO*, No. 4 (1962), 82–87; translated in JPRS 14,607.

## Soviet Writers on the Developing Areas

Vatolina, L. N., "Rost natsional'nogo samosoznaniya narodov Arabskikh stran (1945–1955)" [The Growth of National Self-Consciousness in the Arab Countries 1945–1955], SV, No. 5 (1955), 58–68; partial translation in Walter Laqueur, ed., *The Middle East in Transition* (New York 1958), 487–496.

### D. *Latin America*

Danilevich, N., "Dvizhushchiye sily osvoboditel'noy bor'by v Latinskoy Amerike" [Motive Forces of the Struggle for Liberation in Latin America], MEIMO, No. 9 (1960), 90–99. Translation available ($1.25) from Slavic Languages Research Institute, 1 Seymour Place, White Plains, N.Y.

### III. *Surveys of Soviet Orientology*

### A. *Soviet Writers*

Several works of this nature have been noted in the footnotes, and one has been partially reprinted in the text (No. 4). In addition, a few of the more recent and interesting articles of this type are:

"XXI S"yezd KPSS i zadachi vostokovedeniya" [The 21st Congress of the CPSU and the Tasks of Orientology], PV, No. 1 (1959), 18–25; summarized in *Mizan Newsletter*, ɪ (No. 5), 11.

Gafurov, B. G., "O perspektivakh razvitiya Sovetskogo vostokovedeniya" [On the Perspectives of the Development of Soviet Orientology], SV, No. 3 (1957), 7–16.

Neresov, G. A., "Koordinatsiya issledovaniy sovetskikh afrikanistov" [Coordination of Research by Soviet Africanists], *Vestnik AN SSSR* [Herald of the Academy of Sciences of the USSR], No. 7 (1962), 109–112; translated in JPRS 16,512.

Pavlov, N. S., "Osuzhdeniye itogov raboty Institutov Vostokovedeniya i Kitayevedeniya AN SSSR za 1958 god" [Appraisal of the Results of Work of the Institutes of Orientology and Sinology, Academy of Sciences, USSR, for 1958], *Voprosy Istorii*, No. 4 (1959), 201–206; translated in JPRS 3,012.

Potekhin, I. I., "Nekotoryye problemy afrikanistiki v svete

resheniy XXII S"yezda KPSS" [Some Problems of African-istics in Light of the Decisions of the 22nd Congress of the CPSU], NAIA, No. 1 (1962), 6–16.

"Proyekt Programmy KPSS i nekotoryye problemy natsional'no-osvoboditel'nogo dvizheniye narodov Azii i Afriki" [Draft Program of the CPSU and Some Problems of the National Liberation Movement of the Peoples of Asia and Africa], NAIA, No. 5 (1961), 3–14.

Zhukov, Ye. M., "Protsess likvidatsii kolonial'noy sistemy i zadachi ego izucheniya" [The Process of the Liquidation of the Colonial System and the Tasks of Its Study], *Vestnik AN SSSR*, No. 2 (1961), 5–10.

B. *Western Writers*

Bolton, A., *Soviet Middle East Studies* (Bibliography) (London 1959).

Central Asian Research Center, *Soviet Writing on Africa: An Annotated Bibliography* (London 1963).

Clubb, O. Edmund, "Soviet Oriental Studies and the Asian Revolution," *Pacific Affairs*, xxxi (December 1958), 380–389.

Dallin, Alexander, "The Soviet Union: Political Activity," in Zbigniew Brzezinski, ed., *Africa and the Communist World* (New York 1963), esp. 7–20.

Gasteyger, Kurt, "The Soviet Union and the Tiers-Monde," *Survey*, No. 43 (1962), 10–22.

Holdsworth, Mary, "African Studies in the USSR," *St. Antony's Papers*, No. 10 (Carbondale, Ill., 1961).

——, ed., *Soviet African Studies, 1918–1959: An Annotated Bibliography* (issued in two parts, Oxford 1961).

Laqueur, Walter, *The Soviet Union and the Middle East* (New York 1959), 159–75.

Morison, David L., "Communism in Africa: Moscow's First Steps," *Problems of Communism*, x, No. 6 (November–December 1961), 8–15.

——, "African Studies in the Soviet Union," *Russian Review*, xxii (July 1963), 301–14.

## Soviet Writers on the Developing Areas

Rubenstein, A. Z., "Select Bibliography of Soviet Works on South Asia," *Journal of Asian Studies*, xvii (November 1957), 43–54.

Seton-Watson, Hugh, "The Communist Powers and Afro-Asian Nationalism," in Kurt London, ed., *Unity and Conflict* (New York 1962).

*The Soviet Bloc and the Developing Countries* (Hanover, Verlag für Literatur und Zeitgeschehen, 1962).

Urban, Paul, "Orientalistik und Asienpolitik der Sowjets," *Osteuropa*, No. 12 (1958), 797–805.

### IV. Symposia

The Soviets are very fond of organizing symposia on various subjects, and several recent ones on the third world are of some interest. In addition to the papers presented (or a summary of them), subsequent publication frequently includes a summary of the ensuing discussion that gives an interesting glimpse into the differences of opinion and approach among the participants. The following list is chronological:

"Disintegration of the Imperialist Colonial System in the Post-War Period," organized jointly by the journal *International Affairs* (Moscow) and *Shihtze Chihshih* (Peking), *International Affairs*, No. 3 (1959), 64–86.

"Nauchnaya Konferentsiya: Natsional'no-osvoboditel'noye dvizheniye v Latinskoy Amerike na sovremennom etape" [Scientific Conference: The National Liberation Movement in Latin America at the Present Stage], MEIMO, No. 9 (1960).

"Paths of Development of the Newly Emergent Countries," *World Marxist Review*, No. 4 (1962), 62–78, and No. 5 (1962), 66–72.

"Sovremennaya epokha i puti razvitiya osvobodivshikhsya stran" [The Contemporary Epoch and the Paths of Development of the Liberated Countries], MEIMO, Nos. 3–5 (1962).

"The Socialist World System and the National-Liberation Movement," *World Marxist Review*, No. 3 (1963), 52–72.

343

# Biographical Information About
# the Contributors

THE following information was supplied through the kind assistance of the Embassy of the USSR in Washington, D.C., and the Novosti News Agency. I have made no changes except to standardize the orthography.

AVAKOV, RACHIK MAMIKONOVICH, born 1927. Senior research worker at the Institute of World Economics and International Relations of the USSR Academy of Sciences. Candidate of Economic Sciences. Specializes in problems of the economic development of African countries.

Author of *Morocco* (1957) and *French Monopolist Capital in North Africa* (1958), and a number of articles published in leading economic, social, and political magazines.

FRIDMAN, LEONID ABRAMOVICH, born 1930. Senior teacher in the department of African Studies at the Institute of Oriental Languages of Moscow State University. Candidate of Historical Sciences. Specializes in problems of economic development of Egypt and in the Near East.

Main work: *Capitalist Development of Egypt and the Position of the Working Masses in 1882–1939.*

GORDON, LEONID ABRAMOVICH, born 1930. Research worker at the Institute of the Peoples of Asia of the USSR Academy of Sciences. Indologist. Candidate of Historical Sciences. Specializes in the history of the workers' movement in India.

Author of *From the History of the Working Class of India: Position of the Bombay Proletariat in Modern Times* (1961) and more than 30 articles. His book *On the Position of the Working Class in Present-Day India* is being prepared for the press.

GRECHEV, MARK ALEKSANDROVICH, born 1909. Master of Economics, and senior research associate, Institute of World Eco-

## Soviet Writers on the Developing Areas

nomics and International Relations of the USSR Academy of Sciences.

Author of monographs: *US Imperialist Expansion in Latin America* (1954) and *US Colonialist Policy After the Second World War* (1958).

GUBER, ALEKSANDR ANDREYEVICH, born 1902. Outstanding Soviet orientalist. Corresponding Member of the USSR Academy of Sciences, Doctor of Historical Sciences, professor.

Author of more than 60 works on the recent and modern history of the Southeast Asian countries. The most outstanding are: *Indonesia: Social and Economic Essays* (1932), *The Philippines* (1937), *José Rizal* (1937), *Indonesia and Indo-China* (1942), *The Philippine Republic of 1898 and American Imperialism* (1st edn., 1948; 2nd edn., 1961), *International Relations in the Far East (1870–1945)* (1951).

Author of a number of textbooks on the history of the East —in particular, a textbook for higher schools, *Recent History of the East* (1961).

At present A. A. Guber is assistant academician-secretary of the Department of Historical Sciences of the USSR Academy of Sciences, editor-in-chief of the magazine *Novaya i Noveyshaya Istoriya,* and chairman of the National Committee of Soviet Historians. Participant in a number of International Congresses of Orientalists (Cambridge, Munich, Moscow), and International Congresses of Historians (Rome, Stockholm).

Chairman of the Board of the USSR-Indonesia Society, member of the Soviet Peace Committee.

MIKHAYLOV, SERGEY SERGEYEVICH, born 1912. Candidate of Historical Sciences, professor, and Director of the Latin America Institute of the USSR Academy of Sciences.

MIRSKIY, GEORGIY IL'ICH, born 1926. Senior research worker at the Institute of World Economics and International Relations of the USSR Academy of Sciences. Specializes in the problems of the national liberation movement in the Asian and African countries. Author of more than 25 works on this subject—in particular: *Iraq in the Troubled Times of 1930–*

345

*1941* (1961), *Suez Canal* (1956). As a co-author with L. V. Stepanov, he wrote the books, *The Prospects of Economic Cooperation of the Asian and African Countries* (1958) and *Asia and Africa on the Threshold of a New Era* (1960).

PANKIN, MIKHAIL SEMENOVICH, born 1922. Chief, Southeast Asia Department, World Market Research Institute, Ministry of Foreign Trade of the USSR. Served as adviser to the Soviet delegation to UN ECOSOC, UN Economic Commission for the Far East, and the Preparatory Committee of the UN Conference on Trade and Development.

POTEKHIN, IVAN IZOSIMOVICH, born 1903. Doctor of Historical Sciences, professor, and Director of the Africa Institute of the USSR Academy of Sciences. Outstanding Soviet Africanist.

Author of more than 80 works on the history and ethnography of Africa. He has written, in particular: *History of Agrarian Relations in the Union of South Africa, Formation of the National Community of the South African Bantu, Africa Looks to the Future, Ghana Today.* He is now working on the book, *History of Ghana.*

I. I. Potekhin participated in the 23rd (Cambridge, 1954) and 25th (Moscow, 1960) International Congresses of Orientalists, and the Congress of Anthropologists and Ethnographers (Philadelphia, 1956). He was an adviser for the USSR delegation to conferences of the International Labor Organization (1956 and 1957), and an adviser and specialist at the 13th Session of the United Nations General Assembly (1959).

Member of the International Africa Institute (London) and the French Africanists' Society. Chairman of the Presidium of the Soviet Friendship Association with the Peoples of Africa.

SHUL'GOVSKIY, ANATOLIY FEDOROVICH, born 1926. Senior research worker at the Latin America Institute of the USSR Academy of Sciences. Specializes in the problems of economic and political development of Mexico. Preparing for the press: *Nationalization of the Oil Industry in Mexico.*

# Soviet Writers on the Developing Areas

STEPANOV, LEV VASILEVICH, born 1929. Senior research worker at the Institute of World Economics and International Relations of the USSR Academy of Sciences. Candidate of Economic Sciences. Specializes in the problems of economic development of the Asian and African countries.

Most important works (co-author with G. I. Mirskiy): *The Prospects of Economic Cooperation of the Asian and African Countries* (1958), *Asia and Africa on the Threshold of a New Era* (1960).

UL'YANOVSKIY, ROSTISLAV ALEKSANDROVICH, born 1904. Outstanding Soviet orientalist. Senior research worker at the Institute of the Peoples of Asia of the USSR Academy of Sciences, professor.

Author of more than 30 scientific works on the history and economics of the Asian countries, in the majority of which the problems of the economic development of India are taken up. Most important works: *Agrarian Crisis in India* (1932), *Main Problems in the Economic Development of Independent India, 1947–1957. State Capitalism* (1958, Vols. 1, 2), *Some Questions of the Struggle for Economic Independence in the Non-Socialist Countries of Asia* (1960), and *Agrarian Reform and the Position of Peasants in the Countries of the Near and Middle East, India, and Southeast Asia* (1960).

Participant in the 25th International Congress of Orientalists (Moscow, 1960).

YUDIN, YURIY ADOLFOVICH, born 1926. Master of Law, and research associate at the Institute of State and Law of the USSR Academy of Sciences.

# Index

# *Index*

# Index

industry, industrialization, 11, 15, 52, 56, 124–26, 136, 166, 172, 182–86
intelligentsia, 25–26, 53, 55, 67, 291, 298, 308, 319, 325. *See also* bourgeoisie
Inter-American Agricultural Service, 319
Inter-American Economic and Social Council, 126
International Bank for Reconstruction and Development, 133, 144, 249
International Labor Office, 281–82
International Monetary Fund, 133
Ioniţa, Gh., xiiin
Iran, 196, 199–200, 208, 210–11, 286, 289, 302
Iraq, 49, 49n, 60, 196, 286, 293, 298
Iskandrov, R. G., 11n
Ismagelova, R. N., 233n
Israel, 7, 157n
Italy, 215, 232
Ivanov, L. G., 7n
Ivanov, N. A., 232n, 235n
Ivory Coast, 268n, 269

## J

Japan, 7, 42, 74, 76, 86, 109, 111, 147–48, 151, 157n, 216, 218, 299, 300
Java, 9n, 64–65, 67, 69, 70
Jinishi, M., 14n
Johnson, J. J., xin
Joly, F., 227n

## K

Kaboshkin, V., 27n
Kantor, H., 330
Kashmir, 212
Katz, S. M., xin
Kautsky, J. H., xin
Kautsky, K., 33, 33n, 316
Keita, M., 25
Kennedy, J. F., 306, 324
Kenya, 232, 242, 244–45, 247, 254, 287

Khrushchev, N. S., 2, 4, 29–30, 40, 51, 78, 95, 104, 254, 272
Kim, G., 13n
Kiselev, V., xiiin
Knorozov, Yu. V., 90
Korea (North and South), 49, 52, 57, 84, 195, 196
Kovalevskiy, M., 208
Kravets, N. A., 227n
kulaks, 12, 162, 162n, 199, 199n, 217. *See also* peasantry.
Kuomintang, 17
Kuusinen, O. V., 39, 82, 82n

## L

landlords, 66, 162n, 196, 214–15, 220–21, 293, 296. *See also* agriculture
Laos, 49, 142
Larin, V., 271n
Latin America, 14, 88–102, 118–137, 284–86, 293, 295, 305–31. *See also* Central America and individual countries
Lavretskiy, I. R., 90
Lebanon, 293, 296
Lemin, I., 1n
Lenin, V. I., 2, 3, 4n, 17, 30–33, 39–40, 80–81, 82n, 139, 155, 160, 161n, 166n, 180, 190, 194, 205, 206 207n 211, 212n, 226, 248, 298, 316
Libya, 49, 227, 234, 282
Lichtheim, G., 4n, 190n
Loewenthal, R., 25n
Loza, R., 323
Lugard, Lord, 237
Lutskaya, N. S., 235n

## M

Madurans, Union of, 70
Mahalanobis, P. C., 9n
Malagasy Republic, 254, 258, 294
Malaya, 115, 146, 204, 282, 293
Mali, 21, 24, 26, 28, 49, 61, 246, 267n, 268n, 270, 294–95, 298
Mao Tse-tung, 29, 189
Mariategui, J. C., 308

# Index

Markov, W., 15n, 20n, 25n
Martynov, V. A., 233n, 246n
Marx, K., 2, 3, 4n, 16, 39, 43, 44, 51n, 152n, 162n, 190, 208, 220, 236n, 240
Masjumi Party, 297
McGowan, F., xin
Medianu, L., xiiin
Mella, J. A., 308–09
Mexico, 90, 113, 119, 122–25, 130, 134, 282, 293, 313
Meyer, A. G., 3n, 316n
Middle East, 27, 83. *See also* individual countries
Mikhaylov, S. S., 119
Mikoyan, A. I., 80
military alliances (blocs), 49, 296
Millikan, M. F., xin
Mirskiy, G. L., xiiin, 5n, 7n, 20n, 21n, 25n, 103, 104n, 154
Mnyanda, B. Y., 230
Mongolia, 24, 195
monopolies, 8n, 47, 85. *See also* capitalism
Morocco, 49, 116, 204, 227, 231–232, 234, 248, 254, 282, 287, 292–93, 298–99
Mossadegh, M., 302
Mozambique, 233
Muhamadja, 70
Mukhitdinov, N. A., 2n
Muñoz Marin, L., 317

## N

Nasser, G. A., 17
national democracy, 27–28, 53, 61, 61n, 196–97, 205, 253, 274, 294n, 302–04
national libration movements, 18, 40–51, 193, 277
nationalism, 26, 44ff, 193
nationalization, 56, 321–22. *See also* state capitalism
Nazi Party, 302n, 305. *See also* fascism
Nehru, J., 17
neo-colonialism, 10, 18, 27, 55–56. *See also* colonialism
Nepal, 295

Netherlands, 62–64, 71–72, 75–76, 109, 141, 147
neutralism, 19
New Zealand, 113
Nicaragua, 8, 136
Niger, 268n
Nigeria, 113, 237–38, 249, 254, 257–61, 270, 272–73, 293
Nkrumah, K., 17, 24, 250, 259, 261–62, 267–68, 269n, 270
North Africa, 244, 284–85. *See also* individual countries
Nyasaland, 244, 254, 262
Nyerere, J., 265

## O

October Revolution, 38, 41, 68–69, 70n
Ofori-Atta, Chief, 265
Organization of American States, 120
oriental mode of production (oriental despotism), 2, 190, 237ff
"orientology", oriental studies (*vostokovedeniye*), x–xi, xiii, 2, 2n, 5, 78–87, 88–102
Orizu, A. A. N., 32
Osmanova, Z., 24n

## P

Pakistan, 49, 52, 109, 141–42, 146–147, 149, 151–52, 196, 200, 282, 286, 293, 296, 298
Pankratova, A. M., 86, 86n
Pant, R., 184n, 185n
Paraguay, 119, 121, 136, 307
Partai Nasional Indonesia (PNI), 75
Partindo, 73, 75
Pasundan, 70
Pavlov, V. I., 25n
peasantry, 11, 53, 66, 85, 171, 287–289, 319; middle peasants, 12; poor peasants, 12–14; rich peasants, 12; *see also* agriculture, kulaks
people's democracy, 27, 48
Perón, J., 17

353

# Index

Peru, 99, 121, 130, 134, 136, 305, 307–08, 327, 329

Philippines, 18, 37, 49, 52, 67–68, 109, 142, 149, 196, 204, 282, 293–94, 296, 300

Pistrak, L., 14n, 82n

Poland, 207

Popov, A., 9n

popular (united) front, 27, 82n

Portugal, 62, 99, 215; colonies, 49

Potekhin, I. I., 1n, 14n, 24, 190n, 261n

Preobrazhenskiy, Ye. A., 39

"price scissors", unequal exchange, 10, 98, 98n, 104–105, 117, 138

primitive (primary) accumulation, 50–51, 98, 98n

proletariat, 15–16, 23, 36, 51, 53, 68, 85, 124, 154–88, 192–93, 196, 203, 219, 286–87, 289, 294–295, 308, 319

Prussia, 207ff

Puerto Rico, 307, 315, 326

Punjab, 212–13

## R

"Radical Concentration" (Indonesia), 71

Raffles, Sir S., 63

Red'ko, I. B., 25n

religion, 55, 201, 235

Rhodesia (North and South), 150, 230–31, 242, 242n, 244–45, 247, 262

Rudenko, B. T., 90

Russia, 207–08, 213–14, 222. *See also* Soviet Union, tsarism

## S

Sarekat Dagang Islam, 69

Sarekat Islam, 68–69, 71, 72

Sarekat Rakjat, 71

Saudi Arabia, 81

Savel'ev, N., 19n

SEATO, 56

Second International, *see* social democracy

sectarianism, *see* dogmatism

Semenov, S. L., 90

Semyenov, A., 28n

seizure of power; violent, 28, 253; peaceful, 01

Senegal, 268n, 295

Shchirovskiy, Yu., 27n

Shinn, W., 24n

Shmelev, N. P., 9n

Shul'govskiy, A. F., 88n

Sigmund, P. E., xin

Singapore, 62

slavery, 239

Sobolev, A., 24n

social democracy (social reformism) and social democrat parties, 26, 68, 70, 97–98, 305–31

socialism, 13, 23–24, 27, 48–49, 214; transition to, *see* seizure of power

Somalia, 293

South Africa, Republic of, 157n, 225, 228–29, 244–47

Southeast Asia, 138–53, 283, 284. *See also* individual countries

Soviet Union, ix–xiii, 1–6, 13, 24–25, 28–29, 33, 42, 59, 61, 76, 86, 89, 98, 118, 132, 152, 252, 272, 329. *See also* October Revolution, Russia; Communist Party, 47, 48n, 51, 53, 58, 61, 78–79, 92–93, 98, 101–02, 155, 301–04

Spain, 90, 99, 215

Spear, T. G., xiin

Stalin, J. V, x, 1, 2n, 17, 21n, 30–38, 39, 78, 86n, 93, 103, 155, 301–02

Starushenko, G., 29n

Stepanov, L. V., 103, 104n, 154, 276

Stolypin, P. A., 211–12, 222

Stroessner, Gen. A., 305

Sudan, 49, 244, 293

Suech, L., 227n

Sukarno, 1, 17, 72–74

Sumatra, 67,

Sumatrans, Union of, 70

Sun Yat-sen, 74

Sure-Canale, J., 273n

Syria, 49, 60, 85, 200, 293, 296, 302. *See also,* United Arab Republic

Svanidze, I. A., 238n

# Index

355